35.78

HARPER TORCHBOOKS / The Cloister Library

[*Selected titles*]

HARPER TORCHBOOKS / The Science Library

(*continued on next page*)

HARPER TORCHBOOKS / The Academy Library

PASCAL

THE EMERGENCE OF GENIUS

by Emile Cailliet

SECOND EDITION

with an Appendix on recent research

INTRODUCTION BY C. S. DUTHIE

HARPER TORCHBOOKS / The Cloister Library

HARPER & BROTHERS, NEW YORK

To the memory of the
REVEREND THEODORE CARSWELL HUME,
*killed on a mission of mercy when his
neutral transport plane was shot down
in flames off the coast of Sweden*

PASCAL: The Emergence of Genius
Copyright 1945 by the Westminster Press
Copyright © 1961 by Emile Cailliet

Printed in the United States of America

This book was first published in 1945 by the Westminster Press
and is here reprinted by arrangement with the author.
The Introduction by C. S. Duthie is reprinted, slightly altered,
from and by permission of *The Scottish Journal of Theology,*
in which it first appeared in the June 1948 issue.

First HARPER TORCHBOOK edition published 1961

CONTENTS

INTRODUCTION TO THE TORCHBOOK EDITION

by C. S. DUTHIE

Today, especially in philosophical and religious circles, a new interest is discernible in Pascal and his thought. At the turn of the century his interpreters most congenial to the English-speaking world were men like Vinet, the Swiss Protestant, and Laberthonnière, the French Catholic. There was a reason for this. The prevailing climate of thought made it almost inevitable that Pascal should be read and studied selectively. It was Pascal the Christian layman, Pascal exposing the Jesuits, Pascal the evangelical mystic, Pascal with the *impérieux besoin du vrai* (commanding need for the truth), Pascal the unconscious Protestant fighting authoritarian religion—it was this edited Pascal, for the most part, who fascinated. Thus the vindication of miracle and the doctrine of original sin was not considered important and was rarely seen as part, and integral part at that, of his larger endeavour to present to his age a non-scholastic, Biblical type of theology. To take but one example, John Oman's fine essay on Pascal in his book *The Problem of Faith and Freedom* suffers from this kind of selectiveness.

The modern Christian thinker may be tempted to be selective in another way and to seek to grasp Pascal by the aid of Kierkegaard and that general movement to which we give the name existentialism. He ought, however, to be saved from any gross mishandling of Pascal by the fact that half a century of the most painstaking scholarship has now made a balanced estimate more easy to form. Our own intense pre-occupation with the problems with which Pascal wrestled, such as the nature of man, the source of authority in religion, the hiddenness of God, the relation between faith and reason, ought to help rather than hinder a proper appreciation of the positive results he reached. The Pascal literature of France is immense in its extent and is likely to grow. If we cite the names of Brunschvicg, Boutroux, Strowski, Chevalier, Tourneur, Lafuma, we but mention the more distinguished of a large company of *pascalisants*. Something of the wealth of this writing, as of the heavy debt which French thought in many areas owes

6

to Pascal, has been sensitively and brilliantly conveyed in *The Revival of Pascal,* the legacy of Dorothy Eastwood, a sufferer akin in spirit to Pascal himself. For more than thirty years the late Dr. H. F. Stewart of Cambridge interpreted him to English readers from his own independent standpoint and with full knowledge of what had been done in France. His bilingual edition of the *Pensées* is a useful aid to those who seek to understand Pascal's apologetic purpose, although the more recent work of Louis Lafuma and others now calls for a fresh arrangement of the fragments. More recently Jean Mesnard's *Pascal: His Life and Works* has brought us abreast of the latest French researches, both textual and historical, while Ernest Mortimer has provided a lively portrait of the whole Pascal in *Blaise Pascal: The Life and Work of a Realist.* It is to be expected—and the expectation is already being fulfilled—that the intensive work carried out on the text of Pascal, on his relation to Montaigne and Descartes, on his "Jansenism", on his study of the Bible, and, most of all, on his "apologetic method" will lead to a new concentration on the shape of Pascal's religious thought. The burial of the pernicious idea that he was little more than a purveyor of brilliant but unco-ordinated maxims is long overdue. Already there are indications of the kind of direction which this revived interest in Pascal may give to theological thinking. Pascal is proving a powerful ally to those who are eager to show that a Bible-centered and impenitently supernaturalist Christianity surprises but does not outrage the reason of man, if reason be understood not as a separable faculty of the personality but as the whole man gathered to the pitch and point of decisive personal quest for the ultimate. A diligent and continuous grappling with Pascal could usher in a new stage in the recurring debate about the relation between faith and reason.

In Dr. Cailliet's book we now have a full-length study of Pascal by an established Pascalian scholar who writes out of a rich background of French thought and experience.[1] It is an indispensable aid to the full comprehension of what Pascal was as man, scientist, thinker and saint. Its merits are not far to seek. Professor Cailliet's knowledge of the text of Pascal and of the much larger corpus of books about Pascal is intimate and almost exhaustive. When it was first published in 1945, I thought I had stumbled upon a notable omission when I failed to find any reference to the important investigation of Pascal's

[1] A new Appendix, "The Witness of Recent Research" brings the book up to date.

method in *Les Caractères de la Démonstration dans l'Apologie Pascalienne* by J. F. Thomas (Paris, 1942). On looking again, I discovered that Professor Cailliet had drawn attention to the book, under a slightly different title, in a footnote but had not been able to secure a copy owing to war conditions. This is typical of his thoroughness. His sure grasp of the totality of Pascal's thought enables him, for instance, to correct Vinet when Vinet scores a Protestant point for Pascal against the evidence:

. . . . It is wishful thinking on the part of the Protestant Vinet when he writes: "Let one read the *Pensées* attentively and then answer this one question: Is not Church authority simply a digression in Pascal's system?" The context indicates that he is sure of the reader's acquiescence. How, then, does he come to this conclusion? By identifying purely and simply the heart with the Holy Spirit, according as it is a question of a "new heart with which the Holy Spirit provides us". Truly one seems to be dreaming in reading this gratuitous transposition of Pascal into Protestant language (p. 350).

Although it is not part of Professor Cailliet's purpose to provide the reader with a history of the interpretation of Pascal, the sketch at least of such a history is to be found in the numerous passages quoted from Pascalian scholars and in the comments, critical or approving, made by the writer upon these passages.

But Professor Cailliet is much more than a Pascalian scholar. He is a lover of Pascal who has gladly submitted to the spell of the great Frenchman. Fortunately he is sufficiently aware of the dangers attendant upon such devotion to be on his guard against bias and exaggeration. His self-critical enthusiasm for Pascal, wedded to an astonishing mastery of the material, leads him again and again to make illuminating judgments. This, for instance, is how he describes the method of Pascal:—

The author of the *Pensées,* while he was concerned with the loftiest enquiries that can occupy the human mind, began a new type of apologetic which abandons every instrument of metaphysic and seizes you, as it were, by the lapel of your coat as a man would do in the street if he were trying to save a careless pedestrian whom he saw in danger. Pascal starts from your situation and mine (p. 34).

His analysis of what Pascal set out to accomplish provides us with the proper perspective in which to regard the varying and at times apparently self-contradictory things Pascal had to say about reason:—

The inner drama in the life of Blaise Pascal consisted, on the one hand, in his repudiation of scholastic theology and the incursion of human reason into the domain of faith, and of his ambition, on the other hand, to fashion a rational theology for himself (p. 119).

In fact Pascal was protesting against the contemporary rôle cast for reason and reaching out towards the understanding of reason as a function of the total self, the whole man in his living unity. Tracing the course of Pascal's life from the beginning, he makes skilful and imaginative use of his wide knowledge to expose to our view the growth of a great soul vehemently set upon truth and love and God. On almost every issue that has agitated Pascalian scholarship he has something valuable to say. He shows how deep in the debt of the Jansenists Pascal was without himself being a Jansenist. He corrects the misleading interpretation of the Wager argument along the line of James' "will to believe" by restoring it to its proper setting in the *Pensées*, where Pascal's argument with the freethinker becomes a Biblical challenge, charged with prayer, to the decision of faith, a laying before him of an inescapable choice between life and death. He affirms that the shattering and exalting experience enshrined in the *Mémorial* is the real turning-point in Pascal's search for God:—

Having attained at Port-Royal, that stronghold of the Scriptures, the day after November 23, 1654, the order of charity, Pascal turns from human philosophies; his viewpoint becomes essentially evangelical, Christo-centric, and his language becomes that of a prophet or Biblical mystic (p. 177).

Most importantly, he bends all his energies throughout the book upon proving that the story of Pascal's earthly pilgrimage is the story of a Christian and thinker more and more dominated by the Bible and its message.

This last-mentioned feature of the book is its most significant. Professor Cailliet's thesis is that Pascal's growing concentration upon the Bible is the vital clue both to the content and to the method of his thinking.

Better than any other source, the Scripture points us to the things that are God's. It is to Scripture that we must turn in the hour of our greatest distress: *after completing the full circle of human knowledge, and having come to the end of all those resources known to human nature and to the Church, Blaise Pascal came to realise, in the hour of greatest distress, that the Word has the final word to speak concerning human destiny (p. 124).*

9

A great deal of minute scholarship is expended in the endeavour to substantiate this claim. Whatever attitude be adopted to the claim itself, it cannot be denied that this scholarship is rich with the most fruitful suggestions. Professor Cailliet hardly ever examines without at the same time illuminating. By starting off from the fact that the "Jansenist quickening" brought Pascal far into the world of the Bible, he has no difficulty in showing that the experience of 1654, "the second conversion", owed its form to Pascal's deep love of the Book and may actually have arisen out of an act of sustained, brooding meditation upon some part of it. Nor is it more difficult for him to show that Pascal's plan for his *Vindication of Christianity* was so constructed as to lead naturally to Him to whom the whole of Scripture witnesses, Jesus Christ the Redeemer. So much will be readily granted. But in claiming that the *Pensées*, in which the Vindication is embedded, have what he calls a "Biblical structure" Professor Cailliet seems to be claiming more than this. He seems to be saying that the plan itself is in some special sense "Biblical". It is true that Pascal's order—presentation of the problem (man both great and wretched, seeking for a point of rest beyond himself), statement of the solution (the Christian religion meeting man and answering his needs), the demonstration of the solution (the Christian religion, as revealed from God, fully satisfying man)—it is true that this order may have been derived from the Jansenists, for whom the Bible was the beginning and the end of all theology. But this does not *mean* that the plan was necessarily derived from or suggested by the Bible. The method is precisely that which would present itself to a trained and logical mind like Pascal's as the most fitting for his purpose. As Thomas remarks, "Il y a montrer et démontrer" (there is "showing" and there is "demonstrating" or "proving") and Pascal's "démontrer" (proving) was very near to "montrer" (showing). Nevertheless Thomas seems thoroughly justified in retaining the word "démonstration" for Pascal's vindication of the truth of Christianity. In it he does not abandon his intention of remaining faithful to the same qualities of observation and demonstration which he used when he wrote the *Essay on Conic Sections* and the *Treatise on the Arithmetical Triangle* or when he drew the consequences of the experiments on the weight of air which he got his brother-in-law to carry out at Clermont (Les Caractères de la Démonstration, p. 13). The clue to the method would seem to lie rather in Pascal himself. First he describes the predicament of man. Then, when the full force of this predicament has been brought home, he triumphantly declares the inadequacy of human faiths and philosophies and the adequacy of the Christian religion. Finally, he expounds the internal consistency and reasonableness of this supernatural way. It is the method of the preacher and the evangelist. Perhaps in this sense it may be called Biblical. Professor Cailliet, again, seems to be straining his evidence when he suggests that because Pascal's grasp on the Bible was becoming stronger with the years, the fragments of the *Pensées* might be capable of a chronological arrangement according to the depth of the saturation of each fragment by Biblical ideas. This is to work a hypothesis too hard. It is one thing to say that the Bible is the primary source of influence upon Pascal, quite another to make it a principle which gives unity to the whole field of his thought. Professor Cailliet confesses in his Preface "that every individual point of view has its limitations" and asks the instructed reader to check every step. In defence of Professor Cailliet it must be said that there is always evidence of one kind or another for each part of his hypothesis and that he is careful to point out—to mention but a single other factor—that the tradition of the Church was only second to the Bible in shaping Pascal's mind. A Protestant commentator on Pascal may be motivated to prove that he was dominated by the Bible by an unconscious wish to draw Pascal nearer to Protestantism! Professor Cailliet sees Pascal's affinities with Protestantism without exaggerating them. He paints a vivid picture of Pascal's struggle between loyalty to his evangelical conscience and loyalty to the Roman Catholic Church. But he never allows us to forget that throughout his life and at the end Pascal was her devoted son.

Professor Cailliet is almost too generous in his use of quotation. All his quotations are worth making and reveal his extraordinary intimacy with Pascal literature. Despite the adroitness with which they are woven into the narrative, their cumulative effect is somewhat to blunt the edge of his own positive contribution. Occasionally, too, he lapses into quite gratuitous comment:—

Pascal knows how to keep to a strictly expository method of the Bible, sufficient unto itself. To him a simple presentation of Scripture proves to be the best apologetics possible—truth with which our modern preachers would do well to imbue themselves (p. 337).

The hortatory element is rather out of place in a book of this quality.

Even the good Homer nods. Professor Cailliet knows well that in order to allow Pascal to speak to us, it is sufficient to expound him, as he himself does, with insight and lucidity. And, lest our criticism appear to be carping, let it be freely acknowledged that, apart from such minor blemishes, the exposition is done in a spirit submissive to Pascal's highest order, the order of charity.

Even if the defects of this book were larger and more numerous than those I have mentioned, they could hardly touch its solid worth. In this book Pascal comes alive as a great Christian thinker. There are many who would echo the judgment of Dr Clement Webb that Pascal is not a philosopher "because he lacked that primary interest in speculation on the ultimate structure of reality, for the mere sake of knowing what it is which we nowadays take to be the peculiar qualification of the philosopher, in the strict and proper sense of the word" (*Pascal's Philosophy of Religion*, p. 6). In his book, *Une Vie avec Pascal*, Tourneur gives expression to a very similar sentiment.

I refuse to bestow on him the title of "thinker", of philosopher, because that title seems to me to fit only the man who seeks out the unvarying relations of facts amid the unceasing stream of varying experiences in order to turn these facts into rules of conduct directed to the realisation of a future favourable to happiness, whether it be his own or that of his fellows.

Professor Cailliet would want, I am sure, to give to the words "thinker" and "philosopher" a much wider connotation. We may, in fact, mean by a philosopher one who searches tirelessly into the structure of reality in order to respond to it. By this definition Pascal was a philosopher. The difference in the two types of definition turns upon the question whether we recognise or not that the search for what is ultimate is itself prompted by some dim awareness of that ultimate. Pascal recognised this, believing that the God "qui n'est pas nous" is also the God "qui est en nous". To search with groaning was the seal upon such belief. Péguy says somewhere that a great philosophy is not a philosophy without breaches in the walls, but a philosophy with citadels. Could we not say that Pascal's philosophy is such a philosophy, a philosophy of citadels, Biblical citadels? Because Pascal is a thinker after the fashion of Paul, a thinker whom God has found, his thinking never rests in speculation or even contemplation. It passes over into proclamation, persuasion, evangelism. Because he has seen God, he wants others to see God. Although Boutroux is numbered among those who refuse to call Pascal a philosopher, he has written two sentences which accurately describe the achievement of his thought.

Pascal offered a brilliant example of the possibility of reuniting the highest reason with the most teachable and humble faith.

Pascal, in all sincerity, put the centre of his thought and of his life in Christianity (Pascal, pp. 194 and 193).

Professor Cailliet's book is almost an extended commentary on these words. The greatness of Pascal, this proud and humble genius of the "century of genius", is indeed to be found in the fact that he places the centre of his thought and life in Christianity. At the heart of Christianity he saw Christ Himself. "In Him lies all our virtue and felicity. Apart from Him is naught but vice, misery, error, darkness, despair." And his heart's desire was to lead men to Him. Because Professor Cailliet shares this desire and sustains it with the accuracy and imagination of the true scholar he is a welcome and most trustworthy guide.

The University,
Edinburgh,
Scotland.
January, 1961

PREFACE TO THE TORCHBOOK EDITION

The reason Pascal fascinates one generation after another is that the emergence of his genius continues to confront us all with the enigma of destiny, and this with such vividness that his name has in a unique way remained identified with human anguish.[1] At one time his mood of quiet desperation broke into the aching outcry, "The eternal silence of these infinite spaces frightens me,"[2] possibly the greatest free verse of universal relevance in the original French. Then came the never-to-be-forgotten night watch of November 23, 1654, when the pathetic theme of the misery of man without God yielded to the outburst, "Joy, joy, joy, tears of joy," called forth by the heavenly vision.[3] In the fullness of time Pascal attained to holiness, hidden with the Christ at the higher order of love. From this lofty vantage point it was given to him to behold the depths from which he had emerged, reassessing at true value the achievements of the mind, and, beyond and below, the dross of material enticements. Should it be said that he had found God, or rather that he had been found of Him? The answer Pascal himself gave was crystal clear. Never could a lower order account for the uniqueness of a higher order.[4] This was the case as one proceeded from the material to the intellectual realm, and infinitely more so as one was raised from the realm of intellect to the supernatural realm of love. The perspective made sense only when viewed from the higher order down, and emphatically not from the lower up. Pascal's emergence into the Light cannot be understood in terms of an anthropology of naturalistic inspiration.

Therefore, let Pascal's outlook provide adequate insights into his

[1] I have developed this point at length in *The Tragic Vision and the Christian Faith*, ed. by Nathan A. Scott, Jr., Association Press, New York, 1957, ch. 4, "The Anguish of Pascal", pp. 123–152.

[2] *Pensées*, Section III, Fr. 206, *Oeuvres*, v. *13*, 127. N.B. Throughout this book the word *Oeuvres* refers to the standard edition: *Oeuvres de Blaise Pascal* publiées suivant l'ordre chronologique avec documents complémentaires, introductions et notes, par Léon Brunschvicg, Pierre Boutroux, et Félix Gazier, "Les grands écrivains de la France," Hachette, Paris, 1904–1914. The numerals in bold type indicate the volume, and the following numerals (Arabic or Roman) indicate the page.

[3] Mémorial de Pascal, *Oeuvres*, v. *12*, 5.

[4] Cf. famous fragment 793 on the three orders, *Oeuvres*, v. *14*. 230–33.

strategy. He lays bare the inner logic that lies at the source of human contradictions. When he encounters a network of difficulties, a skein which appears hopelessly tangled, he brings to bear upon it the energy of a keen mind, yet always refusing to cut the Gordian knot. Instinctively he gropes for the point at which the apparent antinomy is resolved with divine simplicity. His faith sharpens his understanding. *Intelligere* for Pascal is always *intus legere*. It is as though the universe were to him a tremendous signalling station, his main task being to make out its meaning. And lo and behold, as he strains toward one solution after another, the subsequent stages seem to become easier until the great release comes to pass, until the day the living Word comes to him: "Console thyself. Thou wouldst not be seeking me, if thou hadst not already found me."[5]

As his mind gives less place to worldly concerns,[6] Pascal's hand holds ever more firmly to the Scripture. Here he finds both impulse and insight. In the rapture of his lofty ascent, he catches glimpses of the summit, gleaming peacefully in the blue mist overhead: *O beata solitudo! O sola beatitudo!* He who has once beheld the Christ of the Andes may apprehend the analogy I am trying to suggest—that of Pascal's whole being earnestly longing for his Lord. Maurice Barrès has proposed a similar analogy, one inspired by the ineffable outreach of Dante's *Paradiso*. He has called the ascent of Pascal "the Divine Comedy" of the French.[7]

When the present work was originally published, I attempted to characterize Pascal's biblical viewpoint in the subtitle, *Genius in the Light of Scripture*.[8] I have since realized that it held too static and too restrictive a connotation. Hence the new subtitle, *The Emergence of Genius*, which more adequately conveys the basic conception of the treatment at hand.

The method of approach reasserted in the preceding paragraphs has been vindicated by recent research, no doubt because it has at every

---

[5] *Pensées*, Section vii, Fr. 553, Le Mystère de Jésus, *Oeuvres*, v. *13*, p. 438.

[6] Barrès, M., "Les enfances de Blaise Pascal," in *Revue hebdomadaire*, No. 28, 32d. year, July, 1923 (Third Centenary of Pascal's birth), p. 134.

[7] *Ibid.*, p. 141.

[8] Pascal: *Genius in the Light of Scripture*, Westminster Press, Philadelphia, 1945. Since he was a Roman Catholic, Pascal used the Latin Vulgate, which he often quoted from memory. He sometimes shortened the text as he quoted it. Sometimes he elaborated on a text, or combined several texts together. Occasionally he would translate directly from the original, with or without the help of other versions. In Chapter XV I have discussed some of the problems raised by these habits of a writer whose mind was so thoroughly steeped in the Scripture.

step kept close to Pascal's own outlook. As a result, the best conclusions of the latest scholarship have been easily assimilated to the main body of the work now brought up-to-date by a new Appendix.

A more immediate result of whatever adequacy there may be in the treatment as a whole is the accession of this title to the Harper Torchbook series, a favor for which I am deeply grateful.

Princeton, January 1961   Emile Cailliet

The Emergence of a Pilgrim

"Truth shall spring out of the earth."

—Ps. 85:11

G od wills it! God wills it! God wills it! God wills it! "
The shout goes up from a thousand throats. Pope Urban II has just finished his sermon in the great square of Clermont " in the presence of four hundred bishops or mitred abbots, and of an immense gathering of the populace." [1] Forthwith each one of these breasts is marked with a cross of red cloth, and, without further tarrying, one hundred thousand poor folk fall into line under the leadership of Peter the Hermit. Eastward moves the endless column — toward the Danube Valley; toward the Bosphorus, where it will be cut to pieces by the Turks; on toward the Holy City, which at any cost must be set free. The nobles will follow later.

To this day, the memory of that uprising of a Christian people hovers over the vast, sloping square of Clermont; it stirs to life the robust, square outline of the basilica of Notre-Dame du Port, which for centuries has served as both church and citadel. This Romanesque structure, the greatest in all Auvergne, is buried like a huge cistern among the surrounding houses. Its sturdy bareness well bespeaks the character of the indomitable soul who reared its walls. Built of arkose, it is still quite light in color, like all the older churches in Auvergne. It will be some time before the builders begin to use stone cut from the lava, which they will prefer because it is more durable. In those early days, however, a single structure — the Cathedral — leaps forth from the soil of Auvergne, with a single heavenward thrust, springing from a single-minded faith, its unobstructed eminence crowning the crest of the hill.

[1] Giraud, Victor, *La Vie héroïque de Blaise Pascal*, Les Editions G. Crès et Cⁱᵉ, Paris, 1923, p. 4.

Riom belongs to the King, Montferrand to the Count. But Clermont belongs to the Bishop, and it is the Bishop's town which is thus dominated by the Cathedral. A walled town it is, embracing the mother church; the cloister; the abbey; the Bishop's palace, with its gardens and chapel; the *officialité;* a prison; and cemeteries.[2]

Clermont is to remain a citadel of the Church, ruled by its bishops, from 1202 to 1551. Divided into the four parishes of Notre-Dame, la Cathédrale, Saint-Genès, and Saint-Pierre, the town also includes the convents of the Cordeliers and the Carmelite Friars, whose huge churches are thrown open to the crowds hungry for sermons. A ring of monasteries surrounds the town on every side: the Priory of Beaumont, the Chamalières' Chapter, the Minims of Saint-Pierre, the Augustinians, the royal abbeys of Saint-André and Saint-Alyre, the Barefooted Carmelite Friars of Chantoin, Jacobins, Ursulines.[3] At the Cordeliers and at Saint-Alyre some relics from antiquity are to be seen.

This land of the Arvernes, where Vercingetorix, who led the Gauls against Caesar, was born about 72 B.C., is the seat of a very ancient civilization. When the Bishop pays a visit to the great seminary at Montferrand, he passes through triumphal arches which bear inscriptions in Latin. At the Puy de Dôme, when the Observatory was being built, they found a statuette of the god Mercury, in the figure of a gay, strapping, young countryman, vigorous in appearance and with enormous fists. This ancient bronze piece was given a prominent place in the historical museum of Clermont, where Mercury stands today, in lieu of a patron saint, as it were, for this borderland of trade, watching over this industrious and practical folk who are at the same time basically religious in spirit.

The Gauls had a sanctuary here, the last stopping place for pilgrims before they reached the sanctuary on the mountain. The Romans named the place Augustonemetum, the city of the Arvernes, and it finally became Clermont in the days of Pepin the Short. If the city of the Arvernes had become the Bishop's town, the real reason was that the bishops were originally leaders chosen by the people themselves.

---

[2] Desdevises du Dézert, G., " Pascal et Clermont," *Foi et Vie,* No. 13, July 1 and 16, 1923, 26th year, Cahier A., p. 712.

[3] *Ibid.,* pp. 711, 712.

The high central ridge where these men were given authority stood as a kind of tangible evidence of the ever surging movement of Christianity within the life of a race and of a region. " What bare strength, what powerful placidity was to be found in ancient Auvergne, sturdy of heart, vigorous with the blood of a great land lying between the four seas. Along with the solidity of your soil and tradition, along with gifts of nature and human wisdom, you possess impulsiveness, audacity and the folly of saintliness. High ridges have pushed their way up in the very heart of the plain, and volcanoes have burst forth, sundering apart the highlands." [4]

The primordial fire made Auvergne what it is, just as Auvergne, fashioned for a destiny surpassing its narrow bounds, made France what it is today. Something more than the geological history of France is recapitulated in this lofty region; in a sense it is the story of the whole world, and perhaps of its civilization. The flickering fires of a primitive culture, that of the Eyzie Grottoes, were first kindled in the valley of the Vézère, in Périgord. In this corner of France the record of our distant ancestors is inscribed in signs and symbols which are only now being deciphered with the aid of modern science. Of this process of unfolding the record of the past, Camille Julian says: " Every Frenchman who reveres his ancestors, every man who has a decent concern to know his own past, should make a pilgrimage to the Eyzies." [5]

THE MARK OF CALVINISM

Shut in by its own highlands, overlooking the highways of civilization from afar, Auvergne finds its chief access to the outer world by way of the deep valley of the Limagne, which extends in a widening valley to the north. From the village of Gerzat, near Clermont in the Limagne valley, came the Bégon family, Blaise Pascal's forebears on his mother's side. Their family record has been traced back to the thirteenth century. Most of them were tillers of the soil; one was a priest, one a notary public. They were well received in local gatherings, and a written record has been preserved of their charitable gifts and of their habits of piety. Pascal's maternal grandfather, Victor Bégon,

[4] Pourrat, Henri, *L'Auvergne. Les Limagnes,* B. Arthaud Succr. des Editions J. Rey, Grenoble, 1932, p. 192.
[5] Capitan et Peyrony, *L'Humanité primitive dans la région des Eyzies,* Stock, Paris, 1924, p. 120.

moved to Clermont toward the end of the sixteenth century and established himself as a merchant. The Pascal family also originated in the Limagne valley, where tradition associates them with the village of Cournon. They were a family of tradesmen — dealers in carts, perhaps — and they made their way up in the world by dint of unremitting toil. Under Louis XI, they were raised to the aristocracy, as members of the petty *noblesse de robe*. For several generations, the family had lived in Clermont, where Jean Pascal, great-grandfather of Blaise, was a *marchand bourgeois*. After making his fortune, he purchased the post of Inspector of Deeds, apparently rather late in life. His son, Martin Pascal, became Tax Collector for Clermont, and later Treasurer of the Bureau of Finance at Riom.[6]

Now it appears to be well established that Martin Pascal, grandfather of Blaise Pascal, was for a time a Calvinist. He was an independent thinker, and, as his grandson said of him, his opinions shifted freely " from *pro* to *con*." Like the grandparents of Blaise Pascal, the Arnauld and the Lemaistre families were also of Huguenot descent, having had Protestant parents and earlier forebears, as Varin has shown.[7] These facts throw a significant light on the development of Jansenism. They have quite a special relevance in the present study. They may even help to shed new light on the problem concerning the versions of the Bible which Blaise Pascal may have used. Personally, we wonder whether he may not have found in the family library a copy of the Bible edited by the pastors and professors of the Church in Geneva, a printing of which was made by Thomas Portau, at Saumur, in 1614. We have come into personal possession of one such copy of the said printing, which served as family Bible, with the initial entry reading: " Mon père an 1560, il mourut 1619." Martin Pascal had great ambitions for his son Etienne whom he sent to Paris to study law. There in the capital the latter doubtless felt the breath of the Renaissance, and it would be less than surprising to find this eager, self-taught man, with his encyclopedic mind, fingering through or even purchasing the Prot-

---

[6] Giraud, Victor, *La Vie héroïque de Blaise Pascal, op. cit.*, p. 2.

[7] Jovy, Ernest, *Etudes pascaliennes*, Librairie philosophique — J. Vrin, v. 7, Paris, 1930: " Le Grand-Père de Pascal et le Protestantisme," pp. 217–224. Ernest Jovy's opinion on this point may be accepted without question. The notes appended to his essay include a complete bibliography on the subject. The Catholic author reviews all the facts brought to light by the most recent works of Pascalian erudition, done in the local archives. He concludes: " It no longer appears surprising that, at one period, Calvinism left its mark upon the Pascal home " (p. 224).

estant edition of the Scripture. His father had given him letters of introduction to the solicitor Arnauld, a brilliant leader of the Paris bar. Arnauld was the father of twenty children who became, as it were, the kindergarten for Port-Royal.

The Pascal family found itself threatened with persecution because of its Protestant leanings. Gaspard Montmorin de Saint-Hérem, Governor of Auvergne during the massacre of Saint Bartholomew's Day, received an order to put to death all Protestants within his jurisdiction. There were very few of them in fact, but the task was most unwelcome. He limited himself to having them all imprisoned. But when the town of Clermont was asked to aid in carrying out these arrests, it calmly decided, with that independence of spirit so admirable throughout its history, that integrity of character in its sons and citizens should take precedence over every other consideration. The Town Council decided, at its session of January 16, 1574, to seek a delay. The Governor insisted, and declared the town of Clermont to be ill-managed. A stern reprimand was given to the garrison commanders in Clermont, with instructions " to prepare at once a roll containing the name and surname of all those persons held under suspicion, with respect to religion." The town then hastened to send Lieutenant Textoris and one of the magistrates to the Governor to lay before him the serious reasons which the town of Clermont gave for not imprisoning those of its citizens who refused to recant. Saint-Hérem was apparently convinced, for at the session of the Town Council on January 30 it was decided simply to keep matters under surveillance, to read out the roll of names, and to file it at the close of the session. This roll of names may actually be seen among the municipal archives of Clermont, with the records of the corporate proceedings of the town in 1574, under date of January 30.

Among the names of those persons who took up, bore, and employed arms against the King in 1567 may be found the name of Anthoine Audigier, surnamed Le Peuchy, the name of some friends of the Pascal and Périer families. It should be recalled that Gilberte, elder sister of Blaise Pascal, later married Florin Périer. Among the names of those who did recant was that of Master Martin Pascal.[8] His grandson was also to face a bitter struggle within his own soul as he stood years later on the frontier of Roman Catholic orthodoxy. These sturdy souls were gifted with a freedom of spirit which made them critical of authority, if not rebellious against it. Small wonder it is then that we find Etienne

[8] *Ibid.*, pp. 217–219.

Pascal, son of Martin and father of Blaise, protesting at the royal court in 1630 against the founding of a Jesuit college in Clermont.

A GARDEN IN THE MOAT

Etienne Pascal was born in Clermont in 1588, eldest of a family of ten children. After pursuing the studies above referred to, he became *conseiller élu du Roy* in the electorate of Bas-Auvergne at Clermont. We shall have ample opportunity in these pages to become more fully acquainted with this perfect *honnête homme,* in the full sense of the word, a good Christian, slightly given to superstition as men were in those days, but in no sense a mystic. The strain of mysticism in his son Blaise came from his mother's side, a type of mysticism balanced by the common sense and realistic turn of mind so characteristic of this plebeian folk.

As magistrate at the Cour des Aides, Etienne Pascal would normally have made his home in Montferrand, seat of the High Court, but in 1616 he had married Antoinette Bégon, and in 1619 he had bought the Langhac mansion, close by the Abbey, in the Bishop's town.[9]

Let us now wend our way to the Pascal home. The good town of Clermont we enter by a gate leading us through the city wall. The wall is in poor enough repair, and in more than one place it seems about to collapse. What was once a moat has been turned into a vegetable garden by the practical citizens of the neighborhood. We shall need heavy boots, indeed, if we are to go up the narrow, winding alley, which is little better than a mass of mud. Let us hail a sedan chair! Huddled together on either side are tiny houses built of dark basalt, telling a tale of unrelieved penury. Opening upon the street are the windows of a small shop, letting in precious little sunlight through the heavy, half-closed shutters. On one side is the main door and the staircase, where a couple of tiny square windows give what light is needed. On the other side of

[9] This chronology is not yet altogether precise. Victor Giraud (*op. cit.*, p. 8) dates the marriage in "about 1614"; Régis Crégut, diocesan keeper of the archives of Clermont-Ferrand, says, "About 1615 or 1616" ("Clermont et les souvenirs pascaliens," *L'Illustration*, No. 4192, July 7, 1923, p. 2); the same author dates the purchase of the two houses linked by a small courtyard as of February 20, 1614; Professor Morris Bishop gives 1617 as the date of the marriage (*Pascal:* The Life of Genius, Reynal & Hitchcock, Inc., New York, 1936, p. 3). We are following the chronology given by G. Desdevises du Dézert, professor at the University of Clermont-Ferrand ("Pascal et Clermont," *op. cit.*, p. 713).

22

the shop is the entrance into the cellar. Upstairs we find a single large room, with a low ceiling and wide casement window, and above that a tiny attic. That is all. The people of Auvergne know the meaning of poverty. Cut off from the other provinces by the lack of good roads, they import but little from beyond their own borders. On the other hand, the major part of their crops is consumed on the spot, sufficing for the needs of ordinary life, and even for some small degree of comfort, albeit upon a slender margin of monetary income.

This, in general, is the standard of life among the tradesmen of the main shopping streets, by which we entered Clermont. Their earnings, which would seem wretched to us, provide enough for upkeep, and enable them to receive and entertain their friends. Some of them have gallantly taken as their family motto the words: *Bene vivere et laetari.* A good living, as they see it, doubtlessly means just enough to treat one's friends for fifteen or twenty sous, and to buy a fine gown for a daughter's wedding. In the way of art there is hardly anything to speak of. Exteriors appear to mean little to the people of Clermont. Such painting as we find consists of a few portraits, while the only sculpture in the community is found inside a few of the more elegant homes. These folk are already living by Jansenist standards, even though the term has not yet been heard of.[10]

Along the Rue des Gras and the Rue des Chaussetiers are to be found a few mansions of moderate scale, but they offer little in the way of outward appointments. Here an ornate doorway, there a family crest carved above the lintel, indicate to the passer-by the owner's social standing. Except for the churches there is little to satisfy the sensitive eye. We enter the Gothic cathedral, with its choir reminiscent of Beauvais. Perchance we shall find Antoinette kneeling in prayer, caught by a ray of sunlight flooding in rich color through the resplendent stained glass.

The Pascal home is only a few steps from the cathedral door, but we shall not find our way to it without some difficulty. Etienne Pascal does indeed live in the house at the corner of the Rue des Chaussetiers and the public square just south of the Cathedral, but he also occupies another house close by, opening on the Rue des Gras, the street named because of the steps by which it leads up to the very front of the Cathedral.[11]

[10] In reconstructing this scene, we have borrowed material from the essay by G. Desdevises du Dézert, " Pascal et Clermont," *op. cit.*

[11] *Gras,* from the Latin *gradus* (step).

The fact is that the two houses are connected by a tiny courtyard, so that the Pascal family finds it easy to live in both houses at the same time.[12] The two houses once formed part of a huge, five-storied structure, built around a court, the Hôtel des Vernines, dating back about a hundred years. Etienne Pascal, being a practical man of affairs, had no sooner pocketed the title to the property than he remodeled the stables into a row of shops, which he rented out, and thus augmented the income which has made him one of Clermont's forty-three leading taxpayers.

PATRIARCHAL FAMILY DISCIPLINE

There it was that four children were born: Anthonia, in December, 1617, who died shortly after her baptism; on January 1, 1620, Gilberte, who was to become Madame Périer; on June 19, 1623, Blaise; and on October 5, 1625, Jacqueline.

Christened on June 27, 1623,[13] Blaise began life as a sickly child. He was barely a year old when he developed an alarming tendency to listlessness, and for months his life was feared for. Etienne was wild with anxiety. Believing the child to be the victim of an evil spell, he sought out the supposed enchantress, forced her to confess her crime, and made her transfer the spell to a black cat, which promptly expired! A poultice was applied to the wretched infant, made from nine leaves of three herbs gathered before sunrise by a seven-year-old child. Soon afterward Blaise was well again. Such evidences of superstition need not trouble us overmuch, for they were deeply rooted in the customs of the people, to whom they would not have appeared in the least out of the ordinary. We mention the incident merely to recall some of the trials which beset Etienne, and to note that Blaise, from his earliest years, was a victim of poor health. There is little doubt that he was already " given to intense, but balanced, hypersensitivity." [14] The phrase is borrowed

[12] Crégut, Régis, " Clermont et les souvenirs pascaliens," op. cit., p. 2.

[13] The following entry marks the baptism of Blaise Pascal in the register of baptismal records in the parish of Saint-Pierre, kept since the Revolution at the town hall of Clermont:

" Le vingt-septième jour de juin 1623, a été baptisé Blaise Paschal, fils à noble Estienne Paschal, conseiller eslu pour le roi, en l'Election d'Auvergne, à Clairmont et à noble damoiselle Anthoinette Bégon; le parrin noble Blaise Paschal, conseiller du roi en la Sénéchaussée et siège présidial d'Auvergne audit Clairmont; la marraine dame Anthoinette de Fontfreyde.

" Au registre ont signés Paschal et Fontfreyde."

[14] Chevalier, Jacques, Pascal, Plon, Paris, 1922, n. i, p. 49.

24

from Jacques Chevalier, who goes on to add however: " Despite the symptoms, evident from infancy, of some ailment which may have been congenital, Pascal never, at that time or later on, showed any sign of mental disorder or hysteria, nor of superstition on his part." [15] An inner flame, out of all proportion to his bodily strength, was already burning in the mind of Blaise.

The " very pious and very charitable " Antoinette died in 1626, leaving President Pascal alone to raise and train three children, all of them quite young. We must admire the understanding integrity and devotion which he brought to this task. As regards their formal education, it may well be said that genius is a matter of infinite patience. Nature never succeeds at a single bound in producing those happy phenomena we call geniuses and saints. Fitting indeed is the comment of Maurice Barrès, as he thought of Blaise Pascal and his father: " Our sons resemble our most profound thoughts." [16]

Young Blaise was " an only son, between two much-beloved sisters, now left without . . . a mother, to be brought up by a father who was a lonely and somewhat saddened man." More than likely it is that Blaise was " fondled and admired, as well as having to grow up under the shadow of this sorrow. Who can say what mark this may have left upon his later years? His imperious manner, his impatience with opponents, his extremely sensitive nature, his hasty temper, his inclination to sorrowful brooding. To his sisters he owed the feminine strain in his own nervous manner, and, no less, that grace and charm which won him so many devoted friends." [17]

What noble spirits they were, both of these sisters! The elder, Gilberte, took her mother's place in the home, where she assumed a measure of responsibility beyond her years. Well she deserves the happy title " the Martha of the family," given her by Fortunat Strowski. Among the many who have written of her brother's life, Gilberte alone, according to Vinet,[18] truly understood that great soul. In the following pages

[15] *Ibid.*, pp. 48, 49. Fortunat Strowski absolves Pascal from any superstitious practice, adding that he spoke adversely of reason, but that he was consistently and invincibly reasonable, worthy of a disciple of Montaigne (*Pascal et son temps*, Plon, Paris, 1909–1913, v. **2**, 5).

[16] Barrès, Maurice, " Les Enfances de Pascal," an address delivered at Clermont-Ferrand, in the name of the Académie Française, on July 7, 1923, *La Revue hebdomadaire*, No. 28, 32d year, July 14, 1923, p. 141.

[17] Strowski, Fortunat, *Pascal et son temps*, *op. cit.*, v. **2**, 3.

[18] Vinet, Alexandre, *Etudes sur Blaise Pascal*, Edition augmentée de fragments inédits publiée avec une préface et des notes par Pierre Kohler, Professeur à l'Uni-

we shall refer often to her impressions.[19] As for Jacqueline — or Jac-
quette, as she was called — who later entered a convent under the name
of Sister Sainte-Euphémie, we may again recall Vinet's estimate: " As
we think of her, we cannot withhold a feeling of admiration even more
unqualified, and marked by more genuine respect, than for him [Blaise].
It is to be doubted whether we shall find anywhere a more accomplished
character, in man or woman, than that of Jacqueline." [20]

As we look back at this family, one feature is strikingly evident,
namely, the patriarchal tradition of family discipline. If the men and
women of that period did not turn to the teachings of the Bible for
precise guidance in the domain of politics, they accepted its authority
unchallenged in the realm of family life, where patriarchal authority
was sustained with the full force of law and custom.[21] However, this
fundamental respect for patriarchal tradition did not in any way shut
them from the new light of the Renaissance.

THE NEW LIGHT OF THE RENAISSANCE

From the second floor of the Pascal mansion there opened a huge
window, for the house was built in the sixteenth century, when men
felt the need of more light to read by. It was a century that opened
many windows of the mind! This style of residence was common among
Clermont families of standing equal to that of Etienne Pascal, for if
there was little in the town that deserved the name of art, Clermont had
reason to be proud of its intellectual tradition. It numbered four or five
hundred students in its college, whose affairs were directed by six
regents, along with the principal, " men of property, of upright life,
and worthy example." A chair of philosophy had been established by
a generous patron, Michel Paschon. M. Savaron, a deputy at the 1614

---

versité de Berne [enlarged ed. of fragments unpublished, with a preface and notes
by Pierre Kohler, professor at the University of Berne]. Payot et Cᵗᵉ, Lausanne-
Genève-Neufchatel-Vevey-Montreux-Berne-Bâle, 1936, p. 3.

[19] Why does Fortunat Strowski feel obliged to cast doubt upon this testimony?
" I have so often found it misled or misleading," he says in a note [n. 3, p. 8] in
Pascal et son temps, v. 2, *op. cit.* The foreword to the new edition [v. 4 to 11] of the
Œuvres, v. 4, iii, puts the mat er more happily: " The precision of Madame Périer
[Gilberte] has in almost every case overcome the suspicions of critics who do not
recoil from bold hypotheses."

[20] Vinet, Alexandre, *Etudes sur Blaise Pascal, op. cit.*, p. 322.

[21] Hubert, René, *Les Sciences sociales dans l'encyclopédie.* La philosophie de
l'histoire et le problème des origines sociales, Alcan, Paris, 1923, p. 29.

Estates General, had published in 1607 a very interesting volume on the origins of the town of Clermont. M. de Champflour, a technical adviser at the Cour des Aides, prided himself on being a connoisseur of architecture. The priests of the several religious orders, the canons of the Cathedral, and not a few of the *bourgeoisie* and aristocracy were noted for their wide learning and urbane manners.[22]

Etienne Pascal had a hobby. He was deeply versed in ancient languages and mathematics. As we look back upon the accomplishments of the seventeenth-century provincial *bourgeoisie,* we cannot withhold our admiration. They leave us feeling quite humble by comparison! One of the counselors at the Parliament of Toulouse, for instance, a man named Fermat, whose relationship to the Pascal family will shortly become clear, was one of the great mathematicians of his day. A student of Greek literature, he wrote poetry of his own, and " amused himself " with scientific investigations which were always in his mind during hours of relaxation. It was an age when men were not consumed, as in our day, by a concern to escape from themselves, nor by an incessant feeling of rush and haste. Men in such an age gave themselves to pastimes which served to stimulate the loftiest attainments of the human spirit. They were fully aware of the fact that Time is a somewhat austere personage who respects only that which is carried through in his company. Yet the intellectual activity of a man like Etienne Pascal, seen against the background of his time, must be regarded not only as recreational in inspiration but also as sportive and playful in character.

This would need elaboration because Blaise started out in the same spirit, throwing himself into all that he did, we may well say, as into a game. Then as a result of and in the midst of circumstances we shall try to recapitulate, his disinterested and playful attitude later gave way to a more urgent concern. When, at the age of nineteen, he invented the calculating machine, patiently assembling it piece by piece, it was primarily with a view to helping his father, who used to sit up late into the night over his figures. With the machine at last ready to operate, the pride of Blaise in his achievement inspired something less than modesty in his letters of dedication. In the course of the controversies aroused by his scientific work, his sharp, even biting, style displayed all too well his stubborn determination to be right. His father never failed to stand by him, and to strengthen his spirit of defiance, which in some cases became almost threatening. Little by little his motives were

22 Desdevises du Dézert, G., " Pascal et Clermont," *op. cit.,* pp. 712, 713.

purged and clarified, yielding at last to a single-minded passion for truth, above all else. What passionate minds this Pascal family had!

Etienne believed himself the victim of a pedagogical method of which he could not approve, and thus it was that, after long brooding on the whole matter of education, he had decided to take the training of his children into his own hands. The methods he had chosen to apply seemed to him more reasonable, more direct, and more effective than those he found current in the schools. His main principle was this: "Always hold the child above his task." Keeping this maxim in mind, he taught young Blaise to observe everything with the utmost care, and to reason out the course of his observations at every step, so that he was able to give an account of everything that happened, stage by stage.

Father and son held frequent conversations during the course of each day. These amounted to vital lessons drawn from actual experience, by means of which Etienne filled the receptive mind of young Blaise with a rich store of impressions concerning the thousand-and-one phenomena he met in everyday life. The lad was thus "encouraged in his own instinctive desire to know the reasons and causes of things, and the discipline he received in the habit of rigorous thinking paved the way for decisive experiments later on."[23]

DEMAND FOR TRUTH

From the observation of physical objects, President Pascal proceeded to a consideration of the use of words, which for Blaise were always inseparable from objects. Through all his life, he felt a natural discontent for empty jargon. Even in boyhood he worked out for himself a rudimentary philosophy of words, which one day was to impel him to inquire into the structure and purpose of grammar. Once fully attained, his sense of the meaning of words was never lost, and this explains the intense vitality of his mature style and the unusual syntax he employed. This is, at least in part, the basis for the comment made by Dr. H. F. Stewart: "No man has written with more magic and mastery of phrase. And this triumph is more than verbal; it is the triumph of a personality: 'Le style c'est l'homme.' Of no one is this more true than of Pascal."[24]

[23] Giraud, Victor, La Vie héroïque de Blaise Pascal, op. cit., p. 21.
[24] Stewart, H. F., The Secret of Pascal, University Press, Cambridge, 1941, pp. 56, 57.

The primary purpose of all genuine education is the attainment by each individual of self-direction. In one sense education thus tends to make itself superfluous. This truth gives special point to the remark of St. Cyres concerning Pascal's education: "The boy's best teacher was himself. Very soon he began to notice the little everyday oddities of Nature, and puzzle over their explanation." [25] If this same reasoning be carried a bit farther, we should be prepared to defend the seeming paradox that the best teacher is one who trains a student to be self-taught. God only knows whether we are justified in laughing, as we often do, at self-taught men. Yet Fortunat Strowski seems to be doing so in the ironical comment: "Whatever it is that Pascal has to say in his *Pensées,* he always shouts it aloud like Christopher Columbus discovering America." [26] We are inclined to agree, nor would the Pascal of the *Pensées* question the point: "People are generally better persuaded by the reasons which they have themselves discovered than by those which have come into the minds of others." [27] But Pascal also went on to say: "Let no one say that I have said nothing new; the arrangement of the subject is new. When we play handball, we both play with the same ball, but one of us places it better.

"I had as soon it were said that I used words employed before. And in the same way if the same thoughts in a different arrangement do not form a different discourse, no more do the same words in their different arrangements form different thoughts." [28]

We are able to agree more fully with Fortunat Strowski when he points out the subtle, penetrating quality of mind which emerges from the kind of education Blaise received at the hands of his father: "It encourages the habit of digging down to the foundation of ideas; it keeps one free from the association of ready-made notions and conventional patterns of thought. It emancipates the mind from those bonds of tradition and social pressure, which make themselves felt as truly in the intellectual as in the physical world. All this was characteristic of Pascal." [29] This last phrase disposes of the matter too easily, however, in that it deals only with method, with the discipline of the mind.

Of greater import is the growth of that *demand for truth,* which is the fruit of intellectual discipline. Pascal's elder sister was well aware of

[25] Viscount St. Cyres, *Pascal,* E. P. Dutton & Co., Inc., New York, 1910, p. 5.
[26] Strowski, Fortunat, *Pascal et son temps, op. cit.,* v. **2,** 8.
[27] Section i, Fr. 10, *Œuvres,* v. **12,** 23.
[28] Section i, Fr. 22, *Œuvres,* v. **12,** 33, 34.
[29] Strowski, Fortunat, *Pascal et son temps, op. cit.,* v. **2,** 9.

this distinction, which she seeks to make clear in the biography of her brother, Blaise. She undertakes to show the relation of method to content: " Thus from his childhood, he would not yield to anything short of the truth, as it appeared to him; so that, when no satisfactory explanation was offered him, he undertook to find it for himself; and when he became absorbed in such an inquiry, he would not think of turning from it until he had found an explanation which satisfied him." [30]

Let such a soul feel the touch of the Divine Hand, and we may guess what inward hunger and thirst were henceforth to torment him! We may well understand why Pascal's favorite psalm was to be the long 118th (known to us as the 119th), for it is essentially a passionate prayer for light and guidance for man's mind. Pascal knew this psalm by heart, and he used to repeat its passages, over and over, with increasing intensity: " Blessed are they that search his testimonies: that seek him with their whole heart. . . . O! that my ways may be directed to keep thy justifications. . . . With my whole heart have I sought after thee: let me not stray. . . . Open thou my eyes. . . . Make me to understand the way of thy justifications. . . . Give me understanding, and I will search thy law . . . and take not thou the word of truth utterly out of my mouth: for in thy words I have hoped exceedingly. . . . I have thought on my ways: and turned my feet unto thy testimonies." [31]

Young Blaise was still very far from these spiritual heights of dedication to God. As yet he was exposed to little more than the teaching of the Roman Catholic catechism, as were boys of his age. Coming home from church, he would then study under his father's guidance. What this home training did for him, as he started out in life, was to stir deep within a passion for excellence, that *libido excellendi* in which Blaise later came to trace, in its most refined form, " that spirit which is contrary to the spirit of Christianity." [32]

[30] " Sa *Vie* par Madame Périer," the manuscript belonging to Faugère in 16°, 82 pp. " Prosper Faugère l'avait acquis de la Bibliothèque d'A.-A. Renouard, qui le tenait lui-même de M. Dequin (1804)." *Œuvres*, v. 1, 49.

[31] We repeat that the version of the Bible cited in these pages for each general reference to the Bible is that of the Latin Vulgate, first published in English by the English College at Douay, in A.D. 1609, for the Old Testament, and by the English College at Rheims, in A.D. 1582, for the New Testament. Unless special mention is made, our text is taken from the translation published with the approbation of His Eminence James Cardinal Gibbons, Archbishop of Baltimore, John Murphy Company, Publishers, Baltimore, Maryland, Printers to the Holy See.

[32] *Œuvres*, v. 1, xlvi.

A BASIC DISTINCTION

Not that Etienne Pascal was a freethinker. On the contrary, he always displayed an attitude of submissiveness and sincere respect toward religion. He held that an object of faith could not, by its very nature, be an object of reason, still less subordinated to the dictates of reason. On the other hand, he maintained that faith had no competence whatever in the field of natural phenomena.

Deeply impressed by the lofty influence of his father, whom he respected alike for his great wisdom and for the clarity and force of his reasoning powers, Blaise thus learned from early childhood to draw a clear line of demarcation between objects of reason and objects of faith. When the freethinkers of his day — in our time we should call them " modernists " — gave first place to the claims of reason, and undertook to submit everything to rational judgment, Blaise was in a position to detect at once their basic heresy. The distinction taught him so well by his father was deeply rooted in his mind, and it enabled him to exercise untrammeled freedom of thought in the domain of pure science, and yet to retain a childlike spirit of submissiveness in the domain of religion. This does not mean, of course, that he kept his thinking in compartments with respect to different types of subject matter on the same level. It was evident to him that above the level of reason there emerged, at the level of faith, a new *order,* other than the order of nature, and in this sense supernatural.

We may note at this point, in the basic distinction taught him by his father, the first appearance of the three orders of reality: namely, the order of matter, the order of minds, and the order of charity. In this hierarchy, values were to be separated to the point that communication between one and the one immediately above appeared inconceivable. To quote from the famous Fragment 793 of the *Pensées:* " All bodies, the firmament, the stars, the earth and its kingdoms, are not equal in value to the lowest mind; for mind knows all these and itself too; and these bodies know nothing.

" All bodies together, and all minds together, and all their productions, are not equal in value to the least feeling of charity. This is of an order infinitely more exalted.

" From all bodies together, one cannot draw forth one tiny thought; that is impossible, and of another order. From all bodies and minds, one cannot draw forth a feeling of true charity; that is impossible, and of another order, supernatural." [33]

It seems clear that the seed thought of the notion of the three orders lay hidden in the early teaching Blaise Pascal received from his father. We can well imagine Etienne, as he followed his son's questions back step by step in considering some matter that claimed their attention, suddenly stopping with an upraised hand, or lapsing into reverent silence, when they found themselves at the threshold of a question concerning God: " That, my child, is not for us to talk about! " What a reverent spirit it was that molded the mind of this gifted child, and what fruitful results were to issue from it!

The basic distinction which Etienne Pascal taught his son helped not a little to save Blaise from the scholastic way of thought. His own theology was always " positive theology," or, we should say, " Biblical theology." It was from the pages of the Bible that Blaise Pascal received the stimulus to search for himself into the secrets of a God who was self-concealed. Etienne Pascal, as we now can see,[34] prepared the mind of his son for the influence of the Bible.

To sum up: Just as it would be a mistake to suppose that Etienne Pascal was a freethinker, it would be a mistake to call him a devout man in the ordinary sense. We could not even call him a religious man. His chief interests, in the leisure hours left him after faithfully discharging his public duty, were mathematics and ancient languages.

[33] *Pensées,* Section xii, Fr. 793, *Œuvres,* v. **14,** 233.

[34] According to Lhermet, it was when the lad began to inquire as to the how and why of things that Etienne Pascal was led to formulate the noted distinction we have described. Lhermet interprets it in the sense that Etienne Pascal had in mind " not to separate, but wholly to reconcile faith with reason." His evidence? It appears to be convincing enough for Lhermet: it is that this maxim is in effect a happy condensation of Paragraph I of the Preface to the *Catechism of Trent.* This is offered as proof that Etienne Pascal taught his son Church doctrine according to this book, in which the following phrase is indeed found: " The realm of faith begins where the realm of reason ends." In support of this contention, Lhermet cites Pascal's letter to Father Noël, which to him, Lhermet, is nothing other than Thomist in spirit! Furthermore, how does he explain that one of the results of this education was " to divert his inquiring mind from subtle questions of theology "? There are in fact two kinds of theology: positive and scholastic, Lhermet answers. According to him, Pascal was to take up the first, but not the second, . . . save in the *Lettres Provinciales* (Lhermet, J., *Pascal et la Bible,* Librairie J. Vrin, Paris [The title page bears no date, but, on p. 691, the endorsement of the Dean of the Faculté des Lettres of the University of Paris is dated January 24, 1930], pp. 22–32).

We have made a special point of adducing for the record these views of a Catholic writer. In our judgment they err in giving too large a place to conjecture.

Scientific discussions were exciting to him. We should also remember that he emerged from a Christian tradition which as an *honnête homme* he did not like to discuss in public, however firmly he might hold to it in personal conviction. He paid his formal respects to this tradition, at a safe distance, when occasion required, but it would be too much to say that President Pascal would ever seek out the occasion. Every Sunday without fail he made his way through the tiny passageway leading from his house to the Cathedral. The passageway was in a sense a symbol: it served as a link to keep the oratory in touch with the laboratory.

Etienne was of a stanch, legal temper, rigorous in its concepts of right, taking but slight account of the whims of popular feeling, but finding deep rootage in the soil of Auvergne. This same temper reappeared, in a loftier and purer form, in his son, who was one day to vindicate the Jansenists against the Jesuits in his *Lettres Provinciales*. As it developed, it was enriched by a stream flowing from Christian faith and from the Bible. It came to take full account of the nature of the human soul, and of the scene of humanity in general. Blaise Pascal believed in human beings as so many distinct personalities, with a responsibility to God and society to suppress all corruption. Of this he was persuaded from having listened as a child to a voice speaking clearly and distinctly of delinquents, accused persons, guilty and condemned criminals, and about the moral law and the law of God. He himself was one day to devote his life to building up cases, when his conscience as a man and as a Christian was laid under constraint!

As to the end product of a long tradition, we can understand how there came to take shape in Blaise Pascal " the most fully rounded mind, the best balanced, the most trustworthy in the realm of the sciences, and at the same time the most restless in its quest for perfection and for certainty, that France has ever produced." [35] A blunt man, full of common sense, a man who handled things and invented useful devices — the calculating machine, the barometer, the omnibus — Pascal felt instinctively that man is a totality, intent first and foremost upon self-preservation. His realism was of the utilitarian sort, craving always for certainty. It was in this spirit that he read the Bible. He was not sentimental or mystical in his first approach to the Bible, but hardheaded, in the manner of one who knew that there is a rule of life, which can be set down in definite propositions, which must be understood and

[35] Fabre, Lucien, " Pascal et les sciences," *La Revue hebdomadaire*, No. 28, *op. cit.*, p. 242.

obeyed. Man's salvation, after all, is basically a matter of self-preservation. And if man is to preserve himself, he dares not dissipate or waste his efforts. In Auvergne men never wasted their resources. A wise economy starts out from a prudent conduct of everyday affairs; it continues unbroken in the intellectual economy of a man of genius, in his search for the inner logic of things, once he is persuaded basically that God is simple, and that all complexity is a mark of imperfection. In the case of Blaise Pascal, his reading of the Bible was a spur to his scholarly inquiry, and assured him of the reality of the Light behind the curtain.

This prudent, practical genius always considered himself the very opposite of a metaphysician. He always demanded certainty. There was nothing vague or abstract about the God he learned to know. He was the " God of Abraham, of Isaac and of Jacob," the Living God of the Bible. For Blaise Pascal there was no such thing as a substitute or counterfeit; nor could there be. Pascal's God was Jesus Christ, God on our earth, God in history and in our own history. His final conviction was to be: We do not know God except through Jesus Christ.

Starting with all the realistic good sense which he owed to his native Auvergne, to the common folk and tradesmen of the Limagne valley, and to a line of men of law in his own family, Blaise Pascal was prepared to believe " only those accounts of which the witnesses would die to vindicate their testimony." He observed that Christianity is primarily a doctrine resting upon facts, and he came to be devoted to the Bible because it was presented as a record of facts. His own Christian faith, in turn, was to be the faith of a witness, and his argument for Christianity took the form of a testimony. " He had the spirit of a witness and a martyr; he was prepared to sacrifice even life for his faith, since he had already sacrificed, for the sake of his faith, something to which his heart was far more firmly attached, namely, his prestige, his human pride, science, and even the love of his family." [36]

The author of the *Provinciales* is properly called the creator of French prose primarily because his realism, smacking of the soil, made him the forerunner of Molière's laughter and the " veritable eloquence " of Bossuet. The author of the *Pensées,* while he was concerned with the loftiest inquiries that can occupy the human mind, began a new type of apologetic which abandons every instrument of metaphysics and seizes you, as it were, by the lapel of your coat as a man would do in the

[36] Chevalier, Jacques, *Pascal, op. cit.,* Foreword, p. vi.

34

street if he were trying to save a careless pedestrian whom he saw in danger. Pascal starts out from your situation and mine. He shows that practical good sense which led the good people of Clermont to plant vegetables in the old moat around their city wall. With every word, his style calls up some image to the mind. Here you see a row of judges, in their ermines and scarlet robes; here a preacher, with a rasping voice and a queer twist to his features, ill-shaven by the barber, and still further besmeared by a chance mishap; here a group of soldiers, drunken brutes in arms with bloated faces, with hands and strength to serve only themselves.

With a sensitive touch Paul Bourget traces the example of Blaise Pascal, as he reflects upon the inequality of our human lot. Speaking of a certain great one, Pascal says: " He has four lackeys, while I have but one. If we settle matters by counting, it is plain that I must give way. By this means we shall find ourselves at peace, which is the greatest of all blessings." Look a bit closely at this last phrase. Bourget writes: " Here you will become fully aware of the transition from physical realism to moral realism. Whatever just and accurate observation Pascal makes concerning even the slightest phenomenon in the material world, he adds an equally precise observation of some psychological truth. Every comment concerning human sentiment which Pascal makes in his *Pensées* is so accurate that it remains true for all time." [37]

A BIBLICAL HORIZON

After speaking of the " motionless convulsion " which lends to Auvergne such a tragic horizon, even during wintry days when the snow lies like a white cloth over the huge layers of volcanic rock, leaving one to guess the force of the subterranean fire and the violence that must have accompanied the eruption, Bourget ends: " By one of those analogies that defy adequate expression, the *Pensées* are very much like the Auvergne landscape; the similarity will be noted by one who is fond of Auvergne and of Pascal. That he belonged in this respect to his native province explains . . . the powerful attraction exerted by this genius, at once so personal in its character, and yet at the same time so representative of a race, of a whole region." [38]

These motionless convulsions, which lent a tragic horizon to Pascal's

[37] Bourget, Paul, " Sur Pascal," *L'Illustration*, No. 4189, June 16, 1923, p. 595.
[38] *Ibid.*, p. 596.

thought, he found quite as much in the Bible, whose intimate realism he loved, as in the landscape of Auvergne. He overheard, in his own heart, a profound echo of the voice of the prophets. He came to love the rich language of the Book, pulsing as it did with vitality. He felt at home with Hebrew notions of the supreme objects of religious devotion, ideas clothed in flesh and blood, taken from life itself. That is one reason why he felt that he must make his own translations from the Bible, and why he often appended an exposition to his own version, always going to the heart of the experience. That is in a sense why his theology came to be Biblical, as the wide gap between the substance of certain doctrines and what the theologians called their " Scriptural foundations " became so evident to him.

This man from Clermont had a natural distrust of all subtlety and circumlocution. It was the substance of things he must grasp. He went straight to his mark. One of the ablest critics of literary style, Edouard de Rougemont,[39] made an analysis not long ago of Pascal's method of writing. It is, says he, distorted by the excessive speed of composition; he resorts to frequent abbreviations (this was common, it is true, at the period when Pascal was writing); words are often illegible, owing to Pascal's astonishing rapidity of writing. Threadlike streaks stand in place of whole syllables; at the same time, it is evident from the coherence of his thought that there is nothing flighty about his mind. All this notwithstanding, there is still an amazing interval between the swift conception of his thought, and the setting down of the words, however rapidly, on paper. It is rare to find this interval so marked anywhere, save in the writings of Napoleon or of Beethoven. Reference to such names should remind us, if ever we should be tempted to lose sight of it for an instant, that large place must be given, in any such analysis, to the working of genius.

" What an enigma it is we confront, almost religious in character, whenever a genius appears! " exclaims Maurice Barrès. " How comes it about that the spark gleams in this child, but not in that one, when both are born of the same parents, and under the same sky? How is this point of perfection attained, this perilous equipoise? What shall we make of such an extraordinary blend of saint and sage, of observer and visionary? Pascal rigorously applied the scientific method, but he sensed all the while the reality of supernatural aid. Since we have no other lan-

[39] Quoted by Fortunat Strowski, " Le Manuscrit des Pensées," *L'Illustration*, No. 4189, June 16, 1923, p. 599.

guage in which to describe this sublime compounding of qualities, must we then call it a miracle? Was Pascal a black stone that fell from heaven into Clermont on 19 June 1623? Not at all. Rather was he a block of genuine Auvergne basalt. This noble flame leaped from the same sparks we find in our humblest pebbles." And the writer adds that, if the divine factor in the fashioning of this genius perforce escapes our reckoning, " we may at least understand him in his early actions and his early nurture, until the time when God lifts him, now fully formed, above the level of earthly influences, in order to shape him according to His own design." [40]

This is what we are seeking to accomplish in part, in these opening pages, though we are deeply aware that, in the interplay of these " earthly " influences, the larger part already belongs to God.

[40] Barrès, Maurice, " Les Enfances de Pascal," *op. cit.*, pp. 133, 134.

II

An Open Mind in the Making

" Train up a child in the way he should go: and when he is old, he
will not depart from it."

—*Prov. 22:6*

Even among the loftiest souls, indeed chiefly among them, maxims of conduct are not so rigid as men like to assume. There is always room for individual initiative, and for a man to maintain it in the course of his life and labor. Montaigne, accustomed to ponder on his life from day to day, called the account of his reflections his " Essays." For him the word " essay " means the same thing as " experiment." Montaigne *essays* the ancient ways and seeks to determine on what conditions he may make them vitally real to himself. The closing chapter of his book he appropriately calls " De l'expérience." This type of " essay," with the connotation of experiment, was transplanted to England by Francis Bacon, who had read Montaigne.

What, in fact, is an experiment? It is a conversation with life. There is danger that life may take you unaware if you approach it without due preparation; but if you have already in mind a solid notion of what you want to say and of what you intend to do, you will then be in a position to pose your questions first. Soon the conversation may take an unexpected turn; life may confront you with new situations, which, for a time, disturb your security and threaten to call in question some position of which you had felt quite sure. Then you will state your views in a new form, and life will reward you with a glimpse of hitherto unguessed horizons. It may even whisper some of their secrets into your ear, at least enough to pique your curiosity. Thus your conversation with life goes on, by means of successive restatements, each one of which offers you ample scope to *essay* your principles. These will stand firm if you are firm and faithful — faith is faithfulness, having originally stood for confidence — but they will stand firm as the members of a living organism endure, always adapting themselves to new conditions and new circumstances. The great principle in the life of Etienne Pascal, which we have suggested by the symbol of the oratory and the laboratory, is no exception to this rule.

EARLY RELIGIOUS EDUCATION

When Blaise was seven years old, his father sold his post of Second President of the Cour des Aides to a brother, converted his property into Government bonds, and settled in Paris with his family. From 1631 to the end of 1639 he devoted himself to science and to the education of his children.

We are left very much to our own conjecture on the point of the early religious education of Blaise himself. Lhermet leans heavily indeed upon conjecture, as it seems to us, when he undertakes to reckon up the sum total of religious knowledge that Blaise had acquired by the time of his first communion: according to this Catholic writer, Etienne Pascal *must have* treated " questions of canonicity and inspiration, and *must have* laid down the rules of the sacred hermetic. The study of each book [of the Bible] need not have been according to the traditional order, as fixed by a canon of the Council of Trent." [1] To Lhermet it seems certain " that they lingered more over those dogmatic and historical passages, which are the foundation of the Christian faith. This was the traditional method followed by the Church in the teaching of Scripture," according to the *Manuel Biblique,* by Vigouroux. [2]

Having decided, for our part, to keep to the solid basis of known fact, we prefer to abide by the briefly stated conclusion of the distinguished Pascalian scholar, Victor Giraud, who is himself a Catholic: it does not seem clear, to him, that previous to 1646 Blaise " had much contact with the Scriptures, especially with the Early Fathers, the Scholastics, and the medieval theologians: that, in any case, such reading had little influence upon him [the same could not have been said of Descartes] — that they added nothing, or, at most, very little, to those lessons in piety he had received from his family; a rather lukewarm Christianity, but quite enough for Pascal at that period." Concluding his hasty notes on this subject, Giraud remarks that Pascal's other reading " must have corroborated the elder Pascal's prudent ' maxims ' concerning the rela-

[1] Lhermet, J., *Pascal et la Bible, op. cit.,* p. 19.
[2] 13th edition, 1913, v. 1, 349 ff., quoted by Lhermet, p. 20.

tion of reason to faith, and must have supported a latent Stoicism in the youth's mind."[3]

A YOUTHFUL PRODIGY

If we turn now from his religious development to his literary and scientific upbringing, it is to see what marvelous progress the young lad was making under his father's direction, aided, of course, by his native genius.

His wide-awake mind let nothing escape. One day at the family table, when Blaise was only eleven, he noticed that one of the porcelain plates vibrated when a knife struck it, and that the noise stopped as soon as someone's hand touched the plate. His father, who was interested in harmony, helped him to account for this singular phenomenon. But it was a singular phenomenon nonetheless; could he not make further observations of a like nature? Might they not lead to sound inductions? Already his distinctively scientific mind was at work. He devoted himself to a series of experiments, and proceeded to write a treatise on sound, which proved to be quite well thought out.

At the age of twelve, the boy was set by his father to the study of Latin. Etienne wished him to get through the study of languages before he undertook geometry. The reason for this, so Madame Périer reminds us, was that Etienne knew mathematics to be " a subject which fills and gives much satisfaction to the mind," and he did not wish his son to have " any knowledge whatever " of it as yet, for fear it would tempt him to neglect Latin and the other languages in which he wished him to be proficient.[4] Madame Périer's interpretation on this point calls for a further remark: what if a mind be indeed filled and satisfied prematurely before it has been prepared by proper earlier training and by maturity? Is not then the danger, precisely, that such a mind will be satisfied too easily and too soon? Etienne Pascal was afraid that he might shape a *closed mind!* In this respect he was looking beyond languages and mathematics alike.

While the father was pondering such matters as these, and trying to keep Blaise at a prudent distance when groups of scholars met at his

[3] Giraud, Victor, *Pascal, l'homme, l'œuvre, l'influence*, notes of a course given at the University of Fribourg, Switzerland, during the first semester of 1898, 3d edition, revised, corrected, and considerably enlarged, Albert Fontemoing, editor, Paris, 1905, pp. 24, 25. See also *Œuvres*, v. 10, 387.

[4] *Œuvres*, v. 1, 53.

home, the young lad himself was down on all fours in a corner, drawing lines and circles on the floor. Thus the father's neat pattern of instruction went awry.

The pedagogue might insist that it would really be better to wait before studying geometry, but it was useless. Geometry? " But what is geometry? " the lad asks, now all eyes and ears. " That, my child, is the noblest and loftiest form of human knowledge." So the teacher replies, meaning to put an end to the argument once and for all. Geometry, that is to say, is something not made for a twelve-year-old child. " Well, anyway, how do you do geometry? " This time Etienne answers quite simply and bluntly, thinking to dispose of the matter: " Geometry is the study of the proportions between different figures, and the manner of stating them with unerring precision." That was quite enough for young Pascal! His mind was seething with ideas now, and he took his bit of charcoal and went back to his corner on the floor, back to more lines and more circles.

The teacher did not wholly disarm him now, but he did put away under lock and key every manual and treatise on mathematics, and made his friends promise to be silent on the subject in the boy's presence. One day he came into a room where the boy had escaped his watchful eye. There he found Blaise just about to finish demonstrating the thirty-second proposition of the First Book of Euclid, having rediscovered for himself every one of the principles that preceded it! [5] Frightened now by his discovery, Etienne turned for advice to Le Pailleur, who told him to let his son have access to every available book on the subject. This he did, and the boy eagerly read them, soon making such progress in geometry that his father allowed him to accompany him to the weekly gatherings of the Académie Mersenne.

From that time on the thirteen-year-old boy, every Thursday afternoon at the Académie Libre, which became in due time the Académie des Sciences, took an active part in the discussions, and his opinion was greeted with respect. Numbered in this group were Father Mersenne, friend of Descartes, and patron saint of all *secrétaires perpétuels* of the Académie des Sciences, always on the watch for new publications and new talent in the scientific field; Desargues, that geometer from Lyons who suggested to Blaise the idea of starting from his knowledge of perspective and reducing the properties of conic sections to a small number

[5] *Œuvres*, v. 1, 53–56. The account by Madame Périer. Cf. notes of Brunschvicg for variants.

of propositions; the epicure Le Pailleur, a self-taught man who proved himself competent in solving some of the most difficult problems; Roberval, professor of mathematics at the Collège de France, opponent of Descartes and precursor of Newton, one of the glories of French science; and Carcavy, and Mydorge, maker of lenses, and the mathematician Hardy, learned in Oriental languages. During the winter of 1636–1637 Hobbes was present on the occasion when Etienne Pascal, Roberval, and the illustrious Fermat launched an attack upon Descartes concerning one of the points in his geometry. Blaise Pascal, mere youth though he was in so distinguished a company, had the culture of an educated man of thirty, and his native genius to boot.

It was this genius, together with this quite extraordinary training, that led him, in 1639 when he was barely sixteen years old, to produce an *Essay on Conic Sections,* of which a summary was published in 1640 for the use of the scholars of the day.[6] Having already advanced well beyond the views of projective geometry held by Desargues, our young savant next discovered the noted lemma which is known in the history of mathematics as the Pascal Theorem. All the properties of conic sections are included in it, and Pascal's mathematical method has already become clearly evident in its essential points. Apace with his mathematical discovery, Pascal's religious faith was also asserting itself: "After which," he concludes, "if this matter be deemed worthy of further consideration, we shall attempt to push it to whatever point God shall give us strength to carry it."[7] Nor was this by any means an empty manner of speaking.

We may go still farther: mathematical thinking, after it had attained a certain level, would compel Blaise Pascal to give further consideration to the distinction between what depends upon reason and what depends upon faith.

PASCAL'S MYSTIC HEXAGRAM

Leibnitz, who passionately admired Pascal, later discussed at some length Pascal's work on conic sections. He summarized it in his letter to Etienne Périer, under date of August 30, 1676,[8] and his summary is the more valuable to us in that Pascal's own papers on the subject have been lost, except for his single essay *Generatio conisectionum,*[9] which

---

[6] *Œuvres,* v. 1, 245.   [8] *Œuvres,* v. 2, 220–224.
[7] *Œuvres,* v. 1, 260.   [9] *Œuvres,* v. 2, 234.

he completed only in 1648, and of which, again, Leibnitz has preserved the only known copy. Now, in this *Essay on Conic Sections*, of which Leibnitz knew, Pascal gave the name of " mystic hexagram " to a hexagon inscribed within a conic section. According to the Pascal Theorem, as quite precisely stated, such a hexagon has this property, that the meeting points on opposite sides are always found to be in a straight line.

Ravaisson clearly saw that this discovery was based upon Pascal's notion that " the properties of a complicated figure may be considered as modifications and resemblances of a simpler figure," [10] such as a circle, when seen in perspective in the third dimension. On this point, Jacques Chevalier comments: " We find here again the Platonic idea of participation, according to which all things found in nature are images or imitations of Ideas; and we thus anticipate the Pascalian doctrine of orders, which sees, in genuine art, the imitation of a natural model possessed of superior charm and beauty; in morality, once again, the imitation of a supernatural example, namely, of God; and in nature generally a type, or a distorted image of grace." [11] Chevalier may have extracted from this notion of the mystic hexagram somewhat more than is justified by Pascal's original discovery. Allowing for exaggeration, however, it is nonetheless clear that the development of Pascal's thought along mathematical lines led him to bring together two orders of thinking which had hitherto been distinct. The line of demarcation, separating oratory from laboratory, was no longer hard and fast.

SCIENCE AND RELIGION

Blaise Pascal's acquaintance with eminent scholars compelled him to reconsider his father's famous maxim, in the infinitely vaster field of the rights of science, as against the claims of theology and of Holy Writ.

A battle was actually under way over Galileo. Two groups of scholars were concerned with the issue: one group, centered about Father Mersenne, held its meetings at the Hôtel des Minimes; the other, led by the Abbé Bourdelot, met at the Hôtel de Condé. Be it said that Pascal rarely appeared at the latter group. It was actually started in 1638, and Etienne moved to Rouen, as we shall see, on January 2, 1640.

[10] " Ravaisson," *Revue des deux mondes,* March 15, 1887, p. 414, quoted by Jacques Chevalier, *Pascal, op. cit.,* p. 56.

[11] Chevalier, J., *Pascal, op. cit.,* pp. 56, 57.

The time was thus short. Another consideration lay in the fact that the Abbé Bourdelot was unorthodox. According to Sainte-Beuve he is supposed to have tried to burn a fragment of the true Cross. Here was a man who took real pleasure in watching science batter down the dogmas of Christianity, and in finding among the many diverse scientific opinions reflected in his group that no question was regarded as sacred, that is to say, untouchable. In such a company, Etienne and Blaise must have felt somewhat ill at ease. That they were found in the group occasionally gives indication of their liberal spirit. At the Hôtel des Minimes, the men around Father Mersenne were not quite so bold. It caused no little anxiety among them when they learned that the Florentine scholar had been condemned by the Inquisition because his conclusions in astronomy were held incompatible with the sacred texts.

In the matter of Biblical interpretation Lhermet makes an interesting comparison between Galileo and the Pascal of that period: " Pascal displays a greater timidity, in the matter of Biblical exegesis, than Galileo. He is in all respects as loyal to Tradition as regards the value to be attributed to Holy Scripture. Assuredly both of them, being convinced Christians, are in full agreement on the question of principle: they affirm categorically the inerrancy of the inspired writers. Is not Scripture the treasure of truths which God has revealed to men? " [12] In that case, how can anyone call in question the truths contained in the Bible? Is it possible for truths of the natural order to clash with truths of a supernatural order? Whereas Galileo imperiously claimed certain rights for science, Pascal was more reserved. The whole Copernican system, in fact, had not yet emerged from the realm of hypothesis. Its evident probability was of no avail; it did not have the Scriptural texts on its side.[13] Galileo insisted that it was for the theologians to reconcile the sacred texts with the new discoveries of science. Pascal was more circumspect, and confined himself to the traditional hypothesis.

Pascal's attitude, in a word, was that of a son always keeping in mind the teaching of his father who was, as it were, his constant companion,

[12] Lhermet, J., *Pascal et la Bible, op. cit.*, pp. 63, 64.
[13] In his treatment Lhermet errs, as we see it, in using a method of concordance which puts the whole of Pascal on the same level and ignores his evolution. Thus he refers to the eighteenth *Provinciale* (v. 7, 51, 53, 54) where Pascal relies on the authority of Saint Augustine and Saint Thomas, and on Fragments 72 and 218 of the *Pensées*. Now we shall see that from the Biblical point of view in particular the Pascal who wrote the *Provinciales* and the *Pensées* is indeed far from the Pascal who paid visits to Abbé Bourdelot and Father Mersenne.

and who doubtless lent added strength to views held by his son. The attitude of Blaise was that of a good Catholic, withholding judgment until the Church had made its pronouncement. During the years of his childhood and youth, " there was no trace of doubt concerning revealed truths; there was no trace of scorn nor indifference toward the practices of piety." [14] We may well wonder, however, whether his serenity of mind was altogether untroubled. Whether he would or no, he was henceforth to confront the question of reconciling experimental science with revealed truth. Before long his mind was bound to be torn by a travail of which he might be but partly conscious. A " conversion " never occurs suddenly; it only appears so to those who look on the surface of things.

THE GOLDEN AGE IN THE MAKING

Everywhere about the Pascal household intellectual life was in a state of intense ferment. How could Blaise escape the influence of this fresh atmosphere so characteristic of Paris in the days of Richelieu at the very time when he was coming of age? The Académie Française, emerging as the fruit of some literary gatherings at the home of Conrart, was organized in 1635, and gave its blessing to the language reform initiated by Malherbe and Balzac. The Hôtel de Rambouillet revived an ancient courtly tradition by adding a touch of refinement to the new school of writing. It prepared the way, in a polite society, for the reign of the honnête homme.

A psychological crisis, marked by conflicting sentiments and emotions, was bound to afflict the chosen souls of the early seventeenth century in France. Such souls were at once self-conscious, inwardly torn, and seeking light from Neo-Stoicism under a Christian name.

Corneille gave eloquent expression to this spiritual crisis in Le Cid (1636), in which Mondory created the hero's role at the Théâtre du Marais. Etienne Pascal was overcome with admiration, and invited the celebrated actor to give private lessons to little Jacqueline, who had fallen in love with the stage. Before long, Jacqueline herself played her part in Scudéry's L'Amour tyrannique to such perfection that she won the heart of Cardinal Richelieu, whom she complimented with some pretty verses at the close of the performance.

Poetry was nothing new to Jacqueline; at the age of eleven she had

[14] Lhermet, J., Pascal et la Bible, op. cit., p. 68.

written a five-act comedy, with the aid of two small friends. The play was presented before the Queen, and Jacqueline, in her small way, became the court poetess. Corneille admired her poetry. One day at Rouen, when she was awarded the *de la Tour* prize for some lines on the Conception of the Virgin, in the annual palinods competition, the author of *Le Cid* improvised some complimentary verses in her stead. Blaise was envious of the Muses, and later took his revenge for the loneliness of that day when his talented sister deserted him, by flinging some rather sharp shafts at poetry in the pages of the *Pensées*.

In the philosophical world, the libertinism native to Paris — there were fifty thousand freethinkers there at the time — was concerned with freedom of manners. These were the *libres viveurs* to whom the author of the *Pensées* was to allude twenty years later. At the moment, Blaise himself took quite an interest in that breviary of skepticism, so eagerly acclaimed by the freethinkers as their authority, namely, Montaigne's *Essais*, and his own thought was steeped in it. This was soon supplanted, in turn, in the world of thought, by the intellectual autobiography of an *honnête homme*, the *Discours de la méthode* (1637), by Descartes, which appealed to reason as the ultimate arbiter, reason, that is to say, which is essentially good sense.

CONCERN FOR THE INNER MAN

More and more attention was directed to the life of that inner man, who alone was deemed worthy of interest. It was the inner man that chiefly concerned the painters of the day, who concentrated their talent upon capturing the meditative mood in their portraits. Their paintings revealed a serious, serene maturity of outlook on the part of men who were aware of their responsibility as human beings, absorbed in moral problems and in the preoccupations of religion.

Religion, for its part, bore the stamp of austere severity of a new type of Stoicism, revived by Guillaume du Vair (1556–1621), of Auvergne, and by the learned Justus Lipsius (1547–1606), of the University of Louvain. The painter Philippe de Champaigne (1602–1674), who, like Jansenism, came from Flanders, reflected, in the rather chilly hauteur of his portraits, something of that way of thought, for which religion is primarily a principle of moral guidance, rather than a metaphysical answer to the questions of life. This austere tradition stands in contrast over against the exuberant buoyancy, and the kindliness which overcomes all disputing, such as we find in Saint François de Sales (1568–1622), as expressed in his *Introduction à la vie dévote* (1608) and in the *Traité de l'amour de Dieu* (1610). Saint Vincent de Paul (1576–1660) made himself the advocate of this type of Christian charity, to the point of becoming its veritable incarnation. The men who founded or restored religious orders complete the picture of this glorious spiritual awakening: Bérulle founded the Oratoire in 1611, and in 1608 Angélique Arnauld reformed Port-Royal.

We must not lose sight of this basic picture of the period if we are fully to appreciate the events which find echo in the next chapter. The Pascal family could hardly remain unaffected by such surroundings as Paris offered between 1631 and 1640. This seething ferment of ideas, sentiments, and emotions on every hand could not fail to leave its mark upon them. They could not help being " obsessed and burdened " with the peculiar concerns of the day. On all sides, from this time on, the atmosphere of the oratory was to press upon, and even oppress, the intellectuals of the laboratory. Around them, on all sides, men were offering themselves to do battle for causes held to be sacred.

The armor was being made ready, individual discipline was revived in a remarkable degree, not unlike the political preparations being carried forward, in the course of this great century, by Cardinal Richelieu. It was just at this point that Richelieu took a hand in the affairs of the Pascal family, with a summons to action.

ENTER RICHELIEU

In the month of March, 1638, the royal treasury was facing difficulties, and the interest was sharply reduced on the bonds of the Hôtel de Ville. Etienne Pascal, finding his personal income directly affected, joined with a number of other bondholders in lodging a formal protest. Richelieu, who was not a man to trifle with in matters of authority, countered by having three leaders of the group thrown into the Bastille. Fearing for his personal safety, Etienne Pascal went into hiding at the home of some friends. Jacqueline was shortly afterward taken with smallpox, and Etienne came out of hiding, risking arrest in order to stay by his daughter's sickbed. Once she was well again, he took refuge in Auvergne.

The smallpox attack left little Jacqueline quite disfigured. As she gazed into the mirror at the " pits " that the disease had left on her face, this young girl decided, quite of her own accord, to consecrate them to God, and wrote some *Stanzas* on the action of divine grace:

> These I accept, my sovereign Lord!
> As token seals that Thy blest Hand
> Would guard henceforth my innocence.

That was Christian stoicism, indeed, in such an age, and in such a family!

Notwithstanding this handicap, Jacqueline was invited by Madame d'Aiguillon, in 1639, to take a part in Scudéry's play *L'Amour tyrannique,* then being arranged for the pleasure of the Cardinal, who was very fond of the theater. It was on this occasion, at the end of the performance in which her acting had won Richelieu's favor, that Jacqueline, as we have mentioned, paid him a compliment in verse. The Cardinal was enchanted, lavished " extraordinary caresses " upon Mondory's young pupil, and promised to grant any boon she might ask. Whereupon Jacqueline, quite spontaneously and with an altogether feminine finesse, asked the great man not to be angry any longer with her father. Richelieu promptly summoned Etienne Pascal to Rueil, along with all his family. There he received him with greatest courtesy and then turned him over to his squire, ordering him to let the guests see everything in Rueil, and to entertain them handsomely.

Richelieu had, indeed, been forewarned by Madame d'Aiguillon, and now he was greatly impressed by the Pascal family. In Blaise he seemed to sense the presence of a genius, as he had done in the case of Corneille. The stately figure of Etienne also impressed him. And here is a feat quite characteristic of the great administrator: a little later on, in September, 1639, Richelieu, finding himself in great need of a well-qualified deputy to reorganize affairs in Normandy, which was passing through one of the worst crises in its history, forgot all past grudges and called upon Etienne Pascal to fill the post. Appointed His Majesty's Deputy Commissioner in Upper Normandy for the levying of taxes and duties, Etienne Pascal arrived early in 1640 in the good city of Rouen, which was plunged in great misery and desolation. He took his work very much to heart. His scrupulous honesty won him such esteem from the people that, on a certain New Year's Day, the magistrates of Rouen presented him, in the name of the town, with a purse of silver pieces coined especially in his honor.

But what a task it was he had undertaken! For a period of four months, as he himself admitted, he did not get to bed before two o'clock in the morning, except half a dozen times. Blaise, who had just turned sixteen, kept wondering how he might help to relieve his father's heavy load. This led him to conceive, and then to contrive in all its details, the calculating machine, the very idea of which was wholly new, and which was by no means easy to carry out at that time. It cost him enormous effort, and he had many obstacles to overcome, including the rivalry of a certain clockmaker in the town. At last it was finished. Morris Bishop has examined one of the ten known models of Pascal's machine, at the Conservatoire des Arts et Métiers, in Paris, and he has given a detailed account of its working, to which the reader is referred.[15] This stroke of genius on Blaise's part seemed to him to mark the triumph of the mathematical mind.

On this point once again, the testimony of Pascal's elder sister, Madame Périer, is of capital importance: she says that this achievement, referring to the calculating machine, " was looked upon as a novel thing [in] nature, to have reduced to a machine a science which resided wholly in the mind, and to have found a way to perform all the operations with complete accuracy, and without making any use of reason whatever." [16] Strange eulogy that was, for at the same time that it lauded a great triumph of the mind, it went on to point out the negative limitations of the achievement. The mathematical mind attained its greatest success by a means which rendered itself superfluous!

It is in the light of a revelation like this that we must later read Pascal's own eloquent treatment of the theme. He points out that what we have, in the mathematical mind, is the interplay of certain principles, substantial, palpable, *capable of being tested by measuring and counting*. What shall we say, then, of a geometer who is only a geometer? The reason why such a geometer has no *finesse* is that *he does not see what is in front of him*. We judge him, in other words, like a machine! What profound irony! How wretched is any man in whom man does not surpass man! Blaise Pascal must have been, indeed, already deeply divided

[15] Bishop, Morris, *Pascal:* The Life of Genius, Reynal & Hitchcock, Inc., New York, 1936, pp. 28-31.
[16] *Œuvres*, v. 1, 58.

within himself when, in 1645, he voiced his youthful pride in the Dedicatory Letter addressed to Monseigneur le Chancelier, and in the instructions needed by those who might wish to inspect the calculating machine, or to use it.

At this point the objection may, of course, be raised that in her statement Madame Périer took too much account of the subsequent development of Pascal's thought, since she was writing twenty years later. Nevertheless it must have been disturbing for Blaise Pascal to realize that " a science which resided wholly in the mind " could be reduced to a machine, and a machine, at that, which enabled a person " to perform all the operations with complete accuracy "! At the very least, such a science was quite evidently narrow: it did not begin to exhaust the resources of the human mind; it hardly scratched the surface of things; at the very least, it called for a supplementary inquiry, if not for wholly new ways and new methods of knowledge. Pascal was already experimenting with the " vacuum," in one sense, before he used the term. The need for some supplementary inquiry can be read between the lines of the Dedicatory Letter to Monseigneur le Chancelier.

The lines themselves, however, express a boundless confidence on the part of Blaise Pascal. The young scientist is evidently engrossed in the practical application of his newly acquired knowledge, as may be expected of a child reared in a town where the neighbors turned an abandoned moat into a vegetable garden; or by the son of a young *president de tribunal* who had remodeled the stables of an old house into useful shops; of a young lad who wanted to bring material relief to his overburdened father, but in a way congenial to his own interests. All this is quite true, and we shall have to stress repeatedly the *continuity* of Pascal's thought. In whatever direction his genius moved, it was to show itself pre-eminently practical, and when, before long, we find him turning to the Bible, it is in this spirit.

It should further be added that the inventor of the calculating machine, in contriving this instrument, was in every sense a child of his own age, which looked upon an inventor, not as a man who conceived ideas, but as one who could apply them in practice. Even the science of mathematics, which men like Desargues and Roberval extolled to young Pascal, was not thought of as purely theoretical.[17]

The Dedicatory Letter went farther, however: it exalted that type of science which not only favored the legitimate, needful, unity of theory

[17] Strowski, F., *Pascal et son temps, op. cit.*, v. **2**, 73.

and art, but which should bring into a single, radiant focus " the lights of geometry, physics, and mathematics."

Fortunat Strowski has clarified this final point in a happy phrase: The period of apprenticeship, he says, through which Blaise Pascal passed in working on the calculating machine, " prevented him from falling into the excesses of mathematical physics. Pascal knew better than anyone else in his day how to plan an experiment, how to carry it out, and how to describe it. He never allowed himself to be carried away by the mania for speculation, by the intoxication of grand generalizations. He always maintained a profound respect for the experimental method, and for facts.

" But what attracted Pascal to physics was this: it was the truly general and philosophical science of the universe. The point of departure, indeed the very basis, for any metaphysics which sought to explain the nature and being of the world was physics." [18]

Etienne Pascal had nothing to fear. Even if his talented son had upset the plan of instruction so carefully prepared, and dipped into mathematics too soon, he, the teacher, had certainly not produced a closed mind. Or rather, mathematics itself had opened up to Blaise, on the one hand, a marvelous vista in the direction of the higher orders; and it had, on the other hand, set limits, so far as Blaise was concerned, to the competence of mechanical science, to its spirit and to its methods.

[18] *Ibid.*, 62, 63.

III

The Jansenist Quickening

"Moreover whom he did predestinate, them he also called."
—*Rom. 8:30*

One icy day in January, 1646, Etienne Pascal hurried out on foot to prevent a duel about to take place. He fell on the hard, frozen ground and dislocated his hip. Two pious gentlemen were summoned to attend him — Adrien Deschamps, Sieur de la Bouteillerie, and Jean Deschamps, Sieur des Landes — men who practiced medicine and surgery and were also dedicated to good works.

THE OCCASION OF GOD'S PURPOSE

These two brothers were recent converts to Jansenism, an evangelical theology derived from the teachings of Saint Augustine, and adapted to the needs of the seventeenth century by Cornelius Jansen; hence the name of their school, whose center was Port-Royal. Jean Duvergier de Hauranne, Abbé de Saint Cyran, had been appointed in 1633 confessor of this convent by its Mother Superior, Angélique, one of Antoine Arnauld's daughters. These fundamentalists, exalting the grace of God, had set out to reform Christianity while insisting that personal salvation was possible only in and through the Church of Rome. Conflicts were to be expected; one must note, in passing, the imprisonment of Saint Cyran in 1638 and also the issue of a Papal Bull, in 1641, forbidding discussion of questions of grace with special reference to the *Augustinus*. This bulky quarto, a sum of Augustinianism, had only been published in 1640, two years after Jansen's death. Furthermore, the substance of the *Augustinus* had been expounded for the general public by Antoine Arnauld in a work, *La fréquente communion* (1643), and this book was immediately the object of passionate debate.

The Pascals were well aware of the storm which spread eventually to the region of Rouen. They were naturally curious to hear all about Jansenism. The Deschamps brothers had quickly won their confidence and respect, and within three months after the dislocation of his hip Etienne Pascal was completely cured.

Morris Bishop pertinently brings out the fact that these men " were in their own persons admirable representatives of the Christian ideal, fulfilling itself in self-abnegation and service to one's fellows. Blaise was of an age to yield readily to hero worship. He was instinctively disposed in favor of the doctrine which had changed their lives, which, they hinted, might change his own." [1] The truth which emerged from that sublime Biblical doctrine, from the very outset, was that man of himself is helpless, and that this helplessness is illustrated by our physical sufferings. Blaise found his own health deteriorating at the time; hence the argument struck him with especial force. He knew from experience how helpless doctors might be — that helplessness which gave Molière material for some of his best scenes: we must not forget that Pascal was living in the middle of the seventeenth century.

The cure the Deschamps brothers were able to achieve being in itself an illustration, Pascal was naturally disposed to follow the teaching of Jansen, who proceeded from concern for bodily suffering to deeper concern over the suffering of the spirit. This all came about, as we have seen, on the plane of personal experience in the Pascal family, at a level familiar alike to father and son. Now, the Bible as experience — or, better, the Bible verified at each step by experience — shows that natural man is not in the state which God originally willed for him: he is a fallen creature. The sin which is rooted in the very core of his being attacks his several faculties, chiefly his will, as the very substance of his being. A vicious circle is thus set in process, by which sin is self-perpetuating, and this vicious circle cannot be broken save by the grace of God. Jansen stands, in this regard, in the line of succession from Saint Paul and Saint Augustine directly. Nothing less than the intervention of divine grace in our lives can free us from helpless mediocrity, from this hidden bondage. Equally true is it in human experience, however, that certain lives are thus regenerated, while others remain in a wretched state in which they appear content. The action of God is the prior fact. It is God's choice which in each case decides. So far, however, from rendering our own energies wholly vain, the grace of God uses them, sustains them, and repairs their faults and weakness by raising them to a higher order of being.

It was to an attainment of this state, no less, that Blaise now aspired.

[1] Bishop, Morris, *Pascal:* The Life of Genius, *op. cit.,* p. 41.

He was himself attracted to the higher life, before he sought to attract others. His youthful ardor was the first to be quickened by the new doctrine. Passionate soul that he was, he at once turned missionary, winning first his " little " sister Jacqueline, of whom he was particularly fond. The two of them appealed to their father, and that lofty soul quietly yielded to the truth, once he recognized it as such. " My ideas resist me," Malebranche was soon to write. Toward the end of the year, Gilberte, the elder daughter, who was married now and had a family of her own, came to Rouen and was won over in turn, along with M. Périer. The latter was to lend himself body and soul to good works all the rest of his life; as for Madame Périer, she and her children henceforth withdrew from all gatherings of a social nature, and she herself gave up every sort of feminine adornment.

The events of our life, as Pascal was one day to say, are lessons which God himself has set before us. In this sense the accident that befell his father appeared to Blaise, as he looked back upon it, to be at once the sign and the occasion of God's purposes for the family. Is it not clear, from what we know of Pascal, that he had already felt growing within his mind " that profound sense of predestination, which gave such a dramatic quality to his work and to his life "? [2]

One point needs clarification here, if we are to remove any trace of misunderstanding which may persist in the minds of readers familiar with the mistaken phrase, " Pascal's first conversion." The term " conversion " had a very special meaning in the seventeenth century; it did not then signify, as it does today, that deep-seated transformation which makes a believer out of an unbeliever; it meant, rather, especially in Jansenist wording, " the transition from a more or less dissipated and worldly life to a life of austere and profound piety." [3]

Let us be even more specific: many writers, when they treat of Pascal's " first conversion," describe it as primarily intellectual, not to say superficial and transitory, in nature, as shown by the fact that Pascal soon thereafter " resumed " his scientific labors. The truth is that Pascal never interrupted his scientific studies at all, and that he had no reason to interrupt them, according to the teaching of Saint Augustine, who greatly influenced his thinking at the time. What was really blameworthy, as he saw it then, was not the study of physics, nor its *employ-*

[2] Barrès, Maurice, " Les Enfances de Blaise Pascal," in *La Revue hebdomadaire*, No. 28, 32d year, July 14, 1923 (Third Centenary of Pascal), p. 140.

[3] Lhermet, J., *Pascal et la Bible, op. cit.*, p. 69.

ment in the sincere quest for truth, but the study of science merely for one's own *enjoyment*. To make *enjoyment* the chief end of research was quite evidently to corrupt it, to the degree that it became a sort of greed or lust for learning, a profligate appetite for knowledge, in the form of *libido sciendi,* or even *libido excellendi.* Such a study of science sprang from a prior concern for the self as the center of things, rather than a concern for seeking out, amid all surrounding natural phenomena, the presence of God and his glory. The very basis, indeed, of this type of intellectual dissipation implied an inversion of the prime principle of eternal Order; it was in essence the *avertio mentis a deo.*[4]

His first contact with Jansenism undoubtedly helped the young scholar, as further evidence will perhaps make clear, to a fuller awareness of this primordial truth. But even at this point it was not really a matter of " conversion "; still less was it so in view of the spiritual heights and depths Blaise was yet to traverse. In the period just following the events we have described, Pascal was as yet far from that mood of complete consecration which marked the closing months of his life.

CONFRONTING THE BIBLE

The Jansenist quickening in the soul of Pascal stirred him to a growing interest in books, which had hitherto played a very limited role in his education. For him, science had been essentially a conversation with nature, needing only the slightest reference to the written word. The problem of religion gave evidence of another Order, quite different from that of experimental science: whereas the latter, under the steady pressure of duly proved facts, sought to free itself — prudently enough, withal — from bondage to ancient Tradition, theology was pre-eminently a matter of authority. This distinction, which became more and more clear to Pascal, seems to us to have clarified in Pascal's thinking the distinction between truth dependent upon the oratory and truth dependent on the laboratory. If we examine it more closely, indeed, the new formulation appears as a reshaping of the earlier principle inherited from his father. Once again we find continuity in Pascal's experience.

Now, authority in the field of religion is quite naturally associated with the authority of certain books, and first of all with the sacred writings. It was thus inevitable that Pascal should be led to confront the

4 *Œuvres,* v. 1, xlvi.

Bible. His first significant encounter with the Holy Book came at a decisive moment in his life. Victor Giraud, who has made a study of Pascal's reading, is persuaded to give first place in importance to the Scriptures, of which Pascal was, as he says, " an assiduous reader," and which he was to know one day almost by heart. Giraud expresses the fervent wish for a book on *Pascal et l'Ecriture*, to stand as companion to the *Bossuet et l'Ecriture*, by the Abbé de la Broise. Pascal's reading of the Bible has not been, in his opinion, sufficiently explored: it would shed new light upon " the religious, Biblical, and evangelical tone of the *Pensées*." Special attention, he thinks, should be given to the epistles of Saint Paul, to the writings of Saint Augustine, and to Jansen's *Augustinus:* " There you will find the substance of Pascal's religious thought and of his mysticism." [5]

The doctrinal views of Jansenism accepted by Blaise, at this period, were closely bound up with the Scriptures. This helps further to account for his turning to the Scriptures, by way of Saint Augustine. The Jesuits were following the doctrine of Molina (1535–1600), a Spanish theologian of their religious order, who aimed at a conciliation of human freedom with divine grace and foreknowledge. In this Molinist doctrine Jansen sensed a mortal threat to Catholicism. As he saw it, it was the revival in disguised form of early Pelagianism, which rooted back, through Origen, directly in pagan philosophy. " Seneca had said: To the immortal gods we owe life, to philosophy we owe the good life. According to Jansen, this same human pride, which raised itself against God and even above God, was the very heart of Molinist theology. On the one hand, Jansen was unwilling to concede to the Protestants that God Himself forced man to sin; nor, on the other hand, would he grant to Baïus that there could be sin where there was no free will. To steer between the two rocks, he resolved rigorously to follow Saint Augustine." [6]

The luminous and solid condensation which Brunschvicg gives of the

---

[5] Giraud, V., *Pascal, l'homme, l'œuvre, l'influence*, pp. 119, 120. Note further that these notes of a course taught at the University of Fribourg, Switzerland, date back to 1898, and that the third edition from which we have taken this quotation dates back to 1905. Since then there has been much progress in the knowledge of this subject. What interests us here is the emphasis that an illustrious student of Pascal places on the important study of the Bible for an understanding of Pascalian thought in its highest expression.

[6] Boutroux, Emile, *Pascal*, Collection " *Les grands écrivains de la France*," 10th ed., Hachette, Paris, p. 109.

teaching of the *Augustinus* [7] will suffice to indicate the extent to which this work is based upon Holy Scripture, as interpreted by Saint Augustine. " It was from this stream of Christian Tradition that Pascal drew inspiration and nourishment, from the time when he first encountered the doctrines associated with the group around Saint Cyran. Jansen was, in his eyes, the authentic interpreter of Christ." [8] The *Augustinus* was for him the book of true doctrine, the spiritual hearthstone about which his other reading centered. Turning back to Saint Augustine he read, in the original tongue, his letters, his sermons, his essays on *Christian Doctrine* and the *Utility of Believing*, the books against Pelagius, the commentaries on Scripture. He read the *Discours sur la réforme de l'homme intérieur*, which Arnauld d'Andilly had just translated and which the Deschamps brothers had warmly commended to him. Here he found lengthy discourses on the vain desire of knowledge, and on pride, which amply justified the text from Saint John with which the book opens: " All that is in the world is the lust of the flesh, the lust of the eyes, and the pride of life." He read Arnauld's *La fréquente communion*, of which four editions were exhausted in six months, and the Letters of Saint Cyran, which were also read by his family: " We have here the letter by Monsieur de Saint Cyran, recently published. . . . We are reading it, and will send it to you soon," wrote Jacqueline and Blaise to their sister Gilberte on April 1, 1648.

But what was the most direct result of all this reading? It was essentially to interest Blaise in making a deeper and more consecutive study of the Bible. From this time on the Scripture held a new meaning for him, which was this: it showed the way to bring about a transformation of heart.[9] It became a rule of life and a means of self-dedication. Madame Périer was doing no more than anticipating the fruits of this Biblical discipline when she wrote: " When he was not yet twenty-four years old, the Providence of God having brought about an occasion which obliged him to read the writings of piety, God illuminated him through this sacred reading in such fashion that he understood perfectly that the Christian religion obliges us to live for God alone, and to have no object at all other than Himself, and this truth appeared to him as so manifest, so inescapab'e, and so useful, that he terminated all his research: so that from this time on he renounced all other forms of

[7] *Œuvres*, v. 12, lxxxii–lxxxix.
[8] *Ibid.*, lxxxii.
[9] *Œuvres*, v. 2, 379, 380.

learning in order to devote himself solely to the one thing which Jesus Christ called needful." [10]

The above statement is, of course, too categorical and is contradicted by the plain facts, if taken literally: we know that Pascal's scientific activity from then on took its place within a Christian order, according to the teaching of Saint Augustine and Saint Cyran on the subject. In whatever he was to do, Pascal always gave first place in his thought to the God of Jesus Christ. The laboratory had become an upper room, and the Bible held the place of honor therein. From this exalted point of view Pascal more and more dominated the human scene as it appeared to him in a fresh perspective. When he intervened in ecclesiastical, scientific, or moral controversies, it was because the sacred cause of truth seemed to him in peril — in the last analysis, the cause of Almighty God; the one thing Jesus Christ has called needful.

A LAYMAN'S BURDEN

At the moment Pascal's attention was absorbed by the case of a certain Jacques Forton, who took the name Saint-Ange. This elderly Capuchin friar of curious repute was understood to be candidate for an ecclesiastical appointment in Normandy. Would he, if he won the appointment, continue to preach his strange philosophy? He held, for example, that the body of Jesus Christ was not formed of the blood of the Holy Virgin, but of a different substance created for this purpose. He held other beliefs of a similar nature. After all, what was the real point at issue? Pascal knit his brow.

We must remember that in the seventeenth century he was one of the first Christian laymen of his day, one of a few devoted men who considered it not only their proper business, but indeed their prime concern, whenever the cause of religion was at stake. Notwithstanding the harsh epithets of Sainte-Beuve, who called Pascal a " denouncer and quasi-inquisitor," [11] and Jovy's description of the incident as " a theological ambuscade," [12] it was perfectly natural for him to proceed in the

[10] *Œuvres*, v. **1**, 59.

[11] Sainte-Beuve, *Port-Royal*, v. **2**, Hachette, Paris, 1878, ed. in-12, 481, n. 1, quoted by Jovy, Ernest, *Etudes pascaliennes*, v. **1**, " Pascal et St.-Ange," Jacques Forton, sieur de Saint-Ange, ses écrits et ses infortunes, Librairie philosophique — J. Vrin, Paris, 1927, p. 3.

[12] Jovy, Ernest, " Pascal et St.-Ange," *op. cit.*, p. 73 [to be found on page 4 of this small book is a bibliography of the Saint-Ange case].

manner that he did, in the circumstances as we understand them. At most, the charge of excessive zeal might be leveled at Pascal, but even that is a matter of opinion.

In his *Introduction* to the record of two conferences, which took place on Friday, February 1, and Tuesday, February 5, 1647, dated April 30, 1647, Brunschvicg recalls one aspect of the reform undertaken by Saint Cyran, which largely explains the immediate hold he had upon French Catholicism. Saint Cyran had in mind the reformation of the nation's clergy, and insisted upon the pre-eminent dignity of the sacred office, with the agonizing, almost crushing, responsibility which every priest assumes in relation to his people. Brunschvicg further reminds us that four years earlier, also at Rouen, Father Maignart, from the Oratoire, resigned his cure at Sainte-Croix-Saint-Ouen, in consequence of some scruples stirred in his own conscience by a conversation with Saint Cyran. Was it then surprising that Pascal, when he heard that Jacques Forton had been nominated for a curacy in Normandy, refused all compromise, and carried the affair to the very limit with the Archbishop of Rouen? [13]

Let us now see how he went about it: he went directly to Saint-Ange with two of his friends, the promising young mathematician Adrien Auzoult, and Raoul Hallé, son of a municipal magistrate, and asked him about the theories attributed to him. The replies Saint-Ange gave them indicated a rationalism at once so peculiar and so dangerous in a preacher, as it seemed to them, that the young men sought to turn him from his errors; but Saint-Ange held firmly to his views, as Madame Périer tells us, " so that, having deliberated further among themselves as to the danger of allowing a man of such erroneous opinion the freedom to instruct youth, they resolved to warn him first, and then to denounce him if he still held out against their warning. That is how the matter ended, for he misjudged their warning." [14]

The three friends actually called upon the Archbishop, Monseigneur de Harlay, who was away at the time, having withdrawn to his château de Gaillon because of illness and fatigue. In his place they found the Bishop-Coadjutor, Camus, a man of conciliatory and sweet temper like his master, Saint François de Sales. Camus was inclined to accept as satisfactory the reassuring explanations given by Saint-Ange.

The young men then took the matter straight to Monseigneur de Harlay, who reopened the case three separate times, examined Saint-

[13] *Œuvres*, v. 1, 352, 353.   [14] *Œuvres*, v. 1, 61.

Ange himself, and compelled him to sign an unequivocal statement that he repudiated the errors imputed to him. It should be added that the Archbishop was not a little annoyed " to see young laymen surpassing his grand vicar *in pontificalibus* in zeal for the purity of the faith." [15] Monseigneur de Harlay thereupon issued instructions to his Coadjutor, reviewing the controversy, recording the submission of Saint-Ange, and remanding the accused party, with some further counsel as to the disposition of the case. Whereupon Camus, " after taking cognizance of Jacques Forton, a man capable and of orthodox opinion, and after administering the oath required by the canons," [16] appointed him on April 12, 1647, to the cure of Crosville. He never set foot in his parish there, doubtless because of his heretical repute, but transferred instead to Sartrouville, where his appointment was again called in question. It is believed that he died in Paris.

Saint-Ange was certainly made to suffer from the controversy associated with his name, but any man who expresses ideas in public must be prepared for such vicissitudes. Would to heaven the critics who continue to blame Pascal and his young friends were always as forthright in facing the issues at stake, and were always as scrupulous on points of law and of procedure, not to mention caring, as much as Saint-Ange, for God's cause itself!

We have recounted the Saint-Ange affair in some detail, not only because it shows how zealous Pascal had become after his initial contact with Jansenism, but because it indicates the extent to which the Bible had already become a criterion for Pascal. This point requires further attention.

INNOVATIONS IN THEOLOGY CONDEMNED

In the course of his philosophical-theological *Meditations* regarding the succession of God's purposes and decrees, Saint-Ange sets down a sketchy outline, still incomplete but already quite definite, of his doctrine of the Immaculate Conception. According to his view, Jesus Christ was of a quite different substance from ourselves. The same is true of the Virgin, who was by no means " formed of the substance of Saint Joachim and Saint Anne, but of a newly created matter." [17] An important role in redemption is attributed to her.

---

[15] Jovy, Ernest, " Pascal et St.-Ange," *op. cit.*, p. 121. [17] *Ibid.*, p. 104.
[16] *Ibid.*, p. 139.

These teachings about the Virgin are what shocked Madame Périer, as it seems, and they must have astonished Pascal and his friends as well.[18] The doctrine of the Immaculate Conception was indeed becoming recognized, by this time, as a pious dogma of the Church, having been approved by the Council of Trent. The Jansenists, however, were still very reserved in their treatment of the subject. According to their view, the Virgin must indeed have been sanctified very early in life, but they still held that she was included within the curse upon Adam, and thus shared in the age-long misdirection of human life which Christ's death alone could redeem. That was a strictly Biblical doctrine, to which Pascal clung instinctively.

It should further be noted that Saint-Ange was already a " modernist." On that day, February 5, 1647, when Pascal, Auzoult, and Hallé de Monflaines brought to M. Courtin's home, in support of their views, an expert in the person of Sieur Cornier de Sainte Hélène, Doctor of the Sorbonne, the discussion became tense indeed. They put a question to Saint-Ange concerning the number of human beings in the world. By way of evading the mathematical difficulty, he stated that the number of years since creation was not at all clear, that on this point the Bible was *obscure*. Did anyone really know when the world began? How long it had existed? Was it not true that the Chinese could recollect a period covering thirty-six thousand years? The scholarly Saint-Ange, on this topic as on many others, held distinctly original views which were quite advanced for his time. In certain of his tenets he is said to have anticipated Leibnitz, and Viscount St. Cyres calls him " a humble Raymond of Sabunda." [19] At that early date he raised questions regarding Biblical chronology which modern exegesis has admitted as valid.

We need to bear in mind, however, that speculations such as these are still looked upon in our day as attacks upon God's Word. Richard Simon, remember, was still less than nine years old when Pascal was questioning Saint-Ange, and besides this, Pascal, already noted for his prudence, had now become a Jansenist, that is to say, a fundamentalist. It was because of his Bible-centered thinking that he was shocked by the " modernism " of Saint-Ange, quite as much as by the latter's advanced ideas concerning Catholic doctrine.

Thus the conversation, on February 5, 1647, finally led to the point where Saint-Ange declared that the Virgin Mary yielded her obedience

[18] *Ibid.*, p. 92.
[19] Viscount St. Cyres, *Pascal*, E. P. Dutton & Co., Inc., New York, 1910, p. 93.

and her death to God, as truly as Christ, for the redemption of the world. Little wonder that Saint-Ange remarked, as his callers left, that Blaise and his friends did not seem altogether happy about the views he had advanced! Every Biblical Christian will understand their position.

We must never tire, either, of stressing the idea, which became ever clearer to Pascal, in all its implications, that, whereas freedom of inquiry and discussion are the condition *sine qua non* of progress in experimental science, religion, on the other hand, is a matter of authority.

A CREED IN HARMONY WITH SCIENCE

On the other hand, we must note the way in which the authority of the Bible became confirmed in Pascal's mind by the harmony, as it appeared to him, between the Jansenist interpretation of the Bible and the type of science familiar to Pascal himself. The type of experimental science central in his thinking was grounded in the uniformity of natural law, in the possibility of predicting each particular event in the predetermined order of things. " The uniformity of the laws of nature," writes Dr. Charles Hodge on this point, " is a constant revelation of the immutability of God. They are now what they were at the beginning of time, and they are the same in every part of the universe. No less stable are the laws which regulate the operation of the reason and conscience. The whole government of God, as the God of nature and as moral governor, rests on the immutability of his counsels." [20] There is thus no reason whatever to suppose that, " in the higher sphere of his operations, which concern the destiny of men, everything is left to chance and allowed to take its undirected course to an undetermined end. We accordingly find that the Scriptures distinctly assert, in reference to the dispensation of grace, not only that God sees the end from the beginning, but that He works all things according to the counsel of His own will, or according to His eternal purpose." [21]

Experimental science confirmed the views of Saint Cyran so recently adopted by Pascal with respect to Scriptural interpretation, in so far as science could be appealed to without involving rationalistic and naturalistic usurpation of jurisdiction.

[20] Hodge, Charles, *Systematic Theology,* Wm. B. Eerdmans Publishing Co., Grand Rapids, Mich., 1940, v. 1, 539.
[21] *Ibid.,* v. 2, 314.

The adherence of his mind " to a certain view of human nature, a view which, as he believed, was rooted alike in good sense and in the teaching of Saint Augustine, that is to say, of Jansen, . . . may well have come to Pascal by way of the sciences." This statement by Fortunat Strowski confirms what we have said about *continuity* in Pascal, especially at this period. Now, for some further observations which serve to justify the foregoing assertions: " If there is one thing which it is difficult for a scientist to conceive," continues Strowski, " it is the freedom of the will. . . . When the religious sentiment awakened within him, Pascal, more scientist than metaphysician, and perhaps less sentimental than logical by temperament, gladly embraced the doctrine which conformed most closely to his own habit of mind. It was this same doctrine which Arnauld sought to expound with what was, for his day, an implacable rigor, the doctrine, namely, that freedom of choice, the freedom of indeterminacy, was a matter of foolishness and pride." [22] In the fresh synthesis of thought which was now taking shape in Pascal's mind, the " order of the mind " was more and more taking a position subordinate to a higher order. His view of the universe was already taking on the outline of a hierarchy only intelligible when seen from above.

This is not to say, of course, that Pascal's famous page concerning the three orders was already articulate in his thinking. Barely the outline was beginning to appear. In a conversation with his sister Gilberte, on April 1, 1648, Blaise recalled a notion they had often discussed together, namely, that " corporeal objects are only an image of spiritual objects, and that God has represented invisible things to us under the form of the visible." [23] He found this idea, be it noted, in Rom. 1:20. Already it appeared to him " so universal and so useful that no one should let an appreciable time pass by without giving it careful attention." [24] For him it became a primary principle of life, as shown by the fact that, when he was the spiritual adviser of Mademoiselle de Roannez, he developed the idea in his own way in a letter dated at the end of October, 1656. The context of his letter to Gilberte, from which we have just quoted, further shows that this Biblical rule of guidance is already identified in his mind with the notion of figuratives, which was also taken from the Bible. This idea is treated at length in Section x of the *Pensées*, having become a fundamental and permanent element in Pascal's thought.

[22] Strowski, Fortunat, *Pascal et son temps, op. cit.*, v. 2, 213, 214.
[23] *Œuvres*, v. 2, 249.
[24] *Ibid.*

As we now realize, this permanent element can be traced back in the early process of its crystallization about basic views of the Bible. In Pascal, then, the life of the mind was transformed in a most wonderful way by what we have called " the Jansenist quickening " that came to him in the year of our Lord 1646. As is usually the case, he began to derive a fresh understanding from his renewed Christian faith, as the Bible became a light unto his path.

IV

The Physicist Confronting His Bible

" Shall he that contendeth with the Almighty instruct him? "
—*Job 40:2*

In October, 1646, soon after he had stirred his family to a renewed concern for Christianity, Pascal watched Pierre Petit, intendant of fortifications, repeat Torricelli's experiment as he had learned it from Mersenne. Finding justification for his new interest, as we have pointed out, in the teaching of Saint Augustine and Saint Cyran, Pascal now threw himself into the task of physical research. He was filled, at one and the same time, with enthusiasm for science and with zeal for religion, and he set to work with an energy that was truly staggering. Thus he would clarify those grand syntheses of thought, which were to take shape in the conception of " orders," and in which God was to appear as the principle and the end of all things.

Pascal wished to establish, first of all, the *fact* of the vacuum, by infinite variations upon Torricelli's experiment. Thus he altered the size, length, and shape of the receptacles used, and also the character of the several liquids employed. In the course of this research, he invented his famous syringe which was, in actual fact, the earliest pneumatic device. He set down his conclusions in a pamphlet, which appeared in 1647 under the title *Expériences nouvelles touchant le vide,* remarkable in the acuteness of the observations recorded.

SCIENTIFIC RIGOR UPHELD

This did not, however, avert a series of attacks upon his scientific report. The sharpest retort came from a Jesuit, Father Noël, teacher and friend of Descartes. Appealing to the *authority* of Descartes in the realm of science, and to that of Aristotle in philosophy, he roundly declared that the notion of a vacuum, synonymous with *nothing*, was inconceivable. In his reply,[1] which was phrased as courteously as the letter from

[1] *Œuvres*, v. 2, 90.

Father Noël had been, Pascal reminded his correspondent of a universal rule which applies to all particular forms of subject matter, whenever the truth is being sought.

Here is the formula, as Pascal himself gave it: " One should never make a judgment concerning the negative or the affirmative of a proposition, unless that which one affirms or denies has one of the following two conditions: namely, either that it should appear so clearly and so distinctly of itself to the senses or to the reason, according as it is subject to the one or to the other, that the mind should have no means of doubting its certainty, and this is what we call a *principle* or an *axiom*." [2] Thus it is that, if equals be added to equals, the sums are equal, which constitutes the first axiom of the First Book of the *Elements* of Euclid. This being understood, Pascal proceeds to the second condition, in the following terms: " Or that it may be deduced as an infallible and necessary consequence of these principles or axioms, upon whose certainty wholly depends that of the consequences which have been derived therefrom; such as this proposition, the three angles of a triangle are equal to the sum of two right angles." [3] This is the famous Proposition XXXII of the First Book, whose demonstration Pascal worked out for himself at the age of twelve.

Unless these specifications are met, so Pascal pointed out in his reply to Father Noël, it could never be more than a matter of *vision,* of *caprice,* of *fantasy,* of *idea,* or, at best, of *fine thought.*[4] Now, the supposed substance which, on Father Noël's view, was said to fill the vacuum, amounted to one of those arbitrary presuppositions, suspended from unconfirmed facts, which are as difficult to believe as they are easy to contrive.

Consider for a moment the implications of these hypotheses: For any hypothesis to be true, it is not enough that it should be in harmony with all known phenomena; but if it be contradicted by a single one, it is false. Furthermore, it was of no avail for Father Noël to seek refuge behind definitions, however nominally clear they might be; in order to be valid, a definition must correspond to a reality, and no concept in the mind can take the place of facts, nor claim validity counter to facts.[5] Forewarned against scholastic metaphysics by his reading of the Bible, Pascal was no less forewarned by the habits of experimental science.

[2] *Œuvres,* v. 2, 90, 91. [4] *Ibid.*
[3] *Œuvres,* v. 2, 91. [5] *Œuvres,* v. 2, 185.

Fundamentally, the controversy with Father Noël emerged as a natural continuation of his quarrel with Saint-Ange. In this respect, as we sought to bring out in the foregoing chapter, Pascal was a thoroughgoing student of the Bible, who also had the most advanced science of his day on his side. At the same time, he did not in the least confuse what depends upon science with what depends upon religion. Pascal felt that he was on solid ground, for he carried on his scientific work as a disciple of Saint Augustine and Saint Cyran. With an inner strength derived from the serenity of his faith, the experimental physicist insisted upon the need for duly established facts, upon having all the facts confirm each hypothesis, and upon adducing facts alone to support the hypothesis.

USURPATION OF AUTHORITY EXPOSED

But there was another side to the question. It concerned a reversal of values which Pascal felt, whether rightly or wrongly, he must attack; *the very persons who appealed to authority in the field of science were launching a naturalistic, rationalistic method in theology.* To Pascal it appeared that the misunderstanding between Father Noël and himself was twofold; Pascal therefore felt that it was necessary, after restoring to experimental science the naturalistic and rationalistic methods which properly belonged to it, to restore to theology the authority that was its proper due, the sole authority that belongs to it according to the strict teaching of the Scriptures: the authority of the Holy Spirit. He further adds — and it is quite clear from the original manuscript that it is an addition: " We reserve for the mysteries of faith, which the Holy Spirit has itself revealed, that submission of mind which extends our belief to those mysteries which are hidden from sense and from reason." [6]

The controversy with Father Noël thus did more than continue the argument against Saint-Ange. It anticipated the *Provinciales* in that it showed how fundamental was the disagreement already between the Biblical thinking of Pascal and the innovating mentality which, as Pascal held, the Jesuits imported into the field of theology. Let it be understood that we are not taking sides. We are seeking to make Pascal's position clear, and his position is quite evidently exclusive.

This question was already so much on his mind that he developed it at some length in the fragmentary Preface to his *Traité du vide.* In our opinion it is no accident that this fragment appeared at the very time

[6] *Œuvres,* v. 2, 92.

he wrote his first letter to Father Noël.[7] Whenever Pascal was touched to the quick, he became eloquent. The reply to Father Noël was twice as long as the letter itself. Might it not be that the additional note, " We reserve for the mysteries of faith," was expanded in turn into the Preface to his treatise?

In this remarkable fragment, Pascal draws a very sharp line of demarcation between matters in which one seeks only to know what others have set down, as is the case par excellence in theology, and those matters which are subject to sense and to reason. In the former case we must have recourse to books, by whose authority alone we may seek for more light. In them, authority is inseparable from truth, and we cannot know the truth save by this authority: " So that to lend full certainty to those matters which are incomprehensible to reason, it suffices to point to where they are found in the Sacred Books (just as, in order to demonstrate the uncertainty of those most likely things, it is enough to show that they are not therein contained); because its principles are superior to nature and to reason, and, the mind of man being too feeble to attain them by its own efforts, it cannot reach up to those lofty thoughts, unless it is sustained by a strength which is all-powerful and supernatural." Here we find an early formulation of the notion of " orders," which was to become the keystone of the arch of the Pascalian edifice. The first hint of it we found in the symbol of oratory and laboratory, whose vicissitudes we have already traced. What was still required, before it should take shape in Pascal's clear and mature consciousness, was a vital contact with the Word of God. It was the Scriptures which gave to Pascal's thoughts the impulse which was to carry it to its zenith.

In matters which are subject to science and to reason and in which only the natural habit of our thinking is involved, so the Preface continues, " authority is useless; reason alone has grounds for such knowledge." In the question of competence at this level, Pascal is quite categorical in his affirmation. He speaks with the tone of the jurist, as he had learned it from his father, President Pascal.

Two conclusions were to be quite rigorously deduced from this affirmation: on the one hand, we must " complain of the blindness of those who appeal to authority alone as proof in physical matters, rather than to reasoning or to experiments "; but, on the other hand, we should be overcome with *veritable horror* at " the malice of others, who look to

[7] October–November, 1647. Fragment of Preface to a *Traité du vide* is to be found in *Œuvres*, v. 2, 129–145.

reason alone in theology, rather than to Scripture and to the Fathers."
There, indeed, lay the sovereign authority for Pascal in theology: in
the Scripture interpreted according to the Tradition. Should anyone
dare to touch that, it was sure to arouse a holy indignation in his passionate soul. Whereas those persons " who do not dare to contrive anything new in physics " are only " timid fellows," whose courage needs
to be braced up, it was needful, on the other hand, " to confound the
insolence of those rash persons who undertake to launch novelties in
theology." It is clear that the *Provinciales* were already within the perspective of his thinking when he wrote the Preface to the *Traité du vide*.
When Arnauld was to appeal to Pascal, in January, 1656, to be the
spokesman for Port-Royal against the Jesuits, Blaise had only to give
free expression to his profoundest conviction, already of long standing,
and it was as the champion of Scripture and of Tradition that he was
to enter the lists in behalf of a cause long recognized by him as sacred.
Whether his stand, in that instance, was well or poorly taken, *his quarrel with the Jesuits was fundamental in nature*. In this respect there was
never any deviation from the main pathway of Pascal's thought.

GOD, PRINCIPLE AND ULTIMATE END

Over and above the changing currents of human opinion, and anterior to all the truths affirmed by men, Truth itself reigns supreme. On
the one hand, and as it were by condescension, she allows her manifestations to be measured by our experimental methods, ever increasing in
their approach to perfection. Man " is made only for infinity." Progress
is the law of his spirit, and " the entire procession of mankind, down
the course of so many centuries, may be thought of as a single man, who
always lives on, and who is always learning." The ancients represent
our childhood. Let us not allow ourselves to be bound by the boundaries
of their thoughts, but, rather, supported by their achievements, let us
give free scope to the experimental method in the study of nature. Beyond this, however, there enters our thinking the grace of a revelation
whose authority cannot be denied, and should not be doubted.

It would be stimulating to inquire how close Pascal is, in this respect,
to the Thomists, according to whom material substances are placed in
the lowest degree of reality, in a hierarchy whose true order is known
only by reference to God. God created the angels close to Himself, said
Saint Augustine, and He created nature next to nothingness. Now, a

self-taught man like Pascal, having defined the experimental method of studying matter and its manifestations, was on the way to discovering that God alone must be "the ultimate end, as He alone is the true principle." [8]

BEWARE OF IDOLATRY

From henceforth, for Pascal, perfect unity could be found nowhere save in God, and, whatever might be the resemblance of nature to her Creator, whatever unity she might derive from Him, it was not proper to bestow upon any one of the created things, especially the smallest and the most vile, that sovereign respect which was due to the Creator alone: "There is nothing so abominable in the eyes of God and of men as idolatry, whereby men render to the creature that honor which is due only to the Creator." [9]

It was at this very period that Pascal's experiments had drawn the attention of all the scholars of Europe to his work. Pecquet and Gassendi were quoting him admiringly; over in England Boyle was developing the principle of the pneumatic machine, which he said was due to "the most ingenious Pascal." [10] It was a dangerous day for him!

Turning to the Scripture, he discovered, in Ex. 20:4, 5, what vengeance God took upon idolaters. With reference to the *Deus zelotes*, in v. 5, Pascal came to the conclusion that, since God was even more jealous of our affections than of our respect, there was no crime "more injurious or more detestable" to Him than to give His creatures first place in our affections, even though they might represent Him.[11] Was he writing here simply in terms of intimate counsel to his elder sister? May we not trace in these words something of the inner anguish of a disciple of Saint Augustine and of Saint Cyran? Blaise knew full well that scientific labor was praiseworthy to the extent that it was a quest for truth, but that it became culpable the very moment when, the means being mistaken for the end, the search for truth was turned into a search for oneself. As is pointed out in another of Pascal's fragments, preserved for us in the second Guerrier Collection, it is impossible for God to be the end at all, if He is not also the principle. This same fragment goes on with this terrible warning: "We lift our eyes on high, but lean upon

[8] *Fragment d'une lettre à Madame Périer*, April 1, 1648, *Œuvres*, v. 2, 250.
[9] *Œuvres*, v. 2, 251.
[10] Chevalier, Jacques, *Pascal, op. cit.*, p. 66.
[11] *Œuvres*, v. 2, 251.

72

the sand; and the earth will dissolve, and we shall fall whilst looking at the heavens." [12] Might Pascal himself one day fall? It is so difficult to be in the world without being of the world!

RUNNING THE RACE

Ah, let him not relax for a single moment in his striving for sanctification! From the first moment when he clearly saw that God is the principle and end of all things, it was likewise clear that His children must set no limits to their striving for purity and for perfection. They are all members of one body, wholly divine and infinitely perfect. Jesus gave form to this principle in His words: " Be you therefore perfect, as also your heavenly Father is perfect." [13] Our divine Master thus set no limits to His commandment of perfection, and He offered us at the same time the example, in Himself, whereby infinite perfection was actually attained.[14]

Opposition and personal malice, by irritating our pride, may easily become occasions for stumbling. Let us not retaliate. Let us keep from all controversy. Father Noël had just written a second letter to Pascal.[15] In May, 1648, he himself published a short treatise on *Le Plein du vide*, in which he now accepted Pascal's view of the physical vacuum, while still holding to his earlier thesis concerning the metaphysical issue.[16] This time it was Etienne Pascal, rather than Blaise, who took pen in hand to reply to the somewhat ungracious statements Father Noël had included in the Letter of Dedication to Monseigneur le Prince de Conti: Blaise had come to believe, so the father explained, " that he could not retort to these words, nor address his retort to you, lest in repulsing your unexpected injuries he might provoke further discourses of a similar category, and from a desire to practice the Gospel precept, namely, to make our complaints and brotherly corrections directly to those who have given us grounds for the same. And . . . he has deemed it more fitting to beg me, as he has indeed done, to take pains to practice this

[12] Section vii, Fr. 488, quoted from *Œuvres*, v. **2**, 250, n. 2.
[13] Matt. 5:48: *Estote ergo vos perfecti, sicut et pater vester cœlestis perfectus est.*
[14] *Œuvres*, v. **2**, 252.
[15] *Œuvres*, v. **2**, 107. (Pascal criticizes this letter in his letter to Le Pailleur, *Œuvres*, v. **2**, 179–211.)
[16] Father Noël will finally yield to Pascal, in his *Gravitas comparata*, that the weight of mercury balances that of water, and that it is the weight of air which explains the suspension of liquids.

same Gospel precept myself, in making you understand his just complaints." [17] Continuing with numerous citations from the Bible, Etienne Pascal made his point with Father Noël in such terms as to reveal how closely father and son were now at one in their ideas and principles, having doubtless studied the Bible together.[18]

THE EAGLE'S FLIGHT

Pascal could not limit himself, however, to the Scripture in his search for maxims of perfection: the passion for perfection laid hold of him no less intensely in the domain of science. Having firmly established the fact of the vacuum, Pascal went on with rigorous logic to interpret its significance, in seeking the cause of the phenomenon and in giving clear demonstration of his conclusions.[19] His ingenuity set to work the method of difference and variations; he established his first proof by experimenting with a vacuum within a vacuum,[20] and his second proof by an ordinary experiment with the vacuum at the base of the Puy de Dôme mountain, and then at its summit.[21] Descartes, by now jealous of the young scientist, claimed that it was he who suggested the idea of the latter experiment. This is not the place to enter into that dispute.[22] Following the Puy de Dôme experiment, repeated and verified at the tower of the Eglise Saint-Jacques, and then in a private home, it was definitively established that the column of mercury fell in proportion as one mounted to a higher elevation, in proportion, that is to say, as the

[17] *Lettre d'Etienne Pascal au P. Noël*, March or April, 1648, *Œuvres*, v. 2, 257.

[18] *Œuvres*, v. 2, 269.

[19] October, 1648. See in *Œuvres*, v. 2, 370, 371, in the account of the great experiment of the balance of liquids, the denunciation of " l'horreur du vide " (horror of the vacuum).

[20] *Lettre de Pascal à M. Périer*, November 15, 1647, *Œuvres*, v. 2, 155–158.

[21] On November 15, 1647, Pascal wrote to his brother-in-law, Florin Périer, then conseiller général à la Cours des Aides de Clermont-Ferrand, to present to him the statement of his work on the vacuum, and to give him instructions for the final experiment. (*Œuvres*, v. 2, 153 *sq.*) Périer, engaged in his official duties and prevented by bad weather, was only able to make the experiment on September 19, 1648. He gave an account of it to Pascal in a letter dated September 22 (*Œuvres*, v. 2, 349 *sq.*). For the *Récit de la grande expérience de l'équilibre des liqueurs*, by Pascal, see *Œuvres*, v. 2, 363 *sq.* (2 inset plates).

[22] See on the subject of this quarrel: Rougier, Louis, " L'Affaire Pascal," *Mercure de France*, November 1, 1931 (we borrow this reference from Morris Bishop, *Pascal, op. cit.*, n. 5, p. 357). Descartes paid a visit to Pascal on September 23, 24, 1647, and Pascal returned the call a few days later.

pressure was reduced in the column of air which balanced the column of mercury.

Pascal began to think of applications of this phenomenon, of which a few are found sketchily hinted in the notes he rapidly jotted down: the barometer, the forecasting of weather, the calculation of altitudes, the correction of thermometers. But even this would be to underestimate the scope of genius, were we to suppose that he would stop with such practical applications. His thought was dominated by the principles we have sought to make clear, and he went on to seek for universal Truth behind every particular truth. His treatise on *La Pesanteur de la masse d'air* was soon to be followed by another on *L'Equilibre des liqueurs*,[23] and between them these two treatises were to achieve the ultimate standard of perfect scientific work.

Scarcely a word will need to be altered by future physicists. To the book of modern science Pascal thus contributed whole chapters in their ultimate form: the equilibrium between a gaseous mass and a column of liquid is presented as simply one particular instance of the equilibrium attained by two liquids in communicating vessels. Thus he formulated the fundamental principle of hydrostatics, which was able to clarify and co-ordinate the scanty experiments already conducted in this field by Stevin, Galileo, Torricelli, Mersenne, and Descartes.[24]

In the course of his work he contrived the notion of the hydraulic press, without having as yet a chance to build it,[25] and he then related all these laws, concerning the equilibrium of liquids and gases, to the laws of general mechanics, of which, in turn, they were essentially but special instances. Still later, having broadened his geometrical view of the physical universe in the course of his new discoveries, he finally arrived at the audacious and fertile concepts of *universal, physical relativity*,[26] as he formulated it in his famous fragment on *L'Esprit géométrique*.[27] Spiritually, his thought ranged even more widely in extent, to the universe, of which each individual is materially a part, and which

---

[23] *Œuvres*, v. **3**, 156–266.

[24] Chevalier, Jacques, *Pascal, op. cit.*, p. 71.

[25] " In fact, the hydraulic press, which now, in the hands of Professor Bridgman, of Harvard, exerts a pressure of 1,440,000 pounds per square inch, which aids a thousand heavy industries and smoothly brakes millions of automobiles, was not effectively constructed until Bramah (1749–1814) found a way of packing pistons against leakage." (Bishop, M., *Pascal, op. cit.*, p. 68.)

[26] Chevalier, Jacques, *Pascal, op. cit.*, p. 73.

[27] *Œuvres*, v. **9**, 255.

encompasses him, in an antithesis which summarizes the entire philosophical problem of knowledge: " By space the universe encompasses and swallows me up like an atom: by thought, I comprehend the universe." [28] It was not, then, from space at all that a man must seek his dignity, but from his own thought and from the government of his thought. " Thought constitutes the greatness of a man." [29] That is why the principle of morality is to endeavor to think well.[30] We have reached one of the peaks of Pascal's thought at this point, already so early attained. But shall we be able to stop at this point?

" LIBIDO EXCELLENDI "

Already a restlessness disturbs this mind which has just attained such excellence. What does it mean to " think well "? Does it mean to think about religious truths or about secular truths? The difference is already present in Pascal's thinking, and is a matter of great concern to him: " Physical science will not console me for the ignorance of morality in the day of affliction. But the science of ethics will always console me for the ignorance of the physical sciences." [31] And Pascal entitles this fragment *Vanité des sciences*.

We have no way of knowing whether these particular lines were written at the time of the events we are about to describe. The comparison of evidence, however, is a matter of no little interest. At the very hour when this scholar was being acclaimed by the world of secular science, he was urging his sister Gilberte to mark the great difference between religious truths and secular truths. The distinguishing mark of secular truths is this: It is enough to learn them once, and to retain them well in the memory, so that there is no further need to be taught them again. Religious truths, on the other hand, can never be reduced to impressions in our memory. A person knows religious truths only in virtue of the inward operation of God's Spirit.

In order to understand this secret language, which remains alien to all who are alien to the ways of Heaven, grace is needed. Grace alone can open the way to the initial understanding of religious truths. Having done this, the same grace is needful to *continue* this understanding,

[28] *Pensées*, Section vi, Fr. 348, *Œuvres*, v. 13, 263.
[29] *Pensées*, Section vi, Fr. 346, *Œuvres*, v. 13, 261.
[30] *Pensées*, Section vi, Fr. 347, *Œuvres*, v. 13, 262.
[31] *Pensées*, Section ii, Fr. 67, *Œuvres*, v. 12, 68.

which it keeps forever vividly present by retracing it *ceaselessly* in the hearts of the faithful, so that it may always be *vital truth*. In italicizing such phrases we are seeking to emphasize the truth so often reiterated by Pascal, who proceeds to set it in bold relief by an arresting illustration: " Just as, in the lives of the blessed, God continually renews their blessedness, which is an effect and a fruit of grace." [32] Of what use would it be for Pascal to rank as acknowledged master in the domain of natural sciences, if he were to lose his own soul in the process?

Pascal's God is the God of Saint Augustine, involved in His creations; it is the God of election, the God of the Bible, who blinds man and lights his way, who hides Himself and lets Himself be found. No man ever finds Him until He has already been found of Him. Not to seek Him is to be abandoned by Him. Without God, man can do nothing: " Perseverance of the faithful in the ways of justice is nothing else than the continuity of grace, it is not a single manifestation of grace which persists forever." [33] Might a man, then, be deprived of this grace? Certainly. The vacuum thus created must be something unbearable indeed. Oh, the misery of man without God!

Our salvation is of God. Let us work out our own salvation. Being a student of the Bible, Pascal quite evidently recognized the cogency of these two affirmations, which seem contradictory only when viewed at the level of nature. Furthermore, the absolute necessity of sanctification recurred in his thoughts with ever-renewed insistence: " Thus we must strive unceasingly to purify our inward heart, which is always being soiled by new blemishes, as well as clinging to its old ones, for without assiduous renewal a man is not capable of receiving this new wine, which will never be put into old vessels." [34] From now on the language tends to be Biblical no less than the thought.

Alluding to the condemnation of Jewish literalism by Saint Paul,[35] Pascal returns, in this same letter, to the distinction between secular truths, which it suffices to commit to memory, and the truths which are the fruit of the Truth in us. He has just remarked that, on the whole, it is as easy to learn by heart an epistle of Saint Paul as a book of Vergil, but that, in that case, it is simply a matter of pure memory. Oh, what

[32] *Lettre de Blaise Pascal à Madame Périer sa sœur,* November 5, 1648, *Œuvres,* v. 2, 380.

[33] *Ibid.,* v. 2, 380.

[34] *Ibid.*

[35] II Cor. 3:6.

terror! Where there is no grace, religious truth is no more than secular truth; it is nothing but dry bones without the vivifying breath of the spirit. The voice which reads the Bible may be no more than a sounding brass. Nay, a man may know the whole Bible by heart, and yet be damned! " Our memory, along with the instructions it retains, is only a lifeless, Jewish body without the capital spirit that must give them life." [36]

His sister had congratulated him, and it must be admitted that he deserved her compliments; but was it not dangerous that men should flatter him thus? All of scholarly Europe was quoting him in a mood of emulation. Descartes was jealous of him. Descartes. Why not God? Ah, let him thrust aside these idolaters and the idol worship! Let him be swift to repel such fateful flattery: " Just as the Angel refused the adulation of a saintly servant like himself, we shall say to thee, in begging thee henceforth not to employ such language of any human acquaintance, that thou guard thyself against paying such compliments to us, for we too are disciples even as thou." [37] He was still on that November 5, 1648, a disciple and saintly servant. But his restlessness was evidently considerable, as he watched the springs of grace dry up within himself, because of his lust, of his search for the good things of the creative order, such as science and the honors it yields to those who pursue it with a passion for excellence.

ADDED TRIALS

Since the middle of 1647, Pascal had been living in Paris with Jacqueline. Their father was preparing to withdraw from public office, somewhat troubled, perhaps, by the notoriety that had been brought to his door by the controversy between Blaise and Saint-Ange. He had asked them to precede him to the capital, where Blaise might, further, be able to consult the best physicians.

Blaise's health was much worse. For a time he was paralyzed from the waist down. He could not walk without the aid of crutches. His legs and feet were chilled, and had to be kept wrapped in bandages soaked in brandy. The pains in his head and abdomen were more than he could bear. He could not take any liquid unless it was heated, and then only one drop at a time, even in the case of the most obnoxious medicaments.

[36] *Œuvres*, v. 2, 381.
[37] *Œuvres*, v. 2, 379.

Whether his was a case of syphilis as Léon Daudet supposes, of ophthal-
mic headaches as Onfray thinks,[38] of cancer as de Sinéty diagnoses it,[39]
of neurosis as Cabanès believes,[40] of hereditary tuberculosis or of arterio-
sclerosis,[41] the fact is that Pascal was a sick man, and we should never
lose sight of that fact. Not at all, of course, with a view to discrediting
Pascal's thought as the philosophy of an invalid, as Aldous Huxley
tries to do: is his philosophy any the less valid because of this fact?
The question is pertinently put by Professor Henri Peyre, of Yale University: " A good portion of humanity is not composed of healthy and
absolutely normal people. As to the rest, the vision of a Proust or of a
Pascal continues to be more revealing than that of a healthy optimist
who has never suffered from dyspepsia." [42]

When Descartes came to pay him a call, on Monday, September 23,
1647, he found Pascal exhausted by bleedings and purges; he returned
the following day and advised him to keep to his bed as long as possible and to take only bouillons for nourishment. The patient was given
his first bath, which proved to be too hot, and so gave him an added
headache. His health went from bad to worse. In January, 1648, he enjoyed only rarely an hour of relief from pain. From March to September
his condition kept growing worse, until his doctors ordered him to give
up all consecutive work.

This was indeed an added trial for the patient; he kept saying over
and over that his infirmities were keeping him from his research, and
this greatly distressed him. But with an excess of Christian stoicism he
bowed to his lot in a mood of renewed religious fervor. It was at this

[38] Onfray, R., " Où l'on voit que Pascal avait des migraines ophtalmiques,"
Chronique médicale, June, 1926. See also in the *Chronique médicale,* September, 1926,
the work of Dr. E. Roux on " La Maladie de Pascal." [References borrowed from
the article mentioned in n. 42 below, by Professor Henri Peyre, of Yale University.]

[39] Sinéty, R. de, " La Maladie de Pascal," in *Etudes sur Pascal,* Beauchesne,
Paris, 1923. [*Ibid.*]

[40] Cabanès, *Les grands névropathes,* Paris, 1930.

[41] Pascal's autopsy increased the discussion about his illness. Concerning this
see the evidence of Marguerite Périer (*Œuvres,* v. 1, 135), and of Maire, Albert,
Bibliographie générale des Œuvres de Blaise Pascal, L. Giraud Badin, Paris, 1925–
1927, v. 5, pp. 59–83.

[42] Peyre, Henri, " Pascal et la critique contemporaine," *The Romanic Review,* v.
21, No. 4, October–December, 1930, p. 326. An excellent short " état des études " on
Pascal, pp. 325–337, followed by a " Bibliographie," pp. 337–340. The work in question by Huxley is headed " Pascal," and is to be found in *The Realist,* April, 1929
(19–37), May (28–40), June (103–117). We are also indebted for these references
to Professor Henri Peyre, *art. cit.,* 326, 338, xlvi.

time that he wrote the letters to Madame Périer which we have just been citing, in which he expressed so forcefully the need for continual grace and his fear of being deprived of it. The theme was altogether Pascalian in spirit and one which never failed to recur in the great hours of his life; we shall find it again in his nights of ecstasy, and even at the hour of his death. It is quite natural that this minor mode should express the inward anguish of a soul which was searching itself, naked and alone before God, in the silence of his own chamber.

Ominous rumblings came from the outside world as well. The Paris to which Blaise and Jacqueline had returned was no longer the Paris of Richelieu's day, of whose orderly discipline we have spoken. The royal finances had been badly managed and were now in deficit. Mazarin was trying to increase the taxes, which were already enormously high. The Parliament, led by its counselor Broussel, refused to vote the added subsidies. Cardinal de Retz, resorting to various schemes of intrigue in order to seize Mazarin's post for himself, was but one of a host of ambitious self-seekers, all inciting the people to revolt. The insurrection of the *Fronde* broke out in Parliament; that of the aristocracy was soon to follow. In such an atmosphere of civil discord, every man felt himself driven back upon his own resources.

Pascal was a parishioner of the Eglise Saint-Merry, which had just welcomed a new curate in the person of the eloquent Monsieur Duhamel, an ardent Jansenist. He confirmed Blaise and Jacqueline in the advice given by their Jansenist friends in Rouen, that they should hear the sermons of " Monsieur " Singlin at the Eglise de Port-Royal-de-Paris. The eloquence of this saintly disciple of Vincent de Paul was matched only by his gift as a spiritual adviser.

Jacqueline was overjoyed to find Monsieur Singlin speaking of the Christian life in a way which was in full accord with the notion she had conceived of it when God had first touched her soul. When she realized, furthermore, that this same Monsieur Singlin was in charge of the Port-Royal convent, she concluded that a person could " be a nun reasonably in such a place as that " [43] — an experience wholly typical of a member of the Pascal family! Mother Angélique, expert counselor in spiritual matters that she was, was greatly impressed with Jacqueline's attitude, and before long Monsieur Singlin, who was likewise impressed, declared to Blaise that he had never seen such a clear sense of calling in anyone. As a devout child of God, Blaise was glad, although an inward pulling

[43] *Œuvres*, v. 1, 153.

at his heart warned him that the " petite " of whom he was especially fond was henceforth lost to him.

Well, Blaise was at least to share in the same upward pilgrimage, so that, in one sense, they were to remain in more intimate communion than ever, in the service of God! Blaise sought out Monsieur de Rebours who, after being converted by Saint Cyran, had become Monsieur Singlin's assistant, and was serving as one of the confessors at Port-Royal. Having exchanged the usual courtesies, Pascal asked him for permission to visit him from time to time, and this permission was granted.

When Pascal returned to talk with Monsieur de Rebours, he wished to come to a full understanding with him, the sooner to achieve a basis for intimate conversation. Pascal began, therefore, by saying " that we had read their books and those of their opponents." Monsieur de Rebours showed some delight at this. Filled with eagerness, and as it were to break the ice, Pascal then said that he thought a man could demonstrate in religion, following the very principles of common sense, many things which the opponents of religion claimed were contrary to it; and that reasoning actually led men to the gateway of believing, although they ought to believe without reasoning. Monsieur de Rebours found his argument rather strange, for it seemed to him, beyond all doubt, to proceed from a principle of vanity and of confidence in the power of reason. This suspicion was further enhanced by the fact that the argument came from a mathematician. It made Monsieur de Rebours resolve to give Pascal a reply marked by utter humility. Sensing that he was suspected of pride, Pascal wished to justify himself, and to demonstrate the innocence of his motive in asking the question; he was concerned, so he explained, only with Christian charity in suggesting the usefulness of reason in turning the souls of men toward the Truth. The grace of God would do the rest, and the prerogatives of divine grace were, in his view, altogether beyond question. Pascal's attempt at self-justification, however, only served to enhance the doubts in the mind of Monsieur de Rebours, who interpreted all Pascal's excuses as obstinacy. Pascal, for his part, considered the fine discourse, which was now directed at himself, as wholly superfluous, although it would indeed have rescued him from his pride had any question of pride been involved. He therefore sought to evade the points as Monsieur de Rebours aimed them at him, and this only served to redouble his counselor's efforts. The more intensely Monsieur de Rebours tried, the more Pascal showed by his profuse thanks that he did not consider these particular efforts to be needed.

The misunderstanding grew worse, to such a point that it was useless to hope the embarrassment could be removed by further conversations. The account of the whole matter given by Blaise to his sister Gilberte, on January 26, 1648, closes with an admission of helplessness on his part: the experience had left him with a sense of impotence, and of his lack of understanding. Doubtless it also left him with a sense of his human solitude. In this sense it was that Matthew Arnold was one day to say, " We are islands! "

INNER SOLITUDE

In his inner solitude Pascal proceeded to a fresh searching of his conscience by the light of Scripture. All our actions, as he there learned, may have two sources. He read in I John 2:16: " For all that is in the world is the concupiscence of the flesh, and the concupiscence of the eyes, and the pride of life, which is not of the Father, but is of the world." Saint Augustine had developed this thought at great length in the *Confessions* and in the *Traité de la véritable religion,* which Arnauld had translated. So also Jansen, in his *Discours sur la réforme de l'homme intérieur,* which the translation by Arnauld d'Andilly had made available among the friends of Port-Royal, and in his *Augustinus.*[44] There Pascal found the phrases *libido sentiendi, libido sciendi, libido dominandi,* which served as text for the superb meditation in Fragment 348 of the *Pensées* in the Brunschvicg edition: [45] " Wretched is the cursed land which these three rivers of fire enflame." Whether or not this fragment was written at the time of the events just recounted, we would naturally not presume to say. It is at least plausible to suppose that it was.

One thing seems certain, however: the searching of conscience which Pascal undertook by the light of Scripture, and of the commentators of Port-Royal, accounts for the focus of interest in his letter of November 5, 1648, also addressed to Gilberte, in which he draws a clear line of demarcation, as we have seen, between religious truths and secular truths. Pascal was overcome with chagrin at the misunderstanding with

[44] *de Statu naturæ lapsæ,* v. **2,** viii.
[45] *Pensées,* Section vii, Fr. 458, *Œuvres,* v. **13,** 369, 370. In our commentary we use the bibliographical indications of n. 4, 369, 370.

Monsieur de Rebours. Certainly his reflections, resulting from this incident, were not lost when he returned to his great theme, in projecting a vindication of Christianity, of which many of the *Pensées* stand as eloquent testimony.

For the time being, the misunderstanding between Port-Royal and himself continued to be very painful to him, the more so when he contrasted it with the divine calling that had brought such happiness to Jacqueline. Blaise felt at odds with himself, and his solitude was thereby accentuated.

To carry on scientific research in the spirit of Saint Augustine and Saint Cyran was evidently a more delicate undertaking than he had at first believed. A threefold concupiscence beset him at every step of the way. His Bible told him that it was expedient for him that one of his members should perish, rather than that his whole body should " be cast into hell." [46] The physicist confronting his Bible was not yet, however, resigned to such mutilation. An even wider range of experience must be his before he would agree to this radical operation. But by then the operation would have to be all the more radical because of the long delay upon which this passionate soul had insisted before yielding his consent. And then, by a stroke of irony which tells us a good deal about the misery of our human situation, when he finally did consent, it was in response to that very *libido excellendi* which pressed upon him and which carried its own stumbling block within itself.

When Paul Valéry writes that " this French Hamlet of Jansenist persuasion " [47] has " fearfully exaggerated the opposition between knowledge and salvation," [48] he does something less than justice to the immense effort of good will with which Pascal entered on that pathway in which there are so many pitfalls — pitfalls which Paul Valéry, as it happens, does not even believe exist.

[46] Matt. 5:29.
[47] Valéry, Paul, " Variation sur une *Pensée*," *La Revue hebdomadaire*, No. 28, 32d year, July 14, 1923, p. 164.
[48] *Ibid.*, p. 170.

V

The Source of Our Unhappiness

*" For all that is in the world, the lust of the flesh, and the lust of the
eyes, and the pride of life, is not of the Father, but is of the world."*
— *I John 2:16*

The author of the *Pensées,* having set himself to consider the several
kinds of restlessness that disturb men, and the perils and pains to which
they expose themselves, which give rise to so many quarrels, passions,
bold and often bad ventures, was one day to discover that " all the
unhappiness of men arises from one single fact, that they cannot stay
quietly in their own chamber." [1]

LONELINESS IN THE HOME

Pascal's loneliness was now aggravated by a fresh misunderstanding,
this time with his intimate companion and constant counselor — his
own father. In the spring of 1648, the elder Pascal had returned to
Paris with the honorary rank of *conseiller d'état.* He was now sixty years
of age, and looked forward to enjoying a period of quiet retirement in
the circle of his family. It was just at this moment that Blaise came to
him, at Jacqueline's special request, to tell of his young sister's decision
to leave home and to enter the convent of Port-Royal as a nun.

Stung by disappointment, the old gentleman, who by law held a considerable power over his daughter, appeared to forget, for the moment,
the whole of the religious experience he had shared with her. Not only
did he refuse his consent to her plan, but he went on to declare somewhat
bitterly that he had lost all confidence in Jacqueline, and even in Blaise,
whom he held to be her accomplice. He even went so far as to place
both young people under the surveillance of the old nurse who had
brought them up.

Jacqueline was not allowed to visit Port-Royal, save by stealth. She
could not see her adviser, Monsieur Singlin, except by subterfuge. This

[1] *Pensées,* Section ii, Fr. 139, *Œuvres,* v. 13, 52, 53.

served only to increase the ardor of her conviction. Shortly thereafter the family moved to the parish of Saint-Jean-en-Grève, and this gave Jacqueline time to deepen her sense of vocation in her solitude. In a letter [2] to her father, dated June 19, 1648, marked by a beauty of style worthy of Racine, she avowed her complete submission to her father's will, asking only for the privilege of undergoing the discipline of a fortnight's retreat at Port-Royal, where she might hold solitary converse with God.

Blaise was left more than ever alone in his ailing condition, and he therefore welcomed the cordial advances of the young Duke de Roannez, who was serious of purpose despite his mediocre training, and who was obsessed by a thirst for knowledge. Was it, perhaps, this latter trait that made him so appealing to Pascal? We love those who need us, most of all when those we love find ways of living without us.

Paternal affection soon gained the upper hand once more with Etienne Pascal. What is more, he realized that he was growing old. Disarmed by the gentleness of Jacqueline's spirit, and by the sincerity of her utter devotion as shown in her letter of submission, their misunderstanding wholly vanished from memory. Blaise and Jacqueline told their sister Gilberte, in the letter of November 5, 1648, already mentioned several times in these pages, that all the difficulties that had "troubled the peace of the home both outwardly and inwardly" had, after a frank explanation on both sides, become wholly a thing of the past. Among such choice souls as these, indeed, the misunderstanding must have seemed the more serious because it was so unheard-of in this family. A spirit of tolerance, shown on both sides, now ruled in the home. In the world beyond its walls, civil war was now raging, in the insurrection of the *Fronde*.

Etienne Pascal, being prudent by temper and royalist by persuasion, and knowing only too well the horrors of civil disorder after his experience in Normandy, left Paris with his family in May, 1649, and moved south for a time to Clermont, where he visited at the Périer home.

Having fulfilled the decent demands of courtesy, Jacqueline quietly retired to her own apartment in the home, where she lived a life of solitary meditation, to the benefit of them all. Mother Agnès, through her letters from Port-Royal in Paris, furnished guidance and encouragement from afar. A local priest asked Jacqueline to translate into French verse the hymn "*Jesu, nostra redemptio*," [3] and the young woman, finding

[2] *Œuvres*, v. 2, 341 *sq.*   [3] *Œuvres*, v. 2, 424.

that her poetic talent could be thus consecrated to God's service, accomplished the task so beautifully that the priest urged her to continue along this line. Jacqueline turned to Mother Agnès for counsel. The latter, who had a very profound understanding of human nature, and who recognized in Jacqueline the signs of that passion for excellence which was found in the very heart of every Pascal, ordered her to bury this talent in the ground.[4] Monsieur de Rebours had not been able to talk so categorically to Blaise.

THE DISCOVERY OF SOCIAL LIFE

The latter sought relaxation in Clermont, as his doctors had advised him to do when he was leaving Paris. In the circle of local society he found that his youthful talents were fêted on every possible occasion. He went to scientific gatherings at the home of Monsieur de Ribeyre. He is said to have taken quite an interest in a certain beautiful and scholarly lady, " the Sappho of the land." He formed a friendship with Domat, the noted jurisconsult, who did a well-known portrait of Pascal in red chalk, often seen in reproduction. It gives us a good idea of what Pascal looked like just before the age of thirty, showing how attractive was his intelligent face with its touch of irony.

Etienne, Blaise, and Jacqueline returned to Paris probably in September, 1650.[5] Once it was understood that she would not take the veil during her father's lifetime, Jacqueline was quite free to devote herself to the disciplines of piety. Her ardor found expression in May, 1651, in an essay on Le Mystère de Jésus,[6] which must be carefully distinguished from the later work by Blaise bearing the same title.

Now that his health was so greatly improved, Blaise continued to enjoy the social life of Paris as he had done in Clermont. We should remember that, during his lonely days, in the summer of 1648, he had formed a close friendship with the Duke de Roannez, who was awaiting his return from Clermont with impatience. Our promises sometimes prejudge the course of events, and occasionally lead to premature commitments. This may embarrass our freedom of action, or it may be fortu-

[4] *Œuvres,* v. 2, 419. *Lettre de la Mère Agnès à Jacqueline.* See, on p. 426 *sq.,* other letters from Mother Agnès.
[5] *Œuvres,* v. 2, 480. Pascalian chronology is somewhat uncertain in this period. We adopt objectively what seems to us most likely. See nn. 37 and 58 in this chapter.
[6] *Œuvres,* v. 2, 452 *sq.*

nate if our nobler purposes gain thereby in strength. Our commitment becomes a hindrance or a blessing, according to its intrinsic quality. To guard the character of our commitments is to protect our character, after a fashion, against evil.

This friendship with a young admirer of his own age was a delightful experience for Pascal, who had enjoyed no normal companionship as a child, and had associated with older people all the while he was growing up. The young Duke, on his part, had rubbed shoulders all his life with soldiers and worldly folk, and hence enjoyed the novelty of contact with a man of such devoted spirit, from whom he had so much to learn. He literally drank in Pascal's every word. He was fascinated by his knowledge and his wisdom. It was not long before Blaise had his own apartment in the ducal palace, which stood at the corner of the Rue Taillepain and the Rue du Cloître-Saint-Merry. Friendship, like love, has its honeymoon period, during which it first expresses itself, gains in strength, and lives apart. Being timid as yet, it hesitates to make claims which may encroach upon the life of the beloved. Thus the Duke showed great respect for the scientific studies undertaken by Pascal, whose active work at this time was being done upon the *Traité du vide,* of which we have some fragments [7] written in the middle of 1651. In July or August of that year, he corresponded with Monsieur de Ribeyre regarding the theses of the *collège* in Montferrand,[8] and his concern for his own reputation is clearly evident in his lines.

DEATH OF ETIENNE PASCAL

A great personal trial was soon to bring him to a new sense of reality. Etienne fell ill in September. Jacqueline nursed him with touching devotion, and when she was not needed at his bedside, she retired to her room to prostrate herself in tears, and to pray for him. Blaise's own anxiety was poignant. Surely he must have repeated to himself, at this time, that events are teachers sent us by the hand of God. On September 24, 1651, Etienne Pascal died. What an immense vacuum was now left in the home, most of all in the heart of Blaise!

This sense of emptiness was all the more distressing to Blaise, in that it was mingled with a sense of regret for the misunderstanding which

[7] *Œuvres*, v. 2, 511 *sq.*

[8] *Œuvres*, v. 2, 475 *sq.* See facsimile, p. 48; the reply of M. de Ribeyre, p. 496 *sq.*; and the reply of Pascal, p. 500 *sq.*

had, in his father's last days, marred the intimacy of their lifelong relationship. What we regret most keenly, as we stand before an open grave, is not the happy hours lived together and now taken from us, so much as the opportunities we have missed; not the persons we have loved, so much as the fact that we did not know how to love them better. In an epitaph whose stately phrases conceal but dimly the depth of emotion behind them, Blaise sketched for posterity a portrait of his departed parent. Above all he sounded the note of praise to the Grace " which had ordained that his great love for God was the foundation, the support, and the acme of all his other virtues." [9]

Our heaviest trials have a way of forcing us to face basic truths. Overwhelmed and chastened to the very depths of his soul, Blaise now recovered again the richness of a religious experience which even then was but slightly hidden from his full consciousness. Now he went to the very heart of Scripture, to Jesus Christ. The letter he wrote to M. and Madame Périer makes it clear that this severe blow gathered meaning for him in the light of the sacred text: " We should call nothing evil save that which renders the victim of God's will a victim of the Devil, but we should call that good which renders the victim of the Devil through Adam a victim of God; following this rule, let us consider the nature of his death." [10] Starting thus with the theme of divine illumination, his thought moves on to a fuller reference to Jesus Christ.

" In considering this matter, we need to turn to the person of JESUS CHRIST; for everything in men is abominable, and since God never regards men save through the Mediator JESUS CHRIST, men ought not to regard one another nor themselves, save through the mediation of JESUS CHRIST, for unless we employ that medium, we find in ourselves only veritable unhappiness, or abominable pleasures; whereas if we regard all things through JESUS CHRIST, we shall find full consolation, full satisfaction, full edification." [11] Those biographers of Pascal who enjoy tracing a series of " conversions " in his life may find ample evidence in this letter of an authentic " conversion ": his candid confession of " abominable pleasure," which makes men victims of the Devil and constitutes the essence of evil in unregenerate man; his repe-

---

[9] The epitaph of Etienne Pascal composed by his son is to be found in *Œuvres*, v. **2**, 562.

[10] *Lettre de Pascal à M. et Madame Périer sur la mort de son Père*, October 17, 1651, *Œuvres*, v. **2**, 542.

[11] *Ibid.*, p. 543.

tition of JESUS CHRIST, JESUS CHRIST, JESUS CHRIST, with an intensity unmatched save in the *Mémorial* we are soon to consider; his self-abasement at the feet of the Saviour and of the divine Majesty; the identification of his own suffering with the agony of the Redeemer and the illumination which thereby comes to him — all these constitute the most complete record of a mystical experience, after a season of dryness.

Pascal continues: " Let us look upon death through JESUS CHRIST, and not without JESUS CHRIST. Without JESUS CHRIST it is horrible, it is detestable, and the ultimate horror in nature. Through JESUS CHRIST it is quite otherwise: it is lovable, holy, and the joy of the believer. All is sweet in JESUS CHRIST, even death." [12]

And he proceeds to ponder the place death holds in the " continual sacrifice " of Jesus Christ. May we not regard this as an anticipation of *Le Mystère de Jésus,* where he is to say: " Jesus will be in agony until the end of the world; we must not sleep during all that time "?

But it is not enough for a creature to abase himself in the presence of divine Majesty, in adoration of the sovereign Existence. God must accept the sacrifice, as the Scripture declares: " And the Lord smelled and accepted the sweet savour of sacrifice." [13]

" All these things were fulfilled in JESUS CHRIST. In entering the world, He offered Himself.[14] Jesus had to endure suffering in order to enter upon His glory," as is recorded in Luke 24:26: " Ought not Christ to have suffered these things, and so to enter into His glory? " Although He was the Son of God, He had to learn obedience; but in the days of His flesh, having cried " with strong crying and tears unto Him that was able to save Him from death, He was heard in that He feared," as we read in Heb. 5:7, 8.[15] The Acts of the Apostles, moreover, declares explicitly that He was received into Heaven, as if to assure us that the holy sacrifice He accomplished upon earth was acceptable to God, and was received into His bosom where it burns from everlasting to everlasting.[16]

[12] *Œuvres,* v. **2**, 543.

[13] Gen. 8:21.

[14] Heb. 9:14 and 10:5–7: *I leo ingrediens mundum dicit: Hostiam et oblationem noluisti; corpus autem aptasti mihi. Holocaustomata pro peccato non tibi placuerunt, Tunc dixi: Ecce venio: in capite libri* [Ps. 39:7] *Scriptum est de me: ut faciam, Deus, voluntatem tuam.*

[15] *Œuvres,* v. **2**, 545.

[16] *Œuvres,* v. **2**, 546, 547.

We ought then to look upon the conditions of our life as we have seen them manifested in our sovereign Lord; we ought not to sorrow like pagans who have no hope. Yes, let us no longer look upon death as pagans do, but as Christians, that is to say, with hope, as Saint Paul exhorts us to do.[17]

The whole of this letter, of which we have caught only a few glimpses, and which fills twenty-four pages in the great Brunschvicg edition,[18] really amounts to a sermon on death worthy of Bossuet, of whom Pascal is the forerunner in more ways than one. His argument rests squarely upon Scripture interpreted according to Tradition, particularly according to Saint Augustine,[19] or Jansen's commentary on Saint Augustine.[20]

When we remember how close Pascal was to his father, and the degree to which these two humans, father and son, were bound to one another in spirit, our imagination must be moved by the impressive scene hinted at in this letter: here was Blaise, turning now to the Bible, his eyes dimmed by tears, hoping to find in Scripture some word concerning the secret of human destiny.

When his back was bent under the heavy blow that had come to him in the loss of his nearest and dearest, his language was so shaped by the thought of the Bible that we cannot tell at times whether it is Blaise speaking, or whether we are reading the Bible itself: " that thus, in hallowing the name of our Father, His will may be made our own; that His grace may reign." [21] It is the theme of the Lord's Prayer, and the human father now blends in thought with the Heavenly Father. The mood then changes and becomes quite simple again, altogether human, unadorned, as a new resolve takes shape in the peace which floods into his heart: " I have learned from a saintly man during our affliction that one of the most solid and useful acts of charity toward the dead is to do those things they would have ordered us to do if they had been still in the world, and to practice the holy counsel they have given us, and for their sake to keep ourselves in that state in which they now wish us to be." [22] Blaise still felt a great need of the guide of his youthful years: he admits that he would have been utterly lost had his father gone six

---

[17] *Nolumus autem vos ignorare, fratres de dormientibus, ut non contristemini sicut et ceteri, qui spem non habent.* I Thess. 4:12.

[18] *Œuvres*, v. 2, 537–561.

[19] Examples: *Œuvres*, v. 2, 550, 555.

[20] Example: *Œuvres*, v. 2, 551.

[21] *Œuvres*, v. 2, 556.

[22] *Œuvres*, v. 2, 558.

years earlier, and, while he now felt less absolutely dependent upon his counsel, he knew that he really would have needed his father for another ten years, and that his presence would have been useful all the rest of his days.

Victor Hugo was to rediscover, one day, the noble simplicity of Blaise Pascal, at a tragic moment in his own experience: his daughter Leopoldine and her husband were drowned in an accident in the Seine quite soon after their marriage. In a poem entitled *A Villequier*,[23] after meditating at length on the theme of death and the divine purpose, the sorrowing father closes with a lament in which he pours out his mood of humble submission in artless words which bespeak Hugo's human weakness: *Thou seest Lord, how needful are our children to us.*

Thus Blaise earlier had said: *I really should have needed my father.*

Human affliction thus gives voice to the soul in familiar accents, at those moments when God permits the events of life to touch our flesh to the quick.

How were Jacqueline and Blaise to fill the vacuum that yawned at the center of their lives and in the depth of their hearts, now that their father was gone? How would they employ their new-found liberty? To use an expression later made famous by Blaise Pascal in his argument on the " wager," they were by now already " embarked." [24]

SERVING GOD AND MAMMON

Between October 19 and October 26, Blaise and Jacqueline exchanged gifts between themselves. The entire property went to Blaise, with the understanding that he would provide his sister with an income for life, which should cease, however, on the day Jacqueline should take her religious vows in the convent.[25] What was now to be done about it? We know from Gilberte's account that Blaise hoped his sister would stay with him, for the sake of Christian charity, for at least a year. We also know that a woman who enters a convent becomes the bride of Christ. Her soul dies to this world, and the nun, reborn under a new name, henceforth wears on her finger the wedding ring of the Heavenly

[23] *Les Contemplations.*

[24] The word is Pascal's own and is in the argument of the wager. (*Pensées*, Section iii, Fr. 233, *Œuvres*, v. **13**, 146.)

[25] Deeds executed by a notary and signed by Pascal (October 19 to 26, 1651), *Œuvres*, v. **2**, 567 *sq.*

Spouse who promises her eternal life. At the time of her holy marriage she brings her dowry: all her worldly possessions she makes over to the convent. Was Blaise intending to lay hands upon this sacred dowry for himself, or did he suppose that he could delay her entry upon her chosen vocation by bringing pressure through his control of her material legacy? Better than anyone save Jacqueline herself, he knew how sacred her vocation was in her eyes.

There was still another aspect of the question: assuming that Jacqueline should be cut off from her patrimony when she took the veil, would not Blaise feel some obligation to divide the family estate with Gilberte? Would Blaise take advantage of Gilberte's absence to lay claim to two thirds instead of one half for himself? However we look at the matter, we cannot avoid the unhappy impression that Mammon had suddenly invaded the Pascal home.

There can be only one explanation for this whole sorry business: Blaise was now in great need of money. This suggests that he must have been more deeply involved in worldly affairs than we had reason at first to suppose. He knew now from experience that " we distinguish men by external appearances rather than by internal qualities! Which of us two shall have precedence? Who will give place to the other? The least clever? But I am as clever as he. We should have to fight over this. He has four lackeys, and I have only one. This can be seen; we have only to count. It falls to me to yield, and I am a fool if I contest the matter." [26] What a confession indeed! " Men would not have me honor a man clothed in brocade, and followed by seven or eight lackeys! Why! He will have me thrashed if I do not salute him. This costume, 'tis a force." [27] Poor Blaise: he was indeed caught in the toils!

Who could have foreseen this? Who would have believed it? Three weeks after Blaise wrote the beautiful letter on the death of his father, Jacqueline was saying prayers for her brother's " conversion." From November 2 to 5 she entered upon a retreat at Port-Royal. When this was completed she had a visit from Gilberte and her husband. She confided to her elder sister her irrevocable decision to enter the convent as soon as the estate was settled. But she wanted nothing said to Blaise about it, lest it disturb him. Did Madame Périer perhaps overstate the facts, in her account of this incident, in her *Vie de Jacqueline?* We are afraid this is the case. The truth is that the Périers, during several fam-

---

[26] *Pensées*, Section v, Fr. 319, *Œuvres*, v. **13**, 238, 239.
[27] *Pensées*, Section v, Fr. 315, *Œuvres*, v. **13**, 236.

ily conclaves which took place in a poisonously embittered mood, entirely agreed with Blaise in begrudging every farthing that was to go to Jacqueline, as if they had never heard of Christian charity.

Once the family estate was straightened out, on December 31, 1651, Jacqueline set the date of January 4, 1652, when she would enter Port-Royal. On the preceding day, according to Gilberte, she asked her elder sister to tell her brother during the evening, lest it come as a surprise. She did so with the greatest care she could; but, though she told him it was only a retreat to help Jacqueline to become a bit familiar with this type of life, he could not help being greatly affected. He retired in great sorrow to his apartment, without seeing his younger sister, who was at the time in a little room where she customarily said her prayers. She did not come out until after her brother had left, fearing it might be too great a shock for him to see her.

Victor Giraud goes into ecstasy over this last scene. To him there is nothing more filled with quiet pathos, in all the plays of Racine: the calm, final night's sleep of the future Sister Sainte-Euphémie, and then her silent departure for the cloister. " Thus *she got up, dressed, and went her way,* moving about now as at all times with an inconceivable tranquillity and equanimity of spirit. *We said no farewell, for fear that we might be too much moved, and I turned aside out of her way, when I saw that she was ready to go.*"[28] We are inclined to accept Victor Giraud's judgment as we recall the women in Racine's dramas.

Once at Port-Royal, the novice was so exemplary that the authorities decided to reckon as part of her novitiate the time of her earlier retreat, conducted when she was still living in the world. Her betrothal to Christ was hence set for Trinity Sunday, May 26, 1652. She sent word to her brother in a letter which was at once firm and yet permeated by her eager wish that he might repent of his ways.[29] She also wrote to Gilberte a fortnight before the ceremony.[30] This second letter indicates something of the effect of Jacqueline's words upon Blaise. He had come to Port-Royal the very next day, " quite beside himself, with a severe headache occasioned by the news, and yet quite calmed down."

The seeming contradiction in this description suggests that Blaise was now a deeply divided soul. He was overwhelmed with love for

[28] Giraud, Victor, *La Vie héroïque de Blaise Pascal, op. cit.,* p. 68.

[29] *Œuvres,* v. 3, 9 *sq., Lettre de Jacqueline Pascal à son frère sur sa profession.*

[30] *Œuvres,* v. 3, 19 *sq., Lettre de Jacqueline Pascal à Madame Périer sur sa profession,* May 10, 1652.

Jacqueline. Yet, upon Jacqueline's special plea, Monsieur d'Andilly had to send for him and put the matter before him with much ardor and skill. Blaise next tried to have the ceremony delayed. Failing in this, he finally declared that he himself preferred Trinity Sunday. Why, then, had he sought a delay? On July 8 he made a gift, apparently with some reluctance, to the abbey of Port-Royal, in the amount of four thousand pounds; this gift would not become effective, however, until his death, and then only if he should die without issue.[31] Why, again, was Blaise so eager to have the ceremony on Trinity Sunday? God is sometimes involved in a curious way in these monetary and mundane affairs, as the latter become mixed with scientific considerations.

BLAISE AND THE QUEEN OF SWEDEN

On April 14 there was a gathering at the home of the Duchesse d'Aiguillon, who had once arranged the happy encounter between Etienne Pascal and her uncle, Cardinal Richelieu. They were a colorful company, according to Loret's *La Muse historique:*

> Duchesses and *cordons-bleus*,
> Eager now to snatch a view
> Of an arithmetical device
> Mathematical and nice,
> Holding secrets passing rare;
> One named Pascal now would dare
> Tempt a theory profound,
> So persuasive, yet so sound;
> " Calculus " and " common chance "
> Win our praise at every glance.

The truth is that Blaise was impelled by the need to add to his income, so that he might cut more of a figure in society. He was also spurred on by his scientific curiosity and his passion for excellence. Perhaps, too, he was thinking of his father, whose memory was associated with the calculating machine. So he proceeded now to perfect his working model. He described it to Bourdelot, the personal physician and confidant of Queen Christine of Sweden. In his letter to Bourdelot, Pascal paid a lively tribute to the Queen. She replied in turn, through Bour-

---

[31] See *Extraits d'actes notariés,* July 8, 1652, *Œuvres,* v. 3, 39 *sq.*

delot, on March 14, 1652. Her Majesty would be happy to accept the calculating machine from Pascal, together with the accompanying statement; she admired the clarity of his reasoning, and always preferred solid proofs to mere appearances; and Pascal was " one of those geniuses for whom the Queen had been searching."

Pascal hurried the work along, and wrote a letter to the Queen, about June, 1652, which tells us a good deal about his state of mind at the time. He had conceived the plan to offer his calculating machine to the sovereign chiefly because her sacred person so happily combined two qualities which filled Pascal with admiration and with respect, namely, sovereign authority and solid science.

Pascal professed " a quite peculiar veneration for those who have attained the highest rank, whether in power or in knowledge." It is understood, of course, that such a principle would place Pascal himself on the same level as the Queen, although he did not at all intend to injure her feelings. He even found a way to slip in an additional word of flattery for the sovereign herself: " It is Your Majesty, Madame, which manifests to the world that unique example hitherto lacking to it. She it is in whom power is exercised by the light of science, and science is advanced by the luster of authority."

Clearly the authority acknowledged by Pascal at this time was an authority of political power and of the mind; and, since these two types of authority were united in the person of Her Majesty the Queen, she could not see *anything that might be superior* to her own greatness. We find Pascal thus revising, for the time being, his notion of three orders, which, as we have seen in the foregoing chapters, were slowly taking shape in his mind: " The power of monarchs over their subjects . . . is simply one manifestation of the power of minds over other minds which are inferior to them, over whom they exert the right of persuasion, which among them is similar to the right to command, in political government. This second empire appears to me to be of an even more exalted order than that over men's bodies, and hence more equitable, in that this power cannot be exercised or conserved save by merit, whereas the other may depend wholly upon birth or fortune." [32] Here we see how Pascal took revenge for having only one or two lackeys, and for being compelled to salute a man's clothes!

A man's clothes, for that matter, were no less a mark of rank in scientific circles than in the world of affairs: " We can only think of Plato

[32] *Lettre de Pascal à la Reine Christine de Suède, Œuvres,* v. 3, 29 *sq.*

96

and Aristotle in grand academic robes. They were honest men, like others, laughing with their friends." [33]

MÉRÉ, MITON, AND ROANNEZ

Pascal himself had learned to laugh by now. Who had taught him? These gentlemen in whose company he was now spending his time and who had become his models.

Most of all, one Chevalier de Méré, a professional gentleman, as Taine has called him. He was indeed one of a type: he knew Greek, Latin, Italian, Spanish, some Arabic, something of mathematics; he practiced the art of war, which he described as the finest calling in the world. He was a knight of the Order of Malta, and between campaigns he was known as a wit and a man of the world. He was found in every salon noted for good conversation, in company with the leading authors of the day. He even became an author himself. Leaving this *grand monde*, he knew also how to turn to the *demi-monde*, slipping from the formal setting of royal society into ladies' boudoirs. He was a gambler. He had his mistresses; Ninon de Lenclos loved him. He was at home in every sort of company, but he belonged nowhere in particular. He was not known as a poet or mathematician, but he was something of both, and a good judge of both. He was an arbiter of good form in any field. He fitted in quite naturally to the mood of each new group with which he associated. He was always perfectly at ease. He could pick up the conversation where it was, no matter on what topic, when he entered a room.[34]

Here was a new ideal of character for Pascal henceforth to emulate with the same passion for excellence he had shown in every other field that had claimed his attention. He did not want anyone to be able to say of him, " He is a mathematician, or ' a preacher,' or ' eloquent,' but, ' He is a gentleman.' That universal quality alone pleases me. It is a bad sign when, on seeing a person, you remember his book." [35] Here was Pascal, himself an expert, proceeding now to burn up everything he had once held in reverence. When are we to suppose he wrote the following fragment: " It is far better to know something about everything than to know all about one thing. This universality is the best "? [36]

[33] *Pensées*, Section v, Fr. 331, *Œuvres*, v. 13, 250.
[34] Cf. *Pensées*, Section i, Fr. 34, *Œuvres*, v. 12, 44.
[35] *Pensées*, Section i, Fr. 35, *Œuvres*, v. 12, 45, 46.
[36] *Pensées*, Section i, Fr. 37, *Œuvres*, v. 12, 47.

May it not have been in the spring of 1653, when he made a trip to Poitou in the company of Méré, Miton, and the Duke de Roannez, jotting down notes on his pad, from time to time, about his traveling companions? The Duke had been appointed Governor and Lieutenant General of Poitou [37] on August 22, 1651, and had invited his friends to make a trip with him to his estates in Oiron, near Poitiers.

There is no better way for men to learn to know one another intimately than to travel together. As they started out, Blaise tried to put himself at ease with his companions by quoting a few *bons mots*. Suddenly he realized that Méré was watching him with a shrewd look, and he stopped in the very midst of a sentence. From now on he listened. Chiefly to Méré. Miton was less interesting to him, with his droll stories about women, told in the "manner" which gave rise to the verb *mitonner*. This Miton was at bottom an egotist!

Was there not, perhaps, a conversation going on all the while in Pascal's own soul, which he also set down on his pad? "Self is hateful.

[37] This chronology is uncertain. Cf. in *Œuvres*, v. **3**, the account of a journey undertaken by Méré, and discussion of the account of Méré, 105 *sq*. Ch. H. Boudhors, "Pascal et Méré, la date du voyage en Poitou," *Revue d'histoire littéraire de la France*, v. **29**, 338, and the excellent nn. 13 and 31, pp. 360–362, in the *op. cit.* by Morris Bishop. A comparison between the known dates of the lives of Pascal, Roannez, and Méré leaves only three dates possible, concluded the author of *Pascal: The Life of Genius* (p. 361): the spring of 1651, the spring of 1653, and July, 1653. Professor Bishop chose the spring of 1651 because of conclusive evidence: the conversation that Méré mentions is plausible in 1651, but not so in 1653. Miton gets married in February, 1653 (Grubbs, H. A., *Damien Miton*, Princeton, 1932, p. 23). Pascal was disgusted with this world at the close of 1653, and to choose the summer of that year reduces the worldly period of Pascal inordinately.

The solution of Professor Bishop makes him then situate the trip to Poitou *before* the death of Etienne Pascal, which leads him to interpret severely the attitude of Blaise at that time: certainly he is "deeply moved" (p. 123) but "it seems not unjust nor cheaply critical to suggest that under all the grief welled up an irrepressible feeling of release" (p. 126). As for the letter of Blaise on the death of his father, it is nothing more, according to Professor Bishop, than "an intellectual exercise on the nature of grief"! (p. 125).

We have given our own interpretation of this letter. We agree that it has something formal, something too didactic, and too logical; that something alive is missing which should put one more at ease. Certainly, Blaise has already taken a step in society, and that is what we meant when we said he was already "embarked." We are not quite satisfied, however, with the idea of ascribing this long Biblical meditation of evident sincerity to a man returning from Poitou. Also since it is a matter of inner evidence, we believe that a man newly converted by Méré would not have written in this manner the type of letter that Blaise wrote on the death of his father. This is decidedly not the letter of a backslider.

See further the remarks of n. 58.

You, Miton, conceal it. You do not for that reason destroy it; you are, then, always hateful. No; for in acting as we do to oblige everybody, we give no more occasion for hatred of us." [38] We can detect here, it would seem, something of the struggle now going on in Pascal's own mind, whatever he may have added later by way of excuse to conceal it. Here was a young man, finding himself " taken along with their luggage by a duke and a peer," [39] his eyes positively dazzled as they opened on a new and a very unfamiliar world. For him it was the discovery and initial understanding of a new generation, now coming to replace the generation of Voiture and the early *précieux;* of a generation which was to stress the return to straightforwardness and to simplicity in place of artificial rules of language and elaborate codes of feeling.[40] As Méré put it: " I am a man of the world, with as little affectation as possible." [41]

A NEW WAY OF KNOWLEDGE

Pascal so promptly assimilated these new ways of thought that, even before they arrived at Poitiers, he was able to meet his companions on their own ground. He was amazed at the transformation in himself, and enjoyed it hugely: " I had been living in exile," he told them, " and now you have brought me back to my own land." Home again from this trip, Blaise still hung eagerly upon every word of his new *directeur de conscience,* who had opened up for him nothing less than a new way of knowledge, infinitely more subtle and of infinitely wider significance than could be known by the mathematical mind: it was the *esprit de finesse* — the intuitive mind, as we should say.

Méré made fun of Pascal's " long-drawn-out reasoning in a straight line," which was not only quite foreign to the mysterious depths of that nature by which " man infinitely transcends man," [42] as Pascal was soon to recognize, but actually *prevented* him from attaining that loftier knowledge which is never deceived, whereas a mathematician never sees what is in front of him! [43] It is not to the mathematical reasoning that

[38] *Pensées,* Section vii, Fr. 455, *Œuvres,* v. **13,** 367, 368.

[39] A delightful remark by Mauriac, François, in *Blaise Pascal et sa sœur Jacqueline,* Hachette, Paris, 1931, pp. 128, 129.

[40] Faguet, Emile, *Revue des cours et conférences,* April 9, 1896, p. 135 (quoted by Brunschvicg, *Œuvres,* v. **3,** 110).

[41] *Œuvres,* v. **3,** 110.

[42] *Pensées,* Section vii, Fr. 434, *Œuvres,* v. **13,** 347.

[43] *Pensées,* Section i, Fr. 1, *Œuvres,* v. **12,** 11.

we must turn, then, but simply to the intuitive mind, to that innate good sense, that instinctive awareness, which we find within us, and which, when properly refined by use, divines the loftier truths of the human order. Thus it was that Méré, an agnostic, forced Pascal to prick up his ears.

Pascal had already tried more than once to sketch out the several levels of reality, and the very multiplicity of his attempts indicated their imperfection. Now suddenly a light flooded into Pascal's mind as he came upon this passage in a letter from Méré: " Beyond this natural world, which is known by sense experience, there is another invisible, and . . . it is in the latter world that you may attain to loftiest science. Those who are in touch only with the corporeal world judge of things in general quite badly, and always grossly, like Descartes, whom you so greatly esteem." And Pascal noted on his pad: " Descartes useless and uncertain." [44]

Truly the purposes of God are inscrutable. For Pascal, in reading such words as these from the pen of a cultured worldling, found new light shed upon the structure of his own thinking, as it took shape in the hierarchy of three orders, and as it was soon to welcome and to understand the charity that is in Jesus: " In this invisible world, which is of infinite extent, we may discover the reasons and principles of things, we may discover truths hitherto largely concealed, notions of propriety, of justice, and of proportion, the true original and the perfect idea of that which we are seeking." [45]

Pascal derived from his new knowledge literary gifts to lend more suppleness to his style, in such a way as to make it the prototype of French prose. He came to grasp the concept of a type of rhetoric which enabled him, in the pages of the *Pensées* to challenge the mind of a libertine, yet withal in such words as the latter might understand. In his *Discours sur les passions de l'amour*, Pascal clearly formulated this principle thus: " There are two types of mind, the one a mathematical mind [*esprit géométrique*]; the other which may be called the intuitive mind [*esprit de finesse*].

" The former takes a slow, hard, inflexible view of things; the latter has a suppleness of thought which it applies, at one and the same time, to the several lovable parts of the beloved object. From the eyes it moves

[44] *Pensées*, Section ii, Fr. 78, *Œuvres*, v. **12**, 98.
[45] *Œuvres de M. le Chevalier de Méré*, Mortier, Amsterdam, 1692, v. **2**. Cf. *Lettre XIX à Pascal*, 60 sq.

to the heart, and from each outward movement, it can tell what is taking place within." [46] In the *Pensées*, this sketchy outline is more amply filled in: in the mathematical mind, the principles are palpable, but removed from common sense; so that it is difficult to turn one's mind in that direction; but if one turns it thither ever so little, one sees things fully, and it is almost impossible that they should escape notice.

In the intuitive mind, on the other hand, the principles are naturally those of ordinary life. It is only a question of good eyesight if you want to see. But it must be good, for the principles are so subtle and so numerous that some may all too easily escape notice. Now, the omission of a single principle leads to error! Pascal can still hear Méré making fun of him, complaining about mathematicians " who are mathematicians and nothing more," and who make themselves ridiculous and intolerable by trying to treat even the most delicate matters mathematically!

We can easily mark a new stage in Pascal's thought, as he thus describes matters of intuition: " They are scarcely seen; they are felt rather than seen; there is the greatest difficulty in making them felt by those who do not of themselves perceive them. These principles are so fine and so numerous that a very delicate and very clear sense is needed to perceive them, and to judge rightly and justly when they are perceived, without for the most part being able to demonstrate them in order as in mathematics; because the principles are not known to us in the same way, and because it would be an endless matter to undertake it." [47] It is in such a context that we should think of Pascal's famous statement of principle: " The heart has its reasons, which reason does not know." [48] But in doing so, we need to remember that Pascal's understanding of the unique character of intuition was attained through personal experience, namely, in thinking through the things Méré had said.

At one time Pascal was in love,[49] or perhaps we should say that he felt a certain tender sentiment for Charlotte Gouffier, the sister of his closest friend, the Duke de Roannez.

[46] Cousin, Victor, *Des Pensées de Pascal*, new edition revised and enlarged, Librairie philosophique de Ladrange, Didier, Paris, 1844, pp. 397, 398.

[47] *Pensées*, Section i, Fr. 1, *Œuvres*, v. **12**, 11, 12.

[48] *Pensées*, Section iv, Fr. 277, *Œuvres*, v. **13**, 201.

[49] Consult circumspectly Chamaillard, E., *Pascal mondain et amoureux*, Les Presses Universitaires de France, Paris, 1923.

" DISCOURS SUR LES PASSIONS DE L'AMOUR "

Charlotte was barely eighteen when Blaise first met her, and he was ten years her senior. Was she not a member of the aristocracy? Well, what of it! This great soul moved in an aristocracy of his own, which was not in the least inferior to hers. It may be that we should trace to this experience the source of Pascal's rather immodest profession of faith, as he declared it to Queen Christine of Sweden. It may account also for the reservations written into the legal documents drawn up on July 8, 1652 — the letter to the Queen was dated in June — allowing for the possibility that Blaise might have children.

As we have seen, Blaise was terribly divided within himself at this time. He was repeating experiments with the vacuum, indeed, but the vacuum was then still more within his own heart. Thus it may be that we find a hint about this experience in a passage of the famous letter written at the time of his father's death. In this passage he declares that man, having fallen into sin, has lost his primary love — his love for God — and that " his love for himself being left within so great a soul capable of infinite love, self-love thus expands and overflows in the vacuum which God has left behind." We have shown, at more than one point already, how Pascal's letters of counsel contained a note of soliloquy which revealed more than he knew of himself. His utter sincerity is beyond question.

So we find him returning to the theme in his *Discours sur les passions de l'amour:* " Notwithstanding that man seeks for something to fill up the great vacuum he has caused by going out of himself, still the need cannot be satisfied by every type of object. His heart is too vast. He needs something which at least resembles himself, and which is as close as possible to himself." [50] He goes on to point out that nature has foreseen this need, by limiting and including within the difference of the two sexes the very fitness and resemblance which provides the beauty man requires for happiness. Nature has impressed this truth, indeed, so well upon our souls that we find the matter well cared for. There is a place in our hearts to be filled, and it can thus be filled effectively. [51] " Man is born for pleasure: he feels that this is so, and no other proof is needed. He then proceeds to follow the dictates of reason in his search

[50] Cousin, Victor, *Des Pensées de Pascal, op. cit.*, p. 399.
[51] *Ibid.*, p. 399.

for pleasure. But he often feels a powerful emotion arising in his heart *without knowing from what source it has arisen.*" [52] We have italicized this last phrase with a full awareness of the question concerning the authenticity of the passage.

Henri Jacoubet has published the results of his inquiry into the matter in the *Revue d'histoire littéraire de la France*,[53] in which he concludes that "the problem of the *Discours* is primarily a problem regarding the manuscript. To solve this problem, we must place ourselves in the position we should occupy if we had in front of us, not the authentic text of the *Pensées,* but one of the copies from which the Port-Royal edition was prepared. There are perhaps two elements combined in the *Discours,* the genuine core written by Pascal, and a more or less discreet, more or less felicitous, wrapping." [54] This represents our own understanding of the matter. Let us therefore admit that we never escape wholly from the mood of conjecture, in considering the *Discours.*

The author of the same, then, is concerned with a person of quality of the opposite sex, occasionally encountered by a lonely man in need of some kind of companionship if he is to be happy: " When anyone is in love with a lady of superior social rank, ambition may mingle with love at the outset. But love itself soon becomes the master. It is a tyrant." [55] The involuntary nature of the affair is quite evident throughout the essay: " You feel the fire growing, although you do not dare to speak of it to the one who has caused it." [56] It is the tale of the *Sonnet*

[52] *Ibid.,* p. 401.

[53] Jacoubet, Henri, " Le *Discours sur les passions de l'amour* peut-il être rendu à Pascal? " *Revue d'histoire littéraire de la France,* 45th year, No. 1, January–March, 1938. The work of Jacoubet presents an excellent " état des études " on the question. The same had been treated anew in a masterly way by Lanson, Gustave, " Le *Discours sur les passions de l'amour* est-il de Pascal? " (*French Quarterly,* January–March, 1920). An excellent historical account of the question is to be found in Bishop, M., *Pascal:* The Life of Genius, *op. cit.,* n. 13, pp. 364–369; the note ends with the following call to order: " If we cannot recognize the work of an author by his characteristic thought and style, most of our talk about the value of literature is a cheat of ourselves and others " (p. 369). The work of Henri Jacoubet must therefore be according to the heart of Professor Bishop, in the following final clause: " Together with Lanson, after Cousin, and even were I alone against so many distinguished and well-informed minds, I would not say that I feel, but that I hear Pascal (boldly giving to this last word its sense of understanding)," *art. cit.,* p. 22.

[54] Jacoubet, Henri, " Le *Discours sur les passions de l'amour* peut-il être rendu à Pascal? " *art. cit.,* pp. 21, 22.

[55] Cousin, Victor, *Des Pensées de Pascal, op. cit.,* p. 403.

[56] *Ibid.,* p. 403.

d'Arvers, told in anticipation! There is no remedy for the throes of passion! If, however, " the joy of loving without daring to speak of it brings pain . . . , it brings its sweetness as well." [57] This undoubtedly echoed a theme current in Pascal's day, which had grown especially popular since the appearance of *L'Astrée* (1610–1627).

A contemporary novel, *Clélie* (1654), by Mademoiselle de Scudéry, contained the famous *carte du tendre,* analyzing the different sorts of love. On this map, long roads led from one city to another. They were marked with villages which were so many stages of a laborious journey. We may be sure that Blaise's passionate soul was not behindhand, in this domain, any more than in another. To him also the map proved to be that of a well-known country. He was familiar with complications and delays when it came to the point of speaking to Charlotte herself! His love remained Platonic, in a day when Platonic love was often the theme of conversations, in salons and among the *précieux.*

DISILLUSIONMENT AND UNEASINESS

Blaise had learned the language of Platonic love at the salon of Madame de Sablé. In his case, however, the mood of the day was reinforced by certain other concerns which we have found recurrently troubling his soul. May he not have been haunted by the memory of another marriage, which took place on July 5, 1653, namely, the marriage of Jacqueline to her divine Spouse, which had now been consummated? [58] He may well have been disturbed by the lofty perspective

----

[57] *Ibid.,* p. 405.

[58] *Œuvres,* v. 3, 46 *sq. Lettre de Pascal à Périer,* June 6, 1653, on the profession of his sister. Cf. Introduction, p. 45.

Mother Angélique, whose beautiful soul one cannot admire enough, stating that a miracle of grace was not to be expected of Blaise then, set Jacqueline at ease by telling her that Port-Royal was prepared to welcome her without a dowry. Immediately Jacqueline wrote to Blaise a letter of renunciation in which her pain could be seen through her saintliness. In a fit of remorse of conscience, Blaise went to see her, and in the course of conversation, the expression " receive by charity " (*recevoir par charité*) was spoken by Jacqueline; Blaise, then, all confused, decided to offer to his sister a suitable dowry, viz.: 5000 pounds within six months and an annual income of 1500 pounds to be paid to Port-Royal.

The copy of deed executed by a notary and drawn up for the purpose of a dowry on June 4, 1653, is to be found in *Œuvres,* v. 3, 39.

The financial effort of Pascal was particularly remarkable because he had to provide for the upkeep of his house, Rue Beaubourg, his carriage, two or three maids and lackeys, by an annual revenue of 2500 pounds as estimated by Chamaillard (*Pas-*

from which Sister Sainte-Euphémie, nee Pascal, was now looking down upon him.

It must be admitted that some of the sections of the *Discours sur les passions de l'amour* are marked by disillusionment: " The life of man is terribly short," and yet in the very next paragraph we read: " How happy is a life when it begins with love and ends with ambition! If I had to choose between them, I should take the former." [59] Did Pascal himself really write that? If so, we can see how far the Biblical notion of a *hidden God,* which later came to hold such a place in his thought, was being wrought out in his personal experience.

The *Discours sur les* Pensées, written by Filleau de la Chaise and only published in 1672, is terribly eloquent on this point as it records a lecture which Pascal delivered to a few friends in 1658. It speaks of Adam's fall as " the greatest of all crimes," and goes on to affirm that in consequence Adam, the first man — who stands as the archetype of natural man in Pascal's thought — " by that act lost all the advantages he had been unwilling to use aright; his mind was filled with clouds, God was hidden from him in impenetrable night; he became the plaything of lust and the slave of sin; of all he once possessed of light and of knowledge, he retained only an impotent desire for knowledge, which served but to torment his mind; he no longer exercised his freedom, save to commit sin, and he found himself deprived of all strength for good. Thus at last he became this incomprehensible monster that we call man." [60] *It may have been this new turn in Pascal's life, as described in this chapter, when he had so little direct contact with the Bible, that prepared Pascal to penetrate to the very depths of the Book, in which the very depths of the human heart are laid bare.*

A curious phenomenon occurred in Pascal's inner experience during December, 1653. Blaise suddenly came to feel " a great contempt for

cal mondain et amoureux, 165 sq.). Hence his constant requests or stipulations for delayed payments. These were also causes no doubt for Pascal's journeys at that time; by reason of economy, he spent the winter of 1652–1653 at the Périer home in Clermont. The above considerations can be added to those which make us choose the date of the spring of 1653 for his journey to Poitou. As we see it, Pascal, on his return from Clermont to Paris, met intimidating financial obligations. Just then, the Duke de Roannez, his ever impatiently expectant friend, proposed to share with him, Méré and Miton, carriage and hospitality. Blaise accepted this godsend coming at the right time to suit him, to save his face, while allowing him a complement of inquiry into a society which was for him a new field of interest.

[59] Cousin, Victor, *Des Pensées de Pascal, op. cit.,* p. 396.
[60] *Discours sur les* Pensées, *Œuvres,* v. **12**, ccx.

the world " and " an almost unconquerable loathing for all the persons in it." [61] The sudden nature of this phenomenon deserves attention.

Blaise had just begun to learn to dance, for he said in one of the fragments of the *Pensées:* " Dancing: we must consider rightly where to place our feet." [62] Some time after this, toward the end of September, 1654, Blaise was to confess to Sister Sainte-Euphémie that *for more than a year* he had felt " so great an abandonment on God's part " that he felt *no* attraction whatever in that direction. He thus felt utterly cut off, both from the side of the world, and from God's side, to a degree that he had never known, " nor anything approaching it."

We have one tangible and undeniable proof of all this: Pascal, who in Méré's company had " foresworn " mathematics, now turned to it again with a frantic intensity.[63] The gambler Méré suggested that he should try to discover what portion of the stakes each gambler should recover, when a game was interrupted before it was finished. Pascal set to work. He entered into correspondence on the subject with Fermat,[64] the noted mathematician, whose discoveries turned out to confirm his own. Anticipating Newton in this field, Pascal thus laid the foundation for the calculus of probabilities.[65]

But this interest in mathematics he was now cultivating solely " from habit." His heart was no longer in it. He felt a vague troubling of conscience, all the while, for not adhering to his earlier Christian vocation. He applied himself to the best of his powers to revive his own interest, but he admits that he was spurred on more by his reason and by his own mental effort than by any inward movement of the Spirit of God.

He doubtless continued, in practice, to take the holy water, to have masses said, et cetera. " Even this will naturally make you believe, and deaden your acuteness." [66] So he was to say near the end of his argument about the wager, and his comment is too often misunderstood. As we interpret it, what Pascal had in mind anticipated the theory of feel-

[61] *Extrait d'une lettre de la Sœur Jacqueline de Sainte-Euphémie Pascal à Madame Périer, sa sœur*, December 8, 1654, *Œuvres*, v. 4, 15.

[62] *Pensées*, Section ii, Fr. 139, *Œuvres*, v. 13, 60.

[63] Cf. *Œuvres*, v. 3, 295 *sq.*, *Retour de Pascal aux mathématiques*.

[64] *Œuvres*, v. 3, *Lettre de Fermat à Pascal* (1654), 369; *Lettre de Pascal à Fermat* (July 19, 1654), 375; *Lettre de Pascal à Fermat* (August 24, 1654), 399; *Lettre de Fermat à Pascal* (August 29, 1654), 413; *Lettre de Fermat à Pascal* (September 25, 1654), 421; *Lettre de Pascal à Fermat* (October 27, 1654), 429.

[65] *Œuvres*, v. 3, Introduction: *Pascal et les questions de la probabilité*, 371 . . *Fragment sur le calcul des probabilités*, 594.

[66] *Pensées*, Section iii, Fr. 233, *Œuvres*, v. 13, 153, 154.

ing and will, lately expounded by the Danish physiologist, Dr. Lange, and by William James, notably in chapter 24 of his *Principles of Psychology*. It is the theory that the outward expression of any emotion leads to the experiencing of that emotion itself, and also to the ideas with which the emotion is associated. It is quite wrong to speak, in this regard, of *autosuggestion*. The truth within the paradox lies in quite another direction, so far as Pascal is concerned. When he stated the argument of the wager, in the light of his own religious experience, he knew for a certainty that there was an authentic ground for this experience. If a man of good will expresses in practice the deeds and gestures which normally proceed from religious experience, there is opened in him a channel for the grace of God. There is thus provided a bridge between intellectual assent and the actual experience of God, supplying a continuity otherwise lacking at the end of the argument of the wager. Pascal's mind was haunted by the notion of divine election, and it became clear to him that, if a man is among the elect, such elementary moral conduct as is here in question would provide God with the occasion to indicate the fact of election. There is no doubt that this is the meaning of his phrase: "The mind must offer itself in humbleness to inspirations." [67] The argument of the wager had been wrought out in Pascal's own life. He meant that his advice should be taken quite literally: "Learn of those who have been bound like you." [68]

WEARINESS AND DISGUST

As Pascal was reading Epictetus and Montaigne early in the year 1654, he unmasked the helpless pride of the former and the latter's deceptive "defeatism." But the course of his thought was labored at this time. We may find evidence for his dramatic inner struggle in some of the less familiar fragments of the *Pensées*. Think of the bitterness, for example, with which he diagnosed the masculine virtues held up for praise by the Stoics: "There are feverish moments which health cannot imitate"! [69] Pascal knew only too well that "those great spiritual efforts, of which the soul is sometimes capable, are things on which it does not lay hold. It only leaps to them, not as upon a throne, forever, but merely for an instant." [70] Thus he had read in the pages of Montaigne,

[67] *Pensées*, Section iv, Fr. 245, *Œuvres*, v. **13**, 179.
[68] *Pensées*, Section iii, Fr. 233, *Œuvres*, v. **13**, 153.
[69] *Pensées*, Section vi, Fr. 350, *Œuvres*, v. **13**, 264.
[70] *Pensées*, Section vi, Fr. 351, *Œuvres*, v. **13**, 265.

but everything he found there he was really finding within himself! [71] Montaigne himself would have chosen to be read in just that way.

It took some time for Pascal to reach the point of considering Montaigne "silly" when he undertook to portray his own nature.[72] Pascal first had to realize that Montaigne's "first and chief design" was to demonstrate, from his own life's example, that men cannot really grasp the foundation of things, nor take pride in the capacity of their own reason to determine their own rules of conduct. The closing words of the *Apologie de Raimond Sebond,* after clearly showing that man can never leap beyond his own shadow, agree upon this truth: that man can rise only if God, in extraordinary measure, reaches out a helping hand. Man must renounce his own effort, and permit himself to be lifted and sustained by divine resources alone, if he is to rise at all. Now, it is implicit in "our Christian faith" to *claim* this "divine and miraculous metamorphosis" — to claim it . . . if one is numbered among the elect, so Blaise said to himself! His anguish of soul grew more and more intense. Would he himself be rejected of God?

There came a day when Pascal spitefully denounced Montaigne's "credulity," his "lewd words," and his "ignorance" touching mathematics; when he castigated Montaigne's "indifference about salvation."[73] The contemporary reader will be in a better position than was Pascal to exonerate Montaigne on many of these points. A recent book presents "the true Montaigne" as a theologian and a soldier of the faith.[74] It was so easy for Pascal when he had seen the light to burn up the idols he had worshiped. We know that if he was steeped in Montaigne, it was because the famous essayist had given expression to the doubts that were later experienced by Blaise the backslider.

A great deal of Pascal's criticism of Montaigne originally emanated from a bad conscience and proves to be pharisaical in character. The truth of the matter is that Blaise found himself, in 1654, "astonished at his own weakness."[75] In every sense of the word, he was experiencing the "misery of man without God." He had left Montaigne crippled in spirit. He had found that "what the Stoics propose is so difficult and

---

[71] *Pensées*, Section ii, Fr. 14, *Œuvres*, v. **12**, 66.
[72] *Pensées*, Section ii, Fr. 62, *Œuvres*, v. **12**, 63.
[73] *Pensées*, Section ii, Fr. 63, *Œuvres*, v. **12**, 64, 65.
[74] The work is that of Marc Citoleux.
[75] *Pensées*, Section vi, Fr. 374, *Œuvres*, v. **13**, 284.

foolish!" [76] Ah, indeed it was "not good to have too much liberty"! [77] The outlook of man "under the sun," as expressed in Ecclesiastes,[78] is echoed in Pascal's proposition: "Man without God is in total ignorance and inevitable misery. For it is wretched to have the wish, but not the power." [79] The pursuit of glory henceforth appeared to Pascal as "the greatest baseness of man." [80]

The great philosophers of the past were now silent. God continued to conceal Himself. "As oft as I have been among men," quotes the author of the *Imitation of Christ*, with deep meaning, "I returned home less a man than I was before." [81]

[76] *Pensées*, Section vi, Fr. 360, *Œuvres*, v. **13**, 273.
[77] *Pensées*, Section vi, Fr. 379, *Œuvres*, v. **13**, 289.
[78] Reference to Eccl. 8:17.
[79] *Pensées*, Section vi, Fr. 389, *Œuvres*, v. **13**, 297, 298.
[80] *Pensées*, Section vi, Fr. 404, *Œuvres*, v. **13**, 306.
[81] *De Imitatione Christi*, I, 20:2.

VI

Pascal's Hour of Agony

*" But became vain in their imaginations, and their foolish heart
was darkened."*

—Rom. 1:21

Pascal returned to his own four walls, but the price of having escaped from them was that he found himself condemned to go around in
circles. Granting that this is only a figure of speech, it was nonetheless
a truly vicious circle in which Pascal found himself caught. His research
in the field of physics, which he now resumed and sought to perfect, the
enormous undertaking of work he was preparing for " the most celebrated Paris Academy of Mathematics," the theory of probability he
was undertaking to establish, and the worldly success which so much
achievement brought him — all this only served to aggravate his restlessness of soul rather than to put an end to the turmoil within. It is true
that he kept up the outward forms of religion and retained an honest
allegiance to his faith, but something within him was crushed. The joy
was gone from his religious life, and instead of the serenity he had come
to know in his younger sister when he called on her at Port-Royal, his
own soul was in great distress. His whole religious status was suddenly
called in question, and he felt himself in the position of a backslider.

MAN'S IMPOTENCE

He was much impressed by the fact that the two men in the Bible who
understood and spoke with greatest insight about the misery of man
were Job and the author of Ecclesiastes. Of these, one was the most
unfortunate of men, while the other was the most fortunate. The former,
from his own experience, understood the vanity of the ills of life, while
the latter understood the vanity of life's pleasures.[1] At this period in his
life Pascal came very close to incarnating both of them at one and the

---

[1] *Pensées*, Section ii, Fr. 174, *Œuvres*, v. 13, 91.

same time. His suffering was apparently in vain, his joys too had ended in vanity. How, he asked himself, could men have founded and extracted, on the basis of sheer lust, such excellent rules of polity, morality, and justice, when in reality the vile root of evil in man was thus only concealed and not really removed? [2] Once again, he asked, how could men be rid of this root once and for all, and be set free from their misery? Within himself, Pascal henceforth found nought but doubts, and " in regard to spiritual matters, a state of doubt is a state of misery." [3]

He had been much absorbed of late in physical and mathematical research, and *had come to understand that it was as impossible to establish physics, as it was to establish morality, on a foundation of reason alone*. In the case of one, as of the other, man's impotence was derived from the same source, namely, the inability of reason to penetrate the nature of the infinite: " The final stage of reason is to recognize that there is an infinity of things beyond it. It is but feeble if it does not see so far as to know this.

" But if natural things are beyond it, what will be said of supernatural? " [4]

We acknowledge, indeed, the existence and nature of the finite, because we also are finite and extended creatures. So, too, we acknowledge the existence of the infinite, but we are ignorant of its nature, because it has extension like ourselves, but has not limits as we do.[5] All the properties of infinity are beyond the reach of the human mind; and yet the human mind encounters the infinite in whatever direction it turns! Thus, reason itself establishes the reality of a mysterious and supernatural field,[6] but the content of this vast area eludes the grasp of reason. There is nothing so conformable to reason as this disavowal of reason.[7] What then can we say of it? *Reason carries its own stumbling block within itself*.

But, Pascal now went on to ask, in what does this stumbling block consist? Constantly recurring to his thought, almost to the point of obsession, was the notion of original sin, upon which the Port-Royalists were always insisting. The notion came to be, for Pascal, *the idea in the*

    [2] *Pensées*, Section vii, Fr. 453, *Œuvres*, v. **13**, 366. Allusion to Ps. 102:13.
    [3] Boettner, Loraine, *The Reformed Doctrine of Predestination*, 5th ed., Wm. B Eerdmans Publishing Co., Grand Rapids, Mich., 1941, p. 194.
    [4] *Pensées*, Section iv, Fr. 267, *Œuvres*, v. **13**, 196.
    [5] *Pensées*, Section iii, Fr. 233, *Œuvres*, v. **13**, 144.
    [6] *Pensées*, Section iv, Fr. 273, *Œuvres*, v. **13**, 199.
    [7] *Pensées*, Section iv, Fr. 272, *Œuvres*, v. **13**, 198.

back of his mind, a guiding principle in his thinking. After all, as he put it, if man had never been corrupt, he would enjoy in his innocence both truth and happiness with assurance; and if man had always been corrupt, he would have had no idea of truth or bliss at all.[8] Truth and bliss thus belong together, and *it is the very same impotence which confronts the physicist and the moralist alike:* thus it is not by increasing proofs that a man must endeavor to convince himself, but by the abating of his passions.[9]

Pascal never failed to wonder whether there was not some way to see " the faces of the cards " [10] in the game of life. He had *thought* through, and carefully *weighed,* all the arguments of Pyrrhonism, and this is what put him in a position to write such penetrating fragments [11] directed against Pyrrhonism. Unable to escape the considerations he had set down in connection with his noted *wager,* just as his mind had been intrigued by the notion of infinity, he had found himself driven to carry the inquiry farther.

THE DUTY OF INQUIRY

A central and characteristic theme in Pascal is his sense of obligation to inquire into everything that is most imperious, the impossibility of *not* carrying forward the inquiry. Our very first concern, and no less our ultimate goal, is to consider whether life itself has any meaning, whether life has an ultimate sanction.[12] Pascal developed this thought to the point of classifying men on the basis of the attitude each one takes with regard to this duty of inquiry. There are three kinds of persons: those who serve God, having found Him; those who are busy seeking Him, without having found Him; and, finally, those who live without seeking Him and without having found Him. The first are reasonable and happy; the last are foolish and unhappy; those between are reasonable but unhappy.[13]

Reasonable but unhappy! The very phrase offers a powerfully suggestive clue to the source of Pascal's agony of soul, since he felt himself " utterly abandoned on God's side," at the same time that he was seek-

---

[8] *Pensées,* Section vii, Fr. 434, *Œuvres,* v. 13, 347.
[9] *Pensées,* Section iii, Fr. 233, *Œuvres,* v. 13, 153.
[10] *Ibid.*
[11] Example: *Pensées,* Section vi, Fr. 392, *Œuvres,* v. 13, 299.
[12] *Pensées,* Section iii, Fr. 194, *Œuvres,* v. 13, 103.
[13] *Pensées,* Section iv, Fr. 257, *Œuvres,* v. 13, 188, 189.

ing " with much moaning." His misery was, at the same time, a mark of his nobility, but it choked off the very breath of his spirit. Now it was that he felt dumfounded with consternation at the sight of those insensate persons who, not having found God, yet went on living without seeking Him. He spoke of them as being, in all respects, like men in chains, all condemned to death: every day some are killed in the sight of the others; those who remain see their own fate in that of their fellows, and yet all they do is await their turn, looking at one another sorrowfully and without hope.[14] Dumfounded, Pascal thought of the case of a man in a dungeon, ignorant whether his sentence had been pronounced, having only one hour to learn it and yet with this hour enough to win his reprieve; yet spending this hour, precious beyond all others, in playing cards.[15] Truly there must have been a growing heaviness of the hand of God, to permit such blindness as that!

Man without God is miserable; but this very misery is a blessed misery for the man who becomes conscious of it. Blessed, because it bears witness to his greatness.[16] In this sense, it is the misery of a powerful lord,[17] a revelation rich in promise. Promise of a God who, for the time being, is hidden from our sight,[18] but whose presence is evident in the hour of our darkness, as the dawn brings its promise of light.

Might not this dawn, however, be merely a mirage born of man's agony? The being of God remains beyond our comprehension, the creation beyond our understanding. Even the fingerprints of the Creator's hand have been obliterated in His works, leaving human intelligence to be deceived, and man's conscience perverted, so that certain passages of Scripture, even, are presented under a repelling guise. It may have been the sun, indeed, but with spots that are surprising.[19]

However much Blaise Pascal may have been struggling in the chiaroscuro of the dawn, he would have had to admit that he was much more stirred by his reason, and by his own mind, than by the mind of God. He now distinguished, with a pitiless clarity, between such efforts to his own behalf, and the movements of divine grace. The frank confession

---

[14] *Pensées*, Section iii, Fr. 199, *Œuvres*, v. **13**, 124.
[15] *Pensées*, Section iii, Fr. 200, *Œuvres*, v. **13**, 124.
[16] *Pensées*, Section vi, Fr. 397, *Œuvres*, v. **13**, 303.
[17] *Pensées*, Section vi, Fr. 398, *Œuvres*, v. **13**, 303.
[18] *Vere tu es Deus absconditus* . . . , Isa. 45:15.
[19] Sully Prud'homme, *La vraie religion selon Pascal.* Research on the purely logical order of his *Pensées* regarding religion followed by an analysis of the *Discours sur les passions de l'amour,* Alcan, Paris, 1905, p. 259.

that fell from his own lips,[20] at this very time, refutes once and for all the charge of a will to believe, equivalent to a kind of autosuggestion, of which he is sometimes accused.

THE SIN OF SELF-SUFFICIENCY

Let us review the main outlines of the situation. Pascal was a Roman Catholic. He had received the gift of grace in baptism, and sought its sustaining power in the Church's sacraments. By profession and practice he was a Christian, and yet he felt himself abandoned of God. Here he was, indeed, a creature of contradiction. At Rouen he had experienced a divine kindling, by which he had felt his life to be wonderfully stirred. He gave evidence of genuine zeal, he put the Scriptures into practice, he converted his own family.

Still, he had become separated from God. He fled from Him, renounced Him, crucified Him, as he was shortly forced to confess. What could have caused such a backsliding? Secretly, gradually, making prayer difficult for him, making the Scripture obscure for his mind. Blaise had not yet attained a fully clear understanding of his own condition. Like a deposed king,[21] he fell at the very moment of his pride. He had made himself the center of his own being.[22] His fatal sin had been self-sufficiency. Like a prodigal son, he must now live for a time upon husks. The husks were doubtless choice morsels for the swine who devoured them, but it was a tasteless, insipid diet for one who cherished the memory of feasts in his father's house. It was just because Pascal recalled with a sense of remorse the actions of divine grace to which he had not fully yielded himself that he now felt his misery all the more keenly. The intense realism of Pascal's diagnosis of " the misery of man without God," as we find it in the *Pensées*, is to be traced to his own inner experience at this time.

Not only its realism, but also its penetration, may be attributed to his personal experience. No man becomes a saint by the exercise of his own powers. No one who doubts this knows what a saint or a man really is: " Grace is indeed needed to turn a man into a saint." [23] Pascal had

---

[20] *Lettre de la Sœur Jacqueline de Sainte-Euphémie Pascal à Madame Périer, sa sœur*, January 5, 1655, in which she tells about the conversion of Blaise. Cf. *Œuvres*, v. 4, 61–68.

[21] See n. 17 above.

[22] *Pensées*, Section vii, Fr. 430, *Œuvres*, v. 13, 330.

[23] *Pensées*, Section vii, Fr. 508, *Œuvres*, v. 13, 404.

learned this truth from the Jansenists: " Does it not appear," Jansen had said, " in what measure nature falls, by its own weight and from its own bent, into vice, and how much help is required if it is to be delivered? " [24] This " mother idea " [25] was now beginning to bear fruit. In the light of his own experience, Blaise was beginning to share the insight he had gathered from the experience of others before him. There is no genuine knowledge save the knowledge that has been personally *lived through.*

A DIZZYING MOUNTAIN DIVIDE

Here we see Blaise Pascal, then, standing for a moment on the border line of two worlds, poised upon a dizzying mountain divide. On one side, the world he had come to analyze so perceptively appeared to him bereft of God; that other world, however, was not to be reached save by an act of faith. We see Blaise Pascal driven to view one world with the eyes of a searching but exhausting criticism, which now could see so clearly its whole pitiable condition. On the other hand, Pascal hoped that the veils might fall away which concealed that other world from his vision. Was it his own sinfulness which alone wove the fabric of these concealing veils? Why was it that the sacraments, of which Blaise partook so faithfully, did not provide the means of grace which might have torn those veils aside?

THE EXPERIENCE OF A PRE-CATHOLIC

In addition to two passages in the Epistles to the Corinthians, in which the conversion of Saul of Tarsus is recorded,[26] in its *outward* aspect, with remarkable completeness, we should also draw special attention to a passage in the Epistle to the Galatians,[27] in which Paul reveals something of the *inward* aspect of his conversion. Sabatier, starting from this evidence, declines to regard the Apostle as an example of religious illuminism, as a sort of Swedenborg, who may have mistaken his own thought for a genuine revelation of God. According to Sabatier, Paul's thought " doubtless followed a logical development, but it was gradual and labored, so that outward circumstances and struggles, together with practical exigencies, made a profound impact upon his

[24] *Augustinus (de Nat.: lapsa*, II, 2), quoted in *Œuvres,* v. 13, 404, n. 1.
[25] The expression is, we think, Henri Poincaré's (1854–1912).
[26] I Cor. 9:1; I Cor. 15:8.
[27] Gal. 1:12–17.

mind." [28] The first important issue is then to recapture and to set down the historical development of the outward setting.

If we pause to examine carefully the circumstances surrounding Paul's experience on the Damascus Road, it will by no means deflect our thought from the main concern of this chapter. We shall be brought, indeed, to the very heart of the matter. *Paul's experience stands, indeed, as the prototype of every subsequent instance in which Christ reveals Himself to the self-assured.*

Saul of Tarsus was, in one sense, a pre-Catholic, a Catholic under the ancient Covenant.[29] He had staked his confidence both in natural man [30] and in the tradition of his ancestors.[31] These traditions had been crystallized in a priestly institution which prescribed good works and ceremonials for the faithful. To Saul's way of thinking, man's native capacities, which he regarded as intact or at least effective, combined with the influence of the ceremonial cult to provide the means of salvation. As he saw it, man could work out his own salvation by himself, with the aid of the ritual through which the Church mediated the divine energy. He felt quite secure in his views, quite capable of obeying the law of his choosing, since God's business was wholly compounded with the business of His Church.

For Saul, man had preserved intact, or nearly intact, his gifts as *homo sapiens:* the capacity to know God in this existence and in His attributes as Creator, the ability to obey the moral law and to do a certain amount of good, which God would reckon toward man's salvation, quite apart from the action of divine grace.

Thus, the naturalistic optimism of the Pharisee of the Jewish Church was to find its way into the Judaeo-Christian Church, and later into a Pagan-Christian Church which adopted — and adapted — Aristotle and his humanism. The truth is, however, that the Fall had disrupted man's communion with his Creator, a contact which involved certain supernatural gifts; but the Church then compensated by prescribing the beliefs and the rituals of which it was the sole guardian, and which thus placed the Church in the position of supervising or controlling the contacts of God with men.

---

[28] Sabatier, A., *L'Apôtre Paul, esquisse d'une histoire de sa pensée* [sketch of a history of his thought], 4th ed. revised, Fischbacher, Paris, 1912, p. 82.

[29] Cf. Gal. 1:13, 14; Phil. 3:4–6.

[30] I Cor. 2:14.

[31] Gal. 1:14; Acts 22:3.

In the opinion of one who ultimately proved to be rational man, God found it necessary to provide an infallible organ of interpretation for the written Tradition, which might gather up that part of the primitive oral message which may have escaped inclusion in the Scripture itself. Since God created the Church to be the extension of the Incarnation in Christ, the Church controlled the source of the sacraments through which divine grace was infallibly communicated to men. Thus, the Church became the supreme dogma, the indispensable source of all supernatural aid, and hence of all certainty.

But for anyone who turned to the depths within himself, and went to the bottom of problems, was it possible for salvation, which thus owed so much to the postulates of human reason, to provide security unchallenged? If human souls were thus able to enjoy such perfect salvation, would they ever turn to seek it in the quiet retreat of a monastery, in doing good works, and in undergoing mortification? Have we not come to the very point which was involved in what we call *Pascal's agony?* Was not his agony, in the year 1654, altogether similar to that of Saul of Tarsus, the proud inquisitor who was torn at heart, and who now was hurled down, in his distress, to the dust of the earth? Each of these men, in turn, was compelled to abandon all confidence in man, which was essentially blasphemous from the start. This was brought about by the sovereign intervention of a gracious God, infinitely sovereign and infinitely free; a God who had chosen His own, and who called His own, a God before whom all human effort was of no avail, a God who loved Jacob and hated Esau.

Blaise Pascal, who had listened to the Jansenists in Rouen without fully understanding them, was shaken to the roots of his being, very much as Saul of Tarsus had been when the vision of Stephen's martyrdom kept haunting his mind, as he set forth for Damascus, proudly clinging to a tradition which was plausible but lacking Scriptural foundation. Thus it is that the legalistic certainty of *homo sapiens* always leads men toward Damascus! It was on the highroad to some Damascus that this overweening Pharisee came to learn that man can do nothing for his own salvation, and that the sense of divine presence, found in the Bible, must issue at last in recognition of the sovereign grace of God in Jesus Christ!

The dramatic turn in the life of Blaise Pascal came about in the same manner as in the life of Saul. He had yet to learn the full meaning of the Epistles to the Galatians and to the Romans, and particularly of that central feature of the Gospel which Saint Paul, having learned it from Christ, undertook to preach and to set down in writing: the utterly free character of man's salvation. The dramatic tension of Blaise Pascal's inner life arose from this fact: he had been serving two masters, plumbing the depths of Scripture on the one hand, while on the other he trusted in the infallibility of an authority which was charged to interpret this same Scripture, but which often forgot the central point therein contained, and which even went so far as to contradict this central truth. The inner drama in the life of Blaise Pascal consisted, on the one hand, in his repudiation of scholastic theology and the incursion of human reason within the domain of faith, and of his ambition, on the other hand, to fashion a rational theology for himself. He persisted in appealing to *argumenta humana*, instead of placing himself, humbly and with empty hands, under the tutelage of the *argumentum divinum*.

THE BONDWOMAN AND HER SON

Let us hasten to point out that the author of the argument about the wager never followed to its ultimate consequence the inescapable choice between salvation by faith and salvation by works. Notwithstanding Saint Paul's chiding words in the Epistle to the Galatians, Pascal never could bring himself to shut the door, once and for all, against the bondwoman and her son.[32] This is the basic reason, so we believe, for the uncertainty of so many scholars on this point. Some of them still ask whether Pascal ever, in fact, fully emerged from his skepticism. Miguel de Unamuno has suggested that Pascal's intimate tragedy consisted in having " sought his salvation in a skepticism to which he was fondly attached, against an inward dogmatism with which he was afflicted. . . . And his logic was never dialectical, but polemical; . . . he remained . . . in a state of contradiction." [33] Certainly this was true, up to a point. But his inner contradiction was not so much the fruit of the spirit of Montaigne. Rather was it a contradiction in which the bondwoman remained unwilling to yield to the freewoman. As Vinet remarked with great perception: " It is sometimes said that Pascal's

[32] Gal. 4:30.
[33] Miguel de Unamuno, " La Foi pascalienne," *Revue de métaphysique et de morale,* exceptional number for the centenary of Pascal, April–June, 1923, p. 348.

For Montaigne's influence on Pascal see Brunschvicg, Léon, *Descartes et Pascal lecteurs de Montaigne,* Ed. de la Baconnière, Neufchatel, Switzerland, 1942.

skepticism made him a Christian. It would perhaps be truer to say that his Christianity made him a skeptic." [34]

To follow Pascal's own spiritual growth is to witness the stages by which his Christian faith progressively freed him from an extreme tendency to rationalism which has always tended to trespass upon the domain of faith. To follow Pascal's own spiritual growth farther is to see how, in his case, the freewoman mentioned in the Epistle to the Galatians gradually triumphed over the bondwoman, without, however, becoming the unchallenged mistress in the field.

It may seem that we have dwelt too long upon this point, which, in more ways than one, anticipates what is to follow. Moreover, the whole argument is likely to be deemed by many a reader unreasonable, even irrational. Should, however, the reader hope to find a fully rationalized treatment of Pascal, he must seek it elsewhere. [35] This detailed comparison of the experiences of Pascal and Saint Paul seems to us to belong in the center of this chapter, where it may shed added light on the considerations which are to follow.

To believe. One must believe! Pascal was now fully persuaded of this. But how? The counsel he one day imagined himself as giving to a freethinker was inspired, beyond all doubt, by his own firsthand experience. The uneven quality of this counsel betokens the continuing conflict within himself, as we have described it, between the son of the bondwoman and the son of the freewoman.

REASON, CUSTOM, AND INSPIRATION

According to Pascal, there are three sources of faith: reason, custom, and inspiration. The mind must be open to proof, it must submit to the confirmation of custom, and it must humbly offer itself " through humiliation to inspiration." The latter alone can produce a true and saving result, lest the Cross of Christ should be made void. [36] Faith, which

[34] Vinet, A., *Etudes sur Blaise Pascal,* Edition augmentée de fragments inédits publiée avec une préface et des notes par Pierre Kohler, Professeur à l'Université de Berne [enlarged ed. of fragments unpublished, with a preface and notes by Pierre Kohler, professor at the University of Berne]. Payot et Cie, Lausanne-Genève-Neufchatel-Vevey-Montreux-Berne-Bâle, 1936, p. 122.

[35] Cf. Neeser, M., " La Réforme vue à travers Saint Paul," in *Le Christianisme social,* No. 5, July-August-September, 1936, p. 21.

We paraphrase here a remark by Professor Neeser.

[36] *Pensées,* Section iv, Fr. 245, *Œuvres,* v. 13, 179. Pascal's Biblical quotation is taken from I Cor. 1:17.

is a gift of God, and which God Himself puts into the heart, differs from proof, which is human, and which is simply an instrument of faith. Faith cometh by hearing.[37] It is in the heart and makes us say, not *scio,* but *credo.*[38] The outward forms of religion were important to Pascal, who thus showed himself to be the forerunner of those philosophies of feeling and will which came to be developed during the nineteenth century.

We are now in a position to set in its own context, and to develop farther, a Pascalian theory to which an allusion has already been made in the foregoing chapter. According to Pascal, to place sole reliance upon outward form is to show oneself superstitious, but to refuse to submit to any outward form is a mark of pride. We must kneel, pray with the lips.[39] Thus we arrive at a gathering of energies in what we today should call psychological automatism: outward gestures tend to produce those states of soul with which they are normally associated in virtue of having originally been the expressions of those states of soul. " The automaton " must be made to believe " by custom." [40] It is in this sense that we should understand Pascal's formula: " Take holy water and allow your reason to be dulled." Listen. Repeat this symbolic gesture of professing Christian faith. Thus, by means of the gesture, your soul will come to be open to the inspiration of God. You will give God a chance to speak to you.

Pascal very clearly saw that reason is but a superficial activity in men. This is naturally more true for the rank and file of mortal men than for educated folk. It is a man's whole being that must be convinced, and it is a fact that reasoned demonstration plays but a limited part. " Proofs only convince the mind. Custom is the source of our strongest and most believed-in proofs. It bends the automaton, which persuades the mind without its thinking about the matter." It is custom that makes men Turks, heathens, artisans, soldiers.[41] Dangerous reasoning this, someone will object. Pascal is aware of the danger, and so adds parenthetically in the margin: " There is a faith which supervenes in the act of baptism, for Christians, more than for the heathen." [42]

Another weak point of reason, in this connection, is the fact that rea-

[37] Rom. 10:17.
[38] *Pensées,* Section iv, Fr. 248, *Œuvres,* v. 13, 181, 182.
[39] *Pensées,* Section iv, Fr. 250, *Œuvres,* v. 13, 182, 183.
[40] *Pensées,* Section iv, Fr. 252, *Œuvres,* v. 13, 185.
[41] *Pensées,* Section iv, Fr. 252, *Œuvres,* v. 13, 184.
[42] *Ibid.,* 184, 185.

son acts slowly, taking many views of a situation and considering many principles, so that there is a continuous danger that reason itself may wander afield. Pascal makes primary, therefore, his appeal to feeling: "It acts in a moment, and is always ready to act. We must, then, put our faith in feeling; otherwise it will always be vacillating."[43] Henceforth Pascal's constant prayer is that of the psalmist: *Inclina cor meum, Deus*.[44] In the end, "all our reasoning reduces itself to yielding to feeling."[45]

The heart — today we should say, with Bergson, the intuition — possesses a source of assurance and an area of competence quite different from that of the mathematical mind. "The heart has its reasons, which reason cannot know. We feel it in a thousand things."[46] Even its caprices tell us something of the complexity of this human faculty. It is by means of the heart that we plumb the depths of our being. By means of intuition, beyond our understanding, we penetrate to the depths of another soul, and this is a profound mystery on both sides.

It is through the heart that God speaks to us, and that we come to be free enough to make contact with Him: "It is the heart which experiences God, and not reason. This, then, is faith: God felt by the heart, not by reason."[47] But precisely here is the tragedy: *What if the heart does not experience God?* Once again we return with Pascal to the point from which we set out. There is no doubt that during the year 1654 Pascal had been going about in circles which God had not, as yet, deigned to interrupt. For Pascal well knew that "faith is a gift of God."[48]

THE HIDDEN GOD

"Heart, instinct, principles."[49] How moving it is to find these three words, written one below the other, beside a broken line which may have been meant to join them, in the margin of another fragment[50] in which Pascal is arguing about the part each one of us must play in the

---

[43] *Ibid.*, 186.
[44] *Ibid.*
[45] *Pensées*, Section iv, Fr. 274, *Œuvres*, v. 13, 199.
[46] *Pensées*, Section iv, Fr. 277, *Œuvres*, v. 13, 201.
[47] *Pensées*, Section iv, Fr. 278, *Œuvres*, v. 13, 201.
[48] *Pensées*, Section iv, Fr. 279, *Œuvres*, v. 13, 202.
[49] *Pensées*, Section iv, Fr. 281, *Œuvres*, v. 13, 203.
[50] *Pensées*, Section iii, Fr. 237, *Œuvres*, v. 13, 158.

world: assuming that we could always remain in the world, or that we were certain not to remain here long, or uncertain if we shall remain here even a single hour — Pascal adding that this last assumption is our case!

In order to get outside of himself and of the circle of his own thoughts, and doubtless for more than one of the reasons we have considered above, Pascal disciplined himself by saying over the divine service — that is, the prayers in the Roman Breviary — as often as he could. Best of all he liked the short prayers which were made up of verses from Ps. 118 — Ps. 119 in the Protestant Bible. He found so many admirable truths set forth in this psalm that he took fresh delight in it whenever he recited it. Later in life, as he used to converse with his friends about the beauty of this psalm, he became almost ecstatic with excitement.[51] And he kindled a similar enthusiasm among his listeners. We need not be surprised at his feeling in this regard. We never truly know anything except what we are in ourselves. Now, this psalm, the 118th, was the one in which Pascal came to feel that his own experience was best reflected. With no other passage in the Bible, which Pascal was one day to know in large measure by heart, did he identify himself so completely as with the words of this deeply moving prayer.

The reason for this appears transparently clear to us. The path of his anguish had now led him to face the sharp alternative: either God will make Himself known to me, and this will furnish the evidence of my election; this will be life. Or else, God will continue to hide Himself from my view, and this will indicate that I stand rebuked, punished it may be for my infidelity; and this will be death.

Having made this clear, we must note at once that the alternative is not in fact so clear as it seemed a moment ago, because God is always hidden from full knowledge on our part. This is the very name which He gives Himself in the Scripture: *Deus absconditus.*[52] The Bible is careful to point out that God has furnished visible signs in nature and in the Church, to make His presence known to those who sincerely seek Him; He has so disguised these signs, however, that they will be understood only by those who seek Him with their whole heart. It is not enough, if we are to seek God with the whole heart, to question certain Church authorities about the truths of the faith, nor to make a quick search among men or among books. It is not enough, even, to spend a few hours

[51] *Biographie de Blaise Pascal,* by Madame Périer, text of 1684, *Œuvres,* v. 1, 103.
[52] *Vere tu es Deus absconditus, Deus Israël salvator,* Isa. 45:15.

in reading some book of Scripture. Our " first interest," our " first duty," our " ultimate end," is to enlighten our minds concerning this subject whereon depends " all our conduct." [53]

We have already referred more than once to this passage, and we must not tire of turning back to it, and to Pascal's insistence upon this point, which cannot be too strongly stressed. It is in and through the Bible that Pascal knew he must seek, while sincerely bewailing his own want of certainty. Better than any other source, the Scripture points us to the things which are of God. It is to Scripture that we must turn in the hour of our greatest distress: *after completing the full cycle of human knowledge, and having come to the end of all those resources known to human nature and to the Church, Blaise Pascal came to realize, in the hour of his greatest distress, that the Word has the final word to speak concerning human destiny.*

But why, if this be so, does the Bible still point us to a hidden God? The Bible itself answers the query in terms that leave us in no doubt whatever: the fault is with man, who must learn that through sin he has become separated from his Creator. Notwithstanding this, God has shown His concern for us to the point of sending His Son, Jesus Christ, to lead us out of our blindness. Apart from Jesus Christ, " all communion with God is cut off. *Nemo novit Patrem, nisi Filius, et cui voluerit Filius revelare.*" [54]

It is a fact well recognized that not all the *Pensées* of Pascal may be regarded as on the same level: they were written on many occasions, quite markedly differing from one another, and under widely differing circumstances. Some of them are in the form of general propositions, while others are answers to specific objections, or aimed at imaginary opponents. But even when due account is taken of this variety in the *Pensées,* and of the presence of whole sections designed as a clear defense of the Christian religion, there still remain in this great " unfinished symphony " many traces of the doubt in Pascal's mind, and of his agony of soul and of his continuing struggle. We should say, rather, that the " Vindication of Christianity " is all the more convincing because Pascal addressed himself first of all.

At one moment it seems clear to him that it is enough for the sinner to turn toward Christ; but then he realizes that no one turns to Jesus unless God has already inclined his heart in that direction. " Faith is

[53] *Pensées*, Section iii, Fr. 194, *Œuvres*, v. 13, 103.
[54] *Pensées*, Section iv, Fr. 242, *Œuvres*, v. 13, 177.

not within our power." [55] Am I among the elect, or shall I be rebuked? "The elect are unaware of their virtues, as are the damned of the greatness of their crimes: Lord, when saw we Thee an hungred, athirst?" [56] Every human condition is thus seen, in the light of Bible teaching, to be insecure. Even the martyrs must fear, according to Scripture.[57] And Pascal speaks of the supreme pain of purgatory, namely, the uncertainty of the judgment. And he repeats again the phrase *Deus absconditus*.[58]

From all our darkness we can derive but one conclusion: our own unworthiness.[59] Neither the prophecies, nor even the miracles, are wholly convincing. Throughout the whole of Scripture the same half-light (chiaroscuro) remains: evidence clear enough to enlighten some; darkness enough to confuse others. In sum, there is enough uncertainty to disqualify reason and to give first place to grace, and to uncover every lust or malice in the human heart.[60] "We understand nothing of the works of God, if we do not take as a principle that He has willed to blind some, and to enlighten others." [61] What then shall we say? The Scripture is ambiguous: indeed it must be so! Clear to the elect, its obscurity confuses the damned. Do you think that the prophecies cited in the Gospel are related to make you believe? No, it is to keep you from believing.[62]

Suppose for an instant that all the prophecies were perfectly clear; the Jewish people, fleshly depositories of a spiritual covenant, would never have been so zealous to conserve them. By concealing the spiritual meaning within the temporal meaning, God saved the Bible, and succeeded in this paradox, that "those who have rejected and crucified Jesus Christ, who has been to them an offense, are those who have charge of the books which testify of Him." [63] O unsearchable wisdom! Wisdom whose very words are understood by some, but cause others to stumble! Jesus Himself shall be a stone of stumbling, according to Isaiah; [64] Hosea, however, proclaims the blessedness of those who will

[55] *Pensées*, Section vii, Fr. 516, *Œuvres*, v. **13**, 414.
[56] Matt. 25:37, 44.
[57] *Pensées*, Section vii, Fr. 518, *Œuvres*, v. **13**, 415.
[58] *Ibid.*
[59] *Pensées*, Section viii, Fr. 558, *Œuvres*, v. **14**, 7.
[60] *Pensées*, Section viii, Fr. 564, *Œuvres*, v. **14**, 12, 13.
[61] *Pensées*, Section viii, Fr. 566, *Œuvres*, v. **14**, 14.
[62] *Pensées*, Section viii, Fr. 568, *Œuvres*, v. **14**, 15.
[63] *Pensées*, Section viii, Fr. 571, *Œuvres*, v. **14**, 17.
[64] Isa. 8:14.

never be scandalized in Him: " Where is the wise? And he shall understand what I say. The righteous shall know them; for the ways of God are right; but the transgressors shall fall therein." [65] The Scripture having thus a double sense, all things work together for good for the elect, even the obscurities of Scripture. And all things work together for evil to the rest of the world, even with regard to what seems quite clear.[66]

Voltaire undertook, unsuccessfully, to treat this question with a touch of superficial irony: " Why should we always want God to be hidden? We should prefer that His presence were manifest to us." [67] Voltaire's was the kind of mind incapable of understanding Pascal. His *Anti-Pascal* [68] gives ample evidence of this, and the entire philosophical critique of Pascal during the eighteenth century [69] is hardly more than an echo of Voltaire's view.

In his *Vocabulaire des locutions les plus remarquables qui se rencontrent dans les Pensées de Pascal*,[70] Victor Cousin cites [71] numerous passages which reveal how greatly Pascal was obsessed with the idea we have sought to bring out: " under the veil of nature *which hides Him* [God] *from us*." [72] " The veil of nature which *conceals* God." [73] " All things conceal a mystery: all things are veils which conceal God." [74] " He does not emerge from the secret of nature which *conceals* Him." [75]

The basis for this view is evidently the Biblical doctrine of total corruption carried to extremes by Saint Augustine. Total corruption cannot mean that every man is as bad as he can be. Otherwise it would be totally absurd, simply because the conception is self-destroying. As

[65] Pascal compares here Isa. 8:14, 16 and Matt. 11:6 and 14:10 to show that Jesus will be an opportunity of shame for the carnal and of sanctification for the spiritual. Cf. *Œuvres*, v. 14, 20.

[66] *Pensées*, Section viii, Fr. 575, *Œuvres*, v. 14, 22.

[67] *Pensées de Pascal, avec les notes de M. de Voltaire*, Genève, 1778, v. 2, 208.

[68] The best available work on this subject is by Waterman, M., *Voltaire, Pascal and Human Destiny*, King's Crown Press, Morningside Heights, New York, 1942. See her excellent bibliography, pp. 120–126.

[69] Cf. Finch, D., *La Critique philosophique de Pascal au XVIIIe siècle*, University of Pennsylvania, Ph.D. dissertation, Philadelphia, 1940. " Bibliographie," pp. 77–81.

[70] Cousin, V., *Des Pensées de Pascal*, new edition revised and enlarged, Librairie philosophique de Ladrange, Paris, 1844, pp. 453–496.

[71] *Ibid.*, p. 463.

[72] Cousin, V., *op. cit.*, p. 338.

[73] *Ibid.*, p. 339.

[74] *Ibid.*, p. 340.

[75] *Ibid.*, p. 338.

Professor John Baillie has reminded us in his book on *Our Knowledge of God,* " a totally corrupt being would be as incapable of sin as would a totally illogical being of fallacious argument." [76] We should understand this doctrine of total corruption to mean that the depravity produced by sin extends to the whole of human nature, to the point of permeating even human virtue. According to II Cor. 4:3, 4: " If our Gospel be hid, it is hid to them that are lost: in whom the god of this world hath blinded the minds of them which believe not, lest the light of the glorious gospel of Christ, who is the image of God, should shine unto them." In a word, Boettner explains, " fallen men without the operations of the spirit of God are under the rule of Satan. They are led captive by him at his will (II Tim. 2:26). So long as this ' strong man fully-armed ' is not molested by the ' stronger than he,' he keeps his kingdom in peace and his captives willingly do his bidding. But the ' stronger than he ' has overcome him, has taken his armor from him, and has liberated a part of his captives (Luke 11:21, 22). God now exercises the right of releasing whom He will; and all born-again-Christians are ransomed sinners from that kingdom." [77]

A TRAGIC TRUTH

It is a fact that the normal result of the action of the Word of God is that it meets outward defeat. This tragic truth runs through the whole of the Old and New Testaments. The testimony of the Bible, concerning whatever is most profound, most serious, and most true, is that the Word of God provokes man to contradiction, and moves him to disobedience.

[76] Quoted by Whale, J. S., *Christian Doctrine,* The Macmillan Company, New York, 1941, p. 42.

[77] Boettner, L., *The Reformed Doctrine of Predestination, op. cit.,* p. 67.

The author has on the same subject a strong page relating to the parables of Jesus, *op. cit.,* p. 110.

The reader is referred to Mark 4:10–13; Isa. 6:10; John 12:40; etc.; and also with the greatest profit to Guisan, R., *Revue de théologie et de philosophie de Lausanne,* 1923, p. 222 *sq.*; Günther Dehr, *Le Fils de Dieu,* Paris, 1936, p. 84; Godet, F., *Commentaire sur Saint-Luc,* v. 1, 392–398.

The discussion on this extremely delicate point of doctrine has been taken up again and brought up to date in the *Actes du congrès international de théologie Calviniste,* held in Geneva from June 15–18, 1936, ed. Labor, Genève. We would make special reference to the Bible study by Max Dominicé, pp. 11–20.

A good bibliography on the subject is to be found in Boettner, L., *op. cit.,* p. 432. We would select as outstanding the article " Predestination," 67 pp., by B. B. Warfield, reproduced in Hastings' *Dictionary of the Bible.*

We must speak, therefore, of a special measure of grace bestowed upon the closest friends of our Lord, whereby they were enabled to receive and to understand the mysteries of the Kingdom of God. To say that believers come to the Light by faith, and to say that God enlightens the elect, are but two different ways of expressing the same truth. To say that God blinds the damned, and that unbelievers condemn themselves by their own false choice, is once again to affirm the same truth under two different forms, in virtue of the vast dialectical process we call revelation. Even one of Jesus' parables may become a touchstone through which the judgment of God is expressed. We might say the same thing, in a general way, concerning repentance and faith. "We repent and believe," Spurgeon once said,[78] " though we could do neither if the Lord did not enable us." He is simply paraphrasing here the Pauline paradox: It is God that worketh in you. . . . Work out your own salvation.

From a human standpoint, the whole position is untenable. But Pascal was too deeply read in Scripture to have missed finding this truth therein set forth. Thus he came to take a very somber view of life during 1654, not only because of the agony of soul that came from his awareness of the profound Biblical truth, but also because of the conflict between this doctrine and the relative optimism of the Catholic faith, by which men thought they could save themselves, with the aid of the visible Church, and of the sacraments through which the Church undertook to mediate the energies of God.

Blaise Pascal was forced to abandon such optimism in the light of his own experience. Notwithstanding his fervent devotion to Catholic practice, he felt that he was still in a state of " utter abandonment from God's side." Since his Bible told him, at one and the same time, that he must work out his own salvation, and yet that he must look for salvation as the fruit of *grace,* he did the best that he could. However, he knew that his own efforts were the result of stirrings within his reason and his own mind

HUMAN EFFORT AND DIVINE GRACE

He clearly distinguished all such human effort from the movements of divine grace. It was this grace which he felt he lacked, this grace which a hidden and sovereign God bestowed upon some and withheld

[78] Spurgeon, C. H., *All of Grace,* The Moody Colp. Libr., n. 1, p. 89.

from others, whom He chose to leave to their blindness. After a period of further brooding, this failure of grace appeared, to his agonized view, to stand as a kind of divine judgment against himself. Ah, what a day it was for Pascal when he heard Jesus Himself speak the reassuring word! " Thou wouldst not seek me, if thou hadst not already found me! "

But Blaise had not yet come to that point.

Alone in the darkness of his soul, he turned once more to his Bible. He opened it at the seventeenth chapter of The Gospel According to Saint John, in which Jesus is shown preparing Himself for His sacrifice on the Cross. In his own Bible the theme of the chapter was described thus: " Jesus Christ, making ready for the sacrifice of the Cross by the acknowledgment He makes to His Father of His release from His charge, asks that He be granted a manifestation of His glory, respecting His own person, and the conserving of His friends, respecting the body of the Church, to lead all the faithful to the same salvation by the sanctification of faith." [79]

Having given up all inclination to struggle or the slightest pretense to a power he might call his own, and at the same time infinitely weary, Blaise groped for Jesus in order to watch with Him.

[79] Strowski, F., *Pascal et son temps,* v. 2, 356.

VII

Fire in the Night

*" He looked, and, behold, the bush burned with fire, and the bush
was not consumed."*

—Ex. 3:2

In the year of Grace, 1654,
On Monday, 23d of November, Feast of St. Clement, Pope and Martyr,
and of others in the Martyrology,
  Vigil of Saint Chrysogonus, Martyr, and others,
  From about half past ten in the evening until about half past twelve

FIRE

God of Abraham, God of Isaac, God of Jacob, not of the philosophers
and scholars.
Certitude. Certitude. Feeling. Joy. Peace.
God of Jesus Christ.
Deum meum et Deum vestrum.
" Thy God shall be my God."
Forgetfulness of the world and of everything, except God.
  He is to be found only by the ways taught in the Gospel.
  Greatness of the human soul.
  " Righteous Father, the world hath not known Thee, but I have
known Thee."
  Joy, joy, joy, tears of joy.
  I have separated myself from Him.
Derelinquerunt me fontem aquae vivae.
  " My God, wilt Thou leave me? "
  Let me not be separated from Him eternally.
  "This is the eternal life, that they might know Thee, the only true
God, and the one whom Thou has sent, Jesus Christ."
  Jesus Christ.

131

Jesus Christ.

I have separated myself from Him: I have fled from Him, denied Him, crucified Him.

Let me never be separated from Him.

We keep hold of Him only by the ways taught in the Gospel.

Renunciation, total and sweet.

Total submission to Jesus Christ and to my director.

Eternally in joy for a day's exercise on earth.

Non obliviscar sermones tuos. Amen.[1]

AN UNQUESTIONABLE RECORD

The existence of this moving document was discovered only after Pascal's death, in 1662. His family seems to have been in ignorance, until then, of the experience of which Blaise wished to keep an indelible remembrance. Jacqueline, who tells the whole story of this conversion, does not mention the document. Marguerite Périer, in her *Mémoires* of the life of her uncle, makes no allusion to it; she explains that Pascal determined to withdraw from the world after hearing a sermon at Port-Royal-de-Paris on the 8th of December, 1654. She gives us a long analysis of the sermon which we shall mention again later.[2]

L'Ecrit sur la conversion du pécheur, found amongst Pascal's undated pamphlets,[3] seems to be a direct echo of his conversion. Victor Giraud sees in it, " if not a confession, at least a generalization, with scarcely any revision, of a very precise personal experience," while Pascal writes: " The first thing which God inspires in the soul that he deigns truly to touch is a knowledge and a quite extraordinary perception by means of which the soul sees everything, including its own self, in an entirely new light. *This new light makes the soul afraid and*

[1] *Mémorial de Pascal, Œuvres,* v. **12**, 3–7.

This translation of the *Mémorial* differs from the one we gave in *The Clue to Pascal* (pp. 67, 68) in that it leaves the Latin passages as in the original; also in that it is much closer to this original to the point of being a literal translation.

Brunschvicg, L., *Œuvres,* v. **4**, 3, n. 1, draws attention to the remarkable commentary on the *Mémorial* given by L. Pastourel under the title " Le Ravissement de Pascal," in *Annales de philosophie Chrétienne,* October, 1910, and February, 1911.

The best commentary on the Catholic side given in contemporary literature remains that of Bremond, H., *Histoire littéraire du sentiment religieux,* v. **4**, 354–383.

[2] *Œuvres,* v. **4**, 7.

[3] *Ecrit sur la conversion du pécheur,* attributed to Blaise or Jacqueline, *Œuvres,* v. **10**, CLXXXI, 419 *sq.*

brings to it a restlessness that disturbs the peace it used to find in those things which formerly had been its delight. The soul can no longer taste in tranquillity the things that it used to enjoy. *Continual scruples war against its pleasure,* and this new insight no longer allows it to find the accustomed sweetness in the worldly things to which it used to give itself wholeheartedly. *But the soul finds even more bitterness in exercises of piety than in the vanities of the world."* [4]

Father Guerrier reports that a few days after Pascal's death a servant of the house noticed by chance that in the lining of the doublet of the illustrious deceased there was something thicker than the rest. Having unsewn the place to see what it was, he found a little piece of folded parchment covered with Pascal's own writing, and in the parchment a paper written in the same hand. One was a faithful copy of the other. These two pieces were immediately given into the hands of Madame Périer who showed them to a few particular friends. All were agreed that this parchment written with such care and in such remarkable characters could be only a sort of *Mémorial* that Pascal kept very carefully in order to preserve the memory of something which he wished to have always with him. Indeed for eight years Pascal took care to sew and unsew the paper in the lining each time he changed his coat. The original parchment is lost, but the copy written in Pascal's hand has been added to the collection in the Bibliothèque Nationale with the attestations of Father Périer. This copy was also accompanied by an attestation of the same date signed by the canon of the Church of Clermont: " I, the undersigned, . . . certify that the paper attached to this one was written by the hand of Monsieur Pascal, my uncle, and was found after his death sewn into his doublet under the lining, with a band of parchment on which were written the same words and in the same manner in which they are here copied. Done in Paris this 25th day of September, one thousand seven hundred and eleven, P E R I E R." [5] In the front of the volume in the Bibliothèque Nationale is the copy mentioned by Périer. [6]

The text of the *Mémorial* differs slightly from one document to an-

---

[4] Giraud, V., *La Vie héroïque de Blaise Pascal, op. cit.*, pp. 90, 91.

[5] *Œuvres*, v. 12, 3, n. 1.

[6] In the additions made in 1864 to the original manuscript appears, after page 495, another manuscript copy, like those that were made in great quantity in the early eighteenth century. The *Mémorial* of Pascal was first published in the volume of 1740, known by the name *Recueil d'Utrecht*, p. 259. We borrow this information from the *Œuvres*, v. 12, 3, 4, n. 1.

other: it would seem that the autograph was a rough copy, a sort of proof, made before the final parchment was written with care and as though drawn. It was actually a sort of semi-stenographic record of the mystical experience.

How many doubters have not expressed the desire someday to find themselves in the presence of a scholar's record of such an experience? That is certainly what we have here: even the hours are given. Pascal probably had a watch fastened to his wrist. From various facts that we may perhaps amuse ourselves someday by putting together, we are inclined to believe that Pascal was the inventor of the wrist watch.

One last remark before beginning the study of the *Mémorial:* although the habit of carrying papers in the lining of clothes was fairly common in the seventeenth century,[7] it is evident that Pascal attached unique importance to the record of the revelation of the night of November 23. One can imagine him touching his lining from time to time, in hours of trial and temptation, to reassure himself of the real existence of the divine message. Skeptics have denounced this as the practice of magic. Voltaire, in particular, has reproduced the text of the " *amulet* found in Pascal's coat," [8] in the first volume of his edition of the *Pensées* where he adds his own notes to those of his illustrious friend Condorcet. He begs the reader's pardon, but for him, as for Condorcet, this " charm " is a " slip " on Pascal's part, and Voltaire likens it to romantic verses dashed off in similar fashion.[9] It would be hard to imagine a more ludicrous misconception! Dr. Lélut, taking the naturalistic point of view, which so many will exploit after him, treats the whole experience, and particularly the vision of fire, as a " hallucination " in his *Amulette de Pascal, pour servir à l'histoire des hallucinations.*[10]

A MATTER OF INTELLECTUAL HONESTY

In the face of any manifestation of the divinity, there will always be two fundamental attitudes. There are some who will question the very claims of religious experience. When one opens a book on the subject, one is never long in discovering in the author a foregone conclusion, an idea in the back of his mind, which directs the discussion: One man

[7] Cf. what Hermant says about Richelieu in his *Mémoires,* ed. Gazier, v. 1, 81.

[8] *Pensées de Pascal, avec les notes de M. de Voltaire,* Genève, 1778, v. 1, xxxiii.

[9] *Ibid.,* xxxii.

[10] *L'Amulette de Pascal, pour servir à l'histoire des hallucinations,* Baillère, Paris, 1846.

holds belief in God to be a natural function of the conscience; he admits the existence of a " mystical function " in man, to quote an expression of Gilson's. It is impossible, declares the eminent Catholic writer, " to pursue to the end the analysis of human thought, without encountering a specifically mystical element." [11] Naturally, every author who subscribes to this statement will explain religious experience by God's action on the human conscience. Another author will begin to speculate on the part played by tradition, by education, by abnormal psychology, by " the fear that creates gods," by a collective conscience. He will talk of psychoanalysis, of " repressions," of glandular deficiency; . . . no doubt he has started with the postulate that religious experience could not possibly originate in divine action. From there on, his problem is to explain it in some other way, by natural causes. Let us read him without being disturbed. His conclusions were implied in his starting point. We must wager, as Pascal said.[12]

How are we to solve this dilemma in the case of the *Mémorial?* It seems to us that the most elementary intellectual honesty requires that we should read this document in the context of the life and of the entire experience of this hero of research; we should interpret it, in accordance with the beautiful phraseology of the great historian Fustel de Coulanges, by taking the text " in its own literal meaning, without putting into it anything of our own."

What does the text say?

" From about half past ten in the evening until about half past twelve, FIRE." [13]

[11] Gilson, E. (cf. his intervention at the time of the sitting of the French Society of Philosophy, February 15, 1923), in *Bulletin de la Société française de Philosophie,* record of the sitting of February 15, 1923, Colin, Paris, p. 17.

[12] We apologize for referring the reader here to our book *Mysticisme et mentalité mystique,* the study of a problem raised by the works of Lévy-Bruhl on primitive mentality, v. 36 of the *Etudes d'histoire et de philosophie religieuses publiées par la Faculté de Théologie protestante de l'Université de Strasbourg,* in particular to chapter 6, entitled " Après le pari," pp. 158–168.

[13] On the subject of Pascal's FIRE many commentaries have been written. Let us recall some: Bremond's commentary in *Histoire littéraire du sentiment religieux, op. cit.,* v. 4, 367–369; the article under the word " Feu " [Fire] in the *Vocabulaire des locutions les plus remarquables de Pascal,* in the appendix of the work already mentioned by Victor Cousin, *Des Pensées de Pascal,* Ladrange-Didier, Paris, 1844, p. 472; the beautiful book by Baron F. von Hügel, *The Mystical Element of Religion as Studied in Saint Catherine of Genoa and Her Friends,* Dent, London, 1908, 2 v., v. 1, 78; Sainte-Thérèse de Jésus, *Vie de Sainte Thérèse écrite par elle-même,* chapter 30, in *Œuvres complètes de Sainte Thérèse de Jésus,* new translation, Retaux, Paris,

It is not enough to say with Jacques Chevalier: Pascal dismisses his own lights to make room, *in the inner self,* for a superior light, an entirely pure light; light that brightens the mind, fire that warms the heart, force that moves the will." [14] Blaise Pascal wrote, FIRE; and Blaise Pascal was reading his Bible when the supernatural event occurred. Only the Bible holds the clue to the mystery. Only the Bible can give us that clue. The Biblical explanation, the only one that has satisfied us personally, we have found given in the *Expositions of Holy Scripture,* by Alexander Maclaren, in these terms: " The fire is distinctly a divine symbol, a symbol of God. . . . There are the smoking lamp, and the blazing furnace in the early vision granted to Abraham. There is the pillar of fire by night, that lay over the desert camp of the wandering Israelites. There is Isaiah's word, ' The light of Israel shall be a flaming fire.' There is the whole of New Testament teaching, turning on the manifestation of God through His Spirit. There are John the Baptist's words, ' He shall baptize you with the Holy Spirit and with fire.' There is the day of Pentecost, when the tongues of fire sat upon each of them. And what is meant by the great word of the Epistle to the Hebrews, ' Our God is a consuming fire '? " [15] That is the fire which Pascal saw, the fire that is spoken of from one end of the Bible to the other, the fire of the flaming bush, of the ' bush that burned, and did not burn out.' " [16]

THE ELECTION MESSAGE

Another remark needs to be made, so important does it seem. The *Mémorial* contains at least nine Biblical references: Ex. 3:6; Matt.

1907, v. 1, 397. An excellent précis summarizing the essentials of mysticism is: Bastide, A., *Les Problèmes de la vie mystique,* Collection Armand Colin, v. 136, Colin, Paris, 1931. Consult in particular chapter 6, " Les Etats mystiques . . . 2ᵉ degré: l'oraison d'union — 3ᵉ degré: l'extase," pp. 74–78. In English, *An Introduction to the History of Mysticism,* by Margaret Smith, Soc. for Promoting Christian Knowledge, The Macmillan Co., London, New York, and Toronto, 1930, presents in its first chapter (" The Nature and Meaning of Mysticism ") excellent pages on " the final stage of the way . . . the unitive life " (pp. 8–10). E. Underhill's book *Mysticism* remains a classic (London, 1912). For a more detailed selected biography, may we refer you again to our book *Mysticisme et " mentalité mystique," op. cit.,* 189–195.

[14] Chevalier, J., " Des Rapports de la vie et de la pensée chez Pascal," *La Revue hebdomadaire,* No. 28, 32d year, July 14, 1923, p. 217.

[15] Maclaren, A., *Expositions of Holy Scripture,* Wm. B. Eerdman's Publishing Co., Grand Rapids, Mich., 1938, v. 2, 21.

[16] *Ibid.,* is the actual title of Maclaren's sermon: " The Bush That Burned, and Did Not Burn Out," *op. cit.,* v. 2, 19–26.

22:32; John 20:17; Ruth 1:16; John 17:25; Jer. 2:13; Matt. 27:46; John 17:3; and, as one might expect, Ps. 118:16, Pascal's psalm, as we have already mentioned.

The *Mémorial* of Pascal is a document precious above all others: by it the God of the Bible reveals his election to him. This message, which tells Pascal that he is one of the elect, is in reality the very text of the Bible, and God announces the Good News by supernaturally lighting up certain particularly pertinent passages in it. That is, in part at least, the reason for the Fire which illumines the page at the same time that it warms the heart and causes it to beat strangely in a mystical communion that holds the whole being in its grasp. The mystery of God's reign is a miracle that remains incomprehensible to the natural man; it is not within the scope of his imagination, his reason, or his own efforts. Natural reason admits its helplessness; it must give way to the faith which is a gift from God. Let him who has ears to hear, hear! Let him who has eyes to see, see! It is said in Isa. 50:4: " God awakens my ear that I may listen "; and The Acts, speaking of Lydia, the seller of purple, says: " The Lord opened her heart that she might receive Paul's words." [17] So it is with Pascal.

The God who reveals Himself to him in this most moving of encounters is the God of Abraham, the God of Isaac, the God of Jacob, the Living, the I AM THAT I AM. " That is to say, that the fire, which burns and does not burn out, which has no tendency to destruction in its very energy, and is not consumed by its own activity, is surely a symbol of one Being, whose being derives its law and its source from Himself, who only can say — ' I AM THAT I AM ' — the law of his nature, the foundation of His being, (the only conditions of His existence being, as it were, enclosed within the limits of His own nature). You and I have to say, ' I am that which I have become,' or ' I am that which I was born,' or ' I am that which circumstances have made me.' He says, ' I AM THAT I AM. All other creatures are links; this is the staple from which they all hang. All other being is derived, and therefore limited and changeful; this Being is underived, absolute, self-dependent, and therefore unalterable for evermore.' " [18]

Capital revelation for Pascal: he is henceforward chosen by this God:

[17] Acts 16:14 [K.J.V.].
The quotation, Isa. 50:4, which precedes, is also taken from the King James version.
[18] Maclaren, A., *op. cit.*, 23, 24.

" A man, about whom it can once be said that God is his God, cannot die. Such a bond can never be broken." [19] Blaise Pascal is established. Remaining for a while in the frailty of the flesh, he will have occasion to stumble, to hesitate, to be confused, to fear, to welcome opinions based on reason, to listen to authorities that will disturb him. Certainly. But he is established. Not that he has a clear idea of the steadfastness of the saints; but he has caught an intimation of it in his Bible, and the intuition of this truth is an integral part of the feeling that comes to him. Blaise Pascal is established. The pages of his Bible are illuminated by that same fire which floods his heart and in which is supernaturally bathed that very room which one day, to his sorrow, he deserted!

Capital revelation for Pascal from another point of view: when one has had such a revelation from the Living God, one is done with scholasticism forever. He was already suspicious of it by nature, and for the reasons which we have given. All that we have learned about him in the preceding pages, or almost all, predestined his theology to become Biblical theology. Nevertheless because of a state of mind in which we have recently recognized something of the " pre-Catholicism " of Saul of Tarsus, Pascal had indulged in metaphysical arguments quite in keeping with the disposition of a speculative " man of the world," denied, for a time, divine enlightenment. Already, certainly, intuition of the three orders, grown clearer by moments, had tended to resolve for him a number of antinomies. But, as we have insisted in the preceding chapter, for him, the son of the bondwoman had all too often prevailed over the son of the freewoman, spoken of in the fourth chapter of the Epistle to the Galatians. He had persisted too long in considering himself as a little free god before a great God, free doubtless too, the two gods exchanging courtesies and trying to get along with each other.

At the hour of the divine visit, he understands that his freedom is that announced by the Bible, that lived by the men of the Bible, that which empowered the impotent man at the pool of Bethesda to rise, take up his bed, and walk.

" Certitude. Certitude. Feeling. Joy. Peace.

God of Jesus Christ."

Pascal's freedom lies henceforward in believing and obeying. It does not lie in him. It lies in the Son, in His power to liberate him, Blaise. God becomes his Father at the moment in which he receives the Son. The Son brings him this inestimable good: he makes God his Father. The

[19] *Ibid.*, 25.

lie which Blaise had lived thus far was that of his autonomy, of his divinity in a way. Up until now he had attributed to himself that which only divine grace can bestow. Without realizing it, he had believed the lie: " You shall be gods." The false security in which he had lived had actually prevented him from becoming a child of adoption in Jesus Christ. In the hour, then, when the words, " Thy God shall be my God," became his own, he resigned himself joyously to the complete obliteration of self: " Forgetfulness of the world, and of everything except God."

Surely he is through, through once and for all, with scholasticism.

" He is to be found only by the ways taught in the Gospel."

In the same flash is revealed to him the " greatness of the human soul."

It is the greatness of a soul made in the image of God and restored to that image, finding itself at the hour in which it loses its last illusion, according as he who wishes to save his life shall lose it.

" Righteous Father, the world hath not known Thee; but I have known Thee."

And in knowing the Father, he found himself. He was found. He was chosen:

" Joy, joy, joy, tears of joy."

Beethoven's Ninth Symphony will not surpass such heights.

We are wrong in representing Pascal's inner life as being darkened by Jansenism, says Bremond, who, we feel, too often attributes to Jansenism that which has its origin in the Scriptures. But, whence, according to him, comes this " Jansenist " joy? from the fact that the Jansenists believe that " if Jesus Christ did not die for all, He died for them; if grace was lacking and will necessarily be lacking for the crowd, they themselves will not suffer this lack." [20] We say: " Since Christ died for all men, He died for me." Pascal says: " Although perhaps, although doubtless He did not die for all men, He did die for me." [21] This is lending very dark thoughts to that joyous person who is going to want to write a " Vindication of Christianity " in which he will try to influence those who forget their miserable lot, or what is worse, do their best not to think about it. Before speculating on the propositions attributed to Jansenism, Pascal simply rejoiced in the fact that the Good News was for him who, for long months, had wandered

[20] Bremond, H., *Histoire littéraire du sentiment religieux en France*, v. 4, 325.
[21] *Ibid.*, 330.

in an arid and waterless land. To charge him with all the injustice that the mystery of the election may seem to include when seen through our infirmities is, to say the least, lacking in charity. What we shall grant to Bremond, on the other hand, is that Pascal's prayer retains a very natural human interest in his own salvation, in his keen desire for distinct and tangible signs.[22] This is precisely what accounts for his joy when these signs are granted him.

During this period, that is, up to November 23, 1654, Pascal has scarcely found favor with the members of Port-Royal and the Rouen readings are already dim in his memory. Actually we believe that they had hardly gone beyond the rudimentary stage. Moreover, we know only that which we are, and, until then, Pascal had hardly *lived* the doctrines of Jansenism. Tomorrow it will be different. The reader of the Bible who has just seen verified in his case, in an hour of anguish, the essential teachings with reference to natural incapacity and election will be interested in what the Port-Royalists teach on this subject. We shall find that the latter are also devotees of the Scriptures, and it is on the common ground of the Bible that Pascal and the Jansenists will meet and conclude their agreement.

No, decidedly Pascal is not a man with a system. He is a man with a method. For him, knowledge is " a way and a life, inseparable, as is all life, from struggle and fruitful anguish." [23] For him, to know is to seek; but one seeks only if one is sought for, and when one finds, it is because one has already been found. Thus, according to God's impenetrable designs, all real knowledge has its end, as it has its beginning, in God's election. Tomorrow no doubt the Arnaulds will nourish with theological substance this belief; at its origin, however, is found a Biblical experience that has become again a living reality, a life sanctified by God, a way opened by His grace. Tomorrow the thinker that Pascal will continue to be will no doubt seek to understand the universe, but it will be henceforward in a new spirit. His task will be to clarify whatever God lets him glimpse of the order by which He governs the universe. Already, however, he is convinced that a heart full of humility will serve him better than his former presumption.

[22] Bremond, H., *En Prière avec Pascal*, Bloud et Gay, Paris, 1923.
[23] Chevalier, J., " La Méthode de connaître d'après Pascal," *Revue de métaphysique et de morale*, 30th year, No. 2, April–June, 1923, p. 183.

Never to be separated from God, no longer to experience the horrible solitude which is the lot of man without God, such is henceforward the keynote to the Pascal of the *Mémorial:*

" I have separated myself from Him."

But already echoes the verse from Jeremiah:

" They have forsaken me, the fountain of living water."

On this point again the Scriptures search his heart. But let us note the line inspired by Matt. 27:46, which immediately follows: " My God, wilt thou leave me? " Here Pascal holds the two ends of the chain in the middle of which, somewhere, lies the mystery of his salvation. I have forsaken God. . . . Will God yet forsake me?

To say that we separate ourselves from God, or that God abandons us, is really the same thing. The only thing to do, consequently, is to abandon ourselves to God's grace and to be fervent in prayer.

" Let me not be separated from Him eternally."

And this is, strictly speaking, divine logic, the logic of the Scriptures interpreted by the Scriptures, when our logic of little gods has been silenced, and the sovereign Word speaks. Henceforward, in accordance with the powerful words of Calvin, Pascal — I know that he would shudder at the juxtaposition of his name and that of the great reformer — will no longer look for arguments on which to rest his judgment, but will submit his judgment and his intelligence to God, " as to a thing elevated above the necessity of being judged." [24] It is from a higher order that will come to him the ultimate synthesis of truth. He has already outlined the page on the three orders while half guessing at it from the human plane of the order of minds with its irreconcilable contradictions; but the final revelation of the true hierarchy of the universe comes to him from the Bible with divine simplicity. Only the creative Word can be the instructive Word.

This Word, however, is beyond us. It is precisely because of our misery and our infirmity that it became flesh; that, according to the admirable prologue to The Gospel According to Saint John — prologue which is a kind of epilogue — " the Word was made flesh, and dwelt

---

[24] Calvin, J., *Institution de la Religion Chrestienne,* text established and presented by Jacques Pannier, Les textes français, Collection des Universités de France de l'Association Guillaume Budé, Société Belles Lettres, Paris, 1936, 4 v., v. 1, ch. 1, 67.

among us." [25] And thus the *Mémorial* continues, once again following the Scriptures:

" This is the eternal life, that they might know Thee, the only true God, and the one whom Thou hast sent, Jesus Christ.

" Jesus Christ.

" Jesus Christ."

Here is Pascal at the very center of truth, finding himself there at the very instant in which he renounces himself: " God as will and person-ality, in concepts of Christian faith, is thus the only possible ground of real individuality, though not the only possible presupposition of self-consciousness. But faith in God, as will and personality, depends upon faith in His power to reveal Himself. The Christian faith in God's self-disclosure, culminating in the revelation of Christ, is thus the basis of the Christian concept of personality and individuality." [26]

This pertinent analysis of Reinhold Niebuhr's not only happens to summarize that central portion of the *Mémorial,* but it makes us under-stand why, henceforward, Pascal's thinking, for the same reason as his life, will be centered in Christ.

Kneeling, abased at the feet of Christ, Pascal henceforward holds a dialogue with Him. His style is no longer that of one who feels himself alone; it is the style of one who is at peace in his meditations; and it is this quality that wins our hearts. It is the style which Charles Du Bos called the " style of silence." [27]

Thus directly brought into the divine presence, Pascal relives the experience of the men of the Bible to whom this signal favor was granted: a tremendous sense of his own unworthiness, of his sin, a sor-row that is a godly sorrow.

"I have separated myself from Him; I have fled from Him, denied Him, crucified Him."

And the prayer rises to his lips, that prayer which will be his last: " Let me not be separated from Him eternally."

We cannot reiterate this too often. In decisive moments of his life, it was the Bible that was Pascal's means of grace. He was reading it when the fire kindled itself; it was through words of the Holy Book that God spoke to him; it was the central hero of the Book who at last came

[25] John 1:14.

[26] Niebuhr, R., *The Nature and Destiny of Man,* A Christian Interpretation, Gif-ford lectures, Scribner's Sons, New York, 1941, v. 1, *Human Nature,* 15.

[27] Du Bos, Ch., " Le Langage de Pascal," in *La Revue hebdomadaire, no. cit.,* p. 265.

and spoke to him face to face — it is through the Book that he will keep the indescribable Treasure that is his.

" We keep hold of Him by the ways taught in the Gospel."

Pascal has been made whole. The strength of a divine presence has been substituted in him for the weakness of a corrupt nature. However, it would be the supreme temptation of the old pride to rest passively in this ecstasy of divine communion. It would be an undoubted error to transpose the *grace* here below in terms of the *glory* of the hereafter. Our salvation is from the Living God of the Scriptures — let us work out our salvation according to the Scriptures. The Christian ethics of the *Provinciales* are found in the direct extension of this truth. The mystery of divine election continues in the uncertainty of the final judgment, and it would be the worst fallacy in Pascal's view to neglect the Gospel of that Living God in a living story, to return to the school of the old paganism. " When God plies a soul with fears of falling it is by no means a proof that God in His secret purpose intends to permit him to fall. These fears may be the very means which God has designed to keep him from falling. . . . God's exhortations to duty are perfectly consistent with His purpose to give sufficient grace for the performance of these duties. . . . These warnings [of God] are, even for believers, incitements to greater faith and prayer . . . , they are designed to show man his duty rather than his ability, and his weakness rather than his strength . . . , they convince men of their want of holiness and of their dependence upon God." [28] So the only key to this situation of the Saint thus seized by God is the word which comes to Pascal:

" Renunciation, total and sweet.

" Total submission to Jesus Christ and to my director."

AN ALL-IMPORTANT RESERVATION

This " my director " added to Jesus Christ, and on the same plane with Him, in the phrase at least, contains the seeds of possible confusion. This director is Monsieur Singlin of Port-Royal and, in a letter to Madame Périer, dated January 25, 1655, Jacqueline will dwell on the difficulty Pascal has in accepting him as a director, though he can think of no other. At the same time Pascal mistrusts himself; he is afraid of being mistaken about the " vocation of which he saw no certain marks, [Singlin] not being his natural pastor." But consider the interpretation

[28] Boettner, L., *The Reformed Doctrine of Predestination, op. cit.*, pp. 195, 196.

that Jacqueline gives to such scruples: " I saw clearly that it was only the remains of independence hidden in the depths of his heart that made a weapon of everything to avoid a subjugation that could only be perfect." [29] The reader will now understand why we declared in the preceding chapter that for Pascal the son of the bondwoman would never entirely give way to the son of the freewoman. This phrase " and my director," added to the phrase " total submission to Jesus Christ " by the Roman Catholic Pascal, lets us foresee that the " day's exercise on earth " spoken of in the next to the last line of the *Mémorial* will not be without new worries.

And it is almost with a pang that we hear the echo of the beloved psalm: " I will not forget thy words," for we know now that in part these words will come to him after direct and prayerful consultation of the Bible, words learned by heart; and in part from the human director, from an ecclesiastical authority. This authority, moreover, will be divided against itself, since under the distant gaze of Rome the Jansenists will find themselves at grips with the Jesuits.

THE HONOR OF GOD

This reservation made, and it seems an important one, the fact remains that " it was on the night of the twenty-third of November, 1654, that Blaise Pascal sealed his definitive pact with God." [30] The " renunciation, total and sweet," will be taken literally. Pascal will not complete the works which he had just confidently enumerated for the " Académie Parisienne des Sciences "; [31] he will refrain from publishing the treatises on mathematics which were already printed. But there is more, much more, to say on the subject of this renunciation. During Pascal's lifetime nothing more will appear under his name. Before being attributed to a certain Louis de Montalte, the *Lettres Provinciales* will be anonymous; the author of the mathematical treatises published in 1658 and in 1659 will pretend to " reveal " his identity under the name of Amos Dettonville; a note on the manuscript of the " Vindication of Christianity " shows that the author would have called himself Salomon de Tultie, an anagram of the first two pseudonyms. Furthermore, Brunschvicg points out that Pascal will undertake none of these works

[29] *Œuvres*, v. 12, 6, n. 1.

[30] Mauriac, F., *The Living Thoughts of Pascal*, Longmans, Green & Co., Inc., New York, 1940, p. 6.

[31] *Œuvres*, v. 3, 305.

on his own initiative. He will first have to feel, through the force of circumstances, the pressure of that will to which he vowed total submission.[32] This is sufficient testimony of the honesty, the absolute sincerity of the author of those *Lettres Provinciales* which are often discussed with such bitterness.

In a decisive hour Pascal felt in himself the budding of a new vocation; a whole new world was suddenly revealed to his mind. Seized with a passion as commanding as God's voice itself, Pascal has made the promise to his own conscience which will bind him. A new Saint Augustine, " he is seduced by the voice from above which subjugates him and carries him away." [33] The event that has just occurred in his life seems to him to be a counsel from Heaven to break all human bonds and to live in the future for God alone. Renouncing the world, he will keep in touch only with a few of those friends who share his convictions,[34] and are committed to the same maxims. Jacqueline's letters amply show with what mistrust of himself, with what fear of the mystery of divine action, Pascal will undertake to submit his thought, his daily conduct, to the new law.[35]

The hours of perfect communion with God are rare. This is a familiar theme to the reader of the *Imitation of Christ*. Tomorrow perhaps Blaise will find a coldness in his heart. It will then be sufficient for him to touch, through his coat, that paper, tangible evidence of the burning visitation. This certainty of belonging to that small flock of those who shall not perish will bring him closer to the Jansenists. " Before being a heresy," writes a contemporary Catholic author, " Jansenism is a family of spirits issuing from ancient Israel, a certain race of souls stirred by the prophets and naturally God-fearing." [36] Mauriac could not better express the fact that the meeting ground of Blaise Pascal and the Jansenists will be the Bible to which they will show themselves equally faithful. Under the inspiration of Jansenism, of Saint Cyran and of Antoine Arnauld, these disciples of Saint Augustine will work together to maintain in its purity the integrity of the inner life of the Church.[37]

[32] *Œuvres, Introduction à la seconde série des Œuvres de Pascal*, v. 4, xxvii, xxviii.

[33] Vinet, A., *Etudes sur Blaise Pascal, op. cit.*, 315. Vinet quotes here page xxx of Faugère's introduction to his edition.

[34] *Œuvres de Blaise Pascal*, chez Detune, at The Hague, 1779, v. 1, 44, 45.

[35] *Œuvres, Introduction à la seconde série des Œuvres de Pascal*, v. 4, xvii.

[36] Mauriac, F., *Blaise Pascal et sa sœur Jacqueline*, " Le Passé vivant," Hachette, Paris, 1931, p. 145.

[37] *Œuvres, ibid.*, v. 4, xvii.

Won to the truth, won by the Truth, Blaise Pascal will also discover the great inspirational principle of that other lover of the Scriptures, Calvin, the principle of the honor of God. Denouncing with energy " the depraved will " [38] which is " bad and born with us," [39] the author of the *Pensées* will affirm that " inclination toward oneself is the beginning of all disorder "; [40] that " all that incites us to become attached to creatures is bad " since it prevents our serving God, and that " one must love Him only, and not transient creatures." [41] To love only God, to serve Him only, to honor Him only, henceforward this is Pascal's watchword. From this time on " the only real virtue is hatred of self." [42] One cannot really appreciate such exclusiveness unless one remembers the temperament of Blaise and the harsh lessons he was forced to learn before the deliverance of November 23, 1654.

Not more in the case of Pascal than in that of Calvin, however, shall we cry against this harshness: " The God of Abraham, the God of Isaac, the God of Jacob, the God of Christians, is a God of love and of consolation; He is a God who fills the souls of those He possesses; He is a God who makes them realize their own poverty and His infinite mercy, who unites Himself with the depths of their souls, who fills those souls with humility, joy, and confidence." [43] It is a great religious poet who speaks these beautiful words, and what a rich experience they express of that God of Abraham, of Isaac, of Jacob, who revealed Himself during that memorable night!

Sanctified, Pascal has at last understood that truth without charity is but an idol placed midway between monstrous falsehood and the Truth that is God Himself.[44] And this is the place in which to recall a word from the *Mémorial* which we have thus far intentionally allowed to pass without special mention — the word " feeling." One remembers the line:

" Certitude. Certitude. Feeling. Joy. Peace."

A manuscript copy appearing after page 495 of the original manuscript in the additions made in 1864 to the latter says, " *vision*, joy,

[38] *Pensées*, Section vii, Fr. 477, *Œuvres*, v. 13, 385.
[39] *Pensées*, Section vii, Fr. 478, *Œuvres*, v. 13, 385.
[40] *Pensées*, Section vii, Fr. 477, *Œuvres*, v. 13, 385.
[41] *Pensées*, Section vii, Fr. 479, *Œuvres*, v. 13, 385, 386.
[42] *Pensées*, Section vii, Fr. 485, *Œuvres*, v. 13, 390.
[43] *Pensées*, Section viii, Fr. 556, *Œuvres*, v. 14, 5.
[44] *Pensées*, Section viii, Fr. 582, *Œuvres*, v. 14, 26.

peace." [45] We italicize, for the sake of clarity, the word *vision,* which will help us greatly in our comprehension of the word " feeling." This same word should be understood too in the context of all that Pascal says of " the heart," " the spirit of finesse " — intuition. During the night of November 23, it is an intuition of the whole being, itself utterly carried away, that grasps the revelation. This revelation comes to this whole being rich in all the divine attributes, and rich above all in that charity of the God who has defined Himself as Love. Once more we understand the decisive part played by the *Mémorial* in the formulation of the perspective of the three orders, the order of bodies, the order of minds, and the order of charity. At the same time, Pascal has become a dedicated intellectual in whose sight truth and charity are identified. Henceforth, he takes his watchword from I Cor., ch. 13.

We are agreed with Lhermet in our conclusion that if from the time of his first " conversion " — which we ourselves called the " Jansenist quickening " — Pascal was the man of the Bible, it was " especially after the great conversion that he turned the pages of the Sacred Books with assiduity and love." And we are pleased to see that Catholic author add, " The Bible helps him to combat Molinism and casuistry, to shake off incredulity, to lend to the Jansenist doctrine fruitfulness and luster." [46] We are in agreement, however, with this reservation: to judge by its fruits, the Jansenist doctrine was already fruitful; and it owed that fruitfulness to the Scriptures interpreted according to Saint Augustine.

[45] *Œuvres,* v. **12,** 4, n. 5.
[46] Lhermet, J., *Pascal et la Bible, op. cit.,* p. 226.

VIII

Glimpse of a Sanctuary

*" Surely goodness and mercy shall follow me all the days of my life:
and I will dwell in the house of the Lord for ever."*

— *Ps. 23:6*

On the 8th of December, 1654, Sister Jacqueline de Sainte-Euphémie
Pascal wrote to her sister Gilberte: " I notice in him a humility and a
submission even toward me, which surprises me. Finally, I have no more
to tell you save that it appears clearly that it is no longer his natural
mind working in him." [1] That same day Blaise had remained in the
parlor with his sister until time for the sermon, the subject of which
happened to be the beginning of the life of the Christian. The preacher
was already in the pulpit when the new penitent entered, and the latter,
because of his expectant state of mind, felt that Providence was using
this means of instructing him. He was so struck by it that he confided in
his director, Monsieur Singlin, his intention of holding a retreat at Vaumurier, not far from Port-Royal-des-Champs. His friend, the Duke de
Roannez, whom he had just led to Christ and who occupied all his attention, reluctantly allowed him to go. Pascal's director, Monsieur
Singlin, was obliged to stay in Paris, and put his penitent under the direction of Monsieur de Saci. Such, however, was the penitent's need for
solitude that the stay at Vaumurier did not satisfy him. So he left the
house of the Duc de Luynes to go to occupy a cell among the solitary
souls of Port-Royal-des-Champs, under the assumed name of Monsieur
de Mons. He stayed there only a fortnight, but later returned frequently,
thus closely associating himself with the life of the convent.

AN EDIFYING CONVERT

Jacqueline, whom he went to see each time he returned to Paris —
the women's convent had been transferred there in 1626 because of the

---

[1] *Extrait d'une lettre de la Sœur Jacqueline de Sainte-Euphémie Pascal à Madame
Périer, sa sœur,* December 8, 1654, *Œuvres,* v. **4,** 15.

malaria in the Chevreuse valley — rejoiced to find him so gay: she wondered how Monsieur de Saci managed a penitent so full of joy.[2] But it was the joy of the pardoned. In her letter of the 19th of January, 1655, one feels the satisfaction of the shepherdess of souls at the spectacle of the lost lamb returned to the fold, and who replaces the " vain joys and distractions of the world by more reasonable joys and more permissible witticisms instead of atoning for them by constant tears." [3] Scoldings are forgotten.

It is a long time, however, before she feels perfectly confident that her brother's conversion is a genuine one. It is only on the 25th of January, 1655, that she decides to tell her sister all about it: if she waited so long, it was because she was afraid of having to retract if she had told about it sooner. However, one point of doubt remains, and she formulates her reserve thus: " Whatever success it may please God to give it " (that is the story of the conversion). The fact is that Jacqueline writes to her sister to ask for her prayers. Blaise's visits increase, but she, Jacqueline, only " follows him without using any kind of persuasion." But the penitent is transformed: she sees him grow, little by little. He grows in humility, in submission, in mistrust and contempt of self, to the extent of wishing for " annihilation in the esteem and in the memory of man." If God continues with His work, Blaise will be unrecognizable. Such is the state of things, and God above knows what Blaise will be one day.[4]

One cannot help being struck by this attitude which consists in expecting everything from God. It is this same attitude that is shown by Jacqueline and Blaise in their choice of a spiritual adviser, and in that same spiritual adviser — Monsieur Singlin — once the choice has been made. A letter from the latter to Mother Mary of the Angels [5] shows him to be full of humility at seeing among those who seek his advice " people of wisdom, of virtue far exceeding mine, who depend on us for guidance in their conduct, who submit like children to what we counsel." This position of responsibility makes Monsieur Singlin feel very humble particularly at this time when he is submitting himself in strict obedience to the divine will. Mother Angélique, in a letter to Renaud de

[2] *Extrait d'une lettre de la Sœur Jacqueline de Sainte-Euphémie Pascal à Monsieur Pascal, son frère*, January 19, 1655, *Œuvres*, v. 4, 17.

[3] *Ibid.*

[4] *Lettre de la Sœur Jacqueline de Sainte-Euphémie Pascal à Madame Périer, sa sœur*, January 25, 1655, *Œuvres*, v. 4, 61, 62.

[5] *Œuvres*, v. 4, 64, n. 1.

Sévigné,[6] explains Monsieur Singlin's seeming coldness by the feeling of responsibility in a man extremely conscious of the strict accounting expected by God of His ministers concerning those souls committed to their care.

It is the attentive and continuous consideration of God's ways that finally convinces Jacqueline of the reality of her brother's sanctification. We have, for instance, a very touching letter of hers in which she consults Blaise at the request of " our Mothers," and asks him to explain his new method of learning to read. . . . And the example she gives is how to learn to read Jesus! [7] What a richly gifted woman, this Jacqueline, and how beautiful are the brother and sister, once consecrated to God! According to the words of Jean Balde,[8] " they are absorbed to the very depths of their being with what they do " and each act conceived by them is performed in a spirit of consecration.

Pascal seeks in Jacqueline a senior in the spiritual life. By her, and through her, he regains contact with the directors of Port-Royal. For her part, Jacqueline, submitting to the evidence of God's work in her brother, returns all his confidence and more! It is apparently Port-Royal that draws them together again; but it is the Scriptures and a theology drawn directly from the Scriptures, which for Pascal constitute the truth, that provide their real meeting ground. And it is this truth as a way of life that is professed and taught at Port-Royal; so that it is true to say that Pascal, overjoyed by his own personal experience, contentedly becomes part of Port-Royal. Thus he remains faithful to all that scientific methods have taught him.

A REFUGE ACCORDING TO PASCAL'S HEART

What is it then that Pascal's experience has taught him? It has given him essentially a revelation of the Living Christ, and those who don't know Him " are ignorant of that which the most mediocre of Christians know! that the imagination plays no part in it, that no power of feeling

[6] Dated November 13, 1660, *Œuvres*, v. 4, 64, n. 1.

[7] *Lettre de la Sœur Jacqueline de Sainte-Euphémie Pascal à Monsieur Pascal, son frère*, October 26, 1655, *Œuvres*, v. 4, 77, 78.

The *Grammaire générale et raisonnée de Port-Royal*, Paris, 1660, uses and publishes Pascal's discovery: First part, ch. 6, " Concerning a New Way to Learn to Read Easily in All Sorts of Languages." Cf. *Œuvres*, v. 4, 77, 78, n. 1.

[8] Balde, J., " Jacqueline Pascal," *La Revue hebdomadaire*, No. 28, 32d year, July 14, 1923, p. 146.

is capable of producing the smallest drop of that for which they thirst." [9]
The true disciples, henceforward, know that their real strength is not in themselves.[10] The author of *Imitation of Christ* draws this assurance from the lips of the Saviour Himself:

"I am He who made all the Saints; I gave them Grace; I obtained for them Glory. . . .

"I foreknew My beloved ones before the beginning of the world.

"I chose them out of the world, they chose not Me first.

"I called them by grace, I drew them by mercy, I led them safe through sundry temptations. . . .

"I am to be praised by all My Saints; I am to be blessed above all things, and to be honored in everyone, whom I have thus gloriously exalted and predestined, without any precedent merits of their own." [11]

Professor Eugène Choisy, in his Opening Address to the International Congress of Calvinist Theology, held in Geneva from June 15–18, 1936, reminded his " honored brothers " that the doctrine of election and predestination is in Calvin, not only the fruit of the study he made of the Scripture but also a personal experience imposed upon him: " The experience in his own soul and conscience that it is God Himself who gives the certainty of the free remission of our sins by faith in Jesus Christ, and the experiences of his life constantly revealed to him that we are not our own masters, but that an Almighty, the Living God, the sovereign Ruler of the earth, is the master of our destinies and that He often leads where we would not wish to go and places us in positions we would not have chosen and that we would perhaps have wished to flee." [12] It is in this sense that predestination is for the chosen an experienced fact. In his view, an inevitable certain progression toward a predetermined end shows itself throughout the entire course of events; and it is not true that events take place because they have been foreseen: the fact is that they are foreseen because they must certainly take place. It is a matter of predestination, not of postdestination.

These high Biblical views, far from engendering a free and easy way of life, inspire a life of confidence and of absolute consecration. The

[9] Mauriac, F., *Blaise Pascal et sa sœur Jacqueline*, " Le Passé vivant," Hachette, Paris, 1931, p. 144.

[10] Cf. *Œuvres*, v. 13, 415, 416.

[11] *De Imitatione Christi*, III, 58:3, 4.

[12] Choisy, E., Opening Address to the International Conference of Calvinist Theology, Geneva, June 15–18, 1936, " De l'élection éternelle de Dieu," Actes du Congrès, *op. cit.*, p. 10.

only wisdom that leaves us in peace, according to two beautiful verses of one of Pascal's contemporaries, is to " desire that which God desires." [13] Praying to this God is essentially praying Pascal's psalm: " O Lord, teach me Thy justifications. . . . For Thy testimonies are my meditation: and Thy justifications my counsel. . . . Make me to understand the way of Thy justifications." [14]

Pascal learns from Saint Augustine that, because of this state of things, the condemned sinner cannot allege that he is unworthy of his punishment, nor the saint boast that he is worthy of his reward. Pascal goes on to prove by the parable of the Laborers in the Vineyard that the God of the Bible is a sovereign in the dispensation of His gifts. This is also clearly shown by His words to Moses: *I will have mercy on whom I will have mercy; and I will shew mercy to whom I will shew mercy.* [15] And it is Pascal's own experience that he finds thus verified in the Scripture, and justified by it from God's lofty point of view. Already the author of the letter about the death of Etienne Pascal knew that all that has happened has from all time been " present " — the manuscript of the *Oratoire* 160, No. 16, says " *presçu* " (foreknown).[16]

The *Discours sur les* Pensées, in which Pascal will soon show his intentions of undertaking a defense and illustration of the Christian religion, will bring into clear relief man's helplessness.[17] According to this *Discours,* the authors of the books of the Bible, with a sincerity no impostor could ever devise, " assure us that we can do nothing about what they prescribe for us, that we are born corrupt and helpless to resist that corruption, that so long as we act only through our own strength, we will infallibly succumb. It is to God that we should appeal for the strength which we lack.[18]

It may be, as Henri Bremond affirms, that Pascal — like Bossuet — confused original sin with concupiscence.[19] In the matter of corruption,

---

[13] Vouloir ce que Dieu veut, est la seule science
Qui nous met en repos.

(Malherbe, *Consolation à M. du Périer, sur la mort de sa fille,* l. 83, 84.) This poem, the most famous by Malherbe, was written after June, 1599. Malherbe himself died in 1628.

[14] Ps. 118:12, 24, 27 [Ps. 119 in Authorized Version].

[15] Rom. 9:15.

[16] Cousin, V., *Des Pensées de Pascal, op. cit.,* " Appendice, no. 2," p. 312.

[17] " Car les hommes n'y peuvent rien," *Discours sur les* Pensées, v. 12, ccxxxiv.

[18] *Discours sur les* Pensées, v. 12, ccxiv.

[19] Bremond, H., *Histoire littéraire du sentiment religieux, op. cit.,* v. 1, 364, 377, 390.

Pascal was never sensitive to shades of difference. He confined himself to the traditional interpretation of the Scripture. He was firmly convinced that the Augustinian theology was " the only one consistent with the Biblical facts, while the other systems are inconsistent with the truth as revealed." [20]

When Pascal was trying to uphold the authenticity of a religious doctrine he made sure that the doctrine was drawn from the Judaeo-Christian revelation; that it was grounded and supported in the Scriptural texts commented upon by the Fathers of the Church, interpreted by the Councils and the Popes. His supreme authority was " the Bible with the Old Testament containing the primitive, Mosaic, prophetic revelation, the Bible with the New Testament, giving Christ's doctrine, and the teachings of the Apostles, representatives of Christ." [21] However, the writings of the Holy Fathers, whose weight with Pascal we have mentioned, all that apostolic Tradition upon which they comment with authority, the official interpretation of the Councils and the Popes, were in the last analysis to his way of thinking only subsidiary and dependent. This will appear clearly later on in our story after the Pope apparently was surprised and biased by the Jesuits. Thus " the real source of truth, which is Tradition," will have been excluded and the truth will no longer be free to appear. So, Pascal will conclude on this point — and the italicizing is ours — " men no longer speaking of *the truth, the truth must itself speak to men.*" [22] This truth will naturally take a position opposed to the new doctrines which betray their human origins, like artificial flowers " that one tries fraudulently to graft onto the tree of Tradition and that must be mercilessly pruned." [23]

Henceforward we have a clear view of the ground on which Pascal and the Port-Royalists meet. It is the high place of a Biblical domain examined by the light of faith, constituting the one standard by which to measure morality and all feeling of obligation. This high place is reached by the path of Tradition, a royal path honored by the name of Saint Augustine. From this high place, it is in the name of the Bible in the last resort that the judgments which count are pronounced. On this high place stands the refuge, according to Pascal's heart: Port-Royal, stronghold of Scripture.

Thus it is putting the horse before the cart to affirm, as does Lhermet,

[20] Lhermet, J., *Pascal et la Bible, op. cit.*, p. 600.
[21] *Ibid.*, p. 628.
[22] *Pensées*, Section xiii, Fr. 832, *Œuvres*, v. 12, 264.
[23] Lhermet, J., *Pascal et la Bible, op. cit.*, p. 629.

that the Jansenist hold on Pascal was such " that it caused him to find in the Bible the expression of the dogma and morality of the sect." [24] Our Catholic brother should, in our opinion, say that the hold of the Bible on Pascal was such as to cause him to find at Port-Royal the expression of the rules of life of the " little flock."

THE PORT-ROYALISTS

What did it mean to be from Port-Royal? It meant renouncing every-thing, giving up the pursuit of honors, and even the idea of a priesthood, of which the conception is so elevated among the solitary souls that it becomes frightening; it is to do penance, to study, or to do manual work, all to the glory of God. The Solitaries " themselves regulate, indi-vidually, under the guidance of their directors and their consciences, their occupations and their penance. They come together for prayer and worship. They meet too in serious cases to deliberate questions of the common good. They probably pool their resources; and a consider-able portion of each man's fortune goes to the convent. The administra-tion of these resources is entrusted to a few reliable monks." [25] The government and the authority belonged more particularly to the " gen-tlemen of Port-Royal," [26] whose leader was Jean Duvergier de Hauranne, abbé de Saint Cyran.[27]

It was Saint Cyran who brought together at Port-Royal those pious laymen resolved to live in the strictest observance of the Christian reli-gion. It was through Saint Cyran that Jansenism penetrated to Port-Royal. Originally the abbey of Port-Royal, in the valley of the Chev-reuse, six leagues from Paris, was a community of women of the order of Cîteaux, which had been founded in the thirteenth century. In 1602

[24] *Ibid.*, p. 119.

[25] Strowski, F., *Pascal et son temps* (Third Part: *Les Provinciales et les Pensées*), v. 3, 3, 4.

[26] In order to simplify and facilitate research, Augustin Gazier gave a list of the Solitaries and the gentlemen, as made out by Besoigne for the period between 1637 and 1660. It can be found in his *Histoire générale du mouvement Janséniste depuis ses origines jusqu'à nos jours*, Champion, Paris, 1923, v. 1, 72, 73.

This list contains forty-five names, but on page 73 is the note: " *A few others,* of whom the Duc de Luynes." So one should probably show about fifty members.

[27] Consult Laferrière, Abbé J., *Etude sur Jean Duvergier de Hauranne, Abbé de Saint Cyran* (1581–1643), J. Wouters-Ickx, Louvain, 1912.

This work, written from the Roman Catholic point of view, is severe with Saint Cyran. It is nevertheless well done and well informed. A precious bibliography en-riches it, pp. 229–236.

Angélique Arnauld, daughter of Antoine Arnauld the famous lawyer of the Parliament of Paris, had been made abbess. As she was then only eleven years old and a great reader of novels, she hardly thought of reforming the household — although it needed reforming very badly! But in 1608, during the Lenten season, she was deeply moved by a sermon preached by a visiting Capucin. The latter, speaking with vigor on the beauty of the religious life, became the inspiration of a vocation: Mother Angélique was going to bring her abbey back to the strict observance of the old order, and she herself was to become an admirable woman. At first she was to meet serious difficulties, even within her own family: she had to forbid their coming to the house. One may read in the admirable *Port-Royal* [28] of Sainte-Beuve the account of that heroic Day of the Wicket, as it is called, of that 25th of September, 1609, when, having closed the door on her own father, she fainted.

Little by little, she succeeded in reforming several abbeys of her

---

[28] Sainte-Beuve, Ch. A., one of the greatest critics of all time, wrote on *Port-Royal*, from 1837 to 1858, a work which remains a monument, the best all-round work which we possess on this subject. However, Sainte-Beuve's documentation remained very incomplete: at the time of two journeys to Holland, in 1848–1849, to Utrecht and to Amersfoort, he did find some precious data, but he did not work as did the initiates in the library of the " Gentlemen " of the Catholic Meeting where he would have found other treasures and new opinions. Which brings us to a second criticism — the most serious: the *man* in Sainte-Beuve not only lacks the deep faith necessary to interpret Port-Royal, but he is mediocre, almost cynical, the most trained, the most broken in mind to metamorphoses. Let us concede to him the resulting suppleness and also the art of " telling about " Port-Royal which charmed thousands of readers and won fervent adepts to Jansenism. For the writer and the artist in Sainte-Beuve are unrivaled.

The *Histoire de Port-Royal*, by Sainte-Beuve, a course given at Lausanne in 1837–1838, was published in 1840–1848 in 3 v.; 2d ed., 1860, 5 v.; 3d ed., 1867, 7 v. — v. 7: Table.

Our quotations are from the edition in 7 v., Hachette, Paris, 1900.

Let us recall that the great dramatist Racine, a former pupil of the " little schools " of Port-Royal, wrote an excellent *Abrégé de l'histoire de Port-Royal*, which will be found in v. 4 of the *Œuvres complètes*, Paris, 1868. Augustin Gazier gave one edition of it with a preface, an appendix, notes, a bibliographical essay, and three illustrations, Société française d'imprimerie et de librairie, Paris, 1908.

Let us point out: Clémencet, Dom Ch., *Histoire générale de Port-Royal*, from the Reform of the Abbey to Its Entire Destruction, Amsterdam, 1755–1757.

In English, besides the popular work by Romanes, E., *The Story of Port-Royal*, John Murray, London, 1907, we have in particular Abercrombie, N., *The Origins of Jansenism*, Oxford University Press, 1936.

We have already quoted several times the indispensable *Histoire générale du mouvement Janséniste depuis ses origines jusqu'à nos jours*, Champion, Paris, 1923, 2 v.

order, and founded in 1625, in Paris, a new house: Port-Royal-de-Paris. There still survive today, on the boulevard accurately named de Port-Royal, a few buildings hemmed in by the Maternity Hospital. In 1623, Mother Angélique began to consult Saint Cyran, friend and collaborator of Jansen, who was spiritual adviser to her nuns. Jansen died in 1638, having written in manuscript his big Latin work, the *Augustinus*. Saint Cyran won over to Jansenism the whole community of Port-Royal, the nuns of Port-Royal-de-Paris as well as the pious laymen of Port-Royal-des-Champs, so that henceforth Port-Royalist meant Jansenist. Among the gentlemen of Port-Royal, we must especially remember the name of the great Arnauld (1612–1694), twentieth and youngest child of Antoine Arnauld the lawyer, who had died in 1619. Doctor of the Sorbonne, the great Arnauld distinguished himself in 1643 by the publication of the little treatise previously mentioned here: *La fréquente communion*, which, being more easily handled than the voluminous *Augustinus*, was to be more efficacious in spreading the Jansenist doctrines on grace with their tendency toward predestination.

What must surely strike the student of Port-Royal is the fundamentally Biblical character of the institution which Saint Cyran succeeded in converting to Jansenism. Because of that character, Catholic anti-Molinism never sought to exert its influence on men of letters. At Port-Royal men wrote to make themselves understood, not to make themselves admired. The same applied to the arts, architecture, painting, and music, the latter of extreme simplicity — unison plain chant without any organ accompaniment. Nevertheless, a Biblical depth and beauty will be found in the tragedies written by Racine to entertain the young ladies of Saint-Cyr, Madame de Maintenon's school: *Esther* (1689), and *Athalie* (1691); and the look of the Jansenist portraits of Philippe de Champaigne show the meditations of an inner being turned toward the realities of a world which is no longer worldly.

In order to be understood, the Port-Royalists freed theology from a barbarous parlance and an infinity of useless questions. To do this, they dug "into the true sources, that is to say, the Scripture and Tradition." [29] Dom Clémencet never tires of insisting: "They possessed the science of the Scriptures and taught it to us.[30] They gave back to the children the Testament of their fathers by the translation of the Scrip-

[29] Clémencet, Dom Ch., *Histoire générale de Port-Royal, op. cit.*, v. 1, preface, xxvii.

[30] *Ibid.*, cix.

tures and of the services of the Church. . . ."[31] The meditation of God's Word, either in the Scriptures or in the writings of the Holy Fathers, occupied their most cherished moments and was all their delight."[32]

It is precisely the same simplicity of expression that is the beauty of the Port-Royalist art, a beauty that mocks at beauty as Pascal's true eloquence mocks at eloquence: Mademoiselle de Boullogne delights in scenes of Biblical piety, and when she paints the suffering Jesus, she reveals a profound mystery without affectation. We have just spoken of the portraits of Philippe de Champaigne. Let us now pay homage to his Biblical scenes in which he announces the Good News with the utmost simplicity. Here is the *Nativity*, the *Healing of the Paralytic*, the *Meal at Simon the Pharisee's*, the admirable *Last Supper*, in which the Apostles have the features of the Solitaries of Port-Royal — and even Pascal may be recognized among them! — the *Christ on the Cross*, and *Disciples of Emmaus*.

For us one theological proposition had always remained a dead letter until the day when, in the steps of Blaise Pascal, we entered into the company of the Solitaries of Port-Royal: " God is simple." It is this divine simplicity which, enlightening the minds of those whom it penetrated, established the scientific reputation of the Port-Royalists: Godeau, the Bishop of Vence, submits to them for censorship and approbation the translation he has just made of the New Testament. A learned doctor, Monsieur Taignier, asks them to examine and to correct his translation of the *Imitation of Christ*. " The renown of the Solitaries' Biblical knowledge rapidly spread abroad, and the high dignitaries of the ecclesiastical world often had recourse to their enlightenment."[33] These gentlemen of Port-Royal undertake to translate the New Testament themselves, and Pascal will attend the lectures preparatory to this translation, known as the Mons Version. We shall see him correct his own spiritual adviser, Monsieur de Saci; and we shall see the latter thereafter modestly make three drafts of his translation of the New Testament. This translation will grow until it comes to include the whole Bible. We personally have the joy of possessing the eight volumes of that Holy Bible translated into French from the Vulgate, with short notes in explanation of the text,[34] and it is with an inner

[31] *Ibid.*, cx.
[32] *Ibid.*, xxiv.
[33] Lhermet, J., *Pascal et la Bible, op. cit.*, p. 155.
[34] *La Sainte Bible traduite en français sur la Vulgate avec de courtes notes pour*

tremor that we recognize the hand of Pascal in this version or that note of the New Testament! May our reader appreciate with us just one sentence which opens the Preface: " One may consider it as a particular mark of the benediction of God on His Church, that it has pleased Him to allow the Faithful to partake of the truth of His words contained in His Holy Scriptures." [35] What wonderful Biblical piety!

And let us make no mistake about it: it is this piety, fruitful stream gushing forth from the Scripture, which, without ostentation, fertilized the souls of the Port-Royalists, freeing them from human tradition and superstition and kindling in them a purer faith and a firmer attachment to the morals of the Gospel.[36] Farther on we shall have a chapter entitled " The Dictates of Conscience." But from this point on we know in what school was refined that sensitive conscience which Blaise Pascal already possessed as an inheritance from his father. This conscience was to be further refined by the " God of Abraham, of Isaac, and of Jacob " through the trials by which He perfects the instrument for its destined tasks.

The men of Port-Royal are men made by the Bible. In that stronghold of the Scriptures, prayer and meditation are Biblical in matter and in form. Daily life is itself a prayer, a prayer which awaits the command. In daily conversation the Scriptures are constantly quoted, and in difficult circumstances the Scriptures are consulted.[37] Monsieur Nicole wrote a treatise on prayer which is at the same time a treatise on the sovereignty of God: from Him, we must accept everything, accept even His refusal if such is His will; " that will being just, we must not only submit ourselves to it, but also love it." [38]

One can thus appreciate at its true value a silly assertion in the Bossut edition, after having recognized the fact " that the defenders of the dogma of human fatalism professed the strictest morality in theory and in practice," it goes on to say this is because of remorse; it is as though " they had wanted to expiate before human society the destructive

---

l'intelligence de la lettre, par Monsieur de Sacy, chez Eugène Henri Fricx, Imprimeur du Roi, Rue de la Madelene, Brussels, 1701, 8 v.

[35] *Ibid.,* Foreword, v. 1, iii.

[36] Clémencet, Dom Ch., *Histoire générale de Port-Royal,* v. 1, preface, xxvi.

[37] Sainte-Beuve, Ch. A., *Port-Royal, op. cit.,* v. 4, 256.

[38] Monsieur Nicole, *Traité de la prière,* 3d ed., revised, corrected, and added to by the same author, Luxembourg, André Chevalier, 1731, 2 v., v. 2, 103.

The first approbation, signed by Gervais, Doctor of the Société de Sorbonne, is dated from Paris, June 15, 1694. (V. 1 without any page indication — we calculated that it must be p. 30.)

consequences of the morality inherent in their metaphysical doctrine." [39]

Let us correct the above with the judgment expressed on the subject by the editor of the fifth edition of the *Select Memoirs of Port-Royal*. He writes: " I thank God that in these last and perilous times there is such a book in our mother tongue as the *Memoirs of Port-Royal*. In the lives of these persecuted saints, we have the saving and living power of divine grace and of the highest preceptive gospel truths gloriously exemplified in unmistakable combination." [40] The same work also notes the importance of the Bible for the Port-Royalists: " Their directors advised them to begin by studying the Holy Scripture itself, without any commentary, only seeking for edification. They were in the habit also of always reading Scripture with a reference to parallel passages, without which they conceived it could only be very imperfectly understood. They also read the New Testament oftener than the Old, because they considered the former as the best explanation of the latter. The whole of Scripture they were however advised to read in the spirit of prayer. . . .

" But above all, the inhabitants of Port-Royal were taught to search the Scriptures with a supereminent view to Him of whom they testify." [41]

According to the same text again — quoting Lancelot — " the exalted piety which characterized Saint Cyran must be attributed to an unremitting study of the Holy Scriptures, and to the supereminent degree of reverence with which he regarded the word of God." Even the way in which the director of Port-Royal read the Scripture was marked by saintliness: " He often remarked, that in order to be beneficial, Scripture must be read with a portion of the very same spirit in which it was written: with a deep prostration of heart, and with a supreme reverence for the Divine Majesty which resides herein. Indeed he had such a reverence for Holy Writ, that he continually told his disciples they ought to read scarcely anything else. . . .

" Monsieur de Cyran used to recommend his disciples daily to study the Scriptures on their knees." [42]

This was the attitude from top to bottom of the hierarchy: in the simplest as in master of the house. All " prayed, mortified themselves,

[39] *Œuvres de Pascal*, chez Detune, at The Hague, 1779, 5 v., v. 1, 49.

[40] Schimmelpenninck, M. A., *Select Memoirs of Port-Royal*. Taken from original documents, 5th ed. in three volumes. Longman, Brown, Green, Longmans, and Roberts, London, 1858, v. 1, Preface to the 5th edition, p. xi.

[41] *Ibid.*, v. 1, 151, 152.

[42] *Ibid.*, 5, 7.

gardened, took care of the farm animals, read the breviary and the Scriptures, busied themselves with the temporal matters of the monastery." [43] And here is Innocent Fai, one of the carters of Port-Royal, who had the habit of sharing the dogs' bread so that he could give his own portion to the poor, and who, his work done, went and knelt at prayer in the stable. " He also used to be very diligent in reading the Scripture, and, the nuns having given him a little room of his own with a key, he used to shut himself up there and copy out passages of Scripture, that he might learn them by heart." [44]

BIBLICAL CHARACTER OF THEIR DOCTRINE

The work of these Port-Royalists is a true expression of their main concern in life, that is to say that it essentially expresses a Biblical outlook. We have already allowed this side of the Port-Royal doctrine to appear in discussing the details of their lives. How, in fact, even for the sake of order and clarity, could one manage to separate the fruits from the tree? Let us consider, for example, with Sainte-Beuve, Monsieur de Saci's library: it contains " Bibles of all sorts and sizes." [45] The Greek and Hebrew texts are next to the Latin and French translations. He translates from the originals and verifies his translations by those at hand. Such erudition certainly speaks well for the period, but one must bear in mind all that the erudition of the period owes to Port-Royal. Lancelot, Hellenist and Latinist, draws up the chronological and historical notes in the Bible of Vitré. Fontaine publishes the *Figures de la Bible* or the *Bible de Royaumont* which so delighted Madame de Sévigné, as we learn from a letter on the subject dated the 28th of August, 1656. Let us recall to mind the treatise *La fréquente communion*, by Arnauld. We owe to Saint Cyran the *Lettres spirituelles, Le Cœur nouveau*, and other pamphlets. All these works seemed to those who were already Christians in the eyes of the world like a revelation imbued with the pure doctrine of Christ and the Church: " In preferring himself to God, and in refusing divine grace, man has truly lost himself. He is become, to the very roots of his will, the slave of the " me " that has

[43] Hallays, A., " Le Souvenir de Pascal à Port-Royal-de-Paris et à Port-Royal-des-Champs," in *L'Illustration*, No. 4189, 81st year, June 16, 1923, pp. 609, 610.
Consult on the same subject Hallays, A., *Le Pélerinage de Port-Royal*, Perrin, Paris, 1909.
[44] Schimmelpenninck, M. A., *Select Memoirs of Port-Royal, op. cit.*, v. 1, 182.
[45] Sainte-Beuve, Ch. A., *Port-Royal, op. cit.*, v. 2, 388 (note).

hypnotized him. Nor can the return to God consist purely and simply in superimposing a supernatural life over his natural one: life cannot be joined to death. He must, literally, be converted." [46]

By the light of this judgment taken from the best work we possess on Pascal's thought, one can measure the incomprehension of certain Roman Catholic opponents. It is thus J. Laferrière concluded his Study of Jean Duvergier de Hauranne, abbé de Saint Cyran, by the assertion that "reactionary against the spirit of his century, Saint Cyran went beyond reasonable limits. . . . His intervention resulted in curbing the magnificent momentum of religious reform which, in the first half of the seventeenth century, was the cause of a resurgence of new sources of Christian life." [47] No doubt that is true, if one interprets the Christian life according to the Molinists instead of construing it according to the Bible! Neither is it a matter of condemning Jansenism for not having succeeded " in finding a stable balance " between grace and nature, as does Blondel. [48] That is, properly speaking, misconstruing the principal teaching of Jansenism! Finally, what is there to be said about judgments such as those of Henri Bremond on what he calls " the beautiful Phariseeism of the great Arnauld "? The latter, according to Bremond, " unites in his own person, incarnates all the truths of religious falsehood so that none can help us to understand what is *not* religious life as well as he can." [49] And how could one dare assert that for Arnauld it is " the religious man " that seems of little consequence?

We do want to avoid controversy in these pages: we cannot, however, let pass, without denouncing them, assertions such as the following: " To put things crudely " — and how crudely! — Arnauld " does not exist. A syllogistic machine, a theological machine gun in perpetual motion, but absolutely denuded of inner life. Religiously and morally, Arnauld must have died in his fifteenth year." [50] It is because of such intolerance that there continues to be, even in our days, such an immense wastage of Christian energy. The crushing of the Jansenists

[46] Boutroux, E., *Pascal,* Collection " *Les grands écrivains de la France,*" 10th ed., Hachette, Paris, p. 21.

[47] Laferrière, Abbé J., *Etude sur Jean Duvergier de Hauranne, Abbé de Saint Cyran, op. cit.,* p. 206.

[48] Blondel, M., " Le Jansénisme et l'anti-Jansénisme de Pascal," in *Revue de métaphysique et de morale,* 30th year, No. 2, April–June, 1923, pp. 142, 143.

[49] Bremond, H., *Histoire littéraire du sentiment religieux en France, op. cit.,* v. 4, 292.

[50] *Ibid.,* v. 4, 286.

meant the draining of a great reservoir of Christian charity, and was, in our opinion, partly responsible for many of the miseries of eighteenth-century France and of the bloody Revolution into which the nation was plunged. It has now been well established by scholars such as Daniel Mornet in his *Origines intellectuelles de la Révolution Française* (1933) that French Revolutionary thought was first directed against the Church.

The truth about Jansenist teaching is that it was concerned in particular with the capital problem which was being debated between Saint Augustine and Pelagius and this problem involves the cornerstone of Christianity: in his *Augustinus,* Jansen asks himself what connection exists between the nature of man before sin, and the nature of man after redemption. Pelagius identifies these two natures. Saint Augustine and Jansen set them in sharp contrast. What the *Augustinus* presents essentially is the historical and theological justification for that opposition.

Pascal will pursue the task by transposing the debate onto psychological grounds, and will ask the Gospel to resolve it: " We cannot comprehend either the glorious state of Adam, or the nature of his sin, or the transmission of it to us; those are things that happened in the state of a nature entirely different from our own, and which is beyond our present capacity to grasp.

" All that is useless for us in solving our problem; and all that we need to know is that we are poor wretches, corrupt, apart from God, but saved by Jesus Christ." [51]

By this evangelical simplicity, we realize that Blaise Pascal had adopted as his own the method favored by Jansen. " There are two methods," writes the author of the *Augustinus,* " of penetrating the mysteries that divine revelation offers our faith: one is that of human reasoning; that method is followed by the philosophers and is subject to many errors; the other springs from the burning charity by which the heart of man is purified and is illumined so that it may penetrate the secrets of God which are contained in the husk of the Scriptures and in the revealed principles themselves." [52]

In Jansen's view, theology should be defined as " the knowledge of the Scriptures and of the Councils and the Fathers of the Church." [53] He makes certain that the maxims presented in his treatise " are from

[51] *Pensées,* Section viii, Fr. 560, *Œuvres,* v. 14, 8, 9.

[52] *Augustinus,* v. 2, *Liber prœmialis,* c. 7, quoted by Lhermet, J., *op. cit.,* p. 85.

[53] Gazier, A., *Histoire générale du mouvement Janséniste, op. cit.,* p. 41.

Saint Augustine who had enough eloquence to express his sentiments." [54] The title of the voluminous manuscript which he had ordered his testamentary executors to have printed explains this clearly. Translated, it reads: The *Augustinus* of Jansen, Bishop of Ypres, or the doctrine of Saint Augustine touching the state of human nature when still whole, touching its sickness and its healing, against the Pelagians and the Semi-Pelagians of Marseilles. [55]

The *Augustinus* includes three parts: The first treats of the Pelagian heresy, and of its new form, Semi-Christianity, Semi-Pelagianism; it frequently attacks Molina, Lessius, and the Quietists. The second gives the doctrine of Saint Augustine on the state of innocent nature, the state of fallen nature, and the state of pure nature, which state, according to Jansen, is impossible. The author follows Saint Augustine very closely in his description of the state of man after the Fall, showing his guilt and his wretchedness. In the words of Saint Augustine himself, he explains the nature of original sin and its fatal consequences. All men are born in sin and are by nature children of wrath; all are guilty in the eyes of God, and they remain under the domination of sin, seated in the gloom of the shadow and of death, until the grace of the Saviour draws them out and up to the Light. It is He, the Resurrection and the Life, who calls them from that state of spiritual death, and delivers them from it.

At this point, Jansen discusses the diverse arguments relative to an irresistible and indefectible grace. The third part of his work treats of the healing of man; of his re-establishment, through grace, in the liberty which he had lost through sin; and of free and absolute predestination.

The background of the doctrine is not, as is often said, a dark and terrible God: it is a Heavenly Father intervening in a folly of charity, with an intervention as illogical as it is undeserved, to save the slaves born of sin from the deluge of corruption, or the flames of Gehenna, in order to restore them as His children, the redeemed of the Son, the sanctuaries of the Holy Spirit.

The center of the doctrine is the Pauline and Augustinian notion of grace, conceived as the all-powerful operation of God on the inmost part of the soul, or rather as the transfusion of divine will into human

[54] *Augustinus, Liber præmialis*, c. 29, quoted by Gazier, A., *op. cit.*, v. 1, 5.

[55] Michaut, G., in *Les Epoques de la Pensée de Pascal*, Fontemoing, Paris, 1902, *op. cit.*, reproduced in appendix form, a good summary of the *Augustinus* first appeared in the *Histoire générale du Jansénisme* [by Dom Gerberon], Lorme, Amsterdam, 1700.

will, or, as the momentary participation by certain men in the life of God. To defend this *self-efficient grace* is, on the one hand, to explain why the gift of such grace is necessary to human nature, and how that gift agrees either with the free will of the created, or with the justice and goodness of the Creator. On the other hand, it is to determine what the moral life of the Christian, and the conduct of Christian society, can and should be, under the action of such grace: here is the whole program of the Port-Royal theology.[56]

The direct outcome of this doctrine is the Christian morality. This morality resolves itself into two essential points in which is summarized the practice of the Scriptures: to strip the old man, and to reclothe the new man. In effect, man is in need of effective grace because he is fallen, as we learn from the Scriptures, and his downfall is all the greater by reason of his original exaltation. Moreover, it is necessary to consider the nature of mankind as an essence, a unit, an integer, an entity; hence, in its fall, it involves all mankind in a *massa perditionis*. And it is this fallen nature having become hereditary which incites man to seek, not only to *use* the good things created by God, but to *enjoy them*. Whence comes concupiscence, a vainglorious delectation, that engenders ignorance. Thus ignorance and concupiscence are both born of a depravation of the will itself, which they increase in their turn in a vicious circle that forces man to live on the lowest plane.

How, therefore, in these conditions, can the remedy be left to the discretion of the patient? What must be reached and restored is that same will from which proceeds consent. The obstacle to be eliminated is that which the corrupt will places before a redemption offered to all. And it is this obstacle which in the last analysis only God can remove at his pleasure. The predestination of the elect shows itself henceforward to be pure mercy. Its secret remains hidden in the depths of a supreme wisdom unfathomable by ours. May God's *love* make us want the remedy by making us love it, following the formula of the Fathers of the Church, namely, that God loves Himself in the predilection which He shows toward His own. Seen from this standpoint, the love of God is the necessary and sufficient condition for virtue; and the love for God, which is in itself only a reflection of the first, is the sum of all Christian morality. Everything comes back to charity, and it is by charity that all our

[56] Laporte, J., " Pascal et la doctrine de Port-Royal," in *Revue de métaphysique et de morale*, 30th year, No. 2, April–June, 1923, p. 250. (An excellent study to which we owe much.)

antinomies are conciliated. Beyond Saint Augustine, it is the Saint Paul of I Cor., ch. 13, that is rediscovered by the Port-Royalists.

It is in this school, where his experience and his Biblical knowledge are verified and clarified, that Pascal was able to put the finishing touches to his great page on the three orders, that page which we have seen him laboriously seeking to formulate.[57]

Not only did Blaise Pascal change his name.[58] He sold his coach and his horses; his fine furniture and his silverware; yes, even his library. He kept only, with a few devotional books, his Saint Augustine and his Bible.[59]

[57] *Pensées*, Section xii, Fr. 793, *Œuvres*, v. **14**, 233.

[58] Jacqueline, at the conclusion of a letter to her brother, dated October 25, 1655, adds as a P.S.: " Let me know, please, if you are still Monsieur de Mons," *Œuvres*, v. **4**, 80.

[59] Petitot, H., *Pascal, sa vie religieuse et son Apologie du Christianisme*, Beauchesne, Paris, 1911, pp. 400, 401.

IX

The New Vista

" Behold, all things are become new."

—II Cor. 5:17

On this day of January, 1655,[1] Monsieur de Saci, in the company of his secretary, the delightful Fontaine, was hurrying through the cold past the cottages of these " gentlemen." He had passed the farm, its outhouses and barns, casting a hurried glance toward the center of the courtyard, at the well for which Monsieur Pascal was proposing a contrivance which would permit a child of twelve to raise and lower two buckets, holding as much as nine ordinary buckets, one full, the other empty. What a genius, that Monsieur Pascal! Inwardly, Monsieur de Saci was rather intimidated at the thought of the interview for which his illustrious penitent had asked!

Laying his hand on the heavy banisters, Monsieur de Saci, accompanied by Fontaine, mounted the flight of steps. Nowadays, inscriptions over the doors designate the rooms formerly occupied by the famous recluses.[2] Our two visitors had no need then of any indication in order to recognize Pascal's room. The door was soon opened. The new inmate of Port-Royal was ready to do the honors in his " cell," which was badly lighted by a narrow window on this gray day. A welcoming fire crackled in the fireplace, and seats were invitingly arranged.

The civilities took little time: the participants had already met that morning at the five-o'clock service.[3] The communion of souls had been so close that, in the exaltation of divine service, the worshipers had

[1] We know that Pascal had reached the home of the Duc de Luynes, at Vaumurier, on January 7, 1655, and that he had retired to Port-Royal-des-Champs a few days later. As he had returned to Paris on January 21 to put his affairs in order, and had stayed there awhile, the interview between himself and Monsieur de Saci must be placed between these two dates.

[2] We use, for this reconstruction of the scene, the study, already quoted, by André Hallays, " Le Souvenir de Pascal à Port-Royal-de-Paris et à Port-Royal-des-Champs," in *L'Illustration,* No. 4189, 81st year, June 16, 1923, p. 610.

[3] Cf. *Lettre de Jacqueline,* January 25, *Œuvres,* v. 4, 66, 67.

been moved to tears during the singing of the hymns.[4] The passionate Pascal still seemed much agitated by his emotion. Monsieur de Saci spoke gravely. His voice was measured, restrained, it seemed, by the circumspection of a wholly Christian wisdom. Born for solitude, more inclined to meditate than to counsel, the nephew of Arnauld had accepted only under protest and in compliance with the expressed desire of Monsieur Singlin the responsibility of confessing the Nuns and Solitaries of Port-Royal-des-Champs.[5]

Monsieur de Saci had a very exalted conception of his duties as a priest. He felt that he was no longer his own master, that he belonged wholly to those whom God had put in his charge. Henceforward he had to be everything to all, and to maintain with each a spirit of union and of charity. His model in this relationship was Saint Paul. Following in the footsteps of this disciple of Jesus, he had become imbued with the spirit of Christian charity and understanding. Hence, his first counsel was that one should flee rash judgments and uncharitable interpretations of acts whose motives can only be surmised. One must, he used to say, avoid impertinent comment on people's behavior. He said that if there was one word of the Bible to be taken literally it was: " Judge not." What rashness to put an ugly interpretation upon actions which in themselves may be laudable! Only God is in a position to judge them with assurance. A sure source of peace, in Monsieur de Saci's opinion, is to forbid oneself all gossip, a fault which the Scriptures condemn vigorously. " It is the vice," he used to say, " which makes the most trouble in a group of people." Whereupon he would say that a person who repeats what he has been told is a child at the dribbling stage, and incapable of social relations.[6] One should also, according to him, avoid speculation which is motivated by nothing more than scientific curiosity. For example, the Solitaries used to discuss Descartes' animal machine. " What an idea of God's greatness it gives me," commented Monsieur de Saci, " to tell me that animals are nothing but clocks! "[7] And he would laugh gently at those novelties which his good sense disdained. Instinctively he mistrusted the demon of analysis which destroys every-

[4] Dom Clémencet, *op. cit.*, v. 1, Preface, xxiv.

[5] Since January, 1654, during Arnauld's absences. Cf. on this subject a letter from Mother Agnès, of December 3, 1654, in the Faugère edition, v. 1, 345.

Consult also in Port-Royal, by Sainte-Beuve, v. 2, 322, following the excellent pages on Monsieur de Saci (1613–1684).

[6] *Œuvres*, v. 4, 26, 27.

[7] *Œuvres*, v. 4, 28.

thing it touches. Of what use to ask: " What is that red color? What is it made of? " instead of admiring a painting?[8] Wisdom lies rather in recognizing the invisible in the visible. Is it to Monsieur de Saci that the Pascal of the *Pensées* owes in part his admirable use of figurative language? Yes and no, doubtless, since both learned it from the Bible. For Monsieur de Saci, however, the Biblical point of view is not complicated by scientific and philosophical scruples. It is entirely ingenuous.

Pascal's interlocutor owes this attitude to the *Augustinus:* he knows once and for all that, in order not to stray, one must follow what the Holy Scriptures reveal to us, what the Councils have defined, and what Saint Augustine, with the Holy Fathers who followed him, have taught us.[9] Let us immediately make it plain, in order to elucidate the development which follows, that it is this attitude which Monsieur de Saci is going to instill into Pascal. Not that it is new to the latter, but he has not yet achieved a pure and unalloyed conformance with it. It is by thus orienting his penitent's perspective that Monsieur de Saci will reveal to him what we called at the beginning of this chapter a new vista. At that period, it is not in fact a question of degree, in the thinking of Pascal; it is a question of an entirely different content. From a philosophical point of view, Pascal will rise to an evangelical point of view. Will he keep it? That is another matter. At this moment Blaise, still quickened by the illumination of November 23, 1654, but having relinquished none of his scientific concepts, is sitting opposite Monsieur de Saci — as he used to sit opposite Monsieur de Rebours. This time, however, he is ready to receive stronger meat; and Monsieur de Saci is not Monsieur de Rebours. This fact made clear, the contrast between the results of the two interviews will allow us to measure the distance which separates the Blaise of 1655 from the Blaise of 1648.

INTERVIEW WITH MONSIEUR DE SACI

We owe to the scholar Joseph Bédier the critical restoration of the text of Pascal's *Entretien avec Monsieur de Saci.*[10] For this masterly restoration, Bédier started from seven records of the interview — five

---

[8] *Œuvres*, v. 4, 29.

[9] According to the " Jansenist " analysis of Dom Gerberon, *Histoire générale du Jansénisme*, by M. l'Abbé (Dom Gerberon), Amsterdam, 1700, v. 1, 2–7, quoted by Michaut, G., *Les Epoques de la Pensée de Pascal*, 2d edition, revised and augmented, Fontemoing, Paris, 1902. Appendix III, A. *L'Augustinus*, p. 226.

[10] Bédier, J., *Etudes critiques*, Colin, Paris, 1903, " Etablissement d'un texte critique de l'Entretien de Pascal avec M. de Saci," pp. 19–80.

manuscript copies and two early editions. One of the seven sources which he used, source G (Gazier copy), reduces Monsieur de Saci's role in the interview to a minimum. Gazier has supposed that Fontaine was unable to resign himself to assigning an insignificant role to Monsieur de Saci. Whence comes the presumption that the words attributed by other sources to Monsieur de Saci might be additions made by the pious secretary.[11] We refer those of our readers who may be interested in the problem to the erudite account given by Joseph Bédier. We mention the problem here for another reason: in order to point out the fact that, at the time of the interview, it is Pascal who talks the most; Monsieur de Saci is mainly a listener. His acuteness consists precisely in making Pascal talk, and it is with justice that Monsieur de Saci has been characterized as a " Christian Socrates." This wise man understood that what Pascal needed, first and foremost, was to unburden himself, to get rid of a whole mass of human knowledge which seemed to Monsieur de Saci an obstacle obstructing clear vision. It is in the act of unburdening that the salutary aspect of confession appears, and Freud, from this point of view, will not invent anything new.

This Christian Socrates had the gift of persuading the penitents entrusted to him to open their hearts. The essential was to find the word that would unlock the heart. For Monsieur Champagne that word was " painting "; for Monsieur Hamon it was " medicine "; for the surgeon in the house it was, of course, " surgery." For Monsieur Pascal that word would be " philosophy." So Monsieur de Saci questioned Pascal on that subject. Pascal told him that the authors he had read most assiduously were Epictetus and Montaigne; and the penitent praised these two minds highly. Monsieur de Saci, who had always thought it best to read little of these authors, asked Monsieur Pascal to tell him all about them.[12]

What follows in the interview is so wonderful that we personally would not exchange the interview between Pascal and Monsieur de Saci for any dialogue of Plato's! The reader will, we hope, forgive this outburst of enthusiasm — Epictetus and Montaigne discussed by Pascal!

Epictetus is summarized in this formula: " There, sir, . . . are the high lights of that great mind who knew man's duties so well. I would dare to say that he would have deserved adoration had he known his own limitations, in as much as he would have had to be God to teach

<hr />

[11] *Ibid.*, pp. 22, 23.   [12] We follow the Bédier text, *op. cit.*, p. 53.

both one and the other to men. But, being only dust and ashes, he loses himself in the presumption of what man *can* do, after having so well understood what he *should* do." [13]

In contrast to Epictetus — and in these two attitudes Pascal summarizes, in a way, all human philosophies — there is Montaigne:

" Now for Montaigne, of whom, sir, you wish me to speak also. Being born in a Christian State, he makes profession of the Catholic faith, and in that there is nothing strange. . . . He has such a universal and general doubt of all things that this doubt, when he doubts, is carried away by itself, and doubting even that he doubts, his uncertainty revolves in a perpetual and ceaseless circle; he opposes both those who affirm that all is uncertain, and those who affirm that all is not, because he will not affirm anything. It is in this doubt that doubts itself, and in this ignorance that is ignorant of its own existence — which he calls his favorite state of mind — that the essence of his philosophy lies, a philosophy that he has been unable to express in any positive terms. For, if he says that he doubts, he betrays himself, by affirming at least that he doubts; and this being strictly against his intention, he has only been able to explain to himself by a question; so that, not wanting to say, ' I do not know,' he asks, ' What do I know? ' He makes this his motto, inscribing it under the scales which, when they weigh contradictions, remain in a perfect state of balance." [14]

Pascal, who, in the past, has abundantly fed on Montaigne, explains to Monsieur de Saci the insensate destruction of all that men accept as most assured by the author of the *Essais*. As Montaigne weighs the difficulties, they grow; the obscurities are multiplied by commentaries, and the light is dispelled as soon as it appears. The favorite procedures of Montaigne are condemned by Pascal: mockery, amusing paradoxes, the caprice that is charmed by contradictions, a freedom of mind so grounded in universal doubt that it is strengthened equally by its triumph and its defeat. And Pascal appropriates the argument of the *Apologie de Raimond Sebond* in which, castigating all theological doctrines, Montaigne shows, with an incomparable virtuosity, the utter helplessness of human reason. Pascal reveals in his exposition the completeness of Montaigne's work of demolition. This work includes all the sciences, even to the certainty of axioms. By the end of this merciless analysis, reason, robbed of faith, has sunk to the point where Montaigne relegates man to the level of the beasts.

[13] *Ibid.*, p. 55.   [14] *Ibid.*, pp. 57, 58.

It is with a saintly impatience, one may well guess, that Monsieur de Saci follows the subtleties of a philosopher of whom Saint Augustine would say that he pricks and tears himself with thorns of his own making. However, this Christian Socrates, who is a courteous gentleman, discreetly congratulates his interlocutor: Montaigne would be the beneficiary if he were known only through the reports made of his writings by Monsieur Pascal! With roguish finesse Monsieur de Saci adds: " I certainly think that this man [Montaigne] had a good mind; but I am not sure that you don't lend him a rather better one than he had, by the logical sequence that you give so cleverly to his principles." [15] To tell the truth, Montaigne lacks all those qualities which, according to the rule of Saint Augustine, we should seek in our reading. He very visibly lacks humility and piety. His only aim is to live pleasantly, and he reaffirms the doctrine of the Academicians, whose folly in the light of Christian doctrines has been denounced once and for all by Saint Augustine. In all he says, Montaigne puts faith aside. Very well, those of us who have faith should put aside all he says!

And here, on the lips of Monsieur de Saci, is a declaration which seems to us to summarize eloquently Pascal's page on the three orders which probably took its ultimate form at that time: " You are fortunate, sir, to have risen above those men whom we call Doctors, who are exhilarated by the intoxication of knowledge, but whose hearts are empty of truth." [16] The spiritual director calls once more upon the testimony of Saint Augustine, who followed the teachings of Saint Paul and the admonitions of his own experience. And now it is Pascal's turn, as a courteous gentleman, to return the compliment just made him by his confessor: " If I know Montaigne, you, in even greater measure, know Saint Augustine! "

However edified Pascal may be, he cannot resist developing a subject of which he is full. He continues, showing how Montaigne's superb reason is blunted by his own weapons; he professes a practical morality, desiring, above all else, peace of mind; he passes lightly over all subjects for fear of being disturbed by what he might find if he probed deeply into them,[17] and he follows the customs of the country for the sake of peace. Since custom rules, in the state of ignorance in which we have our being, Montaigne climbs onto his horse's back without stopping to ask himself whether it might not be his horse who should be climbing onto his back! Montaigne disciplines himself and avoids certain vices

[15] *Ibid.,* p. 66.   [16] *Ibid.,* p. 67.   [17] *Ibid.,* p. 70.

for the sake of his own tranquillity; he even keeps faith with the marriage vows because of the worries which follow infidelity! His rule of action is governed by convenience and the desire for a quiet life. Rejecting the arduous virtues of the Stoics, he welcomes the blithe and pleasant virtues of the skeptics, confident that ignorance and incuriosity are two soft pillows for " a sagacious head."

Thus starting from two specific cases — that of Epictetus and that of Montaigne — in which the two most famous philosophies of the world are summarized, the two poles of human thought opposed, Pascal, henceforth, in the *Entretien*, builds his case on the ruins of these two systems. The mistakes of both systems seem to him to proceed from a common source, i.e., the ignorance of the fact that man now is different from man at the time of the creation. It is thus that Epictetus, recognizing the signs of man's earlier greatness and ignorant of his corruption, considered human nature as sound and without need of healing, thus placing man in a proudly independent position; on the other hand, Montaigne, aware of man's present misery and ignorant of his earlier dignity, considers human nature as necessarily imperfect and incurable. Despairing of ever attaining perfection, he falls into an extreme laxity. We must consider these two states of nature *together* if we are to arrive at the truth. If we consider one state apart from the other, we shall inevitably become either conceited or lazy.

It would seem that, one system being right where the other is wrong, it would be sufficient to combine them in order to attain the truth; but, as Pascal shows, they can no more go together, because of their oppositions, than they can subsist alone because of their faults. And, like a fencer who lunges for a direct hit, Pascal concludes: Epictetus and Montaigne clash and utterly destroy each other in order to make room for the blinding truth of the Gospel.

In this superior order are resolved all paradoxes, " those opposites which were incompatible in human doctrines. And the reason is that these men who are wise in the ways of the world place the opposites in one and the same subject [i.e., human nature]; for the one attributed greatness to nature, and the other, weakness to that same nature, which could not be; whereas faith teaches us to place them in different subjects: all that is infirm belonging to nature, all that is powerful belonging to grace. There lies the new and surprising union which God alone could teach, and which He alone could form, and which is but an image and a reflection of the ineffable union of two natures in the single person of a Man-God." [18] Is it a question of the grandeur of man? What grandeur could man imagine which could compare with the promises of the Gospel? Those same promises constitute the price of the death of a God. That death, on the other hand, has been the cure for the real weakness of sin, of which natural man has only a vague notion when he is brought to consider the infirmity which is in him. Thus, all find in the Gospel " more than they have desired; and what is most wonderful is that those find themselves in agreement who could not agree on an infinitely lower plane." [19] We recognize once more the language of the page on the three orders now completed in the mind of Pascal. In the order of charity, all paradoxes are resolved in the Light which is called Jesus Christ. It is really this Light which drew Pascal out of the contradictions of the order of minds. And so that Blaise should not become vainglorious because of his liberation, a terribly dark spiritual night preceded the glorious dawn.

Henceforward, it was for Monsieur de Saci to draw the practical conclusions from the masterly account given by Pascal. First of all, the director compared Pascal to those clever physicians who know how to draw healing medicine from poison. The reading of such authors is useful, certainly, but only on condition that the reader remains uncontaminated by it. Many run the risk of being wrongly influenced by it. One must not expose oneself to it lightly. The account of the *Entretien* has already insisted upon this fact: everything that Pascal has demonstrated to Monsieur de Saci has already been discovered by the latter in Saint Augustine. Pascal finds this surprising, because, he says, he never saw those ideas expressed anywhere; he had worked them out in his own mind. Monsieur de Saci replies, " As for us, we are used to seeing them on all sides in our books." [20] Monsieur de Saci and the gentlemen of Port-Royal kept repeating this to Pascal, and it is in view of this fact that they made him go deeper into Saint Augustine and the Bible. Their teaching corroborated the revelation of November 23, 1654, and sorted the dross from the gold in Pascal's store of knowledge.

FINAL FORMULATION OF THE THREE ORDERS

Pascal's philosophy reaches its apogee at the moment in which he realizes that it is henceforth useless. This is, in our opinion, the answer to the indictment pronounced on Pascal's philosophy in general and on

[18] *Ibid.*, pp. 75, 76.   [19] *Ibid.*, pp. 76, 77.   [20] *Ibid.*, p. 53.

the page of the three orders in particular, by Professor Clement C. J. Webb, of Oxford. The author analyzes, for instance, the disparateness upon which Pascal insists as existing between bodies (i.e., material things) and *pensées* (i.e., facts of consciousness), and shows that in reality such a distinction is familiar to Descartes' contemporaries; but under the term " bodies," Webb notes that Pascal puts side by side the life of captains and kings, and the glory thereto belonging. Pascal speaks of the " firmament, the stars, the earth and *its kingdoms* " as belonging to the material order. . . . A confusion creeps in.[21] Continuing in this manner, the scholarly Oriel Professor of Philosophy has no difficulty in concluding: " If we try to think out this *Pensée* of Pascal's, it turns out so unsatisfactory and inconsistent that one may excuse Voltaire for . . . calling it in his disrespectful way a *galimatias*." [22] Dr. Webb continues in the same vein: " Even if we look at his reflections upon the profound religious experience which he unquestionably enjoyed, Pascal was not a great philosopher." [23] I am afraid that here, in spite of the reservations which we shall make in a moment, a misunderstanding falsifies the whole discussion.

We have sufficiently explained, in these pages, the immense labor of exact science and thought which finally brought Pascal to the writing of the pages on the three orders. To cite only one example, the mathematician who wrote the *Potestatum numericarum summa*,[24] where he treated of the summation of numerical powers, on the one hand brought out the wonderful connection which nature, lover of unity, establishes between things which are in appearance the most contradictory; while on the other hand he showed in a treatise on numbers that the lower orders are of no value, and may therefore be disregarded. For him, then, the infinity of mathematics was mathematically comparable to the infinity of the soul. " Studying the ' vast triangled heart of man,' he discovered a calculus of infinities more useful, perhaps, than that of Newton or Leibnitz. He found his certitude in that mysterious region where, as he says, geometrical propositions become emotions, like memory and joy." [25]

[21] Webb, C. C. J., *Pascal's Philosophy of Religion,* at the Clarendon Press, Oxford, 1929, pp. 108, 109.
[22] *Ibid.*, p. 110.
[23] *Ibid.*, p. 114.
[24] *Œuvres*, v. 3, 341 *sq.*
[25] Bishop, M., *Pascal: The Life of Genius, op. cit.*, p. 101. Consult also on this point n. 1 by Brunschvicg, in *Œuvres*, v. 13, 22.

Pascal thus based his conception of the universe on a philosophy which is far from being, as is too often the case, merely pious oratorical unction. His solid speculation is built on scientific facts properly analyzed and arranged. So it is that, at the moment of the sigh, which Paul Valéry says marks the end of all true reflection, the divine Light greets the valiant seeker. And the seeker then rediscovers the powerful poetry of the prophets of Israel in which to exalt his vision of the world.

And what do the Voltaires and the Webbs do with this page? Let the latter forgive us, but, as Molière would say, what was he doing in that galley ship? They do with it what the Latin of the Scholastics did of yore with those Hebraic ideas of religious objects, objects of flesh and blood too lifelike to be called metaphysical in the Greek and Occidental meaning of the word. To illustrate: imagine the myth of Hercules and Cacus being subjected to the steam roller and put through the mill of some college form master concerned with philosophical minutiae!

Try to outstrip the mathematician who, in his own field, outstripped Europe, inspired Leibnitz, and conceived solutions so difficult that sometimes the method had to be abandoned! Follow the physicist through those chapters which he wrote in direct contact with the most audaciously invented and the most strictly conducted experiment; emulate the thinker who discusses a question inch by inch; but, pray, allow the man, who at last emerges into the Light, to exalt his view of things in the language of a great religious poet if he has the gift to do so. Do not quibble, just at the moment when you are beginning to understand him, over the exactitude and pertinence of the terms he uses. What we are denouncing here is a confusion of jurisdiction.

The misunderstanding is all the more distressing in view of the fact that Pascal himself, in that same page on the three orders, warned us of it: each order has its greatness which is its own: " All the glory of worldly greatness has no splendor in the eyes of those who are occupied in the things of the mind; while the greatness of men of mind is invisible to Kings, rich men, military chieftains, and all those who are great after the manner of the flesh. The greatness of that sole true wisdom which has its source in God is in its turn invisible to both the men of the flesh and those of mind. Here we have three orders which differ in kind from one another. . . . The men of great genius have their dominion — the saints have their empire." There is the greatness of Archimedes, and there is the greatness of Jesus. It would have been of no use to Archimedes to be a prince. Just so " it is very idle to be offended by the low estate in which Jesus Christ was born, as though this low estate were low in the same order of values to which belongs the kind of greatness which he came to display." [26] Do the commentators on the page of the three orders not realize that these same considerations apply to Pascal?

At the moment in which Pascal emerges into the order of charity, into the order of Jesus, to judge him by the criterion of the order of Archimedes, in which he did in fact shine brightly, is to fall into the very error against which he warned us. We grant our honorable adversaries this: the Christian who has just been promoted to the supernatural order will have to descend again into the lists in which a cause is fought for; into a world of freethinkers who must be made aware of the problem of destiny. . . . Then he will have to argue. In so doing he will delve into the immense store of knowledge in which the profane rubs elbows with the sacred. He must choose words and arguments that will enable him to meet his adversaries on the latter's own ground. Perhaps such a trial may even cause the herald, who accepts it as a duty, occasionally to lose the order of his choosing. It is so hard for mortal man to emulate the Angel who touches without being touched! Finally, Pascal's prose, nourished by the Bible, will become more and more forceful and persuasive and will often reach that true eloquence which mocks at eloquence, but which is definitely no longer the language of the scholar or technician. From then on his opponents will have an opportunity to cavil over unimportant and irrelevant details, and they will not fail to do it.

Having attained at Port-Royal, that stronghold of the Scriptures, the day after November 23, 1654, the order of charity, Pascal turns from human philosophies; his viewpoint becomes essentially evangelical, Christocentric, and his language becomes that of a prophet or a Biblical mystic. Lhermet pointed out [27] that even the philosophical and profane part of the *Pensées* is dependent on Scriptural teaching: in it Pascal reveals his conviction that the Bible contains the " true wisdom " and the " essential truth," measure of all other. It is to the Bible that he refers all philosophical opinions in order to untangle the true from the false. The analysis which he has just made, first singly, and then conjointly, of the representative thoughts of Epictetus and of Montaigne, in order to bring out their characteristics and to reduce them to their

[26] Here we follow the same translation used by Webb, *op. cit.*, pp. 104–107.
[27] Lhermet, J., *Pascal et la Bible, op. cit.*, p. 494.

constituent elements, perfectly illustrates his new way of seeing things. It is in reality the Bible that intervenes, in the *Entretien avec Monsieur de Saci,* to eliminate or relegate to a lower plane all the falsities and insufficiencies of these systems, or to point out and conserve all that conforms to the revealed truth. Even the so-called philosophical part of the *Pensées,* in appearance profane, is fundamentally composed of elements borrowed from the Bible. Even in the nature of the freethinker, in whom he awakens disquieting thoughts, Pascal finds, in accordance with his readings of Scripture, the traces of lost grace. Those whom he disposes to receive the Light have only to " offer themselves to inspiration through humility " and the voice of God within — what Pascal calls " the heart " — alone will henceforth sound.[28]

One will better understand Pascal's new vista if one recognizes with Charles Hodge that " Theology is not Philosophy. It does not assume to discover truth, or to reconcile what it teaches as true with all other truths. Its province is simply to state what God has revealed in His Word, and to vindicate those statements as far as possible from misconceptions and objections." [29] It is because people have failed to appreciate fully the process of evolution which Pascal underwent that so many impertinent remarks have been made about his skepticism. In 1828 Victor Cousin claimed that Pascal showed himself to be a skeptic, even in Port-Royal and in Bossut editions of his works; in 1842, the critic asserts that the autograph manuscript displays even more skepticism, and his later studies strengthened this conviction. From all sides readers protested: What! Pascal a skeptic! " But pray, gentlemen, let us make ourselves clear," Victor Cousin elucidates in a preface dated December 15, 1844. " I could not have said that Pascal was a religious skeptic; that would really have been too great an absurdity; far from that, Pascal believed in Christianity with all his heart. . . . The essential point of the question must be stated and kept in view: Pascal is a philosophical, not a religious, skeptic; and it is because he is skeptical in philosophy that he is so strongly attached to religion, as to the only haven, the last resource of humanity in the helplessness of reason, in the ruin of all natural truth among men. That is what I said, what I maintain, what emerges irresistibly from the text for any sincere and attentive mind." [30]

[28] Mauriac, F., *Pascal et sa sœur Jacqueline,* Hachette, Paris, 1931, p. 162.

[29] Hodge, Ch., *Systematic Theology,* Wm. B. Eerdmans Publishing Co., Grand Rapids, Mich., 1940, v. 1, 535.

[30] Cousin, V., *Des Pensées de Pascal,* Ladrange, Paris, 1844, Foreword, p. v.

Important reserve not to be forgotten, made by the man to whom falls the honor of having presented to the Académie Française the report on the necessity of making a new edition of the *Pensées* based on the original manuscript.[31]

BUILDING ON THE ROCK

Freed from human philosophies, Pascal turns toward the Jansenist doctrine precisely because the system known as Augustinianism remained fundamentally the same throughout the ages in its basic principles, and in these principles the essentials of the Christian doctrine are summarized.[32] The theology of Saint Augustine represents in Pascal's view " the purest and most wholesome theology." [33] He knows it because his own experience has suggested that theology to him; because his Port-Royalist friends were constantly inspired by it; because he himself, Blaise, tested the doctrine by a long process of personal verification in which he took " as a standard of measurement the successive Tradition of this doctrine from the time of Christ to our own days." [34] Thus it appeared to him that this doctrine was " founded on the unshakable cornerstone of the Gospel of the Holy Scriptures " interpreted, not according to his own mind, but according to the best Tradition of the Church.[35] So Jansen was to his mind " the authentic interpreter of Christ." His *Augustinus* appeared to be " the epitome of restored Christianity," [36] of a veritable Christianity in its purity and its integrity. Considered in this light and compared with Jansen's work, the *Summa theologica* of Saint Thomas Aquinas appeared no more than an " eclectic manual with philosophical and pagan tendencies." [37] Jansen, after having tasted Saint Augustine, had found himself, in his own words, " a little disgusted by Saint Thomas." [38]

In freeing himself from the human philosophies, however, Pascal is

[31] Cousin, V., *Rapport de l'Académie Française sur la nécessité d'une nouvelle édition des Pensées de Pascal,* read at the sessions of April, May, June, July, and August 1, 1842, reproduced in *Des Pensées de Pascal, op. cit.,* pp. 1–251.

[32] Boettner, L., *The Reformed Doctrine of Predestination,* 5th ed., Wm. B. Eerdmans Publishing Co., Grand Rapids, Mich., 1941, p. 339.

[33] *Œuvres,* v. 11, 295 (*Ecrits et fragments de Pascal sur la grâce*).

[34] *Œuvres,* v. 11, 142 (*ibid.*).

[35] *Ibid.*

[36] *Introduction aux* Pensées *de Pascal,* III, i, *L'Augustinus, Œuvres,* v. 12, lxxxii.

[37] *Ibid.*

[38] Letter of March 5, 1621, in Sainte-Beuve, *Port-Royal,* 5th ed., v. 1, 293 (quoted by Brunschvicg, *Œuvres,* v. 12, lxxxii).

in no sense doing a *volte-face*. He rises infinitely higher; but he continues to be himself, to remain faithful to the best in that self, in his methods, and in his intelligence. Only, henceforth he dedicates himself, his reasoning, all that he is, to the task of construing life's meaning according to God: " Submission and a prudent use of reason, in which real Christianity consists "; [39] submission to the Scriptures which are divine, and superior to the arguments of a reason adaptable to everything." [40] Certainly as divine teaching, the Scripture is beyond us; but it is presented to us under the form of a human document, and thus allows for reasoning. This reasoning by a Heaven-illumined intelligence about a Heaven-inspired wisdom liberates religion from philosophy and renders useless a purely human philosophy which is but paste in the presence of the divine diamond. Pascal's new vista opens upon an eternal, a whole truth, given once for all. " The unity of this truth will not fit in the logical frame borrowed by the Middle Ages from Aristotle's tradition." [41]

Henceforward, the Biblical layman who has drawn his faith from the very wellsprings of revelation and inspiration, in the sacred texts and in the writings of the Fathers of the Church, will deny that Aristotle's commentaries have anything at all to do either with the scientific truth derived from experience alone in the order of mind, or with the religious truth which is to be found in the Bible, in the life of the Church, and in the miraculous intervention of God — in the deep and only real drama of the universe which takes place in the order of charity.

SCHOLASTICISM DISCARDED

In the school of Jansen, Pascal will not cease to combat the errors of scholasticism — a scholasticism which more and more ignores the monuments of divine revelation and of the true ecclesiastical tradition. Against scholasticism, and in agreement with his Port-Royalist friends, he will state the principle of positive theology which implies a knowledge of the Old and New Testaments, and interpretation of the Fathers, and loyalty to the decisions of the Councils. In this field Arnauld seems to offer the most complete and considered expression of the common opinion: the Port-Royalists " are unanimous in rejecting the scholastic

[39] *Pensées*, Section iv, Fr. 269, *Œuvres*, v. **13,** 197.
[40] *Pensées*, Section viii, Fr. 561, *Œuvres*, v. **14,** 11.
[41] *Introduction à la seconde série des Œuvres de Pascal, Œuvres*, v. **4,** xli.

method, in so far as it attempts to submit theology to human reasoning, whereas they trust only the authority of tradition, considered as the infallible guardian and interpreter of the Revelation of Christ." [42] Pascal shares these sentiments.[43] The Catholic Victor Giraud concludes from his own investigations that Pascal " seems to have read little and even rather scorned the Scholastics." [44] In this Giraud confirms the testimony of Madame Périer, Pascal's older sister.

This testimony, at this point, constitutes a valuable elaboration of the reasons which Pascal puts forward to explain his turning away from metaphysical proofs: he said that they were too far removed from man's ordinary reasoning; not everyone, according to him, was capable of metaphysical speculation; and even if a man did show himself capable of following the reasoning, the proofs could be valid only for a few moments; an hour later those involved " knew not what to say of it, and thought they had been misled."

But Pascal's essential motive, from which all others originated, was *" that such proofs can lead us only to a speculative knowledge of God; and to know God thus was not to know Him at all."* [45] The italics are ours. And may we also remind the reader that in studying the Preface to

[42] Laporte, J., " Pascal et la doctrine de Port-Royal," in *Revue de métaphysique et de morale*, 30th year, No. 2, April–June, 1923, p. 249.

[43] Beginning with those of Jansen himself, remarks Victor Giraud, *Pascal, l'homme, l'œuvre, l'influence*, Fontemoing, Paris, 1905, p. 121.

Giraud refers one here to *L'Augustinus, Liber præmialis*, cap. iii, col. 5; cap. vi, col. 11; cap. viii, col. 19; etc., and to Monchamp, *Histoire du cartésianisme en Belgique*, Bruxelles, 1886, pp. 100–103.

[44] Giraud, V., *Pascal, l'homme, l'œuvre, l'influence, op. cit.*, p. 120. The controversy on this subject, however, remains considerable on the Catholic side.

Bremond, H., " Pascal et les mystiques," *Revue de Paris*, 1923, p. 743, objects that Pascal is not sufficiently scholastic: " The heart may have its reasons, indeed, but reason knows them perfectly well, since it alone found them, since they are reasons only in as far as reason made them its own."

According to Maritain, J., " Pascal apologiste," *La Revue hebdomadaire*, No. 28, 32d year, July 14, 1923, 198, " in our day a strange thing has happened to Pascal, which shows cruelly how far wrong he went in thinking that he could do without metaphysical wisdom. He has fallen into the hands of the philosophers." What would Professor Clement C. J. Webb, of Oxford, have to say to this?

Maritain regrets Pascal's lack of comprehension of scholastics all the more because Pascal's idea " of faith and of the act of faith has its roots in Thomism." (*Ibid.*, 188.)

According to Father Petitot, in *Revue des jeunes*, May 10, 1923, the incurable mistrust which Pascal shows toward metaphysics appears to be the root of all his weakness, etc.

[45] *Œuvres*, v. 1, 76.

the *Traité du vide* we were careful to note in Pascal's point of view an attitude of long standing that was destined to become a constant in his thinking. In those powerful passages that we subsequently studied, we saw Pascal denounce the double corruption which, on the one hand, substitutes authority for reason in profane matters, and threatens thus to destroy the efforts of generations; and which, on the other hand, substitutes reason for authority in sacred matters and threatens to smother under rash novelties that which is in the order of the eternal.[46] Already at the time of the Jansenist quickening, in a sort of introduction to the Forton case, which showed her brother's conviction at that time, Madame Périer noted that " although he made no special study of scholasticism, he nevertheless was not ignorant of the decisions of the Church against the heresies which have been invented by human subtlety and waywardness; and it was against these sorts of inquiries that he was the most active." [47]

The scruples of a Christian united with those of the scholar in Pascal to challenge any attempt to apply the dogma to the physical realism of Aristotle. The impersonal and abstract deism in which Descartes' geometrical method ended was scarcely better in his eyes than atheism pure and simple, since the true God is the Living God of the Bible who is known only through Jesus, the Mediator.[48] In his denunciation of scholasticism on the morrow of November 23, 1654, Pascal would seem to go even farther than Arnauld, Nicole, and Jansen himself. For them the content of the original Thomism was not contradictory to the teachings of Saint Paul and Saint Augustine. In this Pascal was in accord with the Port-Royalists, but going beyond their considerations, he already saw that, as a result of Saint Thomas' teaching, the balance between the spirit and the letter would be destroyed in favor of the letter. Finally would come the vehement protest of the *Lettres Provinciales;* and the Jesuit of the fifth *Provinciale* would be able to say to the questioner: " I have already noted several times that you are not a good scholastic." [49] Exactly! And Pascal would immediately classify himself as one of those who treat of " positive " [50] theology, that is to say, strictly Biblical theology. This conviction would be so substantially established

---

[46] *Œuvres,* v. 2, 133.
[47] *Œuvres,* v. 1, 60.
[48] Cf. *Œuvres,* v. 14, 11, nn. 1, 2.
[49] *Cinquième Provinciale,* v. 4, 315.
[50] *Ibid.,* v. 4, 316.

that in his " Vindication of Christianity " the author of the *Pensées* would admit to the freethinker that he could offer no rational proofs. His frankness on this point constitutes for Julien Benda [51] Pascal's great originality.

" LE MYSTÈRE DE JÉSUS "

Increasingly aware of the inadequacy of his own thinking, Pascal will summarize wisdom in these three words: *listening to God*. From the peak to which he has attained, enriched by an experience which Fire has purified, we find him Biblical to the very depths of his being, preserved from a comfortable religion of compromise. Moreover, the new vista offers him as a reward the view of a height which will satisfy him forever. It is with joy that he hears Monsieur de Saci's constant exhortation to the gentlemen of Port-Royal: " A drop of water that is not sufficient to a man is sufficient to a bird. The sacred waters are peculiar in that they are proportional, adapted to each: a lamb may walk in them, and yet they are deep enough to allow an elephant to swim." [52]

To listen to God is to ask of His Word all the nourishment needed by the soul. It is to enclose oneself in a sacred solitude in which the essence of faith will make itself felt in the heart: *the mystery of Jesus, Mediator*. Nor should this subject become the occasion for human reasoning which would endeavor to give a rational form to the theology of mediation. Let us not imagine that such a mystery can be integrated into our science, " reveal itself in the rational light of unity rediscovered." [53] To Pascal, Jesus appears differently: isolated on earth, alone in His agony, according to the light of his order. It is a solitary Jesus who speaks to the solitary, and animates him with a sacred passion.

And it is this passion which vibrates in the passage on the three orders, and animates all the material in it. Here we find ourselves for once in agreement with Professor Clement C. J. Webb: what counts is the passion behind the passage, that passage in which he found it so hard to discover on analysis (!!) an intelligible argument; it is, according to him, " that passionate love for God revealed in Jesus Christ, whom by

[51] Benda, J., " Pascal et le ' libertin,' " *La Revue hebdomadaire,* No. 28, 32d year, July 14, 1923, p. 237.

[52] Fontaine, *Mémoires pour servir à l'histoire de Port-Royal,* Utrecht, 1736, v. I, 366.

[53] Brunschvicg, L., " La Solitude de Pascal," *Revue de métaphysique et de morale,* 30th year, No. 2, April–June, 1923, p. 174.

this very capacity to seek him he knows he has already found; whom he hears speaking to him." [54] It is with the *Mystère de Jésus* that what we have called Pascal's new vista finally opens.

Every month at Port-Royal, the faithful were invited to concentrate their meditations on a certain subject. With his brothers, Pascal was invited to direct his thoughts toward the mystery of the death of our Lord. Once again, as at the beginning of the ever memorable night, Pascal watches with Jesus; but henceforth it is in a mystic union with his beloved Saviour whom he knows and who knows him. [55]

In His passion Jesus suffers the torments imposed on Him by men; but in the agony He suffers the torments of His own imposing. . . .

Jesus seeks at least some consolation from His three dearest friends; and they sleep; He asks them to endure with Him a little, and they neglect Him entirely, having so little compassion that it could not for a moment keep them from their sleep. And thus Jesus was abandoned, alone, before the wrath of God. . . .

He suffers this pain and this loneliness in the horror of the night.

I think Jesus complained only this once; but then He complained as though He could not contain His excessive pain: My soul is sorrowful even unto death. . . .

Jesus will be in agony until the end of the world; we must not sleep during all that time. . . .

Jesus being in agony and in the greatest woes, let us pray longer.

We implore God's mercy, not that He should allow us peace in our vices, but that He should deliver us from them.

If God were to give us masters with His own Hand, oh! how gladly we should obey them! Necessity and events are indubitably such masters.

— " Console thyself; thou wouldst not be seeking Me, hadst thou not already found Me.

" I was thinking of thee in My agony; I have shed such and such drops of blood for thee. . . .

[54] Webb, C. C. J., *Pascal's Philosophy of Religion, op. cit.*, p. 110.

[55] The *Mystère de Jésus* is one of the purest jewels of the religious literature of all time. We give only a few extracts from it here. The complete text can be found in *Œuvres*, v. 13, 434–440.

" Let thyself be led by My precepts. . . .

" Thy conversion 'tis My concern; fear not, and pray with confidence, as for Me.

" I am present with thee by My Word in Scripture, by My Spirit in the Church. . . .

" I am more of a friend to thee than such a one and such a one, for I have done more for thee than they and they would not suffer what I have suffered for thee and they would not die for thee in the time of thy infidelities and cruelties, as I have done and as I am ready to do and as I do in My elect and in the Holy Sacrament.

" If thou knewest thy sins, thou wouldst lose heart."

— " Then shall I lose it, Lord, for I believe in their wickedness upon Thy assurance."

— " Nay, for I, through whom thou art taught this, can cure thee, and what I tell thee is a sign that I wish to heal thee. As thou shalt expiate them, shalt thou know them, and it shall be said unto thee: ' See what sins of thine are remitted.' Do thou then penitence for thy hidden sins and for the hidden wickedness of those thou knowest."

— " Lord, I give Thee all."

Upon reaching such heights of the *Mystère de Jésus*, we would not draw nigh, for the place whereon we stand is holy ground.

Let us simply say that every Christian should pause on Good Friday to read the few pages of the *Mystère* and then keep all these things and ponder them in his heart. For, in the words of Blaise Pascal, " Jesus will be in agony until the end of the world; we must not sleep during all that time."

X

Not Peace, But a Sword

" Think not that I am come to send peace on earth: I came not to send peace, but a sword."

—*Matt. 10:34*

Y ou, who are young, you should do something! "

At this direct appeal from Arnauld, the gentlemen of Port-Royal turned toward Blaise Pascal.

On the horizon of the sanctuary, on this January day, 1656, black clouds had gathered; the storm grumbled, threatening. From Rome, from the Court, from the Sorbonne, the news had been so bad that Arnauld, the head of the Jansenists, followed by his faithful lieutenant Nicole, had hastened to the sanctuary to hide; and to seek advice about the decisions to be made. The Jesuits had already obtained a condemnation of Arnauld in the Sorbonne by 124 votes to 71. There had been 15 abstentions. A second and final judgment was to be pronounced in which the whole Jansenist party ran the risk of falling under the blow of the verdict of heresy, in the person of their head. " Heresy, in the seventeenth century, meant every sort of legal and economic disability; it meant social outlawry, and a death illuminated by hell's fires." [1]

UNITING JUSTICE AND FORCE

The situation was certainly desperate.

Pressed to give an opinion in a circle in which popular excitement was at its height, Arnauld had drawn up a new statement of the facts. He had just finished reading it. In the painful silence which had followed, Arnauld had sought in vain for an approving look. Heads were lowered.

Arnauld had understood:

" I see that you find my statement poor and I think you are right."

It was then that he turned to Pascal in the appeal we just quoted.

[1] Bishop, M., *Pascal:* The Life of Genius, *op. cit.,* p. 219.

Pascal had come to Port-Royal to seek peace. He knew this peace had been threatened for years. He had been able to believe, however, that the increasing disagreements since the publication of the *Augustinus* in 1640 by Jansen would end by resolving themselves in accordance with the justice which is essentially spiritual. Alas, we find in a fragment [2] of the *Pensées* the admission that this spiritual quality is misused freely: " It has been put into the hands of force; and thus that is just, which one is forced to observe. Thence comes the right of the sword, for the sword gives true right; otherwise one would see violence on one side and justice on the other." According to Pascal, justice and force must always be together. To effect this, there are but two ways: " Make that which is just strong, or that which is strong just." [3]

When that which is strong seems to him unjust, then the champion puts at the service of that which is just his might — of which he is still partly unconscious: the might of a pen, by which the author of the *Lettres Provinciales* will at the same time become the creator of French prose. But, at the point we have reached, Pascal, in making himself the champion of justice, acts first and foremost as a disciple of Jesus Christ: only " the disciples of Jesus Christ are in the order of truly universal justice, and, carrying their vision into the infinite, judge all things by an infallible rule, by the justice of God." [4]

GRACE VERSUS FREE WILL

The profound disagreement between the Jesuits and the Jansenists is already familiar to us. We need only recall here that which is necessary to an understanding of the *Provinciales*. It concerns essentially the relationship between the grace of God and the free will of man. Should we " rely on ourselves, feel the slightest confidence, even for the most immediate future, in our own capabilities "? [5] How can we, since, after the Fall, as sons of Adam we are incapable of keeping the commandments unless the all-powerful and necessary grace of God come to our aid through the Son and the Holy Spirit? For that is what the Scriptures

[2] *Pensées,* Section xiv, Fr. 878, *Œuvres,* v. **14,** 316.

[3] *Pensées,* Section v, Fr. 298, *Œuvres,* v. **13,** 224.

[4] Filleau de la Chaise, *Discours sur les* Pensées *de Pascal,* ed. Giraud, V., Bossard, Paris, 1922, p. 80.

[5] Brunschvicg, L., *Le Génie de Pascal,* Collection " *Maîtres des littératures,*" Rieder, Paris, 1932; new ed. 1937, p. 194. We recommend this book which is enriched by 60 valuable illustrations.

teach, and the Church whose history "should properly be called the history of truth." [6] In opposition to this teaching is constantly propounded the fact of man's free will. How reconcile this human factor with the divine factor?

But, first of all, is it necessary to make this reconciliation? Bossuet himself will deny it, trusting to God in this emergency. And Pascal will extol the beauty of the state of the Church "when it is supported by God alone." [7] Having meditated upon I Cor. 1:25, he will glorify the folly of the conception of original sin. This folly, he will say, is wiser than all the wisdom of men, *sapientus est hominibus;* and he will bring out its irrational character: "You need not reproach me for the lack of reason in this doctrine, since I give it without reason." [8]

STATEMENT OF PAUL ON THE SUBJECT

The Living God of history is the One who said to Moses: *I will have mercy on whom I will have mercy; and I will shew mercy to whom I will shew mercy;* [9] it is the One who said to Pharaoh: *To this purpose have I raised thee, that I may shew my power in thee, and that my name may be declared throughout all the earth.*[10] "Therefore," adds Saint Paul, "he hath mercy on whom he will; and whom he will, he hardeneth. Thou wilt say therefore to me: Why does he then find fault? for who resisteth his will? O man, who art thou that repliest against God? Shall the thing formed say to him that formed it: Why hast thou made me thus? Or hath not the potter power over the clay, of the same lump, to make one vessel unto honour, and another unto dishonour? "[11] Although implied in the Pauline message of Rom., ch. 9, the thesis of the double, that is to say, supralapsarian, predestination was to be early discarded in favor of a predestination which relied on divine prescience. Thus began a process which tended to make, as rationally and reasonably as possible, God subordinate to man.

[6] *Pensées,* Section xiv, Fr. 858, *Œuvres,* v. **14,** 301.
[7] *Pensées,* Section xiv, Fr. 861, *Œuvres,* v. **14,** 303.
[8] *Pensées,* Section vii, Fr. 445, *Œuvres,* v. **13,** 358.
[9] Rom. 9:15.
[10] Rom. 9:17.
[11] Rom. 9:18–21.

Upon arriving in Rome at the beginning of the fifth century, Pelagius was shocked by the low tone of morality prevalent. What could be done about it? The weak were making an excuse of their weakness. To Pelagius it seemed evident that the Augustinian doctrine of the total depravity of man could not meet the existing situation. What man wanted, Pelagius thought, was a firm conscience of his actual powers, an exaltation of his will. " If I ought, I can," such became the message of this well-meaning reformer, in opposition to Augustine's, which stressed the bondage of will in man's fallen nature.

As is often the case, expediency brought Pelagius to a new formulation of Biblical doctrine. In the long run, he came to deny original sin. In his eyes, there no longer existed such a thing as man's inability to meet the requirements of righteousness. What then was the need for the Gospel of the new birth and regeneration by the Holy Spirit? What was the need for Jesus Christ Himself? Augustine objected to the new tenets, and Pelagius, after some hesitation, came to another compromise: he maintained the availability of divine aid, of grace offered. But according to this " Semi-Pelagianism," in the work of salvation initiative had passed to man.

Pelagius had maintained that man, created good, retained the power to remain so by his own efforts, and that he was directly responsible for his salvation. Augustine opposed him with Paul's doctrine, which, however, he reduced to a single infralapsarian decree: that is to say, the election followed rather than preceded the Fall, whereas from the supralapsarian point of view the contrary is true. The idea of God's discriminating between the elect and the reproved was relegated to the background. Saint Augustine's interpretation constitutes a mean between supralapsarianism, in which God discriminates absolutely, and universalism, in which He does not discriminate at all.

THE THOMISTS

The Church had supported Saint Augustine against Pelagius. Thomas Aquinas, the illustrious Dominican Doctor of the thirteenth century, involved himself farther in compromise by granting more leeway to free will. We must, in all justice, point out that this concession was made possible in his thinking by the exaltation of the merits acquired by all men through the sacrifice of the Saviour. From then on, they were the beneficiaries of a " sufficient grace," which undoubtedly would not in itself allow them someday to see God face to face; but which, if one opened one's heart to it, would save the just man from the Eternal Fire. The word "sufficient," an inadequate translation of *sufficiens*, led to many misunderstandings, and the author of the *Provinciales* took full advantage of his opportunity by pointing out the irritating effects of such subtleties on a simple conscience enlightened by the Bible. This so-called " sufficient " grace was sufficient in the sense that it gave to the will the feeling of right and wrong, and made it capable of doing good if it so wishes. Otherwise this " sufficient " grace was not sufficient for total salvation. For this it was necessary to have, in addition, the grace essential to salvation, the efficacious and irresistible grace which God grants only to those whom He chooses. This grace, as long as it lasted, supported human weakness, and invested with sanctity him who received it. It did not, however, give to the saint a guarantee of continuation. It could be withdrawn without the just man's being entirely abandoned by God; in such a case the just man would retain a " proximate power " of accomplishing God's commandments, " power which he may use badly or well according to his will, incomplete power, power of trial, not power of salvation."[12] A disturbing analysis, but who would dare to look the fearful mystery in the face? The only thing the Thomists know is that God wants the salvation of all men. All have the means of being saved. The decree of predestination can be executed only through the efficiency of created freedom. To know more about it, we should have to penetrate the secret of the divine wish. It is, finally, the triumphant resurrection which will, supernaturally, end the reformation undertaken by God, in the history of a sinning humanity; and it is this ending which is already seen by God alone, who is beyond time.

On one point, however, the Thomists seemed to add to the strictness of Saint Augustine. They wanted to explain that strictness by a system of physical premonition, by which God Himself imprints upon the will the impulse which determines it. Consequently, the Thomists were accused of introducing fatalism, of making God the author of sin, of representing Him as a tyrant who, after having forbidden crime to man, makes its commission a necessity and then punishes him for being a criminal. In their turn the Thomists accused their opponents of trans-

[12] Strowski, F., *Pascal et son temps, op. cit.*, v. 3, 37.

ferring to mortals a power which belongs only to God, and of renewing the mistakes made by Pelagius in destroying the power of grace and making man responsible for his own salvation.[13] In other words the Thomists, desiring absolute conciliation, had incurred the displeasure of the very people they had hoped to conciliate, which seems to be the lot of all conciliators. The reproaches heaped upon them by the Franciscans, however, as to a strictness even greater than that of Saint Augustine, were the very cause of their being akin to the Port-Royalists, and to Pascal himself, who, as we have seen, was generally on his guard against scholasticism. It is thus, in our opinion, that one can best explain the apparent contradiction of a Pascal disciple and critic of Saint Thomas, i.e., disciple in the matter of grace, critic in the matter of scholastics.

CALVINISM

Let us now try to define Pascal's attitude toward the Calvinists. The latter have dropped all the subtle distinctions between the Fathers and the Doctors of the Church, to return to the lofty Biblical doctrine.

It will not be amiss to state at this point that Calvin's *Institution de la Religion Chrestienne* is not, as generally believed (by people who criticized without having even read the *Institutes*), a treatise on predestination. Predestination occupies only one chapter (VIII) in seventeen; and this section, like the rest, we may well believe, is but a part of what Calvin gleaned from the Book. What he attempted to do is essentially this: after careful consideration of the Bible's teachings and the writings of the Fathers and Doctors of the Church, he set out to disentangle the Holy Writ from the tremendous mass of literature that threatened to engulf it. The purpose was to release the pure crystal of Biblical truth from the common alloy that had been heaped upon it, and to mount every gem in the restored Scriptural framework to which it belonged. Let God alone speak to us, this was the cry of the Reformer who had just parted ways with other masters of the Renaissance on the fundamental issue of a basic difference in their conception of human nature. How can two walk together unless they be agreed? The Renaissance was pagan at heart.

According to the Calvinists, sin touched the very depths of human nature. It extended to the whole of it, permeating the whole range of human experience. The faculties of emotion, intelligence, and will power

[13] *Œuvres de Blaise Pascal*, chez Detune, at The Hague, 1779, 5 v., v. 1, 52.

were affected by it in their best impulses and in their apparently most disinterested achievements. The Westminster Confession of Faith, therefore, affirms that " when God converts a sinner, and translates him into the state of grace, he freeth him from his natural bondage under sin, and, by his grace alone, enables him freely to will and to do that which is spiritually good; yet so as that, by reason of his remaining corruption, he does not perfectly, nor only, will that which is good, but doth also will that which is evil.

" The will of man is made perfectly and immutably free to good alone, in the state of glory only." [The Confession of Faith, ix. 4, 5.] Only those whom God has predestined unto life are called out of that state of sin and death, by his Word and Spirit.

According to the supralapsarian view, as we have said, the choice even preceded the Fall, in God's eternal design. Whence the five points of Calvinism: total inability, unconditional election, limited atonement, irresistible — i.e., efficacious — grace, and perseverance of the saints. Note, however, that in practice the Bible appears infralapsarian; that, in the famous Westminster Assembly, the Prolocutor Twiss was one of the few supralapsarians; that the majority were on the infralapsarian side, and that the great majority of Calvinists followed that majority. It is, however, in their most intransigent aspects that the Calvinists appeared to the Port-Royalists and to Pascal. The same goes for the Lutherans who, however, were not to follow for long the intransigence of the author of *De Servo arbitrio*. To tell the truth, Calvinists and Lutherans were fused in the term heretics, and no word caused Port-Royal to tremble more. Speaking on the distinction of the Fact and the Doctrine, *le fait et le droit* — terms which we will explain shortly — Arnauld, in his second *Lettre à un duc et pair de France*, will dwell upon the " entirely catholic spirit " by which the Jansenists are motivated, although their adversaries seek to dishonor them in the Church pulpits " by coupling them constantly with Luther and Calvin, whose heresies they detest." [14]

THE JESUITS

Let us now deal with these adversaries, the Jesuits. They followed, in the matter of grace, the doctrine of Louis Molina, a Spanish Jesuit (1535–1600) who, abandoning the doctrine of Saint Augustine, had

[14] *Extrait de la seconde lettre de Monsieur Arnauld à un duc et pair de France, Œuvres, v. 4, 93.*

tried to liberate free will from the tyranny of grace. His book on the subject had appeared in 1588, under the title *De Concorda liberi arbitrii cum gratiae donis, divina praescienta, providentia, praedestinatione et reprobatione, ad nonnullos primae partis D. Thomas articulos.* This important work had been followed by a *Casuistry* in three volumes in folio, *De Justitia et jure* (1593).

In order to appreciate the efforts of Molina and of the Jesuits, to whom we should like to give the credit which is their due, one must, we believe, remember the efforts of Erasmus. This Prince of Humanists had hoped for a sufficiently solid and self-assured Catholicism to tolerate the greatest freedom of thought in every other field. In this Roman Catholicism which the Protestants called paganism, Erasmus recognized " the most enviable form of a civilization in that it combined all that one could dream of superior culture and delicate pleasures, elegance, and freedom of mind, with powers of saintliness." [15] It was to advance this attempt to Latinize culture that the Jesuits, whose Doctors were to dominate the Council of Trent, organized classical teaching. By their efforts, the study of Latin and of Greek was to become the object of secular culture while the Holy Scriptures, reserved for higher schools of theology, would reach the faithful in measured doses through the catechism and the parochial schools.

The efforts of Erasmus, and of the Jesuits, were to suffer a double blow. In translating the Bible, Luther substituted the German language for Latin; in making it the chief reading of the nation, he opposed to the Occidental Latin and Greek cultures a book which was the product of an ancient Oriental civilization. There was more: he opposed to a culture based on the exaltation of the human a life of humility which expected everything of the Divine. Let us note that the Humanist Calvin deserted the Renaissance for the Reformation when he realized the incompatibility of the two movements. Their conceptions of human nature were entirely different: in one, man was exalted; in the other, he abased himself before God.

The Molinists dreamed of reconciling the human and the Divine — rather, of flattering the human in order to facilitate the instilling of the Divine, of a Divine placed on a level with common sense. Facilitate, that is their watchword, and Christian charity makes it our duty to consider the order of Jesuits, taken as a whole, as being sincere in their intention. It is necessary, from their viewpoint, to satisfy the protests

[15] Poizat, A., *La Civilisation et ses tournants*, Albin Michel, Paris, 1936, p. 294.

of common sense against the concept of predestination, against the concept which is the inevitable consequence of the idea of sovereign and undeserved grace. According to the Jesuits, one must detach morality, and consequently theology, from the state of soul imposed by the severe Augustinian doctrine. One must be complaisant toward human nature. The Jesuits " are equally afraid of rebuffing nature by any strangeness of dogma or by the rigor of obligations. They bring religion down to earth so that access to it may be easy." [16] Following Molina, the Jesuits accept the " sufficient grace " of the Thomists, and teach that, used in saintly spirit and with prayer, it entitles man to the " efficacious grace " which, by the simultaneous concurrence of the will of the interested party and the grace of God, guarantees salvation. Thus human free will is entirely rehabilitated.

In order to understand even better the Molinist viewpoint, let us consider the example of a pious humanist like Saint François de Sales. A witness in Paris of the wars of religion, and of their excesses, a witness in Padua, where he studied, of the miseries of free thinking, he felt the absolute necessity of re-establishing order where anarchy had reigned all too long! But he came up against the problems of grace and predestination. During six long weeks, he lived in anguish and the fear of Hell. It was then that, in the presence of God, he drew up an act of submission dictated by a hopeless love — an act of abandon. If I am to be damned, let me at least not damn Thy Holy Name! In this state of utter submission, he entered the church of Saint-Etienne-du-Mont, in Paris, read a prayer (*Memorare*) and was assuaged. Saint François then accepted unconditionally God's good pleasure, and received a promise of eternal happiness, so that he may be able to sing the divine praises. That took place when, in 1586, he was nineteen. Then and there he resolutely became a Molinist.[17] He was outstanding for his fervent piety and his culture, gifts which he consecrated to spiritual guidance. The *Introduction à la vie dévote* put individual advice at the disposal of everyone, the essential idea of the work being that it is necessary to reconcile worldliness and piety. This is to be done by means of lay devotees who will vanquish one by one the prejudices born of an exaggerated piety.[18]

[16] Havet, E., *Les* Provinciales *de Pascal*, new edition with introduction and comments, Delagrave, Paris, 1885, 2 v., v. 1, xlii.

[17] Feugère, A., *Le Mouvement religieux dans la littérature du XVIIe siècle*, Boivin, Paris, 1938 [" Saint François de Sales," ch. 1, 11–25], p. 15.

[18] Concerning Saint François de Sales, consult Rebelliau, A., *Histoire de la langue et de la littérature française* (published under the direction of Petit de Julleville), v.

THE JANSENISTS

According to Brunschvicg, the difference between the Jesuits and those who are called Jansenists is, in brief, this: " The Jansenists accept the alternative which the Jesuits refuse to see, and they refuse to see it in order the better to reserve for their penitents ' the broad way,' as though unconsciousness of sin could become an excuse for it." [19] What interests the Jansenists is God's Truth, and not the inconveniences which this may entail for the worldly. If the worldly are to make the law in this matter, what shall we see? Let us read this terrible passage of Pascal's — no doubt a rough copy written during the battle: " Sinners purified without penitence, just men justified without charity, all Christians without the grace of Jesus Christ, God without power over the will of man, predestination without mystery, redemption without certainty." [20] We must admit this man knows his Bible!

Is it to be the broad way or the narrow way? The alternative had been propounded, in 1643, by the great Arnauld in his treatise *La fréquente communion,* in which the learned theologian warned the faithful against a sacrament which must not be desecrated, and that may be taken only after a laborious preparation. The Jesuits who favored " frequent communion " felt that the treatise was directed against them, and Father Nouet, in their name, made such a bitter reply that he was obliged to retract what he had said. Encouraged by this victory, Arnauld published, in 1644, an Apology for Jansen which was vigorously disputed.

THE FIVE PROPOSITIONS

After having studied the *Augustinus* at great length, Nicolas Cornet, who was syndic of the Sorbonne, summarized its contents, in 1649, in the five following propositions, which were submitted to Rome, and condemned, in 1653, by Pope Innocent X:

1. There are certain divine commandments which it is impossible for the just to obey as they have not sufficient grace.

3, 355–405; Strowski, F., *St. François de Sales,* new ed., Plon, Paris, 1928; Trochu, Francis, *Saint François de Sales.* Now being published (v. 1, *La Vocation, le Sacerdoce,* was published by Vitte, in 1942), Vincent, F., *St. François de Sales directeur d'âmes,* Beauchesne, Paris, 1932.

[19] Brunschvicg, L., *Pascal, op. cit.,* p. 40.

[20] *Pensées,* Section xiv, Fr. 884 (cf. variant, 884²), *Œuvres,* v. 14, 319, 320.

2. In the state of fallen nature, there can be no resistance to interior grace.

3. For merit or demerit after the Fall, it is not necessary for man to have interior liberty; it is enough that he be exempt from external constraint.

4. The Semi-Pelagians admit the necessity of an interior and prevenient grace, even for the first act of grace; but they were heretical in their view that this grace could be controlled by human will.

5. It is Semi-Pelagian heresy to say that Christ died for all men without exception.[21]

Port-Royal greeted the condemnation with silence. Arnauld, without protesting publicly, was content to say that he too, with Rome, condemned the condemned propositions — a matter of *Doctrine;* but that those propositions were not in the *Augustinus* — a matter of *Fact.*

According to certain authors, that was showing singular obstinacy. " I think," wrote Bossuet, " that the five propositions are in Jansen and that they are the soul of his book." And Fénelon: " The pretended matter of fact is a gross and horrible illusion. No one really disputes the true meaning of the text of Jansen. Never was text clearer." [22] In our day, Bremond echoes them: " Everyone today agrees to recognize in them the quintessence of Jansenism." [23] Brunschvicg, however, admits that if the first and last propositions show some resemblance to the *Augustinus,* the three intermediate propositions justify the Jansenist protests.[24] However it may be — and we shall soon have a chance to present the " Jansenist " side of the question — the Jesuits' triumph was expressed in an almanac of questionable taste, called *La Déroute et la confusion des Jansénistes* (The Rout and confusion of the Jansenists). Monsieur de Saci answered it by the mediocre verses of his *Enluminures du fameux almanach des Jésuits* (Illuminations of the famous Jesuit

[21] Cf. *Œuvres,* v. 4, 86, five propositions declared heretical in an official decree, on March 31, 1653, by Pope Innocent X, according to the official translation which appeared at Vitré's in 1655.

[22] Hémon, F., *Cours de littérature, Pascal,* p. 6, quoted by Desgranges, Ch. M., *Histoire illustrée de la littérature française,* 3d ed., Hatier, Paris, 1917, pp. 359, 360, n. 1.

[23] Bremond, H., *Histoire littéraire du sentiment religieux en France, op. cit.,* v. 4, 119.

[24] *Œuvres,* v. 4, lxvii.

almanac). This last publication was of January, 1654. At this period, we remember, Pascal was still writing and announcing mathematical memoirs.

As early as 1652, the abbé de Bourzeis published a work called *Saint Augustin victorieux de Calvin et de Molina, ou réfutation d'un livre intitulé Le Secret du Jansénisme* (Saint Augustine victorious over Calvin and Molina, or refutation of a book entitled The Secret of Jansenism). This abbot lived with the Duke of Liancourt, a man of great piety whose granddaughter was being brought up in the Port-Royal monastery. Already suspected, because of this fact, of being a Jansenist, the Duke found himself further compromised by his guest's publication.[25] On the 31st of January, 1655, he was refused absolution. This time Arnauld came out of his self-imposed silence and, on February 24, published his *Lettre à une personne de condition* (Letter to a person of distinction). Retorts from the other camp then inspired the great Arnauld to write his *Lettre à un duc et pair de France* (Letter to a duke and peer of France), which was really a whole book. He had devoted several months to it — from February to July! This book was immediately referred to the syndic of the Faculty of Theology, and they nominated an examining commission.

Meanwhile, the hostility to the Jansenists was becoming more pronounced in the Sorbonne. Ironically enough, Saint Augustine himself suffered because of it. For a year, in the prayer books printed by Rocolet, a Palace bookdealer, Saint Augustine's name had been omitted from the list of the Doctors of the Church in the litanies for the saints. Could it be by accident? or by design? The Molinists, it is said, more especially the monks, would like to abolish the doctrine of Saint Augustine. At this point the Augustinian Fathers of the Faubourg Saint-Germain brought a suit against Rocolet at the Châtelet; Rocolet sued his printer; the latter, his proofreader.[26] Finally everything was arranged and Saint Augustine was re-instated! In Rome the representatives of his order were less well treated. A monk who was friendly toward the Augustinians was chased out of the city " for no other reason than the Jesuits' hatred for the supporters of Saint Augustine's doctrine, and the affection which

[25] *Œuvres*, v. 4, 89.
[26] Jovy, E., *Etudes pascaliennes*, Vrin, Paris, 1936, 9 v., v. 9, " Le Journal de M. de Saint-Gilles," 36 (August 2, 1655). (Ernest Jovy having died on April 29, 1933, Saintville, trustee for his papers, edited this volume and will publish what he can extract from the papers of this Pascalian scholar.)

this Pope bears these [Jesuit] Fathers, of whom one is his confessor and the other his preacher." [27] Could it be that the Jesuits had influenced the sovereign Pontiff?

THE JESUITS' INFLUENCE IN ROME

Let us refer to an eyewitness' criticism of the preceding reports. But first let us make it clear to our readers that Monsieur de Saint-Gilles, author of the *Journal* whence we drew the reports, speaks for Port-Royal. He will be assisted in his last hour by Monsieur de Saci. It is precisely this situation which prepares us to understand the conflicts which are becoming increasingly grave in the souls of the Jansenists, on the subject of the Pope, the earthly vicar of Jesus Christ. They would certainly like him to be " infallible in the faith," [28] but what if the Jesuits misinform him? What is to become of a Blaise Pascal, caught between the Scriptures and a pontifical authority which has been led into error? This situation causes Pascal great anguish and distress. It is with a deep sympathy that one reads in the *Pensées* this fragment: " Each time the Jesuits deceive [*surprendront*] the Pope, all Christendom is guilty of perjury. The Pope is very easily deceived because he is very busy and because of the confidence he has in the Jesuits; and the Jesuits are very capable of deceiving him because of their desire to injure their opponents." [29]

It is a fact that Port-Royal and Arnauld are slandered in Rome. A young Italian, Cosimo Brunetti, having seen the Pope and spoken to him of Arnauld, " noticed that much ill had been said of him "; he testifies " that Arnauld is considered in that country [i.e., Rome] as a faction and party leader . . . , and as the author and instigator of all the trouble, a quarrelsome and seditious man; that it is thought that only at P[ort]-R[oyal] are there tempters, . . . and that it is reported to the Pope that if the P[ort]-R[oyal] were to be destroyed, Jansenism would go too." [30] It is thus vain at the time of the " Sorbonne affair " [31] for Arnauld to profess an ardent Catholic faith. In his *Lettre à une per-*

---

[27] *Ibid.*, p. 37.

[28] *Pensées*, Section xiv, Fr. 880, *Œuvres*, v. **14,** 318.

[29] *Pensées*, Section xiv, Fr. 882, *Œuvres*, v. **14,** 319.

[30] Jovy, E., *Etudes pascaliennes, op. cit.,* v. **9,** 79 (December 28, 1655).

[31] The details of the " Sorbonne affair " which occasioned the *Provinciales* are given in Sainte-Beuve, *Port-Royal, op. cit.,* v. **3,** 7 *sq.,* and excellently summarized in Brunschvicg, L., *Œuvres,* v. **4,** 85 *sq.*

sonne de condition,[32] for instance, he affirms, in the name of those people who are being persecuted with such an unchristian animosity, his indefectible attachment " to the only saintly doctrine of the Catholic Apostolic and Roman Church, which the Popes and the Councils assure us to be contained in the works of the great Doctor of grace, Saint Augustine, so often approved and consecrated by the Fathers and the sovereign Pontiffs . . . that *nothing should be innovated; but the ancient Tradition should be kept.*" [33]

A SHOW OF AUTHORITY

Meanwhile, at the Sorbonne camps were forming. Since Arnauld supported the opinion that even Saint Peter himself once lacked necessary grace, was it not the Councils, nay, the Holy See itself, that this audacious man was trying to undermine? At the very least, this Jansenist theologian displayed poor taste and tactlessness. He also set an example of rebellion in a kingdom where memories of the civil war were still vivid. Already the general public was showing a tendency to be carried away by this fight for independence. During the course of numerous and tumultuous sessions, the Chancellor Séguier, using his right to preside over the sessions at the Sorbonne, appeared with a great show of ceremony. In his person, authority exerted its pressure. The Queen Mother, Anne of Austria, herself had decided to increase the block of forty mendicant friars who had already been recruited by the Jesuit forces in order to force a favorable vote. The use of the hourglass was introduced in order to limit Arnauld's speaking time; finally he was forbidden to speak at all. It was decidedly a reign of the arbitrary, in which the Crown joined forces with the Churchmen. In fact, are we not witnessing a kind of prelude to the French Revolution? Seen in this light, the Sorbonne affair becomes singularly moving, and Pascal's role in it, terribly impressive. But let us not anticipate ulterior developments.

Two questions were placed before the Court: Has Arnauld not erred in affirming that the five condemned propositions were not in Jansen? Has he not supported a heterodox opinion by declaring that, however just, Saint Peter lacked grace? We showed, at the beginning of this

[32] The complete title is *Lettre d'un Docteur de Sorbonne à une personne de condition: sur ce qui est arrivé depuis peu, dans une paroisse de Paris, à un seigneur de la cour,* 29 p. in quarto [Feb. 24, 1655].

[33] *Œuvres,* v. 4, 89, 90.

chapter, that Arnauld was condemned on the first point by 124 votes to 71. Fifteen abstained from voting. And it was then, as we said, when the Sorbonne was preparing to condemn him on the second point, enveloping Port-Royal with him under the same anathema of heresy, that Arnauld made his famous appeal to Pascal:

"You who are young, you should do something."

MOTIVES OF PASCAL'S INTERVENTION

Grasping the situation at a glance, Pascal will obey what seems to him to be the double command of good sense and probity. He understands the weakness of the " pretext for this persecution with which the Sorbonne and the royal authority seemed to associate themselves "; he foresees the consequences, terrible ones in his eyes, of this state of things: "spiritual life in France was threatened by authoritarian proceedings copied from the Inquisition, and all morality was threatened at the same time." [34]

For him it is not a matter of defending the doctrine summarized in the five famous propositions made up by Nicolas Cornet, and condemned by the Holy See which attributed them to Jansen. One day he will be able to defy the Jesuits to find in his writings the slightest sign of approbation of " those impious Propositions, which he hates with all his heart." [35] And what he will say can be subscribed to by the Arnaulds and the Nicoles, by the pretended Jansenists, and by Jansen himself, according to Laporte.

The latter adds that the group of theologians who are closely or distantly connected with Port-Royal " defended Jansen only by refusing to recognize the thesis of the *Augustinus* in the condemned *Propositions*." [36] Laporte shows here his agreement with Brunschvicg and with Gazier. In the view of the latter, Jansenism, as understood by the adversaries of the Port-Royalists, is nothing but a " phantom " [37] conceived for the needs of a cause. Brunschvicg points out that Pascal deserves the name " Jansenist " only in the historic sense, and in the

[34] *Introduction à la seconde série des Œuvres de Pascal* (v. 4-11), *Œuvres*, v. 4, xviii.

[35] In the seventeenth *Provinciale*. Affirmation corroborated by Fragments 850 and 929 in the *Pensées*.

[36] Laporte, J., " Pascal et la doctrine de Port-Royal," *Revue de métaphysique et de morale*, 30th year, No. 2, April–June, 1923, 247, 248.

[37] Gazier, A., *Histoire générale du mouvement Janséniste*, Champion, Paris, 1923, 2 v., v. 1, Avant-Propos, v.

sense that the Augustinianism of Jansen is for him " religion in its original purity and integrality." [38] The sacred dogma of the revelation and grace inherited by Pascal from Jansen and Saint Cyran via Port-Royal seem to the champion, according to the words of Victor Cousin, " to be the only source of truth, of virtue, and of merit," and constitute "the foundation and the bulwark of all others." [39]

If Pascal is preparing to intervene in the struggle, it is because he knows, as he will say in a fragment of the *Pensées,* that there exists " a false peace," the same peace that reigned on earth before the coming of Him who said: " I came to bring war," [40] and, to carry out that war: " I came to bring iron and fire." [41] *Not Peace, but the Sword!*

For Pascal, " the most cruel war that God can wage on man in this life is to leave him without that war which He came to bring." [42] All glory to God! It is from Him that we take our watchword, Him whom we should exalt. " All the heresies born in the bosom of Christianity, as all the systems conceived outside Christianity, end either by diminishing man or by diminishing God." [43]

Man must choose: Love God, or love thyself! All concrete will leads back to this alternative of first delectation. To be sure, in each case it is permissible to talk of liberty. If one finds one's delight in man, however, the liberty in question is only apparent; it is essentially " an abandonment to corrupt nature, the slavery of that sin which causes the Jesuits, like the Semi-Pelagians, to refuse to receive the tragic mystery." If, on the other hand, one finds one's delight in God, one attains that essential liberty which lies in the order of true and supernatural destiny. " Such liberty can only be the gift of the one efficacious Grace, of the Grace which must be renewed as must the act of will itself.

" The necessity for such an efficacious grace . . . shows that man can never have confidence in himself. . . . Never is it man's right to enslave God's grace. Man must abandon himself in order not to be abandoned." [44]

In this hour of crisis, Pascal revises his notions of slavery and liberty

---

[38] Brunschvicg, L., *Pascal, op. cit.,* p. 16.

[39] Cousin, V., *Jacqueline Pascal,* Didier, Paris [1844], ed. 1861, pp. 340, 341.

[40] One of innumerable examples of translations taken by Pascal from the Scriptures: here, Matt. 10:34.

[41] *Ibid.,* Luke 12:49.

[42] *Pensées,* Section vii, Fr. 498, *Œuvres,* 398, 399.

[43] Vinet, A., *Etudes sur Blaise Pascal,* Kohler, ed., 1936, *op. cit.,* p. 227.

[44] *Introduction à la seconde série des Œuvres de Pascal* (v. 4-11), *Œuvres,* lvi–lvii.

in the light of Holy Writ. After having read the sixth [c]
Epistle to the Romans, he summarizes the antithesis in
" The Jews, who were called to overcome nations and ki[r]
slaves of sin; and the Christians, whose vocation has been
to be subjects, are free children." [45] It creates a false feeling
that mania for reasoning which destroys all attachment to the documents and traditions of faith, that doctrine which constantly fluctuates
at the mercy of human caprices and continually seeks for novelties.
Neolatry is a form of idolatry. Thus, Molinism appeals to speculative
reason to explain the mystery of the Revelation! It is surely " the value
and authority of the Bible " which separates " the Jesuits and Pascal." [46]
More accurately, it is Jesus Christ who, for the Jesuits, in the words of
Isaiah [47] has been " a stone of stumbling." [48]

The *Ecrits et fragments sur la grâce* [49] reveal, better than anything
else of Pascal's, the profoundly Biblical reasons for his intervention.
They show us a Pascal in distress who gives the problem of grace first
place in his preoccupations. The *Premier Ecrit* constitutes a summary
exposition of the subject; the point in question is whether it is man's
will which determines the will of God, or whether it is God's will which is
" the master, the dominant, the source, the principle and the cause of
the other." [50] The author seeks what the Scriptures say on the subject.
Paul says, for instance, " And I live, now not I; but Christ liveth in
me." [51] He is alive in a different way, since he says again in several
places, " We were dead, and we are alive again," et cetera. *Thus two
truths exist together — note this admission of Pascal, student of the
Bible, who steadfastly holds two contradictory propositions, not wishing to sacrifice one for the other:* " I am alive. . . . I am not alive."
The fact is that Paul's life, although real, does not originally spring
from himself. He is only alive through Jesus Christ, the life of Christ is
the source of his life.[52] Thus Christ says of Himself, " It is not I who do

---

[45] *Pensées,* Section x, Fr. 671, *Œuvres,* v. 4, 107.
[46] Lhermet, J., *Pascal et la Bible, op. cit.,* p. 639.
[47] Isa. 8:14, " a stone of stumbling."
[48] *Pensées,* Section xiv, Fr. 926, *Œuvres,* v. 14, 360.
[49] *Œuvres,* v. 11, 97–205, of undeniable authenticity (v. 11, 97). Brunschvicg
gives us the sources (v. 11, 104–108) to which are added the texts commented or
translated by Pascal (v. 11, 108–127), among which a prominent position naturally
goes to Saint Augustine. The Scriptures are constantly quoted therein.
[50] *Œuvres,* v. 11, 129.
[51] Gal. 2:20.
[52] *Œuvres,* v. 11, 130.

...ks, but the Father which is in me," [53] which does not prevent him from saying, " The works which I have done." An annotation in the margin of the manuscript [54] shows Pascal's drawing an argument directly from this Biblical lesson: " Jesus Christ does not wish to be primary, and you do." The fact is that God Himself is the source of the works. In this sense the Prophet Isaiah was able to say, "Lord, . . . thou hast wrought all our works for us "; [55] and Saint Paul: " I have labored: . . . yet not I, but the grace of God with me." [56] And in Rom. 7:20, speaking of the involuntary movements of his will he says, " No more I . . . but sin that dwelleth in me." Henceforth we consider the dominant will as single, even though it may not be so, " because it is the only one to which the action can be wholly attributed and to which it cannot be refused." [57]

We have just found Pascal in the act of asking the Bible for the guidance he needs in the hour of conflict with the Molinists, guidance which he will naturally interpret according to Saint Augustine. In the final analysis, he continues, has God subjugated man's will, or has He submitted the use of His grace to man's free will? Three opinions are given here: the Calvinists establish absolute will in God, and their " terrible opinion " owns itself " injurious to God and unbearable to man "; [58] the Molinists, hating this awful opinion, have taken a diametrically opposed position whose effect is just as contrary. This opinion, in fact, makes common sense master of one's salvation or one's fall, by excluding from God all absolute will. It makes salvation and damnation proceed from human will, whereas for Calvin both proceed from divine will. Between these two extremes, Pascal reveals the wisdom of the disciples of Saint Augustine, which is rather that of the Fathers and of the whole Tradition, and hence that of the Church, namely, that " salvation springs from the will of God, and damnation from the will of man." [59]

In his appendix to the *Premier Ecrit sur la grâce*, Clémencet adds that, after having thus clarified his opinions and placed the truth of the Church in opposition to the falsehood of the Calvinists and the Moli-

[53] John 14:10.
[54] Note by Brunschvicg, *Œuvres*, v. 11, 130.
[55] Isa. 26:12.
[56] I Cor. 15:10.
[57] *Œuvres*, v. 11, 132.
[58] *Œuvres*, v. 11, 133.
[59] *Œuvres*, v. 11, 138.

nists, Pascal takes for his rule the continuing tradition of this doctrine from Jesus Christ to us: " He proposes to show us that we have learned it of our Fathers; they, from those who preceded them; those again, from others; they, from the ancient Fathers who held them from the Apostles, who received it immediately from Jesus Christ Himself, Who is the Truth." [60] So it is on the unshakable rock of the Gospel that this doctrine is founded; of the Holy Scriptures interpreted, not according to our own minds, but according to the Tradition. Henceforth Pascal is in a position to denounce the novelties which trap those who follow their own reason.

Pascal, in fact, before taking up any position, does over again, for his own satisfaction, the work done by those who have succeeded one another in the Church since the time of Christ, in order to preserve intact and to reveal the truth. From several texts of Saint Thomas, for instance, he is convinced of the Catholicism of the opinion supported against the Molinists according to which " sufficient grace is not given to all men, and that God does not wish to save all men." As for predestination, it is " without prevision of merit." [61]

Is it a question of interpreting a teaching of the Council of Trent? [62] Pascal calls upon the Scriptures. Is it a question of answering the proposition " that the Commandments are not impossible to the Just." The fervent reader of Ps. 118 remembers that the one who said, " Seek thy servant," [63] had, no doubt, " already been sought and found." [64] This echo from Le Mystère de Jésus completes our picture of Pascal's seeking guidance from the Bible, himself rich in Biblical experience.

The theologians debate the question as to whether or not Peter, who was a righteous man before God, ever lacked necessary grace. Meanwhile, Pascal reads his Bible and meditates on the fact of Peter's denial. He learns from it that the saints must live in a state in which hope alternates with fear. There, according to Saint Augustine, is the remarkable example which Christ wanted to give on the Cross, " the abandonment of Saint Peter without grace, and the conversion of the thief through a prodigious effect of grace." Let us then ever humble ourselves under the

[60] Œuvres, v. 11, 142.
[61] Œuvres, v. 11, 143.
[62] Œuvres, v. 11, 156. Alludes to ch. xi of the sixth session of the Council of Trent: That the Commandments are not impossible to the Just.
[63] Ps. 118:176 [Ps. 119 in Authorized Version].
[64] Œuvres, v. 11, 168.

hand of God as beggars, and let us say with David: " *Lord, I am poor, and a beggar.*" [65]

Such was the man who was to respond to Arnauld's appeal. He was to respond with all the fervor born of the luminous night of November 23, 1654, united in mind and soul with his admirable sister and his Port-Royalist friends, enriched by his interview with Monsieur de Saci, awe-struck by the far-reaching vista which Jesus had revealed to him from the summits, and having, Bible in hand, " reinvented the Augustinian theology as he had previously reinvented Euclidian geometry." [66]

The champion who was to enter the lists was not an arrogant man; he was an humble being, painfully clinging to his crutches, who advanced, murmuring, " Lord, I am poor, and a beggar."

---

[65] Once more Pascal elaborates from memory. The text of the Vulgate says: *Ego autem mendicus sum, et pauper* (but I am a beggar and poor).

It is the end of the fragments of a letter on grace, *Œuvres*, v. 11, 241.

[66] Gazier, A., *Histoire générale du mouvement Janséniste, op. cit.*, v. 1, 102, 103.

XI

The Champion

"For necessity is laid upon me."

—I Cor. 9:16

O n this 27th of January, 1656, in the drawing rooms, in the ladies'
boudoirs, people were putting their heads together, with poorly concealed smiles, over the reading of a certain pamphlet, a " little letter of
eight pages dated the 23d " and " written to a country gentleman among
his friends " by a certain Louis de Montalte! [1] After a few lines, the
laughter exploded, a deep, full-toned laughter. Molière would soon be inspired by the comic art of this lively and sparkling prose, by this style

[1] This pseudonym has perplexed the students of Pascal as well as his contemporaries. We have already said that on the day after November 23, 1654, Pascal wanted
to lose his identity as an author, for reasons of Christian humility. At Port-Royal the
penitent assumed the name of Monsieur de Mons, in memory of his paternal grand-
mother whose name was Marguerite Pascal de Mons. If the author of the *Provinciales*
conceals his identity under the name of Louis de Montalte, it is, beyond and above
all, for reasons of prudence: he will be continually spied upon by his adversaries, in-
vestigated by the police, threatened with brutal interference, with poisoning (cf. *Introduction à la seconde série des Œuvres de Pascal*, v. 4, xix). It will not be until 1659
that Father Fabri will point out for the first time that Pascal and Montalte must be
one and the same person (cf. *Œuvres*, v. 4, 108). Montalte seems at first to be an anagram drawn from the birthplace of Pascal: Clermont, *Mons Altus*. Two years later
Pascal will take the name Amos Dettonville, and in the *Pensées*, that of Salomon de
Tultie (*Pensées*, Section i, Fr. 18, *Œuvres*, v. 12, 30). Morris Bishop suggests an
ingenious key for these three pseudonyms: " The three names are anagrams, containing the same letters arranged in new order. Pascal's persistent use of this combination
of letters suggests that it has a private meaning, that it is the anagram of something
else. Let me propose a solution: that the phrase in Pascal's mind was *Talentum Deo
Soli*, ' my talent for God alone.' Such a supposition is at least a reasonable one. Pascal has renounced the world's activities, the world's rewards. Now that he is summoned to the defense of his faith, he remembers the parable of the buried talent,
which returns no interest to the exigent master. He chooses a name which is in its very
composition a vow to God and an admonition to himself." (*Pascal:* The Life of
Genius, *op. cit.*, p. 222.) This interpretation is particularly precious to us, in that it
accentuates, in an important aspect of the sanctified life of Pascal, the part played
by the Bible.

which consists in personifying ideas and attitudes of spirit in grotesque silhouettes, clearly outlined behind the authoritative arguments, in scenes peppered with cutting words, with flashes of wit as ingenious as they are acute. And what naturalness! What an absence of studied effects, of oratorical and academic exordiums!

A BOLT OUT OF THE BLUE

" We certainly were deceived; I learned the true state of affairs only yesterday; up till then I had thought that the subject of the Sorbonic disputes was highly important and of the utmost consequence for religion." When an institution, as eminent as the Sorbonne, is anxious to such a degree and with such an uproar, you would certainly think that the subject in dispute must be something very extraordinary! Well, it isn't so at all: I have just learned the whole of it, and I am going to tell you in a very few words what it is all about.

There are two questions: one of Fact, the other of Doctrine. The honorable Bishops have declared that the propositions condemned by the late Pope are to be found in Jansen's book, and Monsieur Arnauld claims that they are not. Is he not a presumptuous man? In the Sorbonne seventy-one Doctors support the position taken by Monsieur Arnauld: that he has not found these propositions in this book, and that he would condemn them if they were to be found there.

Moreover, some go even farther; they have searched for the propositions in the book, and not only have never found them, but have discovered some absolutely contrary propositions. They have, therefore, insistently demanded that if there be any Doctor who has seen the said propositions in the book, he would have the kindness to point them out. In vain! Eighty secular Doctors and some forty mendicant monks, without wishing to examine anything, even to the point of declaring that it is not a question of ascertaining the truth of the matter, have condemned the " presumptuousness " of Monsieur Arnauld's proposition in his own person. That sums up the question of Fact.

That question doesn't bother me very much in any case, for whether Monsieur Arnauld is presumptuous or not is no affair of my conscience, and if it did matter to my conscience, I could have very quickly enlightened myself by examining the book of Jansen for myself. The question of Doctrine seems to me much more worthy of consideration, for it touches the faith. I have, therefore, taken particular care to inform myself concerning it. But don't be alarmed: it is a question that soon proves to be of as little importance as the first!

The point in question is whether or not grace, without which one can do nothing, was lacking to Saint Peter in his fall. On this point you and I would have thought that the examination of the most fundamental principles of grace was involved. In this we were greatly mistaken. Wishing to examine the matter thoroughly, " I have become a great theologian in a short time, and you are going to see the proofs of it."

At this point in his letter Montalte creates a complete dramatis personae: a gentleman of the seventeenth century, candid, entirely ignorant of these matters and desirous of learning about them, replete with the charm of ingenuousness — and humor is always ingenuous [2] — appeals to the Doctors, to the Jesuits. He consults his neighbor, the Doctor of Navarre, one of those most zealous against the Jansenists, but gets only ambiguous responses which are as hollow as they are solemn. He then turns to a certain Mr. So-and-So. The latter takes him to the house of his brother-in-law, " who is a Jansenist if there ever was one, but a good man for all that." With the Jansenist, Montalte plays the part of a fellow Jansenist, as, with the Jesuit, he had pretended to be a Molinist. This does not prevent him from discovering that at bottom the two are in accord. Sure of having, and so quickly, reestablished peace in the Sorbonne, he hastens back to his first Doctor and says so to him. " Not so fast," the latter cautions him. " You have to be a theologian to see the fine point of it. The difference between us is so subtle that we can hardly single it out ourselves; it is too difficult for you to understand it." [3]

COMPLICATIONS AND " NOVELTIES " DENOUNCED

Already one senses that Montalte is becoming impatient with the complications which are introduced into theology, and which put so many obstacles between men and the simplicity of the Scriptures. And these complications are largely caused by the introduction of certain " novelties." Such is the term " immediate power " with which the Jesuit now confronts him. The term is unknown to poor Montalte. Up to this point he had understood the affair; henceforward he is all at sea. He is not far from believing that this *immediate power* has " been in-

[2] Vinet, A., *Etudes sur Blaise Pascal*, Kohler, ed., 1936, *op. cit.*, p. 271.
[3] *Première Provinciale*, *Œuvres*, v. 4, 130.

vented expressly to confuse him." When he demands an explanation of the term from his Doctor, the latter makes a mystery of it and sends him back to the Jansenists, his memory burdened with the term — his memory only, " for my understanding had no part in it."

When Montalte utters this word *immediate* as quickly as he can, for fear of forgetting it, and demands of his Jansenist whether or not he believes in it, the latter begins to laugh, and then says dryly: " Tell me in what sense you understand it, and then I'll tell you what I think of it."

" Er . . . in the sense of the Molinists."

" To which of the Molinists are you referring me? "

Montalte offers them to him as a group, making up one body and acting in one and the same spirit.

" You know very little about the matter," returns the Jansenist.

And he discloses to the unsophisticated inquirer the deep motive which is hidden behind so many subtleties — it is a desire for domination on the part of the " enemies of Arnauld: they intend thus to " crush him entirely." [4] To realize it for himself, Montalte need only consult the Dominicans, who are called *Neo*-Thomists. Still more novelties! what have they invented, these people? Or rather should we say: What have they abandoned?

Moreover, it would be better to consult these gentlemen *separately*. Really? Once and for all let us reduce all their subtleties by means of a simplicity that is as clear as daylight. Montalte henceforth does it in his inimitable fashion:

" If to have the *immediate power* to do something is to have all that is necessary, so that nothing is lacking: to have the *immediate power* to cross a river, would mean to have a boat, boatmen, oars, and all the rest."

" Exactly."

" And to have the immediate power to *see* is to have good eyesight and to be in full daylight."

" Spoken in a scholarly manner."

This time, Montalte feels sure that he is at the end of his labors:

" Consequently, when you say that all the just have always the immediate power of following the Commandments, you mean that they have at all times all the grace necessary in order to accomplish them; so that nothing is lacking to them on the part of God."

" Wait a bit."

[4] *Ibid.*, 132.

And then come some new subtleties, which Montalte clears up again by a simplicity which should disarm the most malicious. Sure of having grasped Monsieur Lemoine's meaning, he rushes to the Neo-Thomists in order to prove their accord:

"What, he begins, is the *immediate power?* . . . Is it not the power that lacks nothing in order to act effectively?"

"No," they reply in chorus.

"How now! Father, . . . do you mean to say that a man, at night and without any light, has the *immediate power to see?*"

"Yes, indeed; he would have it according to us if he isn't blind." After more hairsplitting, in which Montalte defends the ground step by step, he succeeds in making his Neo-Thomist admit both his agreement with the Jansenists in the same Catholic communion, and his disagreement with Monsieur Lemoine. . . . Ah, but no!

"Yes," the Neo-Thomist goes on, "*but* Monsieur Lemoine *calls* this power *immediate power.*"

"But, my dear Fathers, it is playing with words to say that you are in agreement because of the similarity of the terms that you use, when you are entirely opposed as to the meaning."

Deep silence on the part of the Fathers.

In the meanwhile there appears on the scene the disciple of Monsieur Lemoine with whom Montalte has been talking a little while before and from whom he has just learned their profound disagreement with the Neo-Thomists, notwithstanding their use of a common vocabulary. Picture the astonishment of the ingenuous Montalte! However, he will soon learn that these reciprocal visits are not rare . . . backstage.

It is easy to imagine henceforth what deep-seated plots are being concocted behind the pious façade. It is these that the *Provinciales* will endeavor to bring into broad daylight.

And first comes the unexplained practice of using "equivocal and captious" terms. A layman has a right to the truth from those who are expressly consecrated to the service of God. And it is a fiery Pascal, passionately seeking this truth, who now burst out with a holy impatience:

"Once and for all, my Fathers, tell me, I beg of you for the last time, what I must believe in order to be a Catholic." [5]

Catholic, that is to say, in his meaning: with the assurance of salvation, of the only thing which counts. And since the qualified leaders of

[5] *Ibid.*, 141.

the Church fail him, he is soon going to appeal to the supreme Authority of the Scriptures, not only in the matter of salvation and of authority, but also in the matter of an arbitrary power which he must denounce.

ARBITRARINESS EXPOSED

Follow for yourselves this dialogue in which, as will often be the case in the writings of Molière, the comedy turns to tragedy — and it is that which makes its loftiness and its profundity:

" That is to say," Montalte summarizes in taking his leave, " that it is necessary to give lip service to this term, for fear of being a heretic in name. For, after all, does this term come from the Holy Scriptures? " [6]

" No."

" Is it then from Saint Thomas? "

" No."

" What need then is there to *say* it since it has neither any authority, nor any meaning in itself? "

That is certainly adding something to the precepts of that One who said: " My yoke is light." And, forced out of its hiding place, arbitrariness stands revealed:

" You are obstinate, Louis de Montalte; you shall say it, or you will be a heretic, and Monsieur Arnauld also. For we are the majority, and if it is necessary, we shall bring in so many Franciscan friars that we will prevail."

The latter is an allusion to a speech of the Queen on the strategy which consisted in " packing " the meetings by means of an organized invasion of monks, who were ignorant of the fine points of the controversy, but were well disciplined. The Queen had added that, if it were necessary, they would even make the dead vote.

In a letter from P (Princesse de Guemené?) to (Arnauld d'Andilly), dated December 19, 1655 — a copy made by the secretary of d'Andilly — one reads these words: " I replied that the many Franciscans and other monks who were in the Sorbonne would settle the matter as she [the Queen] wished. She told me that they would hunt up still others, and that they had signed the names of the dead. I do not know what she meant by that." [7] The Prince de Guemené is credited with a pleasantry that has become a proverb: he said that a " fine " thing had been noted

[6] Supreme criterion for Pascal: What is *from the Scriptures,* and what is not!

[7] *Œuvres,* v. 4, 110, December 19, 1655.

in the *Lettres Provinciales,* i.e., that Monsieur Arnauld had been condemned by a majority only because of some forty monks who were at the meetings, and that it is much easier to find monks than to find reasons. After that whenever someone gave the Prince de Guemené a poor reason, he would immediately say: " That is a monk," and when someone gave him a good reason: " That's a good reason, but the other is a monk." [8]

In the same order of ideas, Pascal — I mean to say Montalte — exposes the use of the hourglass: this amounts to gag rule. On January 22, for the first time, the privilege of speaking had been denied to Doctor Bourgeois who was in favor of Arnauld. On the 24th, the chancellor reappeared at the sessions. Having placed before him an hourglass, brought by a Doctor of the Sorbonne fertile in expedients, he again cut off the speech of Doctor Bourgeois and of many others. It was then that sixty Doctors left the hall of deliberations, thus setting forth formally their protest.[9]

In his second *Provinciale,* Montalte is conversing with one of his Neo-Thomists, who has that very morning defended the opinion of his school in the meeting of the Sorbonne:

" I spoke there for my full half hour, and without the hourglass, I would certainly have changed that unfortunate proverb which is already spreading all over Paris: he nods assent like a monk in the Sorbonne."

" What do you mean by your ' half hour ' and your ' hourglass '? Do they set a time limit on your remarks? "

" Yes, since the last few days."

" And they make you talk a half hour? "

" Oh, no. You can talk as little as you please." [10]

The second *Provinciale* had appeared on February 5, Arnauld having been condemned on the 31st of January, by one hundred and thirty votes against nine. After having characterized his proposition as " presumptuous, impious, blasphemous, anathematized, and heretical," the holy Faculty had cast Arnauld out of its society, had erased his name from the list of its Doctors, and had " entirely cut him off from its body." No doubt the second *Provinciale,* taking up the question of " sufficient grace," was already well advanced in composition, and it is the third

---

[8] Jovy, E., *Etudes pascaliennes, op. cit.,* Vrin, Paris, 1936, v. 9, 150.
[9] *Œuvres,* v. 4, 152.
[10] *Œuvres,* v. 4, 162 (*Seconde Provinciale*).

Provinciale which defends Arnauld by demonstrating the " injustice, absurdity, and nullity of his condemnation since it is ' much easier to find monks than reasons.' "

The transition between the first letter which treats of *immediate power* and the second which discusses *sufficient grace* is made in this way: Montalte, speaking to one of his Neo-Thomists, says:

" Well, Father, it seems it is not enough that all men should have immediate power, by means of which, however, they never act in fact; it is necessary for them to have in addition *sufficient grace,* with which they act as little." [11]

FALSE PRETENSES UNMASKED

Speaking of *sufficient grace* and of *efficacious grace,* the layman, Montalte, once more is going to lash out at the theological subtleties, to denounce the jargon, to unmask the subterfuges and the false pretenses: the grace which is sufficient although it does not suffice, i.e., " sufficient in name, but insufficient in fact." [12]

" In good faith, Father, this doctrine is very subtle. Have you forgotten in withdrawing from the world (!) what the word *sufficient* means there? Don't you remember that it includes all that is necessary in order to act? "

All kinds of people, everybody in fact, understand by the word *sufficient* " that which includes all that is essential." [13]

"Easy, now," Montalte's Jansenist friend had already cautioned. " There are two things in this term *sufficient grace:* there is the sound which is nothing but wind, and the meaning which is real and effective."

It is therefore a matter of coming to an understanding: is there agreement as to the *substance* of the term, or only " as to its sound "?

Pascal has recourse to his Bible again, and in the framework of the parable of the Good Samaritan, he tells a parable in which the Church is likened unto a man who has departed from his country on a voyage. He is surprised by robbers who wound him with blows and leave him half-dead. There is this difference, however: it is the firstcomer who proves to be the best. Like a good doctor, he probes the wounds, judges them to be mortal, and tells the victim that his only help lies in God. The wounded man follows his counsel, asks of God the strength which he confesses he does not have within himself, and receives from God

[11] *Œuvres,* v. 4, 162 (*Seconde Provinciale*).   [13] *Ibid.,* 166.
[12] *Ibid.,* 163.

mercy and succor. The second doctor insults the first. A flatterer, he tells the wounded man that he has enough strength to reach his home. A third comes on the scene; he embraces the second and joins with him in chasing away the first, for " they were the strongest in numbers." [14] The patient had naturally concluded that the second and third doctors were in accord. But upon questioning them, he realizes his error: the third doctor speaks in scholastic syllogisms:

" You still have your legs."

Now your legs are " the instruments which naturally suffice for walking."

" But I haven't the strength to use them," sighs the wounded man.

The third doctor agrees with him. It appears, therefore, that he was really of an opinion contrary to that of the second doctor with whom he had allied himself. The sufferer complains " of this strange procedure and of the ambiguous terms of the third doctor."

A LITERARY GENIUS REVEALED

The style of the *Provinciale* has become Biblical. Let us compare the two:

Luke says in his parable of the Unjust Steward: [15]

" And the lord commended the unjust steward, forasmuch as he had done wisely: for the children of this world are wiser in their generation than the children of light." [16]

And Pascal, in his parable of the Church:

" He blamed the third physician for having united with the second to whom he was opposed in sentiment and with whom he had only an apparent conformity, and for having driven away the first with whom he was, in fact, in agreement. And after having tried his strength and learned through experience the truth of his weakness, the wounded man sent them both away."

More and more the style gains in amplitude as Pascal's indignation mounts: he puts forth his power and attains real eloquence. It is not

[14] *Ibid.*, 168.
[15] Luke 16:1-8.
[16] Luke 16:8.

It is interesting to compare this translation with that which Monsieur de Saci gives in his *Bible, op. cit.*, v. 7, 93: " Et le maître loua cet économe infidèle de ce qu'il avoit agi prudemment: car les enfans du siècle sont plus sages dans la conduite de leurs affaires, que ne sont les enfans du lumiere."

only Molière whom Pascal anticipates, but also Bossuet, who will draw from the Scriptures the secret of his oratorical style.

The names, Montalte says in substance, are inseparable from the things; and expedient subterfuges would be odious even in worldly matters when one is speaking seriously of things less important than sufficient grace. And he continues in these terms: " This victorious grace has been awaited by the Patriarchs, predicted by the Prophets, bestowed by Jesus Christ, preached by Saint Paul, explained by Saint Augustine, the greatest of the Fathers, maintained by those who have followed him. . . . This victorious grace which had been placed in your hands, as in deposit, in order that it might have Preachers of a holy and enduring order, who would publish it forth to the world unto the end of time, this victorious grace finds itself abandoned and abandoned for interests so unworthy! It is time that others arm themselves to take up its cause. It demands hearts that are pure and free, and itself purifies them and frees them from worldly interests, interests incompatible with the truths of the Scriptures. Take action in the face of these menaces, Father, and take care lest God remove this light from its place and leave you in darkness and without a crown." [17]

What a magnificent peroration from a herald of the Bible! And what Biblical marrow in the argument also: Pascal has learned from the Scriptures that if one human instrument fails, God knows how to raise up another, that even the chosen people have seen themselves dispossessed for having been unfaithful. Already Pascal proclaims himself as the last Prophet of Israel!

THE TRUTH THAT MAKES MEN FREE

With the third *Provinciale*, as we have said, Pascal passes to the direct defense of Arnauld who has just been condemned by the Sorbonne. Schooled by his friends, who furnish him with the necessary documentation, he has mastered all the doctrines; in reality he has done this from the first letter since he takes his point of departure in the Bible.

Nicole, annotating his Latin edition [18] of the letters, shows, for ex-

[17] *Œuvres*, v. 4, 172, 173, 174 (*Seconde Provinciale*).
[18] Which he signs with the pseudonym of Wendrock. We cite here some notes of Nicole in the annotation of his Latin edition and translated into French by Mademoiselle de Joncoux, for the edition of 1699 (*Œuvres*, v. 4, 145, 146).
One may also consult in *Œuvres*, v. 4, 176, 177, the note entitled *Du terme de grâce suffisante. Qui sont les Dominicains que cette lettre condamne.*

ample, why Pascal rejects the term *immediate power:* " He maintains that one ought not to regard as sacred words in order to express the faith, nor require that anyone should receive, with religious respect, new and barbarous words which are not established by any passage of the Scripture, of the Councils, or of the Fathers." Undertaking in his third letter the defense of Arnauld, Montalte clothes his concise reasoning in literary language; he puts the words into the mouths of too sharp-tongued people who inveigh against the condemnation by the Sorbonne; but the imperishable Pascalian argument remains: " If it is against the words of the Fathers [directly inspired by the Scriptures] that one acts in such a way, what has become of Faith and Tradition? If it is against Monsieur Arnauld's proposition? Let someone show us in what it differs from the words of the Fathers, since there appears to us to be perfect conformity between the two." [19] When Montalte has been shown where the evil lies, one can be sure that he also will hold it in detestation, but not before. Anchored to what he knows for certain to be the truth, he will resist arbitrariness. And the measure of arbitrariness is the Holy Scripture interpreted according to the Fathers and the Tradition of the Church.

Arnauld was given for his examiners his most avowed enemies.[20] These " employ all their efforts to search out something they will be able to criticize." [21] Now one cannot ignore two things that the least-informed know. On the one hand, Arnauld has always avoided saying anything which is not firmly based on the Papal Tradition of the Church. The other is the fact that, despite this irreproachable attitude, his adversaries are resolved to cut him off from the Church no matter at what cost. Since his writings do not afford any matter for criticism to his enemies, they have taken refuge in arbitrariness: " they have deemed it opportune and easier to condemn than to reply, because it is much easier for them to find monks than reasons." [22] How few people will go to the trouble of enlightening themselves as to the grounds of the quarrel! There will be fewer still who, reading about it, will understand! Who, taking the affair to heart, will undertake to examine it thoroughly? That is the most dangerous secret of arbitrariness: it is enough to cry, " Shame," on those whom you want to ruin! " Provided that one cries in

[19] *Œuvres,* v. 4, 214, 215 (*Troisième Provinciale*).
[20] On the procedures used against Arnauld, see *Œuvres,* v. 4, 181, 196.
[21] *Œuvres,* v. 4, 211.
[22] Cf. *Œuvres,* v. 4, 217.
Refer also to our note 8 about the witticism of the Prince de Guemené.

the streets: Here is the censure of Monsieur Arnauld! Read about the condemnation of the Jansenists." [23] The populace will be convinced. What becomes of the sacred cause of liberty in these movements of mob psychology?

It is the absolute lack of liberty that Pascal denounces here, and in this sense he has an obvious place — and a large place — in the history of liberalism. The champion of the Bible will always be, in the last analysis, the champion of liberty. How could it be otherwise? One will excuse our recalling here our chapter " Freedom Under Christ " of a recent work,[24] and in particular this proposition: " In every realm of human activity, a deep-rooted solidarity will be found to exist between Christianity and individual endeavor at its best. Everywhere history shows great battles of liberty won by men whose faith is grounded in Holy Writ." [25] Of this affirmation, the Pascal of the *Provinciales* presents a striking illustration. In this connection we have already pointed out his denunciation of what we call " gag rule " — what the Sorbonic Doctors, who wanted at any cost to condemn Arnauld, called " *la demi-heure de sable* " (the half-hour of sand).[26]

THE JESUITS DIRECTLY ATTACKED

The fourth *Provinciale* attacks the Jesuits directly. It opens with the statement: " There is nothing like the Jesuits." Others only copy them; and to study a thing, it is better to go to its source.[27] What is the source that is in question, on this 25th day of February, 1656? To put the matter plainly, it is a question of the source of a deep-seated immorality, which is forthwith brought to light and stripped of its mask of theological pretenses by this impassioned advocate of real morality. It was perhaps Méré who drew Pascal's attention to the fact that these theological subtleties remained unknown to the general public. Perhaps the author of the *Provinciales* was served by a secret instinct. It is the

[23] *Œuvres*, v. 4, 218 (*Troisième Provinciale*).

[24] Cailliet, E., *The Life of the Mind,* The Macmillan Company, New York, 1942, ch. 3, " Freedom Under Christ," pp. 33–43.

[25] *Ibid.,* pp. 38, 39.

[26] *Œuvres*, v. 4, 220 (*Troisième Provinciale*).

This letter is signed: E.A.A.B.P.A.F.D.E.P. (That is, Blaise Pascal auvergnat fils d'Etienne Pascal et Antoine Arnauld, if we begin with the fourth initial and go back to the beginning when we come to the end of the line. According to Sainte-Beuve the first three initials [Et ancien ami] have been added to mislead.)

[27] *Quatrième Provinciale, Œuvres*, v. 4, 251.

instinct of the man, however, rather than the instinct of the writer. Is not real eloquence, which " doesn't give a straw for eloquence," that which springs directly from a conscience possessed with the grandeur of truth?

This truth is once more expressed by Montalte's Jansenist friend as he answers one of the former's questions: " Take it for granted that never did the Fathers, the Popes, the Councils, nor Holy Writ, nor any book of piety, even in recent times, talk in this manner," [28] i.e., like the Jesuits. They have been brought to the excesses which Pascal denounces because they have distorted the Scriptures themselves in a monstrous manner. Take, for example, the *Somme des pechez*, by Father Bauny. Before he became a friend of the Jesuits, Monsieur Hallier pertinently applied to this author the sacrilegious play on words which are taken from John 1:29, " *Ecce qui tollit peccata mundi* " (Behold Him, who taketh away the sins of the world), which is the counterpart of Montalte's cruelly ironic remark to his Jesuit Father: " It is certainly true, I said to him, that there is a new redemption according to Father Bauny." [29] Pascal's French is doubly ironical because of the word order: not " *une nouvelle rédemption* " (i.e., a new redemption), but " *une rédemption nouvelle* " (i.e., a redemption of a new sort). In like manner another great classic writer, La Fontaine, in a fable,[30] which is really a little comedy in the style of Molière's *Tartufe*, speaks of a *new saint*, i.e., a saint of a new kind!

To tell the truth, one can hardly restrain a shudder at some of Pascal's burlesque scenes. He shows us the good Father, bustling about, hastening to get *his* books. Ah, here is Father Annat's book — let us note in passing that Father Annat was the head of the Jesuit order for France and confessor to the King! — Here is the most recent book he has written against Arnauld. Sins are juggled away by means of a sleight of hand which astounds: Father Annat forgets nothing, neither sins of commission, nor sins of omission:

" What do you say to that? "

" I see in it some *fine* consequences! " Montalte replies with an irony that goes unnoticed by the Jesuit. And Montalte adds, with a comic art into which creeps once more a note of tragedy from the point of view of a man of the Bible who knows:

" But, Father, aren't you cozening me with a false joy? Isn't there

[28] *Ibid.*, 251.
[29] *Ibid.*, 252.
[30] *Le Rat qui s'est retiré du monde.*

something in all this very much like that *sufficiency* which does not suffice? "

At this point the " good " Father begins to get angry and gets himself still farther entangled in the prejudicial concession in which Montalte wants to catch him: up to the moment in which certain reflections occur " in the soul," the action is not, " properly speaking," a sin. And therefore the libertines who never think of God may be said to be in a state of " baptismal innocence." Their vices have conveniently " preceded " their reflections! Their very excesses render their salvation assured!

One may easily imagine the scandalized feelings of the man who is already thinking of addressing his " Vindication of Christianity " especially to the libertine. The Jesuits apply themselves to keeping the libertine in his comfortable state of quiescence. According to them the semi-sinners can perhaps be a little uneasy in their minds, . . . but give me your out-and-out sinner, hardened, without qualms, pre-eminently bad! Hell itself will not hold him. The complete libertine has cheated the Devil by giving himself up entirely to the infernal power! Henceforth, the heresy of the Jansenists will consist in denying the need of a troubled conscience in order to establish the reality of sin! That is certainly a heresy of a new kind! Montalte knows very well — and it is that very knowledge which rends his heart! — that there are thousands of people who sin joyously, without remorse, and who boast of it. How dangerous is that maxim which allows them free rein!

After the Jesuit has mired himself in the quicksands of concession, Montalte leads him on to admit still more: the Father claims that he has the Scriptures on his side. Well, then let one make an appeal to the Scriptures, . . . but, at least, let the Father not try to evade the evidence of the Sacred Word!

There follows a terse Biblical demonstration: God did not reveal his judgments to the Gentiles; He left them to wander in the error of their ways. The Sacred Books show them to us abandoned in outer darkness and in the shadow of death. Even Saint Paul called himself the *worst of sinners,* for a sin which he declared he had *committed by ignorance and with zeal*. Those who crucified our Lord did not know what they were doing. Jesus Christ Himself — the supreme argument, that of His Word! — taught us that there are two kinds of sinners, those who sin consciously and those who sin in ignorance; and that they shall all be punished although, in point of truth, in a different manner.

Hard pressed by so many evidences from Holy Writ, the good Father begins to give ground, and "leaving the Impious to sin without inspiration" (!) he looks about for an honorable means of retreat. Then Montalte falls upon him:

"You are backing down, you are backing down, Father!"[31]

The discussion is continued until once more the Scriptures are brought to witness; and it is a paraphrase of Saint Paul:[32] the most saintly men have to remain always in fear and trembling although they may not feel themselves to be guilty in any way; or it is an allusion to the book of The Proverbs[33] in order to show that the just daily commit sins of which they are not always conscious.

There are two psychologies, two moralities, two religions brought face to face in the fourth *Provinciale,* as Strowski has very clearly shown: either we are beings of "free will," as Monsieur Lemoine wishes to have it; or we are "natures," unsoundable abysses from which come forth continually, "by unpredictable gushes, our thoughts, our sentiments, our acts," according to Monsieur Arnauld. Racine's Phèdre will signalize in this respect the violent reaction of an exacting Christianity against the stoicism that was dominant in the Cornelian hero.[34]

Strowski perhaps flatters Monsieur Lemoine in making him the patron saint of Rodrigue and Auguste; we are in agreement with him in making of Arnauld the patron saint of Phèdre. *Phèdre* is a magnificent Biblical tragedy. And certainly it is necessary to choose between these two types of humanity. It is necessary to "wager," to use the language of Pascal. In the final analysis it will be seen that the wager in question is not far from being a wager for or against the Bible.

Father Bauny, for his part, calls as his supreme authority Aristotle, "that Prince of Philosophers."[35] When he cites the latter, the Jesuit is so moved that he presses the fingers of Montalte as he declaims his Latin. The argument is certainly clinched this time. Savor with me this dart from Montalte:

"It seems that Aristotle is of the opinion of Father Bauny, but that is not without surprising me."

What! Would Aristotle's *Morale* justify the oaths of betting, the excesses of debauchery, the passions of the carnival?

[31] *Quatrième Provinciale, Œuvres,* v. **4,** 261.
[32] Phil. 2:12; I Cor. 4:4; *Œuvres,* v. **4,** 262.
[33] Prov. 24:16; *Œuvres,* v. **4,** 263.
[34] Strowski, F., *Pascal et son temps, op. cit.,* v. **3,** 83.
[35] *Quatrième Provinciale, Œuvres,* v. **4,** 265.

The Jansenist friend of Montalte opens the book at the passage from which Father Bauny has taken his quotation and has no trouble in showing that the context establishes beyond all doubt that Aristotle means to say exactly the opposite of what the Father makes him say! Indignation increases the vehemence of the *Provinciale:* "And who will not be astounded to learn that a pagan philosopher has been more enlightened than your Doctors in a matter of such importance to morality."

It is to such a pass that we have been led by a theology based on ignorance of original sin, on ignorance of the depths of man's nature, and of his need for redemption. It is to this perdition that the broad way leads.

Or is it the other way around? has the profession of a lax morality, which accommodates itself to any purpose, inspired this newfangled theology, so foreign to the Word of God?

The Jesuit has just left the premises, opportunely relieved in the midst of a difficult situation by the visit of Madame la Maréchale de . . . and Madame la Marquise de. . . .

"I shall speak about it to our Fathers; they will certainly be able to find some answer. We have some very subtle ones here."

That is something that Montalte and his Jansenist friend can well believe: one would speak about it again.

And this time they would talk about morals.

XII

The Sign in the Midst of Battle

"For I know whom I have believed."
—II Tim. 1:12*

The Christian who allows himself to be drawn into a war of words, compelled to have recourse to irony, even to sarcasm, comes to feel, sooner or later, a strange sense of aridity: Can this be my rightful role? he asks himself with a perplexity that becomes anguish as a deadening cold invades his heart which only yesterday was afire with the ardor of divine communion. Can all the motives that are animating him be attributed to a holy indignation? Is it possible always to distinguish between an abhorrent cause and the individuals who represent it? Might not the very horror inspired by that cause be, at least in part, an unconscious disguise for old, half-forgotten grudges? The human heart so easily deceives itself!

HESITATIONS AND MISGIVINGS

Just yesterday a Jesuit, Father Noël, had taken up arms against Pascal, the physicist. In earlier days Etienne Pascal had crossed swords with the Jesuits of Clermont over the establishment of a college in that city. In 1646 the Jesuits of Clermont, having never forgotten the old quarrels, had denied the primacy of certain of Pascal's scientific experiments. By its very nature Molinism was opposed to the determinism which is an integral part of the scientific spirit. And perhaps a part of Pascal's own hostility to the Jesuits came from the scientific side of his nature. The desire for and pride in knowledge, and one's self-love, can so easily taint what were at first the purest of religious motives.

Furthermore, is it possible that God, Master of the Universe, has need of us, " feeble servants " that we are, to the point that it becomes necessary for us to defend His cause even at the risk of losing our souls in the enterprise? May not the flattering praises which incite us to re-

* *Scio cui credidi* became Pascal's motto after the miracle of the Holy Thorn.

double our efforts themselves be inspired by expediency and thus add to the confusion of our motives?

There are very few directors of conscience who can think first of the care of our soul and of its salvation when their own existence is in danger. Their attitude is only the more moving for that fact.

Blaise did not fail to be touched by the reserve of Monsieur Singlin and by the words of Mother Angélique which were reported to him: the saintly woman said that silence would have been more noble and more agreeable to God, and that the tears of penitence calm the passions more than eloquence. Eloquence, she added, beguiles more people than it converts.

The author of the *Provinciales* goes into hiding. He changes his residence. He has to pretend innocence when his *Lettres* are read or mentioned in his presence: " He knows," writes Mauriac, " that state of perilous security in which the Christian discovers that his duty and his pleasure are one, and that he gratifies his passion for the greater glory of God." [1]

There might, perhaps, even be occasion to contrast Pascal's state of mind with the tranquillity of Arnauld who had taken refuge in a friend's house on the outskirts of Paris. Monsieur Fontaine, who was doing the office of a friend and was alone with him, sent word from there, by a letter dated January 29, 1656, that he was " in a state of serenity and repose even greater than usual." [2] Arnauld and Nicole will claim the honor of having greatly aided the author of the *Provinciales*, of having spurred him on to what certain ones were already calling " disobedience " and even " rebellion " with respect to the teachings of the Church. A scholar like Jovy will say even of the ingenuity of Pascal: " It is Port-Royal that killed him." [3]

ROMAN CATHOLIC TESTIMONIES

At this point Catholic authors have their testimony to give, and probity demands that they should be heard. [4]

[1] Mauriac, F., *Blaise Pascal et sa sœur Jacqueline,* Hachette, Paris, 1931, p. 167.

[2] Jovy, E., " Le Journal de M. de Saint Gilles," Vrin, Paris, 1936, *Etudes pascaliennes,* v. **9,** 113.

[3] Cited by Professor H. Peyre, in " Pascal et la critique contemporaine," *The Romanic Review,* No. 4, October–December, 1930, v. **21,** 327.

[4] Here is a short, selective bibliography, followed by a brief evaluation of the studies, which may be of use to those scholars who desire to consider at length the Roman Catholic point of view:

The inner conflict of Pascal will stand out more clearly if we remember, and this point cannot be emphasized too often, that his first concern is never to become separated from a Church, outside of which there

---

Première réponse aux lettres que les Jansénistes publient contre les Pères de la Compagnie de Jésus, par un Père de la même compagnie;
Seconde réponse, en 29 Impostures.

(All this contemporary argumentation, of inferior quality, comes from Jacques, from Brisacier, and from Father Annat.)

In 1694 a reply of decidedly superior quality is given by Father Daniel, in his *Entretiens de Clitandre et d'Euxore,* in response to the praise of Perrault in his *Parallèle des Anciens et des Modernes,* Part 2, Third Dialogue.

Concerning Father Daniel, see Sainte-Beuve, *Port-Royal,* v. **3**, 51 ff.

The champion of the Jesuits in the nineteenth century is Father Maynard, author of *Pascal, sa vie et son caractère, ses écrits,* 2 v., 1850. His edition of *Les Provinciales* . . . *et leur réfutation,* 1851, is preceded by an introduction containing the historical background of the controversy and the general principles of the discussion, and " at the bottom of each page some notes pointing out all the errors and falsifications of detail."

Le Dictionnaire apologétique de la Foi Catholique, published under the direction of Father d'Alès, A., of the Catholic Institute, gives in v. **4**, col. 1641–1651, a sketch of the attacks against the *Théologie morale,* and cites in its bibliography the book by Guiraud, J., *Histoire partiale et histoire vraie,* which treats of the subject in v. **4**, part 2, published in 1917. Guiraud is a former professor of history at the University of Besançon.

Le Dictionnaire de Théologie Catholique, begun by Vacant, A. and Mangenot, E., and continued by Amann, E., of the Theological Faculty of Strasbourg, contains in v. **9**, col. 39–86, a sketch of the " Querelle du laxisme en France," an article which goes beyond the problem of the *Provinciales.* Another article, " Pascal, Blaise," v. **11**, col. 2074–2203, by the Abbé Constantin, C., chaplain of the Lycée Poincaré of Nancy, is largely devoted to the *Provinciales,* col. 2083–2110.

Let us add: Bremond, H., *En Prière avec Pascal,* Bloud et Gay, Paris, 1923, and Chevalier, J., *Pascal,* Plon, Paris, 1922.

" I choose the Jesuit," writes Bishop, M., in the conclusion of a conscientious study of the *Provinciales, Pascal:* The Life of Genius, Reynal & Hitchcock, Inc., New York, 1936, p. 251. We refer the reader to ch. 10, " The Polemist," *op. cit.,* pp. 211–258, and particularly to ch. 8, " The Faith of the *Provinciales,*" pp. 250–252, where he sums up the reasons for his verdict in favor of the Jesuit.

The following are some essential considerations and conclusions of Roman Catholic scholarship:

Fénelon, gentle and conciliatory, stated: " The text of the saintly Doctor [Augustine] has without doubt, like that of the Apostle, some passages which are difficult to understand, which biased men twist into a wrong sense, and which they abuse to their own ruin. . . . It is thus that Jansen was misled in reading this text. Would to God that the disciples of Jansen might have wishes to learn humbly from the Church what is the pure and moderate sense that it approves in this text." Fénelon, *Œuvres complètes,* 10 v., Leroux, Paris, 1851–1852, v. **5**, 451.

On Fénelon see Carcassonne, *État présent des travaux sur Fénelon,* Belles-Lettres, Paris, 1940.

is, in his judgment, no salvation. In circumstances which are similar up to a certain point, Fénelon will submit to Bossuet, and will present as a

---

Rare is the charitable vein of a Fénelon; as a rule, harsh words express strong feelings:

" The Jansenist translations of the thoughts of Saint Augustine are, in reality, falsifications," states Boyer, Ch., S.J., in his *Essais sur la doctrine de Saint Augustin,* Beauchesne, Paris, 1932, p. 235. The essays explain that Augustine's works, being for the most part occasional in character, place emphasis only on the contested aspects of the teaching under consideration. Thus: " Most of his works were written as a reaction against a ruling sect or a heresy that was in the process of formation. This polemic orientation gives a particular twist to the thought and explains certain formulas which, taken by themselves, might appear excessive."

[Steenberghen, F. van, and Cayré, F., " Introduction générale à l'édition complète," *Œuvres de Saint Augustin,* 1st series, v. 3, pp. 9–84, Desclée, Paris, 1939 (Bibliothèque Augustinienne).]

" Despite the impulse given by the Jansenists to Augustinian studies, it is not in their works that the genuine interpretation of the texts of the great African Doctor is to be sought."

[Feba, P. Angel, O.S.A., *Introducción a la filosofía de San Agustín,* El Escorial, Imprenta del Real Monasterio, 1928, p. 11.]

Cayré has remarked that the founders of the Protestant and Jansenist movements were false Augustinians; that to be truly an Augustinian it is not enough to seize on some of the great Doctor's expressions, or even some points of his teaching; all the essential points, and above all, the spirit of his teaching must be retained.

[Cayré, F., A.A., *Manual of Patrology,* Trans. H. Howitt, A.A., Paris, Desclée, 1936, v. 1, 715.]

The monumental work of Jansen, according to Catholic scholars, is simply a massive chain of citations from Augustine framed in an expository argument. A recent study contains a tabulation of his references to the works of Augustine. [Remsberg, Robert J., *Wisdom and Science at Port-Royal and the Oratory,* A Study of Contrasting Augustinianisms, Yellow Springs, O., the Antioch Press, 1940 (Ph.D. dissertation, Columbia University, p. 92).] They reach the overwhelming figure of 7,595; the majority refer to the works on grace.

Remsberg records 390 references (p. 94) to the treatise *De Correptione et gratia* (On Correction and grace). Jansen used to a marked degree this all-important " key " to the doctrines of Augustine on grace and predestination. Arnauld translated the treatise into French and drew up an analytical synopsis which forms the introduction to the treatise in certain copies of the first Benedictine edition of the works of Augustine. Richard Simon thought that impartial and scientific consideration gave the same sense as Jansen and Arnauld. Bossuet contested this view at length in the thirteenth book of his *Défense de la tradition et des Saints Pères,* and Fénelon, in his turn, devoted special attention to an explanation of *De Correptione et gratia* in his treatise against the Jansenists. Cardinal Noris, a seventeenth-century theologian of the Order of Saint Augustine and an exponent of the Augustinian system of grace (as contrasted with Thomism and Molinism), called *De Correptione et gratia* " un livre d'or " (a book of gold), " the key with which one can penetrate the doctrine of Saint Augustine in regard to grace." [*Historia pelagiana,* Louvain, 1702, p. 94, translated and cited by Jacquain, M., O.P., " La question de la prédestination aux Ve et VIe siècles," *Revue d'histoire ecclésiastique,* v. 5, 1904, 273, 274.]

gift to his own Cathedral of Cambrai a golden censer showing an angel trampling the condemned book under his feet.[5]

Joseph de Maistre, in his *Soirées de Saint Pétersbourg*, enveloping his admiration for the *Provinciales* in an injurious phrase, will date the beginning of modern French from the *Menteur* (Liar), of Corneille, and the *Menteuses* (Liars, that is to say, the *Lettres*), of Pascal. The Protestant writer, Vinet, however, comments on this judgment: " What one knows of the doctrines of Monsieur de Maistre makes of him a very doubtful judge. One hundred and fifty years beforehand, Pascal had, without knowing it, attacked Monsieur de Maistre by attacking his favorite dogma, that is, the absolute authority of the Holy See." [6]

Victor Giraud tries to show that, far from lowering or degrading the Christian ideal, the Jesuits had as their goal the attainment of the greatest possible degree of moral perfection that is really possible, given the worldly state of man's conscience, and, he says, " nothing is more conformable to the real spirit of the Bible." According to Giraud, Pascal has created the " legend of the Jesuit." Why then hasn't he made a dis-

---

In *De Correptione et gratia* it is indeed true that Augustine does not deny that, in the absence of the gift of perseverance, there cannot exist a power properly so called to do good: the *adjutorium sine quo non* and the *adjutorium quo* refer solely to *final* perseverance — a fact which the Jansenists have not taken into consideration.

Jean Calvet clearly sums up the official position of the Roman Catholic Church on the condemnation of Jansenism in the following terms:

" The Church has condemned under the name of Jansenism: the total corruption of human nature by the orignal sin; the inherent powerlessness of man after the Fall; the all-powerfulness of grace which operates all within us and to which man cannot resist; the dependence of human liberty, subject to the all-powerful delectation from above and from below, now drawn by necessity toward good by grace, now drawn by necessity toward evil by concupiscence; the character of concupiscence which is sin in itself and which causes all the actions accomplished without the operation of grace to be odious to God; all men doomed to damnation as a consequence of the original sin and constituting a ' massa damnata,' from which God, who owes nothing to anyone, chooses without any consideration other than that of His sovereign will, the elect to whom the *sufficient grace* will be given, abandoning the others to their unhappy destiny as children of Adam; the Redemption limited in fact, not in the sense that Jesus Christ would not have died to save all men, but in the sense that His blood and His merits, sources of grace, would only be applied to the elect. Such is, roughly, the doctrine of Jansen, taken from orthodox theses in its point of departure, of which some now form a part of orthodox doctrine, of which others are pushed by an extreme logic to the point of error; and such is the doctrine of the five propositions."

[Translated from Calvet, Jean, *La Littérature religieuse de François de Sales à Fénelon*, De Gigord, Paris, 1938, pp. 158, 159.]

[5] Feugère, A., *Le Mouvement religieux dans la littérature du XVIIᵉ siècle*, Boivin, Paris, 1938, p. 164.

[6] Vinet, A., *Etudes sur Blaise Pascal*, Kohler, ed., *op. cit.*, pp. 153–254.

tinction which stands out so clearly? And Giraud goes on to point out the opposition between the *individualistic* and the *social* conception of religion: for the Jansenists, religion is essentially an instrument for the reformation of the inner man; for the Jesuits, it is essentially a social force, and destined to become more and more so; on this point, " the future has adjudged the case to them." According to Giraud, " the Jesuits admirably sensed that Christianity, in order to live and to endure, could not remain what it was at first "; whereas the Jansenists, like the Protestants before them in the preceding century, wanted to lead Christianity back to what it was in the first centuries. Both the Jansenists and the Protestants lacked — it is still Giraud speaking — " the historic sense, ' that powerful evolutionary spirit that Renan finds even in the Bible.' " [7]

Verily the situation created by the Pascal of the *Provinciales* must be very grave, for a Catholic author thus to call Renan to the rescue in Biblical matters! In Bremond's estimation, Pascal belongs " by his virtues, by his theological tendencies, and by the heedless impetuosity of his polemic arguments," [8] to the Jansenist " *Fronde*," using the term in its widest historical and legendary sense. (The *Fronde* was the faction that caused a civil war during the minority of Louis XIV.) For anyone who judges the *Provinciales* in the abstract, " two seconds suffice " to condemn them. However, in the manner of those confessors whom Pascal " reproves, of those who, faithful to the lessons of Saint Paul, are inclined to believe the good rather than the bad," Bremond is going to equivocate and to pronounce Pascal innocent. Only Louis de Montalte is guilty: " To publish a libel is certainly profoundly immoral. But if the author did not realize what his blows were striking, if he neither foresaw nor desired the disastrous consequences of his undertaking, then the stones fall from our hands." [9]

This whole side of the question seems to us to have been ably and temperately summed up by Feugère: Discussions, he says, are certainly a sign of vitality and are praiseworthy when they are not carried to

[7] Giraud, V., *Pascal, l'homme, l'œuvre, l'influence*, notes of a course given at the University of Fribourg, Switzerland, during the first semester of 1898, 3d edition, revised, corrected, and considerably enlarged, Albert Fontemoing, editor, Paris, 1905, pp. 99–101.

[8] Bremond, H., " Pascal et l'Eglise Catholique," in *La Revue hebdomadaire*, No. 28, 32d year, July 14, 1923, p. 175.

[9] *Ibid.*, p. 176.

(See also Bremond, H., *En Prière avec Pascal, op. cit.*, p. 17.)

excess, but the danger lies in the fact that all discussions tend to degenerate into disputes. The latter " incur the risk of corrupting the heart and spirit of the most respectable champions, of weakening, if not killing, in them the sense of prayerfulness and of reason; till the moment comes when each one is conscious only of the joy of crushing his adversary, and yields himself up to ' whatever god it is that wants one to be the victor.' Battles all the more savage in that they are fratricidal." [10] And it is a fact that Pascal gave no quarter to his adversaries.

THE OBJECTIVE TESTIMONY OF A GREAT SCHOLAR

A very distinguished university man who remains neutral in the debate, Gustave Lanson, recognizes this fact and explains it in this way: In his work of clearing up the obscurities of the case, Pascal suppressed the attenuating circumstances, the justifications, " the circumstances which explain and which soften, and offered his decisions ' in the raw,' so to speak, in the absolute."

The procedure was legitimate, according to Lanson, because Pascal was making war against expedient compromises: he was the advocate in a great cause, but, in the final analysis, he was an " advocate." As a natural consequence he found himself compelled " in his citations as in his arguments " to allow " the least possible advantage to his adversaries." [11] The truth is, according to Lanson, that Pascal, despite his profession of submission to his " director," really submitted only to himself.

Michaut answers Lanson here. He points out that this attitude on the part of Pascal is explained by the very polemic of the *Provinciales*. In Pascal's eyes, the heart of the whole controversy was the fact that " the ' director ' might lead the penitent astray, that the penitent ought to act according to the dictates of his own conscience and not according to the dictum of others." Hence, according to Michaut, " Pascal himself would have been the first to undergo the influence of the *Provinciales*." [12]

[10] Feugère, A., *Le Mouvement religieux dans la littérature du XVIIe siècle, op. cit.*, p. 165.

[11] Lanson, G., article " Pascal " of the *Grande encyclopédie*, 21 col. of small text, pp. 18–31. We refer the reader to this remarkable article by a contemporary scholar who is unequaled in his field.

[12] Michaut, G., *Les Epoques de la pensée de Pascal*, 2d ed. corrected and enlarged, Fontemoing, Paris, 1902, p. 264. (Cf. Appendix VI B.)

It would certainly seem to be necessary to view the whole question from the standpoint of the validity of the individual Christian conscience if one wants to be relevant. It is impossible to discuss the question of the heterodoxy of Jansenism without becoming involved as a controversialist either for or against Rome, remarks T. S. Eliot. And he adds: " But in a man of the type of Pascal — and the type always exists — there is . . . an ingredient of what may be called Jansenism of temperament." [13]

Indeed, the *Provinciales* as prose " are of capital importance in the foundation of French classical style," and as polemic " are surpassed by none, not by Demosthenes, or Cicero, or Swift. They have the limitation of all polemic and forensic: they persuade, they seduce, they are unfair. . . . He undoubtedly abused the art of quotation, as a polemic writer can hardly help but do; but there were abuses for him to abuse, and he did the job thoroughly." [14]

Let us keep in mind the admission of the Anglo-Catholic T. S. Eliot: " But there were abuses for him to abuse." This admission brings out the real reason for Pascal's attitude: the indignant protest of a Christian conscience enlightened by the Scriptures. Let us learn from him, concludes Strowski, " how indignant one can become against the legalistic formulas, the sophisms, the subtle decisions, that complacent moralists employ in order to permit what is never permissible, and which souls without integrity employ in order to deceive themselves. Let us acquire a certain moral intransigence which life will know how to correct. Let us touch, beyond the errors and prejudices of the man, the conscience and the soul of Pascal." [15] That is well said, but it is not saying enough.

PASCAL'S INTRANSIGENCE EXPLAINED

It would be well to add that to the Pascal of the *Provinciales* it is a matter of a conscience consecrated to an all-powerful God whose rights come before all else.

[13] Eliot, T. S., Introduction to Pascal's *Pensées*, Everyman's Library, J. M. Dent & Sons, Ltd., London; E. P. Dutton & Co., Inc., New York, reprint ed., 1940, p. xvi.
[14] *Ibid.*, pp. x–xi.
[15] Strowski, F., *Pascal et son temps, op. cit.*, v. 3, 124.

The intransigence of Pascal is explained — and in our opinion is justified — by his conviction that one cannot hesitate an instant in a choice between human pretensions and the divine prerogatives. Gazier puts his finger on the essential point of so-called " Jansenism " when he concludes in these terms the first chapter of his *Histoire générale* of the movement: " What is improperly called Jansenism is nothing but a movement of reaction against the impious theories of those who exalt free will above the divine power; it is a proclamation of the rights of God as opposed to an audacious declaration of the rights of man." [16] And it is a terrible thing to fall under the displeasure of the Living God!

Pascal must have long weighed his responsibility as a writer during the course of the composition of the *Provinciales*. He knew that " the vocation of an author is a serious one, — serious as it respects the writer, and serious as it respects the reader. That to which utterance has once been given, it is beyond the writer's power to recall; so that, in another sense, it may truly be said of literary crimes, as of the sin of Esau, that no place for repentance is to be found, though it be sought carefully, and with tears." [17] The greatest Biblical Christians of all times have always been profoundly conscious of the reality of this fact. Spurgeon, at the close of his pamphlet *All of Grace*, makes at least the claim that his reader " will not be able to charge me with having idly used the attention which you were pleased to give me while you were reading my little book." [18] And there is nothing in Pascal of the idler or the dilettante. Henceforward the only thing that matters is to know the will of God.

We have tried to give in the preceding pages a cross section, so to speak, of the judgments occasioned by the *Provinciales*. We have done this, not to satisfy the curiosity of the reader, and not solely for the sake of objectivity, but, rather, in order to present, in all its amplitude, the problem which confronted a Biblical conscience.

We are persuaded that Pascal had considered his responsibility for a long time, and that few of the contentions which we have reported would have surprised him. In the final analysis we have found ourselves faced with the alternative, the only consideration which would have had any weight in the mind of Pascal: what is the will of God? Once the

[16] Gazier, A., *Histoire générale du mouvement Janséniste, op. cit.,* v. 1, 17.

[17] Schimmelpennick, M. A., *Select Memoirs of Port-Royal,* 5th ed., Longman, Brown, Green, Longmans, and Roberts, London, 1858, 3 v., v. 3, 63.

[18] Spurgeon, C. H., *All of Grace,* The Bible Institute Colportage Association, Chicago, p. 125.

first *Lettres* had been written and he was confronted with the widely differing reactions, Pascal must have searched his mind and soul for the answer to that question. But only God could decide it.

DIVINE ARBITRATION

And that is what He is going to do by giving to the champion a sign in the midst of the battle: the miracle of the Holy Thorn. " Would Pascal have had the courage to persist, alone against all, if the miracle had not seemed to be the seal of a contract between God and him? God has charged him to defend the truth: what does anything else matter? He will reject all that contradicts the divine Word, be it the Bull of the Pope." [19] No abstract consideration would have sufficed to reassure Pascal: that would have been still a human thing. Pascal could not even invoke the ardor of his piety or of his virtue: who could say that they were agreeable to God? His Christian conscience could bow with fear and trembling only before the mysterious, the indisputable judgment of God. " God Himself must speak: the only mark of piety is that one has merited a response, above all, that one has merited the ability to understand the response." [20] Before the miracles of Jesus Christ, " the prophecies were doubtful; they are so no longer." [21] Before the miracle of the Holy Thorn, " the five propositions were doubtful; they are no longer so." [22] With one stroke, the miracle of the Holy Thorn illuminates the champion of the Bible and the Bible itself in his eyes. The miracles are going to become the keystone of Pascalian thought.

The life of the elect is a life of expectation; his prayer is an anticipation. The supernatural, the divine sign " blazes forth despite all rational skepticism." [23] Without this special sign, how would Pascal have known that he was approved, loved?

Bremond, the ardent Catholic, has thought it possible to compare the " sign " given to Pascal to the witnessing of the Holy Spirit among the Methodists and the Calvinists.[24] In the absence of this token, the Christian would be likely to slip into the habit of compromising. Certainly,

[19] Michaut, G., *Les Epoques de la pensée de Pascal, op. cit.,* p. 159.
[20] *Œuvres,* v. 12, cxxxviii.
[21] *Pensées,* Section xiii, Fr. 830, *Œuvres,* v. 14, 263.
[22] *Pensées,* Section xiii, Fr. 831, *Œuvres,* v. 14, 263.
[23] Sully Prud'homme, *La vraie religion selon Pascal, op. cit.,* Alcan, Paris, 1905, p. 117.
[24] Bremond, H., *Histoire littéraire du sentiment religieux, op. cit.,* v. 4, 336, 338.

declares a fragment of the *Pensées*, one can preserve oneself " by bend-
ing, but that is not, properly speaking, standing one's ground "; thus
there must be either " these compromises or miracles." [25] When the Pope,
the depositary of Tradition, has been biased in advance and deceived,
declares another fragment, so that truth no longer is free to show itself,
" then, since men may no longer speak of truth, truth itself must speak
to men." [26]

That is what seems to free Pascal as a Catholic from responsibility:
it is in the very hour of the eclipse of the qualified power — qualified
according to Pascal — with the Pope misinformed by the calumniators
who surround him, that the voice of the miracle makes itself more unmistakable, more irresistible than ever. If, as we have had to report it,
the Jesuits have deceived the Pope, and if Pascal has found that the
guidance of which he stands in need comes to him falsified, or does not
come at all, then his only recourse is to God.

In this hour, as in the other decisive hours of his life, the Scriptures
would guide him in his vigil. What, then, did they say to him? They
showed him Jesus referring His people to the miracles " as the most
powerful [thing]." And here Pascal, summing up John 10:38, recalls
the words of the Saviour in these terms: " If you do not believe in me,
believe at least in the miracles." [27]

It would seem then that the miracle of the Holy Thorn in the midst
of the battle was a sign all the more precious because the voice of the
immediate chief could be heard only faintly and was, moreover, the
voice of a prisoner in the enemy camp. Finally, the sign accorded was
in conformity with the promises of the Scriptures, and declared beyond
doubt by Jesus Christ Himself.

THE MIRACLE OF THE HOLY THORN

Pascal had a ten-year-old niece, Marguerite Périer, who was a boarding pupil at Port-Royal. She had a lacrimal fistula that was thought to
be incurable. At the inner corner of the left eye, an inflammation, the
size of a walnut, showed a hole which penetrated the bony structure and
seemed to reach as far as the oral cavity. Pus came out of it, accompa-

---

[25] *Pensées*, Section ix, Fr. 614, *Œuvres*, v. **14**, 55.
[26] *Pensées*, Section xiii, Fr. 832, *Œuvres*, v. **14**, 264.
[27] *Pensées*, Section xiii, Fr. 839, *Œuvres*, v. **14**, 268.
One may consult with interest: Brunschvicg, L., *Le Génie de Pascal*, 2d ed., Hachette, Paris, 1925, " L'Expérience du miracle," pp. 161, 162.

nied by an odor so nauseating that Marguerite had to live apart from the others in order not to distress them. Five experts had tried in vain to treat the ulcer.[28] Not only were they unable to cure it, but they saw no way of preventing it from becoming worse.

Only one remedy remained to be tried: cauterization with a red-hot iron. Marguerite's father, Florin Périer, after hesitating for a long time, finally decided to have it tried. On March 24, 1656, a letter had just been dispatched to Clermont, telling him to come to Paris where the operation would be performed as soon as he arrived.

However, at the very moment that the letter was started on its way, the nuns were singing the Introit for the daily mass, Ps. 85: " Incline Thine ear, O Lord, and hear me: for I am needy and poor. . . . O God, the wicked are risen up against me, and the assembly of the mighty have sought my soul: and they have not set Thee before their eyes. . . . Shew me a token for good: that they who hate me may see, and be confounded, because Thou, O Lord, hast helped me and hast comforted me."

This same day, in order to please a relative, who was a friend of Port-Royal and a great collector of relics, the good Monsieur de la Poterie, the Abbess, Mother Agnès de Saint-Paul Arnauld, had consented to expose a thorn that the pious priest said had belonged to the crown of our Lord. They were not worshipers of relics at Port-Royal, and Mother Agnès had remarked that the hour was rather one for prayer and supplication. However, after Vespers, the members of the community filed past the reliquary, and each one kissed it. Little Marguerite came forward in her turn with her teacher, Sister Flavie, a girl of rare faith. " My child, pray for your eye," said the nun. She was later to testify that the little one's eye had never appeared more horrible to her than at that moment when she touched the relic to it.

When Marguerite was back in her quarters, the mistress of the boarding pupils heard her say: " My eye is cured; it no longer hurts me." Indeed, the inflammation had disappeared, and the suppuration had stopped. Overcome with emotion, the mistress ran to make her report to Mother Agnès. Always deliberate, the latter counseled that they should wait to see whether the cure would prove to be permanent. After a week, doubt was no longer possible.

When they sent for Monsieur d'Alençay, the celebrated surgeon, he could not help feeling impatient: had he not already pronounced the

[28] For details, see Jovy, E., *Etudes pascaliennes, op. cit.*, v. 9, 170.

sore incurable? However, he had to yield to the evidence. Face to face with the fact which controverted his judgment, he declared with entire good faith " that he would give his attestation whenever it was required that it was impossible for the fistula to have been cured without a miracle." [29] Let us not waste time on the multiplicity, on the circumspection, on the trustworthiness of the testimonies. Few miracles are better attested than the miracle of the Holy Thorn.[30]

The adversaries of Port-Royal themselves had to yield to the evidence. The persecutions relaxed for a time. Pupils and recluses could return to the shelter of Port-Royal-des-Champs.

The miracle, which was to be the first of a long series of signs of election, had a message, not only for the defenders of efficacious grace, but, in a very special manner, for the family which Blaise Pascal had, in earlier days, led to the fervent and austere practice of Christianity.

The miracle confirmed Pascal himself in his vocation, and in the assurance of the firm foundation of the cause he was defending. It gave him the assurance necessary to sustain the souls who had to fight without truce against the reawakening force of concupiscence. It conferred upon him the right to become a Christian layman, or rather, it consecrated him in the role already assumed, and which he had practiced at least in an intermittent fashion since the Saint-Ange case.

[29] *Extrait d'une lettre de la Sœur Jacqueline de Sainte-Euphémie Pascal à Madame Périer, sa sœur,* March 31, 1656, *Œuvres,* v. 4, 334.

A letter from the same, dated March 29, 1656, *Œuvres,* v. 4, 327–331, contains a detailed account of the miracle.

[30] Cf. *Œuvres,* v. 6, 65, *Sentence de Monsieur le Vicaire général de Monseigneur l'Eminentissime Cardinal de Retz, Archevêque de Paris, portant vérification du miracle,* . . . and concluding " que la dite guérison surnaturelle et miraculeuse arriva le 24 Mars dernier," etc.

Sainte-Beuve, *Port-Royal,* 5th ed., 1888, v. 3, 183, gives an extract of the *Œuvres* of Benoît XIII, in which this Pope invokes the example of the miracle of the Holy Thorn.

See in *Œuvres,* v. 6, 70, the *Attestations des médecins et chirurgiens,* April 14 and 20, 1656 (*Premier recueil MS, du Père Guerrier,* p. 591). There follows, 76–79, *Lettre de la Sœur Jacqueline de Sainte-Euphémie Pascal à Madame Périer, sa sœur, sur la vérification du miracle de la Sainte Epine,* October 24, 1656.

V. 6, 93–98: On Monday, October 30, Jacqueline sends to Gilberte, at Clermont, the detailed account of the ceremony at Port-Royal. After the mass, the *Te Deum* is sung. The church is filled to overflowing. And this time, at the request of Mother Agnès, Jacqueline describes in verse the miracle performed in the person of her niece (v. 6, 103–114).

Morris Bishop cites some interesting views of Dr. Sanford R. Gifford, professor of ophthalmology at Northwestern University. Cf. *Pascal: The Life of Genius, op. cit.,* n. 19, p. 376.

The letters which Pascal wrote at this time to the Duke and to Mademoiselle de Roannez, of which we shall speak again, strove to make them understand "that the violence of inner anguish, the disquietude and tremblings are the signs of a sincere conversion, that they thus constitute the best reason for expecting steadfastness in the faith and the final mercy of God." [31] According to Madame Périer, the reflections suggested to Pascal by the miracle of the Holy Thorn encouraged in him the idea of a " Vindication of Christianity." [32]

The event was so memorable for Pascal that he adopted a new seal on which Heaven was depicted in the center of a crown of thorns, with this text from Saint Paul: *Scio cui credidi* (I know whom I have believed).[33] He couldn't have found a better way of expressing the fact that henceforth he would regard himself as the predestined instrument of Providence. As a consequence, he would act with the assurance of the chosen one, sure of himself because he had been approved from above.

THOUGHTS ON MIRACLES

Madame Périer, having indicated, as we have just said, to what point her brother had been impressed with the significance of the miracle of the Holy Thorn, goes on to say that on the occasion of this particular miracle there came to him many very important thoughts on miracles in general, on those of the Old as well as those of the New Testament.

There are miracles; therefore there is something above what we call nature. Moreover, these miracles bear the marks of their divine origin. They prove God. Those of the New Testament brought into conjunction with those of the Old establish, furthermore, the Messiahship of Jesus Christ. Blaise, his sister tells us, " discerned all that with an admirable

[31] *Œuvres*, v. 4, xx, *Introduction à la seconde série des Œuvres de Pascal*, v. 4-11.
[32] *Œuvres*, v. 1, 73 ff.
See also *Pensées*, Section xiii, and especially Fr. 841.
Le Recueil de plusieurs pièces pour servir à l'histoire de Port-Royal, Utrecht, 1740, declares, p. 300: " Monsieur Pascal was for a long time overcome with wonder, on the occasion of this miracle, and he had reason to be more moved by it than the others. For it appeared that God had granted the miracle, not only as an answer to the prayers and needs of Port-Royal, but also and more especially as an answer to his faith." Some days later, talking with a libertine, he said without hesitation " that he believed the miracles necessary, and that he did not doubt that God performed them continually."
In the interlocutor of Pascal, " one is tempted to recognize Méré," states *Œuvres*, v. 4, 353, n. 1.
[33] In *Œuvres*, v. 4, 352, the seal of Pascal is reproduced among accounts of the miracle, v. 4, 336–353.

insight, and as we listened to him talking, and as he disclosed all the circumstances related in the Old and New Testaments, they appeared clear to us. One could not deny the verity of these miracles, nor the consequences that he drew from them for the proof of God and of the Messiah, without denying the most common principles on which one bases all the things that pass for being beyond question." [34]

Let us not, however, be too hasty in concluding that the fragments on the miracles are all contemporaneous with the event which we have related, that is to say, date from 1656. Many of the *Pensées* relative to the subject are even in Madame Périer's handwriting, dictated by Pascal. One of them is written on the back of a letter dated the 19th of February, 1660.[35] However, whatever may be the date of composition — and this observation holds good for many of the other *Pensées* which were inspired by circumstances — it is natural to refer the inspiration to the event which stirred the spirit.

The proofs drawn from the miracle were, still according to Madame Périer, to constitute the first chapter of the " Vindication of Christianity." That would perhaps tend to prove that Pascal intended to take as his point of departure the conversation which he had " with the irreligious man " on the eve of the miracle of the Holy Thorn, and from there to go back to the beginnings of the Christian religion.[36]

Pascal, abruptly precipitated into polemical controversy, saw the Biblical theory of the miracles link the Church of Jesus Christ to the Church of his own time. The theory constituted an introduction to the polemic between the Jesuits and the Jansenists. In this Pascal saw " the secret and the key of true Christianity." [37] Religion thus becoming clear in his eyes, everything seemed to him to be connected in the verities, each one of which is drawn from the others. He found thus his method of exegesis, which was to consist henceforth in explaining the Bible by the Bible itself. That, as we know, has been the method used by men of God throughout the ages. Pascal was, his sister tells us, " carried away by it," [38] as he said so often.

[34] *Œuvres*, v. **1**, 73, 74.
[35] *Œuvres*, v. **12**, liv.
[36] *Œuvres*, v. **12**, lvi.
[37] *Œuvres*, v. **12**, lx.

Brunschvicg sees, in this way, the last sections of his classification of the *Pensées* fall into a natural order: La *Perpétuité* — les *Figuratifs* — les *Prophéties* — *Preuves de Jésus-Christ* — les *Miracles* — *Fragments polémiques* (*ibid.*, lxi).

[38] *Œuvres*, v. **1**, 75.

The miracles explained to Pascal the method of God. Like the parables, and by the same right, they justified the hardening of the hearts of some, at the same time as the enlightenment of others. Touchstones, they served " not to convert, but to condemn." [39] Thus, Pascal, the polemist, says to the Jesuits only what the Apostles said to the Jews who saw Jesus: referring to John 10:26 and to II Thess. 2:10, he declares that it is a lack of charity which causes some not to believe the true miracles or to pronounce them false.[40] But what joy and trembling for those who, having in their hearts the charity of Jesus, have known how to interpret the Holy Word which came to them! Beyond the human part of their being, dwells the God who became man.

MIRACLES AND THE HIDDEN GOD

The religion of Pascal lies in the order of charity, in the world of the supernatural. With Saint Augustine he confesses: " I would not be a Christian without the miracles." [41] In a sense, either all leads one to religion, or all turns one away from it: the same God dissipates the darkness for us, or increases it if we love darkness better than light. He has not wished complete enlightenment for those unworthy sinners whose natural powers cannot save them. No more has He wished total darkness, and in His goodness He has sent us a Liberator. In short, He has wished enough darkness to blind the unrepentant sinner, and enough light to guide the elect; and it is certainly not human reason which will make the division between light and darkness.

The history of Christianity, by the same token as Sacred History, is ambiguous; and this observation applies to contemporary history which shows Pascal locked in battle with the Jesuits. Heresy having cast doubt upon all doctrine, the miracles have been the intervention of God for the salvation of the Church, in that they have served to indicate the verity. Today, as of old, they condemn those whom they do not convert, and they convert those who are not condemned.

Certainly, miracles are rare in our times: there are few persons " to whom God appears in these extraordinary revelations," [42] Pascal declares to the Duke and Mademoiselle de Roannez; one should profit

[39] *Pensées*, Section xiii, Fr. 825, *Œuvres*, v. 14, 257.
[40] *Pensées*, Section xiii, Fr. 826, *Œuvres*, v. 14, 258.
[41] *Pensées*, Section xiii, Fr. 812, *Œuvres*, v. 14, 246.
[42] *Extrait d'une lettre de Pascal à Mr. et Mlle de Roannez*, October 27 (?), 1657, *Œuvres*, v. 6, 87.

all the more by these occasions. Citing the Revelation of John, the Epistle to the Romans of Paul, and the prophecies of Isaiah, and taking his starting point from these books, he writes a beautiful letter of counsel on the theme of the hidden God. As we already know, that is a favorite theme with him. It is within the framework of this theme that the subject of miracles comes henceforward to find its fullest meaning: " All things cover some mystery," concludes the extract of the letter which we are quoting; " all things are veils which hide God. Christians should recognize Him in everything." [43]

In some fragments,[44] which we must read in their entirety in order to appreciate their profundity, Pascal, studying the foundations of the Christian religion, declares that he is *astounded* — in the strong sense which the seventeenth century gives to this word: *thunderstruck* — by his encounter with the Jewish people and their Law, the first in the world and the most perfect. It is thus that the consideration of the miracles of Moses, of Jesus Christ, and of the Apostles, which at first did not appear convincing, leads him to render homage to the Book which contains " this Law, the first of all," and which henceforth is established in his eyes as " the most ancient book in the world."

THE TOUCHSTONE OF TRUE RELIGION

A miracle has become, in his opinion, a criterion: " At first when one sees a miracle, one must either believe it or discern strange contrary indications. One must determine whether it denies God, or Jesus Christ, or the Church." [45] Thanks to the miracle which for Pascal has become a sign in the midst of battle, this questioning is no longer necessary. " Here is a sacred relic; here is a thorn from the crown of the Saviour of the world, over which the princes of this world have no power, which performs miracles by virtue of the power of that blood which was shed for us. God Himself has chosen this house [Port-Royal] as the place in which to show forth His power.

" It is not men who perform miracles through an unknown or dubious virtue, a virtue which requires of us a difficult effort of discernment. It is God Himself; it is the power of His Passion, which is present in many places at one time, that chooses a certain place and draws men

[43] *Ibid.,* 88–90.
[44] *Pensées,* Section ix, Fr. 619, 620, *Œuvres,* v. **14,** 58–65.
[45] *Pensées,* Section xiii, Fr. 835, *Œuvres,* v. **14,** 267.

from all sides, there to receive the miraculous assuagement of their weariness." [46]

The miracle of the Holy Thorn, taking place between the condemnation of Arnauld by the Sorbonne on January 29, 1656, and the Bull of Alexander VII on October 16, 1656, which transformed the condemnation of the five propositions into a condemnation of Jansen, is a warning from God " that one think not contrary to His Will." [47] Never was such a miracle granted to heretics!

Miracles are the mainstay of religion. They constitute the touchstone of the true religion: they set apart the Jews, the Christians, the saints, the innocent ones, the true believers. It would be something worthy of notice " if a miracle were performed for the Jesuits." [48] Fragment 852 of the *Pensées* is really the rough draft for a *Provinciale*. It opens with this apostrophe: " Unjust persecutors of those whom God manifestly protects." In the manner of the Scriptures and submitting to their teachings, the fragment exalts the miracles which " have served for the foundation and will serve for the continuation of the Church even unto the Antichrist, unto the very end." [49] Section xiii of the *Pensées*, in the edition of Brunschvicg which we are following, closes with a hymn of thanksgiving taken from Fragment 856 " *Sur le miracle. — As God has not rendered any family happier, let it also be said that there has never been a family more supremely grateful.*" [50] An appendix to Section xiii presents some questions on miracles which Pascal put " to the Abbé de Saint Cyran," [51] and reveals to what point the subject was close to his heart.

We shall devote a special chapter to Pascal as a student of the Bible. At this point we should like to draw the reader's attention to the manner in which Pascal searches the Scriptures on the subject of miracles. Fragment 842 contains not less than twelve Scriptural references.[52] To put it plainly, *Pascal scrutinizes the Bible henceforth with the same minuteness that he used to employ in scrutinizing nature*. An excellent example of his method is offered to us by Fragment 819, in which we see him considering the authenticity of the texts, comparing the different

---

[46] *Pensées*, Section xiii, Fr. 839, *Œuvres*, v. **14**, 270.
[47] *Pensées*, Section xiii, Fr. 850, *Œuvres*, v. **14**, 286.
[48] *Pensées*, Section xiii, Fr. 851, *Œuvres*, v. **14**, 288.
[49] *Pensées*, Section xiii, Fr. 852, *Œuvres*, v. **14**, 291.
[50] *Pensées*, Section xiii, Fr. 856, *Œuvres*, v. **14**, 292.
[51] *Œuvres*, v. **14**, 293-299.
[52] *Œuvres*, v. **14**, 273-275.

versions, studying the variants, the etymologies, and clarifying the whole question of the miracles by reference to Jesus Christ: " Jer. 23:32, the *miracles* of the false prophets. In the Hebrew and in the Vatable edition there are *unseemly frivolities*.

" *Miracle* does not always mean miracle. In I Kings 14:15, *miracle* means *fear*, and is so in the Hebrew. The same evidently in Job 33:7. And again in Isa. 21:4; Jer. 44:12. *Portentum* means *simulacrum*, Jer. 50:38, and has that meaning both in the Hebrew and in Vatable. In Isa. 8:18 Jesus Christ says that He and His people will be in *miracles*." [53]

Fragment 827 refers to six Biblical texts in order to prove that there has never been a miracle on the side of error.[54] The counterproof is furnished in Fragment 828: it is always Truth which prevails in matters of miracles. On the witness stand we see: Abel and Cain; Moses and the magicians; Elias and the false prophets; the latter again confronted by Jeremiah, by Ananias, by Micah; Jesus Christ in debate with the Pharisees; Saint Paul and Bar-Jesus; the Apostles and the exorcisers; the Christians and the infidels; the Catholics and the heretics; Elias, Enoch, and the Antichrist.[55]

A NEW RESOLUTENESS

As the tone becomes more vehement in the polemic fragments of the *Pensées*, we realize that this compilation as we know it today lets us into many a secret of Pascal. As, on the other hand, Pascal's " Thoughts " were to culminate in a " Vindication " of Christianity, it seems evident that the *Provinciales* would have expressed therein their final message. We have on this last point precious evidence from Etienne Périer.[56] A fragment such as Fragment 921 in the Brunschvicg classification surpasses in violence any of the *Provinciales:* " [What have you gained by accusing me of ridiculing holy things? You will not gain any more by accusing me of being an impostor.]

" [I haven't said all, you will see.]

" I am not a heretic. I have not defended the five propositions. You

[53] *Pensées,* Section xiii, Fr. 819, *Œuvres,* v. **14,** 252, 253. Compare Douay edition I Kings 14:15 with Authorized Version I Sam. 14:15.

[54] *Pensées,* Section xiii, Fr. 827, *Œuvres,* v. **14,** 259, 260.

[55] *Pensées,* Section xiii, Fr. 828, *Œuvres,* v. **14,** 260, 261.

[56] *Œuvres,* v. **12,** cxcv. See also the Argument of the *Pensées,* v. **12,** ccxxiii. Cf. on this subject our note 32 in Ch. XIV, pp. 274, 275.

say that I have and do not prove it. I say that you have said it, and I prove it.

" You threaten me.

" Will you say that I am an impostor?

" I say to you that you are the impostors. I prove that you are. . . .

" No man has ever had such a good cause as I, and never have any others made themselves so vulnerable.

" You shall feel the force of the Truth, and you shall yield to it.

" To make the world believe you, you would have to threaten it with mortal sin.

" There is something supernatural in such blindness. . . .

" I am alone against thirty thousand? Not at all. Keep, you, the court; you, the imposture; I, the Truth: it is my whole force; if I lose it, I am lost. I shall not lack accusations and persecutions. But I have the Truth, and we shall see who shall win the victory." [57]

Let anyone who cares to, become indignant at Pascal's indignation. It would not have been marked by such assurance if it had not been stamped by the approbation of the divine seal, by the Sign come down from above in the very midst of the battle; it would not have fortified souls, it would not have rendered them moral to such a degree, if it had not sprung from the *fountains of living water — fontes aquae vivae —* " from which Pascal drew the force with which he armed himself in order to fight that which he held in such abhorrence ' as being very hurtful to the Church,' that is to say, baseness, vice, and the corruption of morals." [58]

The *Provinciales* are the fruit of the dictates of conscience, of a conscience enlightened by the Holy Scriptures, set afire by them.

[57] *Pensées*, Section xiv, Fr. 921, *Œuvres*, v. 14, 345–349.
[58] Stewart, H. F., " Deux mots sur les ' Provinciales,' " *Foi et Vie*, Year 1923, p. 779.

XIII

The Dictates of Conscience

" Holding faith, and a good conscience."

—I Tim. 1:19

Four days after the miracle of the Holy Thorn, on March 28, appeared the terrible fifth *Provinciale,* analyzing, with implacable and vengeful irony, the prime features of the morality of the " good Jesuit Fathers."

The latter, in their *Image of the First Century* (*Imago primi saeculi*), set themselves up as " a society of men, or, rather, angels " predicted by Isaiah, and destined to change the face of Christendom.[1] And what can one say of this *Moral Theology* of the Jesuit Escobar, compiled by the latter from twenty-four Fathers of the Society, and compared by him in an allegory to the book of *Revelation* sealed with seven seals? Jesus, Escobar claims, " offers it sealed thus to the four animals Suarez, Vasquez, Molina, Valentia [note the rimes!], in the presence of the twenty-four Jesuits who represent the twenty-four Elders." [2]

Jesuit tactics employ the " severe maxims of the Bible . . . suitable for governing a few kinds of people," on the occasions when they are favorable to the Jesuits. Since these maxims do not agree with the views of the majority of people, the Fathers " leave them with regard to the latter in order to have something to satisfy everyone." [3] One could not be more opportunistic: by this conduct " obliging and accommodating," as Father Petau calls it, they extend their arms to everyone.[4]

By thus carrying water on both shoulders, the Jesuits conserve all their friends and defend themselves against all their enemies: " When charged with their extreme laxity, they immediately produce for public display their austere directors, and some books they have written on

---

[1] *Cinquième Provinciale, Œuvres,* v. 4, 298.
[2] *Ibid.,* 305, 307. See the preface of Escobar and the facsimile, v. 4, 286.
[3] *Ibid.,* 300.
[4] *Ibid.,* 200, 201.

the severity of Christian law; and the simple-minded, and those who never look below the surface of things, are contented with these proofs." [5]

They use the same tactics in the field of missions where Jesuit preaching suppresses, when they think it necessary, " the scandal of the Cross " of which Saint Paul speaks.[6]

THE DOCTRINE OF " PROBABLE OPINIONS "

Montalte then comes to the famous doctrine of *probable opinions,* of which the good Father says that it constitutes " the foundation and the A B C of all our morality." [7] In virtue of this doctrine an opinion is declared *probable* when it appears founded on reasons of some consideration. It is thus that the opinion of a single very serious Doctor can make an opinion *probable.* And as there is nothing one cannot justify by the authority of a Doctor arbitrarily qualified as " serious," so there is no human act which cannot find its justification! The fifth *Provinciale,* and those following will strive to point out to what degree such casuistry ruins morality. Essentially, they will do this by constant references to Scripture, according to which " the law of the Lord which is spotless and holy is the one which must convert souls." [8]

At the root of the moral quarrel carried on with the Jesuits by the fifth *Provinciale* is found the great debate between nature and grace.[9] As the morality of the Jesuits appears quite pagan, confidence in nature is all that is necessary to practice it. When Montalte and his friends uphold the necessity of efficacious grace, they have in view a higher virtue: it is no longer a question only of curing vices by other vices, nor of having men practice the exterior duties of religion in the manner of the Pharisees and the wisest among the pagans. Law and reason would

[5] *Ibid.,* 301.
[6] Gal. 5:11.
[7] *Cinquième Provinciale, Œuvres,* v. 4, 310.
[8] Wendrock (Nicole) adds in his Latin translation *à Scripturâ dicitur.* Cf. Ps. 18:8.
[9] Nowhere, so far as we know, has the opposition between the movements of nature and those of grace been better analyzed than in *De Imitatione Christi,* Liber III, liv, *De Diversis motibus naturae et gratiae.* Personifying abstractions, following a practice familiar to the Middle Ages, the author designs by " nature," the man who lives according to nature, and by " grace," the man who lives according to grace.

Christians of all times will always find an immense profit in submitting themselves to the test of these luminous pages which excel in setting forth in full clarity the most remote corners of the human soul.

be sufficient grace to attain that end. " But to free the soul from the love of the world, to take it away from what it holds most dear, to make it die within itself, to lift it up and bind it to God alone, this can be the work of none but an all-powerful hand." [10]

The casuistry of probable opinions arouses the indignation of a Biblical conscience anxious for certainty and for salvation. Can the Father who exposes the views of the casuists conscientiously share them?

" Certainly not," replies the latter.

" You speak then against your conscience? "

" No, indeed. I was speaking on that point not according to *my own* conscience, but according to that of Ponce and Father Bauny; you may safely follow them for they are able men."

" What, Father! because they have put those three lines in their books, will it now be permissible to seek occasions to sin? I thought I should take only Scripture and the Church Tradition as my rule, not your casuists."

" O good heavens; you make me think of those Jansenists! Cannot Father Bauny and Bazile Ponce make their opinion probable? "

Listen closely to the answer which the good Father receives, for all of Blaise Pascal is in it:

" *I am not content with the probable, I seek the sure.*" [11]

And to appreciate fully this reply, compare the one in Fragment 908 of the *Pensées*, where Pascal is found meditating, pen in hand, on the subject. " But is it *probable* that probability assures? Difference between repose and surety of conscience. *Nothing gives assurance except the truth; nothing gives repose except the sincere search for truth.*" [12] It is we who italicize this noble thought which makes our naked soul touch the naked soul of Blaise Pascal.

Where then can we find it, this assurance of the truth which we need? There is not an instant of hesitation in Pascal: " only in the way of the Bible." [13] When, indeed, the good Father has terminated his exposé of the doctrine of probable opinions, Montalte says to him:

" I understand all that. I see very well that all is welcomed by you except the ancient Fathers; and that you are the champions of the course: you have only to run.

[10] *Cinquième Provinciale, Œuvres*, v. 4, 304.
[11] *Ibid.*, 309.
[12] *Pensées*, Section xiv, Fr. 908, *Œuvres*, v. 14, 336.
[13] *Cinquième Provinciale, Œuvres*, v. 4, 319.

" But I foresee three or four great barriers and some formidable disadvantages which oppose your course."

" What? " asks the astonished Father.

" Holy Scripture, the Popes, and the Councils, which you cannot contradict, and which all follow the undeviating path of the Gospel."

" Is that all? You frightened me." [14]

CASUISTRY IN LEAGUE WITH NATURE

The unswerving way of the Gospel itself loses the simplicity by which it was identified with the truth, as soon as a Vasquez interprets it. The Gospel tells us, for example, to give alms from our excess. But what becomes of this rule when this same word *excess* is understood in such a way that the richest men find that they have no excess? Charitable obligations vanish after Vasquez and Diana have spoken. There are two paths henceforth: the path which leads to almsgiving, and the path which excuses one from it. Both are found to be " sure according to the same Gospel, one according to the Gospel in its most literal sense, and the one easiest to find; the other according to the same Gospel interpreted by Vasquez." [15] It is difficult for Montalte to conceive the utility of such subtle interpretations: utility is here translated by Wendrock [Nicole]: *quanta commoditas;* [16] thus casuistry creates a hopeless situation with regard to a believer anxious to find salvation and to go back to the simplicity of spirit of the Holy Text.

Casuistry at its best appears to be a form of *speculative* theology which seeks in scholasticism " the means of reconciling man's freedom and God's power, both considered as truths of the same breadth and the same level; susceptible, so to speak, of being placed at the two ends of a horizontal chain." [17] Let us not be surprised to see Pascal, a committed student of the Bible, revolt against such an operation which ends in placing God and man on the same plane.

The operation, moreover, is only brought about by an intellectual perversion which, substituting the letter for the spirit, finally confers an occult and magic virtue upon words — as Descartes had already said of the Scholastic definitions: " If in the formula of the rule by which

[14] *Ibid.*

[15] *Sixième Provinciale, Œuvres,* v. **5**, 31.

[16] *Œuvres,* v. **5**, n. 1, 31.

[17] *Introduction à la seconde série des Œuvres de Pascal* [v. **4-11**], *Œuvres,* v. **4**, liii.

the confessor judges the penitent, the word has a value merely as a word, it will be possible to give the appearance of submission and obedience, while violating the moral principle from which the rule drew its value." [18]

There is for Pascal only one means of resolving these disastrous confusions; that is to bring the teachings of casuistry back to their principle by the light of the Scripture: the Christian religion " is very different in the Holy Book and in the casuists," affirms an addition to Fragment 601 of the *Pensées*,[19] written in by Pascal.

Let no one be mistaken about it: it is *nature* in man which makes an appeal to casuistry; and this statement is true of all times and of all casuistry: " The Gospel, expressing a state of soul raised above nature by exaltation, is not always in agreement with pure reason. If it happens, then, in morality that nature is less exacting than the Gospel, it is to nature that casuistry will appeal, to be more freely indulgent, and thus it will find itself nearer to us." [20] It is noteworthy that the study of cases of conscience is as old as morality itself. It has its proper place in so far as we need to reflect on our duties, to make a decision in the midst of circumstances which cause us, at times, to seem to be divided against ourselves, at grips with the best of ourselves for causes which may be very noble. Duty proves to be complex. Often it carries within itself its own stumbling block. Cicero, in the last book of his *De Officiis*, treated of these problems of the inner life from the point of view of Stoicism. However, the very notion of casuistry appears, in its modern sense, as contemporaneous with the Catholic practice of confession. It is not only a question of absolving the conscience of sin, but of directing it; and these two types of obligations pose for the confessor delicate problems whose reality and gravity cannot be doubted. The Protestant ministers are familiar with these difficulties in their personal counseling. A danger lurks at each step on the way of the confessor and the adviser, however: that of being obliged to compromise with nature, even though it be for motives in appearance as powerful as they are noble.

Casuistry finds its natural domain, of necessity, in the vulgarity of appetites, in the violence of egotism, in the everyday fact of human weakness. At each instant, the means runs the risk of becoming an end — one

[18] *Ibid.*, xlvii.
[19] *Œuvres*, v. 14, 40.
[20] Havet, E., *Les* Provinciales *de Pascal,* new edition with an introduction and remarks, Delagrave, Paris, 1885, 2 v., v. 1, Introduction, lxxxv.

of those ends which justify the means. Even before he perceives it, the casuist has relaxed his morality. Casuistry and relaxed morality then follow the famous line of least resistance in accordance with the natural propensity of nature left to itself.

If there is in the Bible one clear precept, it is that the natural man must die within himself to make place for the new man. We must be born again: " That which is born of the flesh, is flesh and that which is born of the Spirit is Spirit." [21] The Cross will become the starting point for the new man only if it has been the terminal point for the old man. These primordial affirmations of the Bible condemn once and for all the subtleties of nature. Nature rebels against it, and few people consent to be broken at the threshold of the narrow gate. That is why the normal result of the preaching of the Word is its failure. Between the single-minded way of the Bible and the others, there is no compromise: " Be not yoked together with the ungodly," remains in this sense the great commandment of the sanctified soul.

Each time the Bible is preached anew in its purity, the unswerving way of the Bible will be contrasted with the devious ways of casuistry — devious because they yield to the propensity of nature instead of sticking to the straight and difficult ridge trail where one can keep one's footing only if one is being assisted. Havet recalls that the Protestants, in the war they waged against the Catholic Church, had taken care not " to forget what compromised it the most," and the Reverend Monsieur Du Moulin, in a book published in Geneva in 1632, *Catalogue des traditions romaines,* had drawn up a veritable list of grievances on this subject. [22]

Pascal, the man of the Bible, came to take his place in the Biblical tradition by writing the *Provinciales* where, above all else, he takes casuistry to task. However, he was an innovator to a considerable extent in the sense that up to that time polemics had found an audience only among the theologians and in the ecclesiastical world. " It is Pascal who brought them before the great public with a repercussion which has been prodigious, since casuistry and the Jesuits have not recovered from it." [23] It is without a doubt this which continues to stir up the worst rancor against Pascal. A professor who teaches a course on Pascal in a graduate school constantly is made aware of this fact.

[21] John 3:6.
[22] Havet, E., *Les* Provinciales *de Pascal, op. cit.,* v. 1, v.
[23] *Ibid.,* vi.

The very unction of the excuses, attributed to the good Fathers by Montalte, exasperates anger even in our day.

" Alas! " says the Father in the sixth *Provinciale*, " our principal aim was to establish no other maxims than those of the Gospel in all their severity," but " men are today so corrupt, that being unable to make them come to us, we have to go to them." [24] And it is thus that the Jesuits are led to have " maxims for all sorts of persons." [25]

" DIRECTION OF INTENTION "

The seventh *Provinciale* takes up the same theme and shows how compromise leads to expedients. The Fathers had to relax a little the severity of religion in order to accommodate themselves to the weaknesses of men. It was for the advisers a question of remaining attached to the Gospel by their duty toward God, and to the people of the world by their love for their neighbor. They needed, therefore, all their cleverness to find expedients and compromises in their efforts to attain the golden mean by which it is possible to " keep entirely together two things as contrary in appearance as piety and honor." [26] You can well imagine that they succeeded.

Montalte would consider this impossible if he didn't already know that the Jesuits " can easily do what is impossible for other men." [27] And certainly if there is an impossibility par excellence it is to ally the Gospel with the world! To attain this end, nothing less than a " marvelous principle," a " great method," would suffice. This method is of such importance in the morality of the Fathers that one would almost dare to compare it to the famous doctrine of probable opinions! It is of the *direction of intention* that the good Father wishes to speak.

To see this great method in all its luster, we must observe its effects in the question of homicide. Would you believe that the direction of intention succeeds in justifying homicide on a thousand occasions? Oh! let us make our meaning clear: it could not be a question of justifying the diabolic attitude of " whoever persists in limiting his desire to evil for the sake of evil." Moreover, the good Fathers, as much as it is in their power to do so, turn men away from forbidden things. But still the mo-

[24] *Sixième Provinciale, Œuvres,* v. **5**, 37.
[25] *Ibid.,* 38.
[26] *Septième Provinciale, Œuvres,* v. **5**, 84.
[27] *Ibid.,* 85.

ment comes when, in spite of their efforts, the good Fathers do not succeed in preventing evil actions. They, therefore, *purify the intention,* and thus correct " the vice inherent in the means by the purity of the end." [28] In this way, " they satisfy the world by permitting evil actions; and they satisfy the Gospel by purifying the intentions." [29] They succeed thus in realizing an alliance " of the maxims of the Gospel with those of the world." [30] Let us consider an example: " Have I claimed," replies the Father at a certain moment, " that one is permitted to kill treacherously? God forbid. I say unto you that one may kill secretly; and from there you conclude that one may kill treacherously, as if it were the same thing." [31] And he sends Montalte off to Escobar.

This poor ignorant Montalte! To confuse " to kill secretly " with homicide by treachery! That is what happens when a man of the Bible takes it upon himself to borrow the language of a learned man! Having cited Escobar on homicide by treachery, the Father triumphs loudly. Let us follow the argument:

" You see now, you do not even understand what the terms signify, and yet you speak like a doctor."

" I confess that this is something quite new to me, and I am learning from that definition that few, if any, were ever killed by treachery; for people seldom take it into their heads to assassinate any but their enemies. Be this as it may, it seems that, according to Sanchez, a man may freely slay (I do not say treacherously, but only behind his victim's back or in an ambush) a calumniator, for example, who prosecutes us at law."

" Yes, but always by directing his intentions well; you forget the main point all the time." [32]

But, among so many subtleties, what becomes of the fundamental Commandment: " Thou shalt not kill "? Let no one worry about this, however: casuistry with its accommodating suppleness knows how to provide for the rigidity of the Scriptures. Listen to the good Father explain it:

" Search in the ancient Fathers to find out for how much money it is permitted to kill a man. What will they tell you, except *non occides: thou shalt not kill? "*

" And who has dared to determine that sum? "

[28] *Ibid.,* 86.
[29] *Ibid.,* 87.
[30] *Ibid.*
[31] *Ibid.,* 93.
[32] *Ibid.,* 94.

" Our great and incomparable Molina, the glory of our Society, who, by his inimitable prudence, has estimated it at six or seven ducats, for which he is certain that one may be permitted to kill, and further, the one who takes them should flee."

Molina adds, moreover, *" that he would not dare to condemn with any sin a man who kills the one who wishes to take away from him a thing valued at a ducat or less."* This is what brought Escobar to establish this general rule: *" that regularly one may kill a man for the value of one ducat."* This elicits the following repartee from Montalte: " O my Father, from what source could Molina have been enlightened to determine a thing of this importance without any help from Scripture, the Councils, or the Fathers? I certainly see that he has special light on the subject, very different from that accorded to Saint Augustine, on homicide as well as on grace." [33]

CARAMUEL'S THEORY

But here is something which is better still, or worse — it all depends on how you understand this teaching of a new type: Let us examine with Montalte the famous theory of Caramuel by virtue of which a *priest* can, under certain circumstances, kill a slanderer; but there is still more: there are certain occasions when that action becomes for him an *obligation:* " etiam aliquando *debet* occidere." [34] This principle is then examined to learn *" whether the Jesuits can kill the Jansenists."* There is a point of moral theology which certainly surprises Montalte! Let him be reassured, however: it was only a false alarm. The fact is that the Jansenists are not at all endangered because they do not harm the reputation of the Jesuits. Montalte, however, is not yet completely reassured:

" I do not consider them in any great security, if that is the case. For if it became at all possible that they were doing you wrong, they are thus *killable* without any difficulty." [35]

A note of the *Œuvres* [36] specifies that the term *killable* was not admitted into the dictionary of the French Academy until 1672. Richelet cites only this example from Pascal; Hatzfeld and Darmesteter cite another from Pierre de l'Etoile. Let us, moreover, point out the comic (!) side of this neologism, another precedent which will make of Pascal

[33] *Ibid.*, 103, 104.
[34] *Ibid.*, 106.
[35] *Ibid.*, 107.
[36] *Ibid.*, 107, n. 2.

Molière's teacher: the latter, in the first scene of *The Misanthrope,* will use a similar procedure, by playing on the word " hang." To Alceste, who declares to him:

> " And if, by misfortune, I had done the same,
> I should go away regretfully, to hang myself at once,"

his " friend " Philinte makes the rejoinder:
" As for me, I don't see that the case is hangable."
A " killable " man, says the Pascal of the *Provinciales.*
A " hangable " case, says the Molière of the *Misanthrope.*

A comedy in both cases, and a tragic one in both; such is the depth of the " comic " in one as in the other. Once more we discover in Pascal an artisan of the great French classic period generally designated under the name of " century of Louis XIV."

Faugère compares to the theory of Caramuel a phrase of the *Aphorisms of Calvin,* where the latter is said to have advocated the use of the same procedure with regard to the Jesuits. But this work is the product of the Jesuit Martin Bécan, who falsely attributes this doctrine to Calvin.[37]

RELIGION MADE EASY

Certainly one is now ready to understand the reflection of Montalte toward the end of the seventh *Provinciale:* " In truth, my father, one might as well deal with people who have no religion at all." [38]

It is the cry of the heart which echoes this remark at the beginning of the eighth *Provinciale:* " It is very painful to see all Christian morality upset by such strange aberrations without openly contradicting them." [39] When the Father points out in his authors " things of such an infamous nature " that he would not dare to quote them, the anxiety of Montalte is not feigned. It is a question of Molina's discussions on the *occulta fornicatio.* To tell the truth, Montalte confesses himself dumfounded in his surprise " to see books of priests full of decisions so horrible, so unjust, and so extravagant all together." [40] The same is true in the ninth *Provinciale* in matters of chastity, where the Fathers consent to treat " rather curious and rather dubious questions, prin-

[37] Weiss, in *Bulletin historique et littéraire de la Société de l'Histoire du Protestantisme français,* 1896, v. **45,** 5 (quotation in *Œuvres,* v. **5,** 107, n. 1).

[38] *Septième Provinciale, Œuvres,* v. **5,** 107.

[39] *Huitième Provinciale, Œuvres,* v. **5,** 136.

[40] *Ibid.,* 162.

cipally for persons who are married or engaged." Montalte learns a lot of things on the subject, things " the most extraordinary and the most brutal that one can imagine." He could " fill several letters " with them. However, he will not even quote them, his end being not to provide " entertainment " [41] for a whole class of readers of the *Provinciales*.

The letters warn against false devotions to the Virgin, and against the false security which their superstitious practices give to the faithful. Montalte is especially vehement against deceptive assurances. These false assurances make those who employ this type of devotions believe, for example, that " without changing their evil life, they will be converted at death, or that God will resuscitate them." This maneuver is especially proper " to keep sinners in their disorders by the false peace that this audacious confidence brings, instead of " drawing them away by a true conversion which grace alone can produce." [42] It is again to the fundamental teaching of the Bible that Pascal has recourse in order to clarify a whole growth of such practices.

The last lines of Father Barry aver that the Virgin answers for the entrance into paradise of the one who, troubled at death, says that Mary will answer for him. Montalte objects: " Who has told you that the Virgin answers for it? " But the only answer he elicits is the amazing response that Father Barry answers for her!

An attractive religion, that of the Jesuits! It is " a quite charming picture of devotion " that the Fathers invent for the use of worldly people! Such is the book *La Dévotion aisée* of Father le Moyne, which gained for him much fame.[43] This same Father, in the seventh book of his *Peintures morales*, pictures the alternative to this " easy devotion " by his presentation of a monk of austere morals with the features of an unfeeling specter, and the eyes and ears of a statue, and who has grimly retired from the world. Montalte, this time, feels that the whole affair has gone beyond the limits of the intelligible:

" My reverend Father, I assure you that if you had not told me that Father le Moyne is the author of this painting, I should have said it must have been some impious man who did it with the design of ridiculing the saints. For if this is not the image made by a man completely detached from the sentiments which the Gospel obliges us to renounce, I confess I understand nothing of all this." [44]

Is it a question of the licentiousness of feminine clothing? Where do

[41] *Neuvième Provinciale, Œuvres*, v. 5, 207.
[42] *Ibid.*, 194.
[43] *Ibid.*, 197.
[44] *Ibid.*, 198, 199.

the Jesuit authors take their maxims, and how do they answer the passages of the Scripture which speak with so much vehemence of the lack of modesty in woman? Lessius, answers the Father, has made a doctoral reply to this objection. According to him, the passages of the Scripture in question " were precepts only with regard to woman of that time, to give by their modesty an example of edification." [45]

The best means which the Fathers have found " to attract everyone and to repel no one is doubtless the softening they brought to confession. And how far they have gone in this direction! The tenth *Provinciale*, which attacks the subject, notes that the Fathers literally " discharged men from the *painful* obligation of loving God," [46] this dispensation from " the annoying obligation of loving God " being " the privilege of the New Testament law above the Judaic." This time Montalte cries out his indignation: " O my Father, there is no patience which you do not stretch to the breaking point, and one cannot hear without horror the things which I have just heard." [47]

SUBVERSIVE INNOVATIONS

Would the Jesuits then reduce to nothing, through their innovations, the best established traditions?

We remember having read in the magnificent work by Emile Mâle consecrated to *L'Art religieux du XIIIe siècle en France* [48] a passage relative to a prescription which, since it is already found in the apostolic constitutions, went back to the first centuries of Christianity. It is the prescription which directs that the head of the church point to the east, that is to say, the part of the sky where the sun rises at the time of the equinoxes. From the eleventh to the fourteenth century, remarks the author, one can scarcely cite any examples of wrongly oriented churches. And he adds: " The rule fell into neglect toward the epoch of the Council of Trent, at the same time as the other traditions of medieval art; the Jesuits were the first to violate the rule." [49] Could this be the

---

[45] *Ibid.*, 209.

[46] *Dixième Provinciale, Œuvres*, v. **5**, 271.

[47] *Ibid.*, 272.

[48] Mâle, E., *L'Art religieux du XIIIe siècle en France*, Etude sur l'iconographie du Moyen Age et sur ses sources d'inspiration [a study on the iconography of the Middle Ages and on its sources of inspiration], new edition, revised and corrected, illustrated with 127 prints, Colin, Paris, 1902.

[49] *Ibid.*, p. 18.

same spirit which inspired the shaking of the very foundations of Biblical teaching?

The tenth *Provinciale* ends with a terrible indictment, an indictment pronounced by the Biblical herald under the compulsion of his conscience.

Indignation is so genuine in Pascal that once more it raises its tone to veritable eloquence: " The license they have assumed to tamper with the most holy rules of Christian conduct amounts to a total subversion of the laws of God. They violate the great Commandment which includes all the Law and the Prophets.[50] They strike at the very heart of piety; they rob it of the spirit that gives it life; they say that to love God is not necessary to salvation; and go so far as to maintain that this dispensation from loving God is the advantage which Jesus Christ has brought into the world. This is the epitome of impiety. Christ's blood, then, was shed to buy our dispensation from loving Him. Before the Incarnation we were obliged to love God; but since *God so loved the world that He gave His only begotten Son,*[51] the world, redeemed by Him, will be discharged from loving Him! Strange theology of our days! We dare to take away the anathema which Saint Paul pronounces against those that love not the Lord Jesus.[52] We cancel the sentence of Saint John: *He that loveth not, abideth in death;*[53] and that of Jesus Christ Himself: *He that loveth me not, keepeth not my commandments.*[54] Thus are rendered worthy of enjoying God in eternity those who never loved God in all their life. Behold the mystery of iniquity fulfilled." [55]

Shaken by the vehemence of this attack, the Society of Jesus multiplies its responses, responses without grace or talent, where the argumentation is dulled under the chaotic mass of insults and vain recriminations.

Public opinion turns against the Jesuits, and the Church of France itself begins to take action. On May 12, 1656, the syndic of the curés of Paris proposes to the assembly of its confreres the examination of the questions raised by the *Provinciales*. Either Louis de Montalte is a slanderer, or the casuists should be condemned! On May 30, Du Four, curé at Rouen, in the presence of the Archbishop and a synod of more than eight hundred members of the clergy, pronounces a sensational

---

[50] Cf. Matt. 22:36–40.
[51] Cf. John 3:16.
[52] Cf. I Cor. 16:22.
[53] I John 3:14.
[54] John 14:24.
[55] *Dixième Provinciale, Œuvres,* v. 5, 273–275.

sermon against corrupt morality; he takes up his case again on July 9. Father Brisacier, rector of the *collège* at Rouen, demands from the Archbishop a "reparation of honor" and the interdiction of the *Provinciales*. The curés of Rouen join with Du Four, and, in a counter-request, accompanied by a report, demand the condemnation of the maxims professed by the Jesuits. They go so far as to ask their confreres of Paris to join them in denouncing these immoral doctrines at the Assembly of the Clergy. When, on the seventh of August, the assembly of curés of Paris concur with their demand, the whole Gallican Church shows itself ready to rally in the same condemnation of the Company of Jesus.

It is the Company of Jesus, taken as a body, that Pascal is going to attack directly, beginning with the eleventh *Provinciale*. The Jesuits have complained that he has turned sacred things to raillery. Ah! Indeed not!: "I have been," he specifies, "as far from making fun of holy things as the doctrine of your casuists is far from the holy doctrine of the Gospel." [56] And he clearly poses the question on Biblical grounds: "It would be an impiety to be wanting in respect for the verities which the Spirit of God has revealed but it would be no less impiety of another sort to be wanting in contempt for the falsities which the spirit of man opposes to them." [57] Not only is Montalte's method justified, it is "used by the Fathers of the Church," authorized by Scripture, by the example of the greatest saints, and by God Himself." [58] Ridicule is a weapon of the Scripture against the impious: according to David,[59] the saints will laugh at the punishment of the evil. Job [60] speaks of it in the same way, and the first words which God addressed to man after his fall contain a discourse of biting irony: Behold the man has become one of us.[61] Such ridicule is only justice.[62] The prophets, filled with the Spirit of God, have used it, as we can see in the examples of Daniel and of Elias. Jesus Himself had recourse to it in his interview with Nicodemus. And what should one say of the Church Fathers and of Tradition? Pascal cites Saint Jerome, Tertullian,

---

[56] *Onzième Provinciale, Œuvres,* v. **5,** 309.
[57] *Ibid.*
[58] *Ibid.,* 310.
[59] Ps. 51:8.
[60] Job 22:19.
[61] Gen. 3:22.
[62] Jer. 51:18. The Douay version reads: "They are vain works, and worthy to be laughed at." The Authorized Version reads: "They are vanity, the work of errors."

Saint Augustine, Saint Irenaeus, Saint Bernard, and the other Fathers of the Church, imitators of the Apostles, and imitated by the faithful in succeeding eras.[63] Montalte therefore does not believe he is wrong in following them.

Let those whom Montalte's campaign irritates consider then before God how shameful and pernicious to the Church is the morality spread everywhere by the casuists; how scandalous and immoderate is the license which they introduce into the Christian way of life. . . . *Woe to the blind who lead, woe to the blind who are led!* [64]

And what do the Jesuits say to legitimize their grievances? That Montalte blackens their character in a spirit of impiety and hatred? Even if it were a question of converting the whole earth, the truth of God would not need our lie, according to Scripture.[65] Whoever uses lying, acts through the spirit of the Devil, and there is no direction of intention which can rectify calumny. In order to dissipate any misunderstanding relative to the reproach which the Jesuits addressed to him, Montalte recalls to his detractors the signs which the Church Fathers have given to us to judge whether the reproofs come from a spirit of impiety and hatred, or from a spirit of piety and charity. The first rule is to speak with truth; the second, to speak with discretion; the third, to mock, when necessary, errors and not holy things; and the fourth, which is the principle and the end of all the others, to have " in one's heart the desire for the salvation of those against whom one is speaking," addressing " one's prayers to God, at the same time that one addresses reproaches to men." [66] It is in a spirit of prayer that Pascal thus declares he is writing his *Lettres Provinciales*.

PRIVATE LETTERS CONFIRM THE " LETTRES "

Could Montalte remain master of himself to this extent? At the beginning of the twelfth *Provinciale,* he picks up in the replies of his adversaries the appellations of Impious, Buffoon, Ignorant, Bad Joker, Impostor, Slanderer, Cheat, Heretic, Disguised Calvinist, Disciple of Du Moulin, Possessed by a Legion of Devils.[67] And everything else you want, he adds. Soon, however, the amused tone of the opening para-

---

[63] *Onzième Provinciale, Œuvres,* v. 5, 310–314.
[64] *Ibid.,* 320.
[65] Job 13:7.
[66] *Onzième Provinciale, Œuvres,* v. 5, 321–324.
[67] *Douzième Provinciale, Œuvres,* v. 5, 361.

graphs becomes bitter: " At least, remember that it is you who oblige me to enter this elucidation, and let us see who defends himself best." [68] He then proceeds to the examination of the *Impostures* of the Jesuits. And from there on, it is a free-for-all which is somewhat painful. Can we imagine the author of such pages searching his Bible in a spirit of prayer? We may doubt it, and we shall not take sides a priori in this quarrel.

It is noteworthy, however, that at the same period we find Pascal, playing his role of Christian layman, director of conscience according to the precepts of the Scriptures. Mademoiselle de Roannez spoke to him about the beginning of a pain. He does not know what is the matter; but he knows that one must expect to bear crosses: " I was reading this afternoon the thirteenth chapter of Saint Mark while I was think- ing of writing to you," says his letter of September, 1656, to the Duke and Mademoiselle de Roannez, " and so I shall tell you what I found there. Jesus Christ makes a long speech to His Apostles on His last coming: and since everything which happens to the Church happens also to each Christian in particular, it is certain that this chapter pre- dicts the state of each person who by conversion destroys the old man in him, as of the entire universe which will be destroyed to make way for new heavens and a new earth, as the Gospel says. And also, I was thinking that this prediction of the ruin of the reprobate man, which is in each one of us and of which it is said there will not be left one stone upon another, indicates that there should not be left any passion of the old man." [69] Here is something which established, if there were any need of this, the absolute sincerity of Pascal, opposing the fundamental truths of Scripture to the easy devotion of the casuists.

It is indeed in the Bible that the author of the *Provinciales* finds the best part of his spiritual diet; in his Bible read in a spirit of prayer. The comparison of texts is striking: we find Pascal in the thick of battle asking from the Scripture the explanation of what is happening to him. This thirteenth chapter of Saint Mark, on which he is meditating, is the one in which Christ foretells the destruction of the Temple, and the signs that shall precede the Day of Judgment. Thus, on one hand, Pascal, faithful in this to his doctrine of symbolism, seizes the oppor- tunity which his text offers him to preach to his correspondents the

[68] *Ibid.*, 363.
[69] *Extrait d'une lettre de Blaise Pascal à Mr. et à Mlle de Roannez*, Sept., 1656, *Œuvres*, v. 5, 405, 406.

necessity of the death of the old man within himself; on the other hand, he applies to himself, in the midst of the circumstances in which he is living, the teachings of the same chapter. His text on this occasion are these words which have just astonished him: *When ye shall see the abomination standing where it ought not, then let them flee without going down into the house to take anything out of it.*

This is a typical example, as we shall see, of the Pascalian method of Biblical quotation: for his immediate need, he gathers together in a striking formula the substance of two entire verses of Mark: Mark 13: 14, 15. Let us now follow the application to his particular case: " It seems to me that this predicts perfectly the time in which we live when the corruption of morality is in the houses of saintliness and in the books of the theologians and monks where it should not be." The moral is, " One must go out after such disorder, and woe to those who are with child or who nurse children in those days, that is to say, to those who have attachments to the world which hold them there." [70] That interpretation of the Bible which offers only maxims of concession and peace at any price is false and sickly. The Bible shows us the One who called Himself " gentle and meek-hearted " with a scourge in His hand, and in His mouth the most stinging denunciations. And yet the Jesus who pronounced them descended from the mountain where He knew how to converse regularly with His Heavenly Father.

The twelfth *Provinciale* was dated September 9, 1656; on September 24, in a new letter to the Duke and Mademoiselle de Roannez, Pascal justified his own violence, and placed it in its proper light: " Our Lord," he wrote, " has said that since the coming of John the Baptist, that is to say, since his coming into the world, and consequently since his coming into each faithful person, the Kingdom of God suffers violence and the violent ravish it."

Having been again with Jesus, and strong from His teaching, Pascal — or, rather, Montalte — was ready to write the thirteenth *Provinciale*, one of the most terrible that came from his pen.

He denounced there the *doctrine of ambiguous statements*, already criticized in the ninth *Provinciale*,[71] and which permits one to read a passage *aloud*, while saying with an inner voice that the author was speaking there of something else.[72] What a shameful business is this

---

[70] *Ibid.*, 406.
[71] *Œuvres*, v. 5, 205.
[72] *Treizième Provinciale, Œuvres*, v. 6, 23.

one of *mental reservations!* He accused the Jesuits of upsetting " the Law of God which forbids homicide." [73]

Having barred the path for any compromise and having retaken the offensive, he unveiled the underlying motive of the Jesuits who treat the State tactfully under the cover of religion, for political ends: " Is it not true, my Fathers, that if you had really any regard for God, and if the observance of His Law had been the first and principal object in your thoughts, this respect would have invariably predominated in all your leading decisions. . . . But if one sees on the contrary that you violate, in innumerable instances, the most sacred commands that God has imposed upon men; and that, as in the instances before us, you annihilate the Law of God, . . . do you not give us grounds to conclude that you have no respect for God in this fear, and that if you maintain His Law in appearance in so far as regards the obligation to do no harm to the State, this is not done for the Law itself, but to gain your own ends." [74]

The Jesuits fear only judges and not the Judge of judges. To be thus " bold against God, and timid toward men " [75] is a frightful perversion absolutely contrary to the spirit of holiness! It is indeed in this principle of differentiating between the Jesuits and their adversaries that one finds " the secret of the influence exercised by the *Lettres Provinciales.*" [76] The Jesuit Generals did indeed foresee that the dissoluteness of their doctrine in morality might be fatal, not only to their Society, " but even to the universal Church." [77]

This terrible danger may have no meaning for the heads of an order which dreams of domination at any cost; it overwhelms Pascal. In an hour of profound emotion, he once more reaches " true " eloquence; an eloquence sustained at each step by consultation of his Bible. The style of Saint John shows forth in this denunciation by Montalte: " Having had among you Doctors who told the truth, you did not dwell in the truth and . . . you have preferred the darkness to the light." [78] May we say in passing that the statistics [79] of Lhermet showing more than

[73] *Ibid.*, 36.
[74] *Ibid.*
[75] *Ibid.*, 37.
[76] *Introduction à la seconde série des Œuvres de Pascal* [v. 4-11], *Œuvres*, v. 4, 1. (See also *Sixième Provinciale, Œuvres*, v. 5, 51.)
[77] *Ibid.*, 41.
[78] *Ibid.*, 42.
[79] Lhermet, J., *Pascal et la Bible, op. cit.*, 186, 187, 229–232.

a hundred Biblical quotations in the polemical works of Pascal tell only of a small part of the role played by the Bible in Montalte's campaign. Only the reading of the text permits one to realize to what degree Pascal was inspired by the Bible. The sap which nourishes these vengeful pages is a Biblical sap. Let us hasten, however, to render to Lhermet this justice: he himself has very closely followed Pascal's text in his work. We should, however, regret his statistics and his tables were they to encourage certain students to dispense with a complete reading.

THE LETTER ON HOMICIDE

As this reading progresses, the Molière, of whom Pascal makes us have a presentiment, gives way to the Bossuet of whom Pascal gives us no less a presentiment: as indignation mounts, comedy makes way for eloquence. In a *Discours prononcé à l'ouverture du cours d'éloquence française,*[80] in December, 1822, Villemain drew the attention of his public to the fourteenth *Provinciale,* the famous letter on homicide. Let any reader who is sensitive to eloquence and accustomed to the genius of Demosthenes, he said, reread this *Provinciale!* And he describes its movement in these terms: " Pascal first traps his adversaries between corrupt religion and outraged humanity: then he advances against them by a slow and inevitable progression, always descending from the highest principles, leaning on all the sacred authorities, and scrupulously using the most rigorous logic in the demonstration of the most manifest truths. He uses, so to speak, a superabundance of force for the defeat of his enemies; and we see that he keeps them for so long a time under the sword of his eloquence less to refute them than in order to punish them. Each time he concludes an argument, the cause is won; but he begins again, in order to drag his vanquished adversaries through all the humiliations of their error." This " administrator of justice " is one in the name of the Bible. These " highest principles " from which he descends, these " sacred authorities " on which he leans, these " most manifest truths " which he demonstrates scrupulously with the most rigorous logic, are derived from the Bible. The eloquence of Pascal is that of one of the last prophets of Israel, and one of the greatest!

What Montalte wants to do in this fourteenth *Provinciale* is to

[80] Villemain, *Discours et mélanges littéraires,* 2d ed. Ladvocat, Paris, 1823, v. 2, 165.

make the world horrified with the Jesuits' opinions on homicide! The permission to kill, which these Fathers grant on so many occasions, makes it apparent that in this matter they have so far forgotten the Law of God, and so far extinguished the very laws of nature, that they need to be sent back " to the simplest principles of religion and common sense." [81] From all times the Commandment, *Thou shalt not kill,* has been imposed upon mankind. The Gospel [82] has only confirmed the Law [83] on this point, and the Decalogue has only renewed the Commandment which mankind had received from God before the Law, in the person of Noah from whom mankind was to be born. For upon that renovation of the world, God said to the patriarch: " I shall demand an accounting from mankind for the life of man, and from each brother, the life of his brother. Whosoever sheddeth man's blood, his blood shall be shed; because man is created in the image of God." [84] It is God alone who may dispose of human life, and when Saint Paul treats of the right which sovereigns exercise in this matter, he makes them spring from Heaven,[85] specifying the obligation of justice.[86] Thus, " to avoid the crime of murder, we must act at once both by the authority of God, and according to the justice of God." [87] It is upon these principles that sacred and profane legislators — the very pagans! — have at all times and places based their laws! The elementary fact brought out henceforth by Montalte is that the relaxing of Jesuit opinions is " contrary to the severity of civil and even pagan laws." [88] What will the contrast be, then, if we compare these same opinions with the laws of the Church, " this chaste spouse of the Son of God, who in imitation of her Heavenly Husband can shed her own blood for others, but not the blood of others for herself "? [89]

" For the Church, men are not simply men but the images of God whom she adores. For each one of them, she feels a holy respect which makes him, in her eyes, venerable, redeemed at an infinite price in order to become the temple of the Living God. And thus she believes that

[81] *Quatorzième Provinciale, Œuvres,* v. 6, 131.
[82] Matt. 26:52.
[83] Ex. 20:13.
[84] Gen. 9:5, 6.
[85] Rom. 13:3, 4.
[86] *Quatorzième Provinciale, Œuvres,* v. 6, 132, 133.
[87] *Ibid.,* 134.
[88] *Ibid.,* 145.
[89] *Ibid.*

the death of a man, slain without the authority of one's God, is not only murder, but sacrilege." [90] What, then, do the Jesuits do in disposing of the lives of men? They commit the supreme sacrilege of usurping God's place. It is to this sacrilege that this fundamental usurpation was to lead them, the usurpation which inspired their anti-Biblical doctrine of grace. " According to your modern laws, there is but one judge: and that judge is no one other than the offended party. He is at the same time judge, victim, and executioner. He demands from himself his enemy's death; he orders it, he executes him at once, and, without respect for the body or soul of his brother, he kills and damns one for whom Jesus Christ died." [91] Thus is consummated the frightful upheaval by which man has made himself God, thus nullifying by the ultimate sacrilege the sacrifice of the Man-God, even our Lord and Saviour Jesus Christ.

Then Pascal thunders forth: " Where are we, Fathers? Are these really monks and priests who speak in this way? Are they Christians? Are they Turks? Are they men? Or are they devils? " [92]

" CHOOSE YE THIS DAY "

The indictment is amplified now: either the Jesuits are on the side of the children of the Gospel, or else on the side of the enemies of the Gospel. It is either the one or the other, and there is no middle ground: *He who is not with Jesus Christ is against Him.*[93] There are two peoples and two worlds spread abroad over the earth, according to Saint Augustine: the world of the children of God, which forms one body of which Jesus Christ is the Head and the King; and the world of the enemies of God, of which the Devil is the head and the king. That is why Jesus Christ is called the King and the God of the world; because He has everywhere subjects and worshipers: and the Devil is also called in Scripture the prince of the world, and the god of this world, because he has everywhere his tools and slaves.[94]

Jesus Christ has imposed upon the Church which is His empire such laws as have pleased Him according to His eternal wisdom; and the Devil has imposed upon the world which is his kingdom such laws as

[90] *Ibid.*, 145, 146.
[91] *Ibid.*, 151.
[92] *Ibid.*
[93] Matt. 12:30.
[94] John 12:31; II Cor., ch. 4; John 16:11.

he wished to establish. Jesus Christ has associated honor with suffering; the Devil, with absence of suffering. Jesus Christ said that those who are smitten on one cheek should turn the other cheek; [95] and the Devil has told those who are threatened with a blow to kill those who would want to injure them.[96] Jesus Christ pronounces those happy, who participate in His ignominy and the Devil declares those in ignominy unhappy. Jesus Christ says, Woe unto you when men speak well of you; and the Devil says, Woe unto those of whom the world does not speak with esteem.[97]

Now that light has been shed on these two kingdoms by these flashing passages from Scripture, the Fathers may see where they stand. Opposite the mystical Jerusalem, and separated from it by an impassable abyss, the judge points out to them " the city of trouble which Scripture calls the *spiritual* Sodom," [98] of which the book of Revelation speaks. To which of these kingdoms do they belong? Henceforth, everything depends on the language which the Fathers understand and speak and here again Scripture has the last word: according to Saint Paul,[99] those who belong to Jesus Christ have the same sentiments as Jesus Christ; and according to Jesus Christ Himself,[100] those who are children of the Devil, *ex patre diabolo,* who have been *murderers* from the beginning, follow the maxims of the Devil.[101]

This peroration of the fourteenth *Provinciale,* by the large picture that it paints, and in which the fundamental issue is shown in all its relief in apocalyptic lightning flashes, presents the conclusion of the great moral debate inaugurated by the *Provinciales,* particularly since the fifth letter. The fifteenth *Provinciale* will add very little. Not that it is inferior in any respect, but its very subject, calumny, is so close to the controversy already raging that it constitutes rather a transition

[95] Luke 6:29, 22, 26.

[96] Pascal alludes here to the adventure of the slap at Compiègne of which the *Treizième Provinciale* speaks: having been charged to prepare a feast for Queen Christine of Sweden who had just arrived in France, Guille, officer of the King, had taken over for that purpose a room of the *Collège* des Jésuites, and Father Borin had slapped Guille. In his *Response à la Treizième Provinciale,* Father Nouet had denied this slap. It is to this reply that the *Quatorzième Provinciale* replies in its turn.

For more details, consult the excellent note of Havet, E., *Les Provinciales de Pascal, op. cit.,* v. 2, 103, 104.

[97] *Quatorzième Provinciale, Œuvres,* v. 6, 153.

[98] Rev. 3:12; 11:8.

[99] Rom. 8:9.

[100] John 8:44.

[101] *Quatorzième Provinciale, Œuvres,* v. 6, 154.

with the last *Provinciales*. The sixteenth does, in fact, continue the castigating of the calumnies of the Jesuits against monks, but it brings back the controversy to the question of orthodoxy.

It seems scarcely pertinent, however, to claim because of this fact that the controversy will end " as it had begun." [102] To us, the situation already appears too profoundly changed for us to subscribe to the preceding judgment. The Gallican Church, as we know, rose en masse behind Montalte and placed itself squarely in opposition to the Jesuit order. Beginning with the seventeenth *Provinciale* Montalte lays the blame on the head of the Jesuit order, Father Annat. Thus the peroration of the fourteenth *Provinciale* seems to us to present the conclusion of the grand moral debate which had been established: those two kingdoms of which it gave such a powerful vision seem henceforth to take form, one around Montalte, the other around Father Annat. Their forces were henceforth completely mobilized. Decisive blows were about to be exchanged. There would be many victims. Jacqueline herself would fall beside her vanquished brother.

My Kingdom, said Jesus, is not of this world.

[102] Giraud, V., *La Vie héroïque de Blaise Pascal*, Crès, Paris, 1923, p. 123.

We cannot end the notes relative to the present chapter without recommending the reading of two excellent chapters of the work of Stewart, H. F., *The Secret of Pascal*, University Press, Cambridge, 1941: ch. 1, " Pascal in Debate," pp. 1–28; ch. 2, " Pascal as Moralist," pp. 29–55.

We have not failed to make use of Stewart's book in the course of the present work. We are happy to state, on the majority of points, our agreement with the eminent *pascalisant* of Cambridge. According to him, " Pascal proclaims the perfect morality. He draws it from the Fountainhead, the Mediator, sole channel of communication with God, the great Lawgiver. Through Him alone are right doctrine and right morality conveyed to man " (*op. cit.*, p. 36). Pascal " set his feet in the straight way to which his reading of the Gospel pointed him " (*ibid.*, p. 41).

One could no better reveal the secret of what the present chapter calls " the dictates of conscience " in Pascal.

Due to the situation created by the war we have been unable to procure the following work recently published in Europe: Thomas, J. F., *Essai sur la morale de Port-Royal*, suivi de *Les Caractères de la morale pascalienne*, 1942, 2 v.

This last reference we owe to Professor Henri Peyre, of Yale University: " Ouvrages français parus depuis la guerre " (September, 1939 to September, 1942), *The Romanic Review*, April, 1943, Columbia University Press, p. 101.

XIV

Fighting a New Inquisition

"These things I have spoken unto you, that in me ye might have peace. In the world ye shall have tribulation: but be of good cheer; I have overcome the world."

— *John 16:33*

On August 3, 1656, a decree of the Index condemned all the writings of Arnauld that had been published since the vote of censure of the Sorbonne. On September 4, the Assembly of the Clergy approved a Formulary which imposed on all of France the obligation to subscribe to the Pope's decisions relative to the five propositions. On October 16, a Bull of the Pope, confirming that of his predecessor Alexander VII, again condemned those five propositions, " applying the same vote of censure to them " with which each one of them " in particular " had been " noted or struck." The new Bull condemned, prohibited, and forbade the *Augustinus*, " with all other books, manuscript as well as printed, and all those which might perhaps be printed in the future, in which that doctrine of the said Cornelius Jansen herewith condemned is or might be established or sustained." [1] One could not be more specific. However, the miracle of the Holy Thorn had to be officially recognized on October 22. The priests of Paris demanded from the Assembly of the Clergy the condemnation of the morality of the new casuists. For the time being, the Assembly had to content itself with an indirect blame, while a *Réponse générale à l'auteur des Lettres* (General reply to the author of the Letters) ordered him to put down the pen he had taken in hand against the innocent, and to cease a war " which should never have been begun." [2]

How could Montalte have done so? Father Annat, head [3] of the Jesuits and confessor of the King, had just answered the *Provinciales*

---

[1] *Bulle d'Alexandre VII*, October 16, 1656, *Œuvres*, v. 6, 61.

[2] *Response generale à l'Autheur des Lettres. . .* , in *Introduction à la Quinzième Provinciale*, *Œuvres*, v. 6, 168.

[3] The exact title of Father Annat in the Jesuit order was that of " provincial."

by a work entitled *La bonne foi des Jansénistes* (The good faith of the Jansenists). In these difficult hours, God seemed to wish to multiply His signs to His small flock of faithful followers. At Port-Royal, a good number of miracles continued to be authenticated, to such an extent that Mazarin himself asked for " linen which had touched the relic " [4] for his sister.

THE ACCUSATION OF HERESY

It was under these circumstances that Montalte, on January 23, 1657, wrote his seventeenth, and, on March 24, his eighteenth *Provinciale*, this time directly addressed to " Reverend Father Annat, Jesuit." As a matter of fact, the latter had hurt Pascal to the quick by accusing him of heresy; and it is a true believer cut to the quick who writes at the very beginning of his reply: " You know very well, Father, that this accusation is so important that to advance it is an unbearable temerity if one does not have the means of proving it." [5] By accusing him of heresy, the representative of the Jesuits struck a direct blow, one which does not cease working upon its victim without his knowledge. There are some words which indeed touch us to the quick and their effect proves lasting. We wish to wipe them from our memory, but they attach themselves there; they work their tenacious penetration into us until one day their subterranean labor allows its effects to appear on the surface.

The accusation of heresy leads Pascal to question his own beliefs and to question himself concerning the Pope and his infallibility. Many fragments of Section xiv of the *Pensées*, according to the Brunschvicg edition, reveal this inner struggle to us: the Pope is first, but it is easy for this primacy to degenerate into tyranny, asserts Fragment 872. Fragment 876 declares that God performs no miracles in the ordinary conduct of His Church, and that it would certainly be a strange miracle if infallibility were in a miracle. If we consider the Pope as infallible, we must declare ourselves his slaves, or we may pass for heretics. As Fragment 879 recalls, Jesus said, " Feed *my* sheep," and not, " *Thy* sheep." The evil lies in the fact that the Pope is easily influenced because he is so busy, and every time the Jesuits prejudice him, Christendom will become perjured (Fragment 882).

What should one do then? Fragment 920 proclaims the answer in the most violent terms: " One must cry out all the louder as one is cen-

---

[4] December, 1656, *Œuvres, Introduction à la Dix-septième Provinciale.*
[5] *Dix-septième Provinciale, Œuvres,* v. 6, 341.

sured more unjustly, . . . until there comes a Pope who listens to both sides." The Inquisition and the Society of Jesus constitute " the two scourges of the truth." It is this same fragment which contains the famous passage: " If my letters are condemned at Rome, what I condemn there is condemned in Heaven: *Ad tuum Domine Jesu, tribunal appello.*"

A LABORIOUS SELF-JUSTIFICATION

The accusation of heresy brings Pascal to a laborious self-justification. Having abandoned the controversy relative to casuistry, to consider, together with the vindication of Jansenism, the question of orthodoxy, he had already made the sixteenth *Provinciale* too long, and had made his excuses for it, saying that he had not had the time to make it shorter. He was, however, to find the time to rewrite thirteen times the eighteenth *Provinciale*, and it is proper to see in this fact more than a concern for literary perfection.

This length, these new beginnings, speak of an ardent need to explain himself, in a Christian whose heart is troubled to the point of anguish by the direct accusation of heresy. The critics still continue to discuss [6] Montalte's assertions as to the incompleteness of his affiliation with Port-Royal. The *Provinciales* brusquely cease appearing after the eighteenth. A nineteenth remains unfinished. The author, according to his profession of faith in the seventeenth *Provinciale*, is determined to live and die in the only Church to which he is attached on this earth, outside of which he is " fully persuaded there is no salvation," in the communion with the Pope, its sovereign head. [7] For the time being, however, Montalte is satisfied with the distinctions which his Biblical assurances dictate to him. And on this point he remains completely clear.

He determines, for example, the understanding of what is *de fide,* that is, what must be believed: " When the Church condemns writings, she supposes that there is an error in them which she condemns; and then one must believe that this error is condemned; but one need not believe that these writings contain indeed the error which the Church presumes to be there." [8] In this statement the reader will have recognized the question of Doctrine and the question of Fact. The ques-

---

[6] See, for example, Spoerri, T., " A propos de la sincérité de Pascal. Discussion d'un point de méthode," in *Revue d'histoire littéraire de la France,* v. 30, 300 *sq.*

[7] Havet, E., *Les* Provinciales *de Pascal, op. cit.,* v. 2, 213.

[8] *Dix-septième Provinciale, Œuvres,* v. 6, 362.

tion of Fact still remains in doubt " without there being any way to establish the fact to the satisfaction of all." Thus, one cannot truthfully make of this question " a matter of heresy "; but the Jesuits could indeed make of it " a pretext for persecution." [9]

To the cry of *heresy*, Montalte replies by that of *persecution:* " All your proceedings are political," [10] he declares to Father Annat. " As a matter of fact, it is not the Pope who was mistaken: it is you who deceived the Pope, which is more scandalous, since we know you so well now." [11]

Alexander VII's Bull, dated October 16, 1656, was officially handed to the King on March 11, 1657. On March 14, the new nuncio Piccolomini, who was very hostile to the members of Port-Royal, gave a copy of it to the president of the Assembly of the Clergy. On March 17, the latter received the Bull officially and decided again to have a single Formulary signed. Here the mention of the Bull replaced the double reference to the declaration of the Assembly of the Clergy on March 28, 1654, and to the Papal Brief of September 29, 1654, contained in the preceding Formulary. The eighteenth *Provinciale*, may we recall, is dated March 24, 1657. Pascal treats his adversaries very harshly in it, particularly Father Sirmard — a fact which does not prevent him from making use of the latter's argument on the wager, as Blanchet has demonstrated. [12]

In the eighteenth *Provinciale*, Pascal leans, not only on the authority of Saint Augustine, but also on that of Saint Thomas. [13] In it, he adopts as his own, and as Port-Royal's, the Thomist doctrine of sufficient grace. Not that he has evolved on this point as much as Bishop says: [14] we have mentioned above to what point certain of Saint Thomas' articles in this respect go beyond Saint Augustine himself. Moreover, in this matter, we have differentiated between what Pascal had been led to think of Saint Thomas, Doctor of grace, and Saint Thomas, the Scholastic. We have thus explained the apparent contradiction between Pascal as a follower of Saint Thomas, and Pascal as Saint Thomas' critic.

[9] *Ibid.*, 367.

[10] *Ibid.*, 369.

[11] *Ibid.*, 366.

[12] Blanchet, L., " L'Attitude religieuse des Jésuites et les sources du pari de Pascal," in *Revue de métaphysique et de morale*, July–August, 1919 (477–516) and September–October, 1919 (617–647).

[13] *Dix-huitième Provinciale, Œuvres*, v. 7, 51.

[14] Bishop, M., *Pascal:* The Life of Genius, *op. cit.*, 247, 248.

We believe that it is proper to reply in this same way to Strowski when he accuses the author of the *Provinciales* of having " fallen heir to the inventions of scholasticsm and to the chimeras of Thomism." [15] To come back to what we were saying of Bishop, we must point out that the Pascal of the first *Provinciale* did not attack Saint Thomas himself on the matter of grace, but the *new* Thomists. This clarification, which reference to Pascal's essentially Biblical inspiration permits us to establish, finally reduces to very little the " evolution " of Pascal on the question of grace.[16] Pascal's anxiety, as we have said, came from another source, i.e., from his growing preoccupation with Roman orthodoxy in order to meet the accusation of heresy.

It is precisely because it was made under these circumstances that the declaration relative to grace and the freedom of the will becomes so important. Pascal marks his position in the matter quite definitely in the eighteenth *Provinciale:* " God disposes of the free will of man without imposing any necessity upon him, and . . . the free will which always may, but never will, resist His grace, whensoever He is pleased to draw it to Himself by the sweet constraint of His efficacious inspirations." [17] By leaning on the authority of Scripture, Pascal places himself between the two extremes: First, "that impiety of Luther " condemned by the Council of Trent: *" We co-operate in no way whatever in the matter of our salvation, any more than inanimate things ";* secondly, " the impiety of Molina's school which will not admit that it is by the strength of divine grace that we are enabled to co-operate in the work of our salvation; and which thereby destroys the principle of faith established by Saint Paul: [18] *" that it is God who worketh in us both to will and to do."* [19]

In short, the principles set up by the author of the eighteenth *Pro-*

[15] Strowski, F., *Pascal et son temps, op. cit.*, v. 3, 207.

[16] We had arrived independently at our conclusion on this subject when our attention was drawn to an excellent note in the *Œuvres*, v. 7, 12, n. 3. The commentator remarks there that the close collaboration of Arnauld, Nicole, and Pascal " destroys entirely " the affirmation that Pascal " had returned to Thomism." (See also *Œuvres*, v. 6, 318.) If on page 30 of the eighteenth *Provinciale*, Pascal speaks of the " divine principles of Saint Augustine and Saint Thomas," this is because he knows how to render homage to Saint Thomas wherever the latter is found to be in agreement with the Tradition of the Fathers.

See also the continuation of our text where we come back to Saint Thomas with regard to the debate concerning grace in the eighteenth *Provinciale*.

[17] *Dix-huitième Provinciale, Œuvres*, v. 7, 30.

[18] *Dix-huitième Provinciale, Œuvres*, v. 7, 31.

[19] Phil. 2:13.

vinciale bring into accord certain passages of Scripture which at first had seemed almost irreconcilable, because of the fact that they assigned our good actions sometimes to God, sometimes to ourselves. Is it not obvious, henceforth, that the principles in question are divine? It is indeed in this way that the author of the eighteenth *Provinciale* spoke of " the divine principles of Saint Augustine and Saint Thomas." [20] Thus he pays homage to Saint Thomas inasmuch as the latter is found to be in agreement with the Tradition of the Church Fathers. Pascal does even more from this time on, and not merely from pure desire for conciliation: He takes pleasure in confirming his agreement on certain points " with the new Thomists *themselves*." [21] It is we who italicize in order to denote clearly that he had distinguished these *new* Thomists from Saint Thomas, in so far as they had become separated from him in the matter of grace. He specifies, furthermore, the reason for this agreement " with the new Thomists themselves, namely, that they vindicate both the power of resisting grace and the infallibility of this grace which they profess to uphold so highly." [22] It is impossible to be more specific. Here is another reason for not arbitrarily simplifying the argument.

THE STRATEGY OF THE JESUITS

Pascal's restatement of facts, as we have said, should be read as an answer to the accusation of heresy which is intolerable to him: No longer give the name of " heretic " to your adversaries, he insists to Father Annat; give them some other name " which would be proportionate to the nature of your differences. Say that they are ignorant and stupid, and that they misinterpret Jansen; these would be reproaches suited to your dispute: but to call them heretics has no connection with the argument." [23] Any name at all — but not heretic! Pascal prefers to be called ignorant and stupid, or to share these appellations with his friends of Port-Royal! He is indeed reduced to the defensive. May we be pardoned for the expression: he is winged, and will soon fall. *The fear of heresy will henceforth be in him an unseen but omnipresent motive, the source* [24] *from which will come his final decisions.*

[20] *Ibid.*, 30.
[21] *Ibid.*, 32.
[22] *Ibid.*, 32, 33.
[23] *Ibid.*, 36.
[24] We hope to be pardoned for the anachronism of this expression of Henri Poincaré (1854–1912).

The strategy of the Jesuits will not miss this point. In this very eighteenth *Provinciale*, Pascal was right when he wrote: "You have made the most desperate efforts to convince people that your disputes involved points of doctrine; and never has it been more apparent that the whole controversy turns upon a mere point of fact." [25] Pascal was right, but did he perceive that the Jesuits had noticed his anguish, and had taken the best possible advantage of it? Did he realize that they had found the chink in his armor, and made it the exact target for their blows?

At this critical moment, Pascal falls back to positions which he had judged safe for a long time; even the author of the Preface to a *Traité du vide* could have subscribed to this proposition of the eighteenth *Provinciale*: "If it relates to a supernatural truth, we must judge of it neither by the senses nor by reason, but by Scripture and the decisions of the Church. If it concerns an unrevealed truth, something within the reach of natural reason, reason must be its proper judge. If it is a question of a point of fact, we must yield to the testimony of the senses, which are the natural judges of such matters." [26] What a magnificent discourse on method by a Christian man of science! And here he applies this rule directly to the interpretation of Scripture: "So general is this rule, that according to Saint Augustine and Saint Thomas, when we meet with a passage even in Scripture, the literal meaning of which, at first sight, appears contrary to what the senses or reason recognize with certainty, we must not attempt to reject their testimony in this case, and yield them to the authority of the apparent sense of the Scripture. We must interpret the Scripture, and seek therein another meaning which will be in agreement with the testimony of the senses. The Word of God being infallible in the facts which it records, and the information of the senses and of reason, acting in their sphere, being also certain, it follows that there must be an agreement between these two truths. As Scripture may be interpreted in different ways, whereas the testimony of the senses is uniform, we must in these matters adopt as the true interpretation of Scripture that view which corresponds to the faithful report of the senses." [27] Thus, Gen. 1:16 seems to say that the moon is larger than all the stars. Unquestionable demonstration proves that this is false. We should not stubbornly

[25] *Dix-huitième Provinciale, Œuvres*, v. 7, 40.
[26] *Ibid.*, 50.
[27] *Ibid.*, 51.

cling to the defense of this literal interpretation, but, rather, search another meaning in agreement with this truth of the fact. One might say, for example, the words " great light " denote the greatness of the moon merely with regard to us, and not the magnitude of its body considered in itself. If one wishes to use Scripture in any other way, one only exposes it to the scorn of infidels.[28] A quotation from Saint Augustine and one from Saint Thomas which confirm the interpretation follow.

Having thus appealed to an interpretation of Scripture faithful to Tradition, Pascal pursues this argument to conclude that we cannot refuse to consider as orthodox " those who would not believe that certain words were in a certain book, where they are not to be found, merely because a Pope by mistake has declared that they are." [29] Resolved according to a Scriptural method, the famous question of *Fact* and of *Doctrine* leaves the orthodoxy of Pascal and Port-Royal intact. And this orthodoxy, as we well know, is to be considered henceforth essential with regard to the author of the *Provinciales*.

We believe that one should take literally the scarcely disguised confession of the fragment of the nineteenth *Provinciale*: " Be comforted, my Father, those whom you hate are in distress." [30] The portrait, which follows, of the members of Port-Royal is one of the most touching pages in Pascal's works: " I have seen them . . . pious, composed and unshaken, filled with a meek deference, love of peace, tenderness and zeal for truth, a desire to know and obey her dictates, fearing their own infirmity, regretting that they should be thus exposed to trial, yet withal sustained by a hope that God will deign to sustain them by His light and His strength, and that the grace of Jesus Christ which they uphold and for which they suffer will be at once their light and their strength." [31] What persuasive and evangelical gentleness does Pascal have in defending his brothers! The best part of his moral and religious conscience [32] is revealed here.

[28] *Ibid.*, 51, 52.
[29] *Ibid.*, 51.
[30] *Fragment d'une Dix-neuvième Provinciale, Œuvres*, v. 7, 171.
[31] *Ibid.*, 171, 172.
[32] The moral and religious conscience of the author of the *Provinciales* is revealed even better in all its aspects — and with all its angles — in the Fragments of the *Pensées* which constitute the rough sketches of " Letters," or notes taken in view of them.
May we cite, for example: *Pensées*, Section x, Fr. 681, *Œuvres*, v. 14, 116: quotations from John 4:23; 1:29 referring to the redemption of a new type, according to Father Bauny (*Quatrième Provinciale*); *Pensées*, Section xiv, Fr. 882, *ibid.*, 319;

THE " PROVINCIALES " INTERRUPTED

Why was the nineteenth *Provinciale* not finished? Why did Pascal suddenly stop in the midst of success? The multiplicity of reasons given leads us personally to suspect the validity of most of them. Everyone knows by experience that man is all the more prone to offer copious explanations when the motive which inspires him is deep-seated. This remark is certainly valid for those students of Pascal who wish to justify a position held from the first.

In the first pages of this chapter we clearly set forth our conviction that in the months and years to come Pascal will be more and more deeply affected by the necessity of freeing himself from the slightest appearance of heresy. After having thus disclosed our opinion, we find ourselves quite free to present objectively the reasons advanced by different sources for the sudden interruption of the *Provinciales*.

God having spoken by the miracle of the Holy Thorn, says one, man had no need to present further arguments.[33] Montalte was a long time in reaching this conclusion! The effect of the miracle appears to us, in these pages, contrary to what Augustin Gazier thus claims: the whole series of the *Provinciales*, beginning with the terrible fifth letter, amply justifies the way of considering the matter which we have called

---

" Every time that the Jesuits surprise the Pope, all of Christianity will be perjured," *ibid.*, Fr. 883, compare Section xiii, Fr. 849 and 851, where it is a question of the " unfortunate ones " who obliged Pascal to speak on the substance of religion " (Fr. 883), or on miracles (Fr. 849, 851); Section xiv, Fr. 886: " You speak like pagans " (v. **14**, 321); Fr. 887: " The Jansenists are like the heretics in their reformation of morals; but you resemble them in yours [i.e., an evil, upside-down reformation of morals] (v. **14**, 321, 322); Fr. 897: " Jesus Christ has told us the end. And you are destroying that end " (v. **14**, 329); Fr. 902: " The Jesuits have not made truth uncertain, but they have made their impiety certain " (v. **14**, 331); Fr. 903, where the Jesuits opposite Pascal appear in the same light as the Jews facing the Prophets (v. **14**, 332, 333); Fr. 904: " Of the exception, you made a rule without exception, so that you no longer want the rule to be an exception " (v. **14**, 333); Fr. 905 (end): You keep in the Church those whom the Jews " would have abhorred as impious " (v. **14**, 339); Fr. 909: " The entire society of their casuists cannot assure conscience in error " (v. **14**, 336); Fr. 919: " The Jesuits have wanted to be loved by the great " — and Pascal considers them in the light of a text of II Tim. 4:3; Fr. 920: what Biblical eloquence in this appeal to the people: " If what I say does not serve to enlighten you, it will serve for the people. If the latter are silent, the stones will speak. Silence is the greatest persecution. The saints were never silent " (v. **14**, 341).

Cf. " A New Resoluteness," Ch. XII, p. 241.

[33] Gazier, A., *Histoire générale du mouvement Janséniste, op. cit.*, v. **1**, 107.

the sign in the midst of battle. Cécile Gazier is more convincing when she remarks that the last *Provinciale* bears the date of March 24, that is to say, that of the anniversary of the miracle.[34] Could it be also that Pascal wanted to spend the Easter holiday in peace this spring of 1657? The long tension of this war had wearied him perhaps or made him sick. Did he give in to the arguments of Mother Angélique and Monsieur Singlin who, as we have said, advocated compassion, charity, and prayer? Had he the hope of seeing a religious peace negotiated at a time when influential persons were intervening with Mazarin and the Queen Regent? Bishop shows him anxious not to be instrumental in perpetuating dissention in the bosom of the Church: " He seems, indeed, to have been much moved by the news of the condemnation of the *Provinciales* by the Parlement de Provence at Aix, about February 21, 1657. (As the magistrates would not give up their copies, the hangman burned an almanac.) "[35] According to Jovy,[36] Pascal was tired of controversy and his profound loyalty with regard to the Pope and the royal power was touched by the open hostility of these two authorities. The appeal of Father Morel, Prior of Sainte Foy, must have moved him: the Jesuit had uttered the wish that after a sincere and lasting reconciliation with his order, Montalte would turn his pen against the impious and the *libertines*. Without following up the request for reconciliation, Pascal, from the month of April, 1657, did address his efforts toward the unbelievers and the indifferent. The project of a " Vindication of Christianity " preoccupied him more and more. He wished to use the strength remaining to him " for a work of which the usefulness seemed greater to him than that of a work of polemics."[37] Most of these considerations, it is obvious, seem to radiate from scruples of conscience. Pascal is anxious above all else to escape the slightest appearance of heresy, and this is, we feel, the essential fact.

But on the other hand, the Biblical herald who remains ardent in Pascal could not forget his duties with regard to what he considers to be the pure and simple truth, according to God. Lanson believes[38] that Pascal was ready to encourage resistance to the Bull of Alexander VII

[34] Gazier, C., " Pascal et Port-Royal," in *La Revue hebdomadaire,* No. 28, 32d year, July 14, 1923, p. 157.

[35] Bishop, M., *Pascal: The Life of Genius, op. cit.,* p. 248.

[36] Jovy, E., *Pascal inédit,* Vitry le François, 1911, v. 2, 30.

[37] Gazier, C., " Pascal et Port-Royal," *art. cit.,* p. 157.

[38] Lanson, G., " Après les PROVINCIALES. Examen de quelques écrits attribués à Pascal," *Revue d'histoire littéraire de la France,* January–March, 1901, v. 8, 1 *sq.*

Ad Sanctam, of which the Assembly of the Clergy had ordered the publication on March 14, 1657. This Bull, as we have said, reaffirmed the Bull *Cum Occasione* of Innocent X and determined the question of Fact. A new Formulary was threatening, which would demand the formal adhesion to the condemnation of Jansen and the *Augustinus.* Port-Royal's tactics would consist henceforth in resisting the Pope's aggression in the name of Gallican liberties. It was, for the Jansenists, a matter of getting the Parliament to refuse to register the Bull. In these circumstances, Pascal would have consented to hold his hand. Thus, the sudden interruption of the *Provinciales* might be due to the fact that " Pascal was busy with other urgent services to the Jansenist cause." Bishop, from whom we borrow this last sentence, sees in this "the likeliest explanation " of the interruption of the *Provinciales.* [39]

THE " PROVINCIALES " CONDEMNED IN ROME

The fact is that at the beginning of June there appeared the *Lettre d'un avocat au parlement à un de ses amis, touchant l'Inquisition que l'on veut établir en France, à l'occasion de la nouvelle Bulle du Pape Alexandre VII* (Letter of a lawyer at parliament to one of his friends, concerning the Inquisition that they wish to establish in France, upon the occasion of a new Bull of the Pope Alexander VII). *Now a comparison of texts reveals that the man who thus dares to denounce the new Inquisition is none other than Blaise Pascal.* It may therefore have been that he left unfinished his nineteenth *Provinciale* in order to write this *Lettre d'un avocat.*

The members of Parliament joyously welcomed the letter; but it irritated the nuncio. By a decree of the Council, dated June 25, the letter was suppressed. The King had to intervene so that Parliament would consent to register the Bull. But this registration did not take place until the nineteenth of December.

In the meanwhile, on December 6, 1657, " Our Holy Father Pope Alexander VII " had forbidden and condemned the eighteen *Provinciales* and the other writings of the Jansenists with the other enumerated works of Antoine Arnauld.[40] This condemnation had been known in Paris on October 18, 1657; the decree had been printed there and was cried in the streets in December. Arnauld was to make the remark

---

[39] Bishop, M., *Pascal:* The Life of Genius, *op. cit.,* p. 248.
[40] For the text of this condemnation, see *Œuvres,* v. 7, 231, 232.

that the *Provinciales* had been inscribed in the catalogue of forbidden books because they had appeared without any author's name, without approbation, and without any indication of the place where they were printed; also because they were not written in Latin.

Pascal's soul was deeply tormented by the inclusion of his letters in the Index. He needed the exhortations of his Jansenist friends to sustain his courage. A touching indication of his state of mind is seen in the fact that he again took up his study of mathematics.[41] Was this from need of relaxation, of diversion?

HOSTILITIES RESUMED THROUGH CHURCHMEN

Some have not sufficiently taken into account the fact that stopping a battle involves at least two men: the champion and the one — or the ones — whom he is fighting. The champion is not free in all his movements. He is not free because of circumstances. That is one reason why Lanson's theory, mentioned above, does not contradict what we have said about Blaise's fear of heresy. All the less since we have insisted on pointing out that Father Annat's direct accusation of heresy would make its effects felt only in the long run. For the moment, with events helping, it only adds to Pascal's trouble, to his inner torture. His courage is all the greater when he follows, in spite of everything, the high route of duty as it appears to his conscience.

But now the adversaries themselves repeat the offense. They have just triumphed, and once more their triumph is noisy. Toward the end of 1657 appears the anonymous *Apologie pour les casuistes contre les calomnies des Jansénistes* (Apology for the casuists against the calumnies of the Jansenists), by a certain Father Pirot, professor of theology at the *Collège* of Clermont and a friend of Father Annat. Gathered together at their synod on January 7, 1658, the curés of Paris undertake to have this abominable piece of writing condemned. They send a digest (*Extrait*) in the form of about sixty propositions with their pressing requests to the Parliament, to the Faculty of Theology, and to the grand vicars. In addition, their commission submits to the synod on February 4, for permission to print, a *Factum pour les curés de Paris*.[42] *The con-*

---

[41] Cf. *Problèmes proposés par Pascal à Sluse* (September or October, 1657), *Œuvres*, v. 7, 233 *sq.*

[42] *Factum pour les curés de Paris, Œuvres*, v. 7, 278 *sq.*, proceeded in the *Œuvres* by an introduction relative to the Assembly of the Clergy against the casuists, 259 *sq.*;

sensus of opinion is that Pascal was charged with editing it. Lanson
points out [43] several notes which form a part of the collection of the
Pensées that were used verbatim in this factum.

The factum begins with a noble profession of faith: " Our cause is the
cause of Christian morality." [44] It denounces " the completely carnal
morality which the casuists have introduced, and which finds its support
only on the arm of the flesh [French: *le bras de chair*], as the Scripture
puts it." [45] Taking up, for example, the question of homicide, it forcefully renews the denunciation of the *Provinciales:* " In the end everything will be permitted, the Law of God will be annihilated, and natural
reason alone will become our light in all our actions, even to determine
when individuals will be permitted to kill their neighbors." [46] Once more,
it is the dictates of a Christian conscience which inspire the writer:
" Were we silent . . . , we would be unworthy of our ministry." [47] Our
ministry! The Christian layman has experienced no difficulty in speaking the language of the consecrated minister! He feels himself bound
by " an indispensable obligation " to speak out at a time when a numerous Company is leading simple people astray without anyone's opposing it. " The judgment of God must not be allowed to come on the
peoples and on their pastors, according to the doctrine of the Prophets." [48] At this hour of crisis, in the night which is threatening from
all sides, once more Pascal appeals to the Bible: " For woe is unto us,"
says the Scripture,[49] " if we preach not the Gospel. The wrath of God
threatens us on the one hand, and the audacity of these men on the
other, and puts us in the necessity either of becoming in fact false pastors and wolves, or of being torn apart as such by the thirty thousand
mouths which disparage us. Here is the subject of our complaints." [50]
A fragment of the *Pensées* clearly constitutes a note in view of the passage below: " I am alone against thirty thousand? Not at all." [51] Con-

---

it presents extracts from the *Apologie pour les casuistes,* 263–274, and the complaint
of the curés, 274 *sq.*

[43] Lanson, G., *art. cit.* in n. 38.
[44] *Factum pour les curés de Paris, Œuvres,* v. **7,** 278.
[45] *Ibid.,* 282. The Biblical allusion is to Jer. 17:5.
[46] *Factum pour les curés de Paris, Œuvres,* v. **7,** 290.
[47] *Ibid.,* 292.
[48] *Ibid.,* 293.
[49] I Cor. 9:16.
[50] *Factum pour les curés de Paris, Œuvres,* v. **7,** 296, 297.
[51] *Pensées,* Section xiv, Fr. 921, *Œuvres,* v. **14,** 349.

sidering themselves to be directly the addressed, the Jesuits answered.

A second *Ecrit* appeared on April 2, 1658. *Likewise written by Pascal*, it advised the casuists to be silent, or to open their mouths only to disavow their errors, " so untenable and so visibly opposed to the truth of the Gospel." [52] Let us welcome upon its recurrence this great Pascalian theme of truth, the " one true way," which is the Bible. For the author of the second *Ecrit*, it is the very doctrine of Jesus Christ which is threatened by those whom he scourges with the name of " Pharisees of the New Law," establishing " their human traditions on the ruin of divine traditions." [53]

PASCAL ON PEACE

Here follows a magnificent meditation on true peace, doubtless inspired in Pascal by regard for Mother Angélique and Monsieur Singlin, who would have found silence preferable: " *We have spoken only when we could not be silent without committing a crime.*" [54] It is we who italicize these unforgettable words, not only for their beauty, but because they give us the key to the inner debate of a Pascal torn between his desire not to disturb the unity of the Church, and the summons of his evangelical conscience: " The true children of the Church know how to distinguish the true peace which the Saviour alone can give from that false peace which the world can indeed give but which is horrible to the Saviour of the world." [55] *There is a true peace and a false peace,* as there is a true charity and a false charity: " The false charity is one which leaves the evil at peace in their vices, while the true charity is the one which troubles this wretched tranquillity." Moreover, it is for that reason, according to Scripture, that Jesus Christ came to bring to the world, " not only *peace,* but also *a sword and division.*" [56] The ultimate end of the faithful is " good and truth." Peace and war are only means to this end, and are on this ground legitimate only " in proportion to the advantage which comes to truth from them." It is in this sense that Scripture says " that there is a time for peace and a time for war." [57] On this subject, the Pascal of the *Pensées* will note that " the

[52] *Second Ecrit des curés de Paris, Œuvres,* v. **7,** 309.
[53] *Ibid.,* 317, 318.
[54] *Ibid.,* 318.
[55] *Ibid.*
[56] *Ibid.,* 319. This last passage is inspired by Matt. 10:34 and Luke 12:51.
[57] *Ibid.,* 320. Cf. Eccl. 3:8.

faith embraces several verities which seem to contradict each other." [58]

Who will give us a book on " Pascal on Peace "? Such a work is much needed by Christian peoples during these troubled times. After citing many authorities who confirm his statement, *Pascal proclaims as "a capital truth of our religion" that there are "times when we must trouble this possession of error that the evil call peace."* [59] A fragment of the *Pensées* echoes the preceding: " It is a false piety to preserve peace at the expense of truth." [60]

Pascal henceforth would answer Mother Angélique and Monsieur Singlin by this conclusion which is not far from being the conclusion of his whole work, and would deserve to become the life motto of a Christian: " One must remain in silence *as long as one can,* and entertain oneself only with God, Whom one knows to be the Truth." [61]

Pascal will never abandon Christian morality, for he loves truth too dearly; but, together with the curés of Paris, in order to testify to his adversaries how much he really does love peace, he will open the door wide for them " as soon as they are willing to abjure the pernicious maxims of their morality." [62] In the tempest and in obscure weather, it is Scripture in all its simplicity and consequently in its perfection which serves him as his only compass: " *We shall be turned aside neither by their cursing nor by their blessing,* according to the words of Scripture. . . ." [63] We shall always present the same face to all their different faces, and we shall oppose to the duplicity of the children of the world the simplicity of the children of the Bible." [64] The point at issue is still the opposition of the " children of this world " and " the children of light " of which the Bible speaks, according to Luke 16:8, and we have shown Pascal fighting a new Inquisition under the sign of this fundamental Biblical distinction.

---

[58] *Pensées*, Section xiv, Fr. 862, *Œuvres*, v. 14, 304 (the context is important).

[59] *Second Ecrit des curés de Paris*, *Œuvres*, v. 7, 322.

[60] *Pensées*, Section xiv, Fr. 930, *Œuvres*, v. 14, 371.

[61] *Pensées*, Section vii, Fr. 536, *Œuvres*, v. 13, 424. The italics are ours.
We must acknowledge that here we are isolating arbitrarily the text from its context; but it is a fact that in a thinker preoccupied with a vindication the same idea may be called to take its place in different lines of reasoning.

[62] *Second Ecrit des curés de Paris*, *Œuvres*, v. 7, 324.

[63] Pascal alludes here to the fragment of II Sam. 14:17: " For even as an angel of God, so is my lord the king, that he is neither moved with blessing nor cursing."

[64] Biblical peroration of the *Second Ecrit des curés de Paris*, *Œuvres*, v. 7, 326.

In response to the Jesuits' answers other writings appear until the month of June, 1659. Of these seven other factums, only two, the fifth and the sixth, can with reason be attributed to Pascal. He is also said to be the author of a project of a *mandement* that has been found among his papers, which he is supposed to have composed for a bishop.[65] The *Cinquième Ecrit des curés de Paris* (Fifth Writing of the curés of Paris) continues to appeal to Scripture.[66] Analyzing the evil in the Jesuits, it affirms that this evil springs from their desire to reconcile the inclination of the world with the severity of the Bible which they corrupt only in order to make allowances for corrupt nature.[67] Similar declarations are found in the fifth *Provinciale*,[68] the *Factum pour les curés de Paris*[69] and the *Pensées*.[70] Also a *Projet de mandement* was found among the papers of Pascal, and was in his own handwriting.

According to Bossut, who published it for the first time, it is a veritable prophetic denunciation literally bristling with Biblical quotations. It proclaims[71] that one does not fall into such errors " except through a lack of understanding of the Scriptures." The editor of the *Œuvres* failed to recognize here the exact quotation of the judgment of Jesus: " You err, not knowing the Scriptures," Matt. 22:29. Since the casuists do not understand the Scriptures, then, the *mandement* will explain it to them, in order that " pious persons be henceforth free from peril, and the impious without excuse."[72] It is indubitable that scandals arise to test the faithful. The Apostle Paul describes to Timothy the seductions of recent times.[73] In the same way, Peter predicts that false prophets will arise within the Church just as they did among the Jews.[74] The time must come of which it is written: And woe to them that are with

---

[65] Giraud, V., *La Vie héroïque de Blaise Pascal, op. cit.*, p. 127.

[66] Gen. 34:30; Ezek. 37:17–20 (*Cinquième Ecrit des curés de Paris, Œuvres*, v. 7, 358).

[67] *Cinquième Ecrit des curés de Paris, Œuvres*, v. 7, 359.

[68] *Cinquième Provinciale, Œuvres*, v. 4, 299.

[69] *Factum pour les curés de Paris*, v. 7, 280.

[70] *Pensées*, Section xiv, Fr. 907, *Œuvres*, v. 14, 335.

[71] *Projet de mandement contre l'apologie pour les casuistes, Œuvres*, v. 7, 381.

[72] *Ibid.*, 381.

[73] At this point follows a long quotation from II Tim. 4:1–9.

[74] II Peter 2:1.

child in those days; and do you believe that the Son of Man, when he cometh, shall find faith on earth? Matthew,[75] Mark,[76] and Luke [77] are successively called upon to give evidence on this point. All things are symbols, the synagogue having been the image of the Church.

It is fitting that the example of the synagogue should enlighten us, according to the Apostle Paul.[78] Scripture teaches us that impiety was originated by false prophets, and then spread among the rest of mankind.[79] First the powerful were corrupted, then the lower classes. But when the very priests took up indulgent doctrines, it was *then* that the scourges of God began to fall without surcease upon this people and there have remained until this day.[80] It is *then* that no more mercy can be expected, because no one is worthy to seek mercy.[81]

Presented with an implacable logic, these Biblical texts under Pascal's pen present the ineluctable conclusion: " Here is the ultimate misfortune to which, by the grace of God, the Church has not yet come, and into which she will not fall so long as it shall please God to sustain her pastors against the corruption of the false Doctors who combat them." [82] A word to the wise is sufficient!

A Pascal preoccupied with heresy, but nevertheless infinitely anxious to follow the dictates of his Biblical conscience, found an ideal solution in his writings destined for the clergy. He must have felt greatly relieved, and the crisis toward which he seemed to be heading — if there was any such crisis [83] — must have been proportionately attenuated.

The question of Blaise Pascal's last days, which continues to cause much ink to flow,[84] cannot, however, make us lose sight of the much more modest problem of Pascal's retirement during the last months of his life. From this point on we are under the impression that the Biblical Pascal probably felt more sure of his orthodoxy because he had

[75] Matt. 24:19.
[76] Mark 13:17.
[77] Luke 18:8.
[78] I Cor. 10:6; ch. 11.
[79] Jer. 23:15.
[80] Jer. 5:31.
[81] Ezek. 22:25–31.
[82] *Projet de mandement. . .*, *Œuvres*, v. **7**, 382–386.
[83] We are thinking here of the last days of Blaise Pascal and of the confidences of Father Beurrier of which we shall speak in our Chapter XVII.
[84] See, for example, in *Studies*, Dublin, December, 1937, the article of Hugh Kelly on the eternal question of Pascal's possible retraction *in extremis*. We treat this question briefly in our Chapter XVII, entitled " Holy Anxiety."

been the authorized spokesman of the clergy. One can say even more: much of the substance of the *Provinciales* had been used in those factums or writings, and could therefore be said to express the best of the clergy's conscience. This statement is even valid for the *Sixième Ecrit des curés de Paris* (Sixth Writing of the curés of Paris), the last one frankly attributed to Pascal,[85] and in which one notes an evident relationship with the fifth *Provinciale*.

SIGNATURE OF THE FORMULARY

In 1660, the measures of harshness against the Jansenists were to increase: not only were the Little Schools of Port-Royal dispersed, but under the influence of the Archbishops of Rouen and Toulouse the Assembly of the Clergy required the signing of the Formulary of 1657, unearthed for the occasion. On September 23, 1660, a decree of the Council of State condemned the Latin edition of the *Provinciales*,[86] a work exposing " things which have been condemned as heretical by the holy pontiffs, by the Gallican Church, and by the Sacred Faculty of Theology of Paris." [87] After Mazarin's death on March 9, 1661, the boarders and the novices of the two monasteries of Port-Royal were to be expelled. Monsieur Singlin was to be obliged to hide, and the grand vicars were told to see that the Formulary was signed.[88] As the grand vicars were at heart favorable to Port-Royal, they published, on June 19, a *mandement* in the writing of which Pascal is supposed to have once more collaborated.[89] This *mandement* cleverly maintained the famous

---

[85] Although no document of the seventeenth or eighteenth centuries ascribes it to Pascal, Bossut has inserted in his edition a *Factum des curés de Nevers* attributed to Pascal. On this subject, see *Œuvres*, v. 8, 65 *sq.* — Introduction 67, *sq.* — Text of the *Factum*, 69 *sq.*

The *Sixième Ecrit des curés de Paris*, of July 24, 1658, shows once more the Bible on one side and the casuists on the other (*Œuvres*, v. 8, 47). The casuists, it says, take good care not to ask for the suppression of the Gospel: they would lose. The fact is that they make use of it at times, finding it as useful as their own writings (*ibid.*, 47). Their theology aims at excluding nothing, to make use of everything. " They unite in a horrible alliance JESUS CHRIST with Belial." [Cf. II Cor. 6:15.]

[86] *Arrêt du Conseil d'Etat condamnant l'édition latine des Provinciales, Œuvres,* v. 10, 13 *sq.*

[87] *Ibid.*, 20.

[88] An excellent résumé of the quarrel of the Formulary is found in the *Introduction à la seconde série des Œuvres de Pascal* [v. 4-11], *Œuvres*, v. 4, lxvi-lxx.

[89] In his " mandement " [*Ordonnance des Vicaires généraux pour la signature du Formulaire, Œuvres*, v. 10, 75 *sq.* (The text begins on page 82)] Pascal appealed

distinction between Fact and Doctrine. On this ground it modified the effect of the Formulary and was therefore supposed to be kind to delicate consciences. Arnauld and Singlin advised a simple signature. Certain priests and nuns, however, insisted upon adding a few words of explanation. As she lay dying, Mother Angélique blessed Heaven that her illness released her from being involved in this " mystery of iniquity." She allowed each one the latitude of acting according to his conscience.

It was then that Jacqueline, in a letter to Sister Angélique de Saint Jean, dated June 22–23, 1661, made her memorable declaration: " Since the bishops have a courage of maids, the maids should have a courage of bishops. If it is not our task to defend the truth, it is ours to die for the truth and sooner to suffer everything than to abandon it." [90] This affirmation is certainly the voice of a Pascal!

When an official inquirer pressed her, August 22, 1661, to tell him why so many souls were lost eternally, and if one should believe that Jesus Christ died for all men, Jacqueline confessed that often, at prayer before the Cross of her Saviour, she herself had felt anguish because of that question. But she added, when these thoughts come to me " I reject them, because I do not believe that I should try to search out the secrets of God: that is why I content myself with praying for sinners." [91] This brave, persecuted woman was far from suspecting that her answer echoed a declaration of the author of the *Christian Institutes:* " For things which it is neither permitted nor possible to know, ignorance is learned." [92]

Jacqueline confessed to Sister Angélique de Saint Jean her excessive grief upon signing under coercion. Unless she saw at least a few people make themselves victims of the truth, she must succumb. Sister Jacqueline Sainte-Euphémie Pascal, sick at heart, finally had to sign; but shortly afterward, on October 6, 1661, she died, literally heartbroken at having been forced to act against her Christian conscience.

---

again to Scripture, and defined the Biblical notion of faith (cf. p. 82, the elaboration of Heb. 11:1), and exalted the good conscience drawing his argument from II Tim. 2:33 and from Titus 3:9.

[90] *Lettre de Jacqueline Pascal à la Sœur Angélique de Saint Jean, Œuvres,* v. 10, 108.

[91] *Interrogatoire de Jacqueline Pascal,* made by Bail, visitor to the convent, *Œuvres,* v. 10, 130.

[92] Calvin, J., *Institution de la Religion Chrestienne,* text established and presented by Jacques Pannier, " Les Belles Lettres," Paris, 1938, v. 3, 80.

Blaise withstood the blow without flinching: " God give us the grace to die as well as that! " he said simply.

His own cross was waiting for him close at hand.

He knew it.

The peacemaking *mandement* to which he had set his hand had been nullified by the King's Council on July 7, censured by a Papal Brief, and replaced by another written with brutal clarity. The Archbishop of Toulouse had edited it, and the nuncio had enjoined the grand vicars to publish it after signing themselves on October 31, 1661. The reading in the Churches, however, took place only on November 20. It was then that the question of signing it became pressing.

Mother Angélique had died. Mother Agnès had been replaced, according to regulation, by Mother Madeleine de Ligny, worthy in every respect of the lineage she was continuing. Strong pressure was exercized on the nuns, and on Mother de Ligny herself, that they should sign the new Formulary: no means was neglected by the authorities. The nuns refused simply to sign their names; they insisted on adding a declaration which in effect annulled the provisions of the Formulary to which they subscribed. As we might well suspect, they were awaiting directions from their Port-Royalist heads.

It was under these circumstances that Pascal was to compose, toward the end of November, or during December, 1661, his *Ecrit sur la signature du formulaire* (Writing on the signature of the formulary). He set forth the problem with the most perfect clarity: " In the truth of things, there is no difference at all between condemning the doctrine of Jansen on the five propositions and condemning efficacious grace, Saint Augustine, and Saint Paul." [93] With one glance, he had measured the alternative created by the new Inquisition. With one stroke of the pen he condemned those who, under such circumstances, claimed to take " a middle course, . . . abominable before God, despicable before men." [94] At Port-Royal, they were not so clear-cut. In his *Examen d'un " Ecrit sur la signature . . ."* [95] (Examination of the " Writing on the signature . . ."), Nicole discussed point by point Pascal's conclusions,[96] and to the latter's " false conclusions," he opposed " true ones." [97] Long discussion ensued, centered about these points. Pascal answered Nicole

[93] *Ecrit de Pascal sur la signature du Formulaire, Œuvres,* v. 10, 171.
[94] *Ibid.,* 175.
[95] *Œuvres,* v. 10, 198–221.
[96] See in particular, 216, 217.
[97] *Ibid.,* 218–221.

and Arnauld with a *Grand Ecrit*. It was necessary to make an end to debate.

THE PRICE OF COMMITMENT

A meeting was called in Pascal's home. He began to speak in order to explain his position once and for all; he undertook this task despite terrible headaches, and in the midst of general tension: the Pope had condemned the sense of Jansen, which was the doctrine of efficacious grace. Now this sense had been recognized as a fundamental doctrine of the Church since Saint Paul and Saint Augustine. It had been confirmed by Tradition, after having been taken from Scripture. To come to the point of condemning it, therefore, the Pope must have been mistaken on a question of fact — doubtless deceived by the Jesuits who surrounded him. But here was Arnauld proposing that the nuns of Port-Royal sign a declaration which indirectly safeguarded the doctrine, but in an ambiguous way, as a concession to unity in the faith. But how could one sign the Formulary, even for the sake of unity in the faith, without clearly safeguarding the doctrine of efficacious grace which was the doctrine of Jansen, and before him, of the Church Fathers, of Saint Augustine, and of the Scripture? Arnauld and Nicole then plunged into interminable theological subtleties, followed therein by the great majority of the Port-Royalists present, all of whom vaguely felt that appeasement would be at the end of speeches whose complexity sufficed to calm the throbbings of conscience.

Exhausted, panting, his head bursting as if under an iron vise, Blaise fastened his glance on the only three loyal ones who remained at his side: Domat, the Duke de Roannez, and young Etienne Périer. Then, as he considered the vague mass of those who were turning away their heads, his eyes grew dim, and he collapsed in a faint.

When he regained consciousness, his sister Gilberte was at his side: " Well, what happened? "

" When I saw all those very persons waver and succumb, who should have been the defenders of the truth, and to whom I believed God had made the truth known, I confess that I was so overcome with grief that I could not endure it, and so collapsed." [98]

Condemned by the Church outside of which there is no salvation, abandoned in the darkening night by those who no longer have the

---

[98] Testimony of Marguerite Périer, *Œuvres*, v. **10,** 401.

strength to watch with him, Pascal feels that everything is now accomplished:

" To Thy tribunal, Lord Jesus, I appeal." [99]

[99] *Pensées,* Section xiv, Fr. 920, *Œuvres,* v. **14,** 243. Cf. Jovy, E., *Etudes pascaliennes,* v. **3,** " Discursions autour de Pascal," Vrin, Paris, 1928, p. 54 *sq.*

Pascal's cry may have been, as Jovy suggests, no more than an echo of Saint Bernard's appeal for absolute justice, to which as a Christian he also aspired (Jovy, E., *Etudes pascaliennes, op. cit.:* D'où vient l' " Ad tuum Domine Jesu, tribunal appello " de Pascal et Saint-Bernard? v. **3,** 85). Steeped as he was, however, in the writings of Montaigne, Pascal had a way of so assimilating what he read as to make the substance of it his own. Jovy admits to some doubt as to precisely what Pascal implied by the Latin quotation in question (" Il resterait à déterminer quelles idées Pascal plaçait sous ces mots," *ibid.,* pp. 85, 86). Henri Bremond takes it to reflect at most a passing rebellious impulse (" Tout au plus velléité passagère de révolte." Henri Bremond adds: " Insensiblement oubliée peut-être, et peut-être aussi, expressément rachetée par une déclaration contraire et les larmes de la pénitence. Cri silencieux de détresse et de confiance, lancé, nous ne savons à quel moment, ni dans quel esprit; intimes colloques avec Celui à qui nous pouvons tout dire; écho résigné à la plainte du Calvaire: *Mon Dieu, pourquoi m'avez-vous abandonné?* En dehors du souverain Juge qui nous comprend mieux que nous ne nous comprenons nous-mêmes, nul ici-bas n'a le droit d'écouter aux dernières portes de l'âme." " Pascal et l'Eglise Catholique," *La Revue hebdomadaire,* No. 28, *op. cit.,* p. 175.) Yet we learn that in the year 1679, when the persecution of Port-Royal was resumed, Mother Angélique placed in the folded hands of a deceased nun a written request to the Great Shepherd of the sheep, the request beginning with a phrase strikingly similar to the words of Pascal and Saint Bernard: " We appeal to Thy tribunal, Lord Jesus." (Sainte-Beuve, *Port-Royal, op. cit.,* v. **5,** p. 177. Quoted in *Œuvres,* v. **14,** 343, n. 3.) Pascal, like the Port-Royal nuns, was carrying his appeal to the supreme Judge of all judges. It was the plea of a man who, through his profound study of the Bible, had come to know God's will in all its directness, and was now taking his stand upon the basis of that knowledge.

XV

" A Lamp Unto My Feet "

" Thy word is a lamp unto my feet, and a light unto my path."
—Ps. 119:105*

It is written . . . and it is written. . . . And this is why Jesus
Christ, who said . . . also said . . . But he did not say . . ." Pascal's thinking in his latter years might well have been summarized in
these five Scriptural propositions, based upon five Biblical texts,[1] forming a solid framework of eight lines in Fragment 949 of the *Pensées.*[2]
Alike in his life and in his work, the Bible came to hold such an important place for Pascal that, if we wish to establish the chronology of some
undated writings of his on a moral or spiritual theme, the surest criterion would be to rely upon the number and character of Biblical quotations or allusions found therein. Whether he was summarizing his
position during a controversy, or establishing the proper ground for
some personal maxim, or giving counsel as a Christian layman, Pascal
came to rely more and more upon the Bible.

BIBLICAL RADICALISM

" Anyone who seeks to give meaning to Scripture, without taking it
directly from Scripture, is a foe to Scripture." This principle indicates
clearly enough the Biblical radicalism of one who had heard Christ Himself say to him: " I am present with thee by My Word in Scripture."[3]
For Pascal, " all depends upon the blessing of God, to be attributed
only to things done for Him, according to His rules and His ways, the
manner being thus as important as the thing itself, and perhaps more."[4]
To hold fast to Scripture interpreted according to Scripture, was to

---

* Psalm 119, numbered 118 in the Douay Bible, was Pascal's favorite.
[1] Eccl. 3:8; Ps. 116:2; John 12:34; John 14:27; Matt. 10:34.
[2] *Pensées,* Section xiv, Fr. 949, *Œuvres,* v. **14**, 383.
[3] *Le Mystère de Jésus, Pensées,* Section vii, Fr. 553, *Œuvres,* v. **13**, 438.
[4] *Pensées,* Section vii, Fr. 499, *Œuvres,* v. **13**, 399, 400.

hold fast alike to the commands of God and to the ways He taught to the man of faith, the man who had prayed to Him, pouring out his heart in the words of Ps. 118: "Make me to understand the way of thy justification." [5]

This man of faith had already come to acknowledge in the words of this same psalm: " By what does a young man correct his ways? By observing thy words." [6] And he had learned that we do not know these ways save through Jesus Christ, that " we know God by Jesus Christ alone," that " we know ourselves only through Jesus Christ "; we know life and death only through Jesus Christ," and that " the Scripture has Jesus Christ alone for its object." [7]

It is Jesus Christ who, in this double capacity, gives meaning to Scripture, as the object of Scripture and as being present in Scripture. That is why anyone wishing to interpret the meaning of Scripture must take it from the Scripture. This came to be the maxim guiding a man whose philosophy was henceforward Christ-centered, a Christian who learned to recognize in the Bible the same Voice he heard speaking to him in his prayers, and who from now on came to pray through his Bible even more than to read in it. After the manner of the brethren in the book of The Acts,[8] he was found " daily searching the Scriptures, whether these things were so." [9]

THE SUPREME REFERENCE

We have not adequately stressed, writes Robert Vallery-Radot,[10] the continued contact, on Pascal's part, with the Bible, and with Saint Augustine, and most of all with Saint Paul. This same writer goes on to indicate, as we have done, that Pascal's devotion to the Bible was inseparable from his love of Christ, which shone forth in his sublime countenance, and thus revealed the central secret of Pascal's genius.

Every scholar who has made a study of Pascal's reading agrees that

---

[5] Ps. 118:27 [Ps. 119 Authorized Version].

[6] Ps. 118:9 [Ps. 119 Authorized Version].

[7] *Pensées*, Section vii, Fr. 548, *Œuvres*, v. **13, 431.**

[8] Acts 17:11.

[9] *Pensées*, Section xi, Fr. 696, *Œuvres*, v. **14, 136.** The entire text of the fragment is taken from Acts 17:11, in the Latin text of the Vulgate. We shall see that these summaries of selected Bible texts reveal a favorite method used by Pascal in his study of the Bible.

[10] Vallery-Radot, R., " Le Secret de Pascal," *La Revue hebdomadaire*, No. 28, 32d year, July 14, 1923, p. 204.

the very first importance must be given to the Holy Scriptures.[11] This preponderant place was apparently given to the Bible, especially after the famous night of November 23, 1654, not only as a result of the special revelation attested by the *Mémorial*, but also from the fact that, after this experience, Pascal lived in close contact with Port-Royal, where the Bible was held in great respect. Pascal was present at the Vaumurier meetings which established the text of the Mons edition of the New Testament. He followed closely the discussions of this whole matter among the Jansenist theologians. He explored the Port-Royal library at length, finding it particularly well-stored in editions of the Bible, and in works relating to the Bible.

When he found himself engaged in full-fledged controversy with the Jesuits, the author of the *Provinciales* turned constantly to the Bible for reference and for guidance. Thus in the first *Provinciale* he examined Arnauld's assertion according to which grace had failed Peter when he denied his Lord. Fragment 744 of the *Pensées* [12] shows Pascal turning to the Bible for an explanation of Peter's behavior. Domat scrutinized the same Biblical texts here annotated by his friend Blaise.[13] The tremendous part played by Scripture in the *Provinciales* and other polemical writings has already been brought out. Likewise our study of the *Pensées* has shown the polemist absorbed in the consultation of Scripture as he was drafting his letters and facta.

Pascal had turned from experimental science to the Bible as his teacher. The only truth that henceforth mattered greatly to him, he found set forth in the texts of revelation which gave him answers to his questions: " He applied all his energy to the interpretation of these texts, becoming a disciple, not only of the Hebrew writers who edited the Old Testament, but also of the Jewish rabbis who had disclosed and established its figurative meaning. Pascal was loyal to the tradition of Saint Paul and to the spirit of Jansen, who unceasingly condemned the corrupting influence of Origen and the Scholastics, and sought to purify religion of all traces of Platonic metaphysics and Stoic ethics, that is to say, of all pagan influences. Pascal sought to rediscover Christianity in its original form, distinguishing it clearly from its later contact with

---

[11] Cf., for example: *Introduction aux* Pensées *de Pascal, Œuvres*, v. 12, lxviii; Jovy, E., *Etudes pascaliennes*, v. 2, 3, Vrin, Paris, 1927; v. 8, 164, Vrin, Paris, 1932; Mauriac, F., *Blaise Pascal et sa sœur Jacqueline*, Hachette, Paris, 1931, p. 193; Strowski, F., *Pascal et son temps, op. cit.*, v. 3, 302 ff.

[12] *Pensées*, Section xii, Fr. 744, *Œuvres*, v. 14, 200, 201.

[13] *Œuvres*, v. 14, 201, n. 7.

the mentality of the West, and welding it solidly to the Judaism which was its prime source." [14]

In this regard Pascal developed the very thesis which, in the years 1847 to 1850, Kierkegaard was to take up with new vigor, and to press to its logical ultimate consequences. In his *Comparaison des Chrétiens des premiers temps avec ceux d'aujourd'hui* Pascal pointed the way for the author of *The Sickness Unto Death* (1849), of *Training in Christianity* (1850), and of the bellicose pamphlet the *Instant* (1855). Both men made quite clear the incompatibility between the spirit which inspired Christianity in its beginnings and its condition in modern times. " This antagonism dates from the day when the Church undertook to enter into intimate relations with ' the world,' with ' this age,' that is to say, with culture as resting upon purely human foundations." [15] It was to find its most vehement expression in Kierkegaard's pained outcry: " The Christianity of the New Testament no longer exists! " [16] The identical protest, in Pascal as in Kierkegaard, roots in a similar evangelical consciousness, whose theme is well stated in the title of one of Kierkegaard's Edifying Addresses *Purity of Heart Is to Will One Thing.*[17]

In his later years Pascal came to acknowledge " that there is one substantial truth, and that that alone is the truth." [18] For him, faith was knowledge in the full sense of the term, " above sense and reason, but not contrary to them." [19] We may note an edifying analogy on this point, between Pascal and Saint Paul.[20] Faith is what reveals to us ourselves, and reveals other men to us for what they are. All genuine

---

[14] *Introduction aux* Pensées *de Pascal, Œuvres,* v. **12**, cxxxii, cxxxiii.

[15] Höffding, H., " Pascal et Kierkegaard," *Revue de métaphysique et de morale,* 30th year, No. 2, April–June, 1923, p. 221.

[16] Quoted by Höffding, *op. cit.,* p. 229.
Kierkegaard's aim was the deplorable state of Christianity in Christendom; his " one thesis " was that " Christianity no longer exists." (*A Short Life of Kierkegaard,* by Walter Lowrie, Princeton University Press, 1942, p. 233.)

[17] Kierkegaard, S., *Purity of Heart Is to Will One Thing; Spiritual Preparation for the Feast of Confession,* translated from the Danish by Douglas V. Steere, Harper & Brothers, New York and London, 1938.

[18] Vinet, A., *Etudes sur Blaise Pascal,* Kohler, ed., 1936, *op. cit.,* p. 133.

[19] Chevalier, J., " La Méthode de connaître d'après Pascal," *Revue de métaphysique et de morale, op. cit.,* p. 193.
Vid. *Pensées,* Section iv, Fr. 265, *Œuvres,* v. **13**, 194, 195; Fr. 273, *ibid.,* 199; Section vii, Fr. 430, *ibid.,* 335, 336.

[20] Cf., for example, I Cor. 13:12, and Pascal's statement: " Par la gloire nous connaîtrons sa nature."

psychology finds its starting point in " the most ancient Book in the world and the most authentic." [21] All history appears as sacred history, once it is seen in the perspective of this Book. Pascal said in his own way, before Bossuet, that man frets, but God leads him.

Indeed Pascal is the forerunner of Bossuet, in the thinking evidenced in the *Discours sur l'histoire universelle* (1681) and in the *Politique tirée de l'Ecriture Sainte* (published 1709). How glorious it was for Pascal " to see with the eyes of faith the history of Herod and of Caesar "! [22] " How fine it is to see, with the eyes of faith, Darius and Cyrus, Alexander, the Romans, Pompey, and Herod working, without knowing it, for the glory of the Gospel! " [23] Faith, by giving us a true understanding of prophecy, draws back the curtain and shows history as a single drama with a unifying theme. The Messiah appeared at the time " foretold by the state of the Jewish people, by the state of the heathen, by the state of the temple, by the number of years." [24] What a wonderful thing! When a human intelligence is enlightened from above, it can trace the conflict of God's purposes at grips with the purposes of man, and watch man's purposes take their proper place at last palpitating within the purpose of God! Is it true that neither Josephus nor Tacitus, nor other historians, spoke of Jesus Christ? " So far is this from telling against Christianity, that on the contrary it speaks for it." [25] The fact is that " if Jesus Christ had come just to sanctify, all Scripture and all things would tend to that end, and it would be quite easy to convince unbelievers. If Jesus Christ had only come to blind, all His conduct would confuse; and we would have no means of convincing unbelievers." [26] As it was, in the words of Isaiah, Jesus Christ would rise *in sanctificationem et in scandalum.*[27]

Pascal frankly faced the contradictions found in Scripture and submitted to them, being convinced that the source of all heresy is the exclusion of one truth on behalf of another.[28] In Fragment 776, for example, he cites Biblical texts which declare in substance: " Fear not,

[21] *Pensées,* Section ix, Fr. 601, *Œuvres,* v. **14**, 40.
[22] *Pensées,* Section xi, Fr. 700, *Œuvres,* v. **14**, 137.
[23] *Pensées,* Section xi, Fr. 701, *Œuvres,* v. **14**, 138.
[24] *Pensées,* Section xi, Fr. 708, *Œuvres,* v. **14**, 141.
[25] *Pensées,* Section xii, Fr. 787, *Œuvres,* v. **14**, 227.
[26] *Pensées,* Section xii, Fr. 795, *Œuvres,* v. **14**, 234, 235.
[27] Isa. 8:14.
[28] *Pensées,* Section xiv, Fr. 862, *Œuvres,* v. **14**, 303-307. The entire fragment is deserving of careful study from this point of view.

provided you fear; but if you fear not, then fear." [29] The statements appear to be mutually exclusive. But Pascal, facing the situation candidly, sets forth the following principle: " To understand Scripture, we must have a meaning in which all the contrary passages are reconciled." [30] To understand Pascal would be to discover just this meaning in his work,[31] particularly in the work of his later years. A detailed analysis of Section xi of the *Pensées* from this point of view would be fruitful and instructive. The *Abrégé de la vie de Jésus-Christ* [32] stands, in our judgment, as the culmination of this effort at clarification, in the light of Pascal's conviction that " in Jesus Christ all the contradictions are reconciled." [33]

It is Jesus Christ, in the final analysis, who gives Scripture its authenticity and its meaning. In Pascal's eyes, however, this authenticity was evident from one end of Scripture to the other. Moses was contemporary with the events he described in this sense that he was brought quite close to these events by the small number of generations that separated him from them,[34] whereas " truth is perverted only by the change of men." [35] Shem, who saw Lamech, who saw Adam, saw also Jacob, who saw those who saw Moses; " therefore the deluge and the creation are true." [36] In this connection, Pascal opposes the sacred writers to " those fabulous historians " who " are not contemporaneous with the facts about which they write." [37] Furthermore the sincerity of the Jews is beyond question, and this lends added distinction to the contrast between sacred and profane writers: Moses does not hide his own shame, whereas Josephus hides the shame of his nation.[38] Isaiah declares: " This book shall be for a testimony," [39] and we must admit this truly extraordinary fact, that the Jews lovingly preserve a book which denounces them.[40]

[29] *Pensées*, Section xii, Fr. 776, *Œuvres*, v. **14**, 219.

[30] *Pensées*, Section x, Fr. 684, *Œuvres*, v. **14**, 122.

[31] Baruzi, J., " Pascal et la ' Vanité de la peinture,' " *La Revue hebdomadaire*, No. 28, 32d year, July 14, 1923, p. 267.

[32] *Abrégé de la vie de Jésus-Christ, Œuvres*, v. **11**, 6 ff.

[33] *Pensées*, Section x, Fr. 684, *Œuvres*, v. **14**, 122.

[34] *Pensées*, Section ix, Fr. 622, *Œuvres*, v. **14**, 65, 66. Cf. also 65, n. 2.

[35] *Pensées*, Section ix, Fr. 624, *Œuvres*, v. **14**, 66.

[36] *Pensées*, Section ix, Fr. 625, *Œuvres*, v. **14**, 67.

[37] *Pensées* Section ix, Fr. 628, *Œuvres*, v. **14**, 69.

[38] *Pensées*, Section ix, Fr. 629, *Œuvres*, v. **14**, 71.

[39] Isa. 30:8; *Pensées*, Section ix, Fr. 630, *Œuvres*, v. **14**, 72.

[40] *Pensées*, Section ix, Fr. 631, *Œuvres*, v. **14**, 72.

O fathomless wisdom of the hidden God! The Jews never understood how it was that God, in carrying out His profound plan, was able to veil the entire life of Christ and of Christianity within the depths of the Hebrew text. The Jews saw in the text only the carnal meaning which suited them, and it was this which actually saved the Scriptures for us. Why was The Book of Ruth preserved? Why the story of Tamar? [41] Everything in the Bible is there for a reason. The more Pascal examined these various books, scattered through the centuries and later miraculously gathered together, the more truths he found in them, the more he found this succession, this religion, divine. The more he admired it in its authority, its duration, its perpetuity, its morality, its conduct, its doctrine, its effects, the more frightful he found the darkness that was foretold for the Jews. And it was with unspeakable exultation that he held out his arms to a Redeemer, foretold for four thousand years, who had come to suffer and to die for him, Blaise Pascal, on earth, at the time and under all the circumstances foretold. [42]

There are clearly two meanings, therefore, in Scripture: the literal, or carnal, meaning and the spiritual meaning. Pascal then proceeds to suggest this principle of interpretation: " When the Word of God, which is really true, is false literally, it is true spiritually." [43] Are there numerous statements and expressions which shock our human way of seeing and speaking? It is because they must be spiritually understood. Such, for example, as these: " God is jealous "; " He accepts the odor of our sweet-smelling savor "; et cetera. The Old Testament is a type, [44] Pascal tells us. The Jews were not able to read it aright because they were carnal; and thus it came about that they misunderstood Jesus in His greatness as foretold; for they sought in Him merely carnal greatness. [45] No man can attain to the full meaning of Scripture save by charity, inasmuch as charity is the unique object of Scripture. Everything in Scripture is figurative, save that which leads to charity.

At this point, however, Pascal would guard against overstatement. There is danger that either of two errors may arise out of what has just been said: The first consists in taking everything literally; the second, in taking everything " spiritually." [46] Pascal consequently promises that

[41] *Pensées*, Section xii, Fr. 743, *Œuvres*, v. **14**, 200.
[42] *Pensées*, Section xii, Fr. 737, *Œuvres*, v. **14**, 196, 197.
[43] *Pensées*, Section x, Fr. 687, *Œuvres*, v. **14**, 125.
[44] *Pensées*, Section x, Fr. 691, *Œuvres*, v. **14**, 129.
[45] *Pensées*, Section x, Fr. 662, *Œuvres*, v. **14**, 98, 99.
[46] *Pensées*, Section x, Fr. 648, *Œuvres*, v. **14**, 89.

he will "speak against excessively figurative language "[47] and "far-fetched " figures of speech.[48] He denounces the "extravagances of the Apocalyptics, Preadamites, Millenarians, etc."[49] We are at a loss, in fact, to know wherein lies our great admiration for this passionate soul, henceforth so completely devoted to the Bible: whether for his enthusiasm or for his firm moderation. Let no one think of Pascal as a romanticist: even in his most enraptured moods, he still remains a classicist — indeed, one of the most eminent craftsmen of French classicism.

A classicist in spirit, and a man of good taste, he admired the Scripture for its fine style no less than for its basic truth. The Port-Royal editors record in their *Préface* [50] that Pascal found elements of beauty, in the Gospels particularly, which it may be no one before him had ever noticed. The simplicity of Jesus' words impressed him above all else, and this he explained by saying that our Lord, finding His own Spirit at home among the most sublime concerns of the Kingdom of God, was enabled to speak of the supernatural with the greatest naturalness. This lent a certain naïve candor to His words, a quality which is only added evidence of His divinity and in no sense contrary to it.

In Fragment 797 of the *Pensées,* under the caption " Proofs of Jesus Christ," we read this charming tribute: " Jesus Christ said great things so simply that it seems as though He had not thought them great; and yet so clearly that we can easily see what He thought of them. This clearness, joined to simplicity, is wonderful."[51] The succeeding fragment stresses the admirable style of the Gospels, and its unaffected modesty. " Who taught the Evangelists these same qualities of Christ," he asks in Fragment 800, " so that they could know how to portray with such nuance the very soul of Him? " Pascal immediately rejects the notion that the Apostles could have been impostors,[52] deceived or deceivers.[53] His conclusion is that the glorified Christ continued to inspire His followers.[54] Pascal's eulogy of the style of the Bible takes the form of a characteristic lapidary formula: " God rightly speaks of God."[55]

[47] *Pensées*, Section x, Fr. 649, *Œuvres*, v. **14**, *ibid.*
[48] *Ibid.*, Fr. 650.
[49] *Pensées*, Section x, Fr. 651, *Œuvres*, v. **14**, 90, 91.
[50] *Préface de Port-Royal, Œuvres*, v. **12**, cxcii, cxciii.
[51] *Pensées*, Section xii, Fr. 797, *Œuvres*, v. **14**, 235.
[52] *Pensées*, Section xii, Fr. 801, *Œuvres*, v. **14**, 238, 239.
[53] *Pensées*, Section xii, Fr. 802, *Œuvres*, v. **14**, 239.
[54] *Ibid.*
[55] *Pensées*, Section xii, Fr. 790, *Œuvres*, v. **14**, 237.

Pascal most naturally uses the Vulgate edition as his chief reference in studying Scripture, since it was, by virtue of a decree of the Council of Trent of April 8, 1546, the only authorized edition in the Roman Catholic Church. Thanks to the aid of Popes Sixtus V and Clement VIII, a revised and corrected text of the Vulgate had now been published, which was regarded as definitive, and came to be known as the Sixto-Clementine Bible. This is the text to which Pascal, as a loyal Catholic, referred when he wrote the *Provinciales,* as well as the *Ecrits des curés de Paris* and the *Projet de mandement* — all drafted for the use of the French clergy. Being the only authorized edition in the Church, it was the only one which might be cited as proof. It will be recalled that the Vulgate originated as the Latin version of the Bible, translated from the Septuagint and corrected by Saint Jerome.

Pascal himself makes no reference to the Septuagint. He set out directly from the Vulgate. He had a thorough knowledge of Latin and translated it freely, as is shown by the corrections and marginal notes in his manuscripts. Even in the words he crossed out, we never find a mistranslation, but only the minor corrections made by a busy man who was summarizing in French the details he found in the Latin text.

We should never lose sight of Pascal's realism. Always he remained the practical man of Auvergne. Born in a town where the neighbors made vegetables grow on an abandoned moat, Pascal wanted things ever to be tangible and sure. He put his questions to the Bible in just the way he had put them to nature, always keeping in mind the distinction between what depended upon authority and what upon experimental science.

Pascal often appeared to be a hasty worker, but this did not mean that he neglected detail. Quite the contrary. The matter in hand was far too important in his eyes for that. Just as in the field of physics he had once exhausted every resource of methodology, of proof, of counterproof, and of verification, so now, as a student of the Bible, he neglected no source of information or verification. As to the content of his inquiry, he displayed great independence of mind, and seems to have felt justified in turning to Protestant sources, and also to the Jewish rabbis.

Whenever he was trying to restore the original form of a Scriptural text so as to meet an objection, or to refute some error, or to discomfit an unbelieving opponent, he was, we find, dominated by a desire for purity of doctrine. In the Vulgate, for example, these are the words in which the irritated Jews accused Jesus of blasphemy: *Quia tu, homo cum sis, facis teipsum Deum,* taken from the Greek: ὅτι καὶ σὺ, ἄνθρωπος ὤν, σαυτὸν ποιεῖς θεόν. The Vulgate puts a conjunctional subordinate in place of the participial clause in the Greek, thus introducing a slight sense of concession into the translation. It stresses the grounds for the grievance, rather than the incompatibility between the divine nature and the human nature. Pascal openly challenges the Latin genius, and observes an absolute literalism in his own translation: *Homo existens, Deum te facis.* He then devotes all his energy to meeting this objection, in order to show that Jesus' claim, as understood by the Jews, merely affirmed the identity underlying these contradictions, and thus led to an absurdity. Pascal's original translation was intended to shed some light upon the course of his reasoning,[56] and it succeeded in its aim.

Did Pascal consult the Hebrew Bible directly? It appears that, in addition to Saint Jerome's translation, he also used that of Vatable,[57] an " apostate " who had gone over to Protestantism. Pascal seems to have had some acquaintance with the Hebrew language. What he learned may have come from working with the *Polyglot Bible,* each page of which was printed in four parallel columns, including: (1) the Greek text of the Septuagint; (2) the Latin text of the Vulgate; (3) a new translation made from the Hebrew by Sante Pagnino; and (4) the

---

[56] Lhermet, J., *Pascal et la Bible, op. cit.,* pp. 224, 225.

[57] *Biblia Polyglotta vulgo dicta Vatabli:* ex officina Sant' Andreana, Heidelberg, 1586 (2d ed., Heidelberg, 1593).

Pascal seems also (cf., for example, Fr. 819 of *Pensées*) to have used the edition given by Robert Estienne in Paris in 1545 and re-edited in Geneva in 1547. This edition provided the text from the Vulgate on the one hand, and on the other a new translation worked out from the original Hebrew. The latter, moreover, was a combination of the translation of Léon de Juda (Tigurina) and that of Sante Pagnino. Also there appeared in 1564 in Bâle an excellent edition of the notes of Vatable and Sante Pagnino, entitled *Biblia Veteris ac Novi Testamenti.* Finally, Robert Estienne incorporated other corrections of Vatable to the Hebrew Bible of Kimchi, 1539–1543, 3 v. Thus Estienne summed up what Vatable had gathered from various commentators, adding to it the benefits of his own strong erudite mind, and what Estienne himself had to say in the form of personal commentaries of Calvinistic inspiration.

An excellent revised and enlarged edition of Vatable was published in Paris in 1745, namely, *Biblia Sacra, cum universis Franc. Vatabli, Regii Hebraicae Linguae quondam Professoris, et varium interpretum, annotationibus. Latina interpretatio duplex est: altera vetus, altera nova. Parisiis.* MDCCXLV.

Hebrew text itself. In the margin of the Greek text appeared a summary in Latin and a concordance of Biblical texts. At the bottom of each page were found, along with Vatable's notes, the diverse interpretations of the commentators, some passages translated by the Fathers, and occasionally a literal translation. " Thus arranged," so Lhermet points out, " Vatable's Bible had a double advantage: it was of great practical utility in that it assembled, one beside the other, all the texts recognized by the Church, at the same time taking account of other editions; secondly, it was scientifically useful, in that, by recording variant readings, it satisfied the inquiring and reasoning mind of Pascal, who made his own choice among them, selecting the one which conformed most closely to the ideas he was developing." [58] This is a fine tribute to this scholarly edition, edited by one of the royal lecturers appointed by Francis I, at the time when the latter was laying the foundation for what was to become the *Collège de France*. It will further be recalled that Calvin studied Hebrew under Vatable in 1531.

A SCRUPULOUS SCHOLAR

Lhermet was of the opinion, formed by selecting such texts as Fragment 434 of the *Pensées,* and more specially the quotation from Ps. 118:13, that Pascal made use of a method of contamination in order to favor the Jansenist position. In Lhermet's view, Pascal was motivated less by the philologist's scruples in finding that translation which would keep most faithfully to the original, than by " the concern of a clever man who wanted to see the triumph of his religious ideas." Where necessary, Lhermet goes on to assert, Pascal resorted to omission and condensation, or borrowed from both versions, i.e., the Vulgate and the Vatable edition, according as the one or the other would bring to light some fact or establish some truth favoring the Jansenist position.[59]

In a very detailed study, published in the *Revue d'histoire littéraire de la France,*[60] Joseph Dedieu takes Lhermet to task on this point. In a devastating critique, he refutes point by point the charge that Pascal deliberately altered the sacred words of Scriptural Tradition with a view to stressing or strengthening the Jansenist aspect of his " Vindication

[58] Lhermet, J., *Pascal et la Bible, op. cit.,* p. 212.

[59] *Ibid.,* pp. 215, 216.

[60] Dedieu, J., " Note sur Pascal traducteur de la Bible," in *Revue d'histoire littéraire de la France,* 40th year, 1933. pp 80–90.

of Christianity." Dedieu declares, first of all, that this accusation shocks every probability. It is no less a shock to " the whole uprightness, inflexible to the point of brutality, which this noble character displayed at every point in his work." [61] After examining closely the texts from the Vulgate, from Vatable, and from Pascal, Dedieu exposes the feebleness of the arguments put forward [62] and shows how very precise the translations of Pascal really were — even to the point of their Oriental manner of phrasing [63] — for Pascal was a scholar who had familiarized himself with the Hebrew commentaries.

Hence Pascal emerges greatly enhanced in stature from Dedieu's critique, which is fully documented. This Roman Catholic scholar of exegesis ends by denouncing the gravity of injustice and the fallacy in an entire school of thought, which is still, alas, deeply rooted in our time. This consists in regarding the theological fragments of the *Pensées* with a measure of contempt. " Pascal brought all his powers of reflection and ingenuity to his study of the Scriptural text. He was familiar with every scholarly scruple and, I would add, retained his full freedom of mind as well. Had he had at his disposal the same knowledge of Hebrew matters that Spinoza had, it may well be that we should have had an extraordinary French version of the Bible." [64] Mauriac, another Roman Catholic writer, echoes Dedieu's view in doing belated justice to Pascal's good name, basing his own opinion upon the testimony of the admirable Père Lagrange: " The contempt which has long been affected toward Pascal as an exegete cannot be sustained in view of the testimony of a scholar such as Père Lagrange: his arguments remain weighty down to our own day, even from the standpoint of modern exegesis." [65] Let us take the liberty of adding, since we have adduced authoritative testimony to counterbalance Lhermet's unfortunate statement, that Pascal himself once wrote a fragment in the *Pensées* " against those who misuse passages of Scripture and who pride themselves in finding one which seems to favor their error." [66] This should suffice to indicate the objectivity, the integrity, and the erudition of Pascal's Biblical research, which has at last received due homage.

[61] *Ibid.*, p. 81.
[62] *Ibid.*, pp. 81–84.
[63] *Ibid.*, p. 84.
[64] *Ibid.*, p. 90.
[65] Mauriac, F., *Pascal et sa sœur Jacqueline, op. cit.*, p. 193.
[66] *Pensées*, Section xiv, Fr. 899, *Œuvres*, v. 14, 329.

Another type of question must now, however, be considered. The specific problem which confronts us here was raised by Strowski,[67] as we know, regarding the night of November 23, 1654. Pascal was fingering the pages of Scripture. The quotations in French which form part of the *Mémorial* are in the archaic French of Lefèvre d'Etaples. Had Pascal been quoting from memory, he would have corrected the archaism of his phrases; but he did not do so.[68] Pascal was reading, then, from some French edition of the Bible. From which one?

In his brief study on *Pascal et la Bible*,[69] Jovy considers the leading French versions of the Bible which might have been used by families in Pascal's time. He lists thirteen titles. This list makes no reference, however, doubtless because of its Protestant origin, to the Bible prepared by the pastors and professors of the Church of Geneva, an edition of which we have a copy in our possession,[70] published at Saumur in 1614. A copy of this Geneva Bible might very well have found its way into the Pascal home, for we have already seen that some members of an earlier generation of the family were influenced, for a brief time, by Protestantism. Can we think of any Protestant family of such standing without its own Bible? Furthermore, this Geneva Bible was the fruit of the best scholarly work of the Renaissance, and we have seen that Pascal's father was reared in Paris during the Renaissance. He was a man of ample good taste and would have doubtless treasured such a volume. He himself might very well have purchased a copy, if he should not have discovered one in his library. Blaise, indeed, was the sort of person who would have put it to good use; we have already noted his eclectic habits when it came to probing Scripture. A man who had not hesitated to look into Vatable would hardly have hesitated to read the Geneva Bible. It is a fact that the French text of John 12:3, so

---

[67] Strowski, F., *Pascal et son temps, op. cit.*, v. 2, pp. 355, 356.

[68] *Ibid.*, 356, n. 1.

[69] Jovy, E., " Pascal et la Bible," in *Etudes pascaliennes*, v. 8, Vrin, Paris, 1932, 153–155, n. 1.

[70] *La Bible* qui est toute la Saincte Escriture du vieil et du Nouveau Testament, autrement l'Ancienne et la Nouvelle Alliance, le tout revu et conféré sur les textes Hebrieux et Grec par les pasteurs et professeurs de l'eglise de Geneve, avec les tables nécessaires pour le soulagement du Lecteur, Saumur, 1614, 2 v., 460 ÷ 138 (sans compter 31 pages non numérotées, d'index et de tables), in 4°.

often quoted in the words of the *Mémorial,* is found word for word in this Geneva edition. It may be that, so far as Pascal is concerned, the passage was drawn from some source common to all the French versions of that period.

These French versions can be traced back to the translation made early in the sixteenth century by Lefèvre d'Etaples. In successive revisions, it became the Louvain Bible first printed in Antwerp in 1534; in Louvain in 1550; by Christopher Plantin of Antwerp in 1578; by Buon of Paris in 1586; by Pillehotte of Lyons in 1603; by Ménard of Paris in 1639. Jovy traces evidence of still another version of the Louvain Bible in the Bible of René Benoist, curate of Sainte-Eustache, later Bishop of Troyes.[71] To us it seems worth pointing out that the Bible named for the Doctors of Louvain, published by Plantin in 1578 with a preface by Jacobin de Bay (1572), was very similar to the Bible of René Benoist,[72] and also to the Geneva version; and that all these versions were only variants of the evangelical one by Lefèvre d'Etaples, which accounts for their similarity. We may willingly admit that it was most probably a Catholic version that Blaise was reading on the night of November 23, 1654. Perhaps it was the Louvain edition or that of René Benoist. Since most of the Old Testament quotations in his writings are from the Louvain edition, we may presume that he read from it. This does not, however, exclude the probability that he had somewhere in his library a copy of the Geneva Bible which contains the exact form of John 12:3 as Pascal quoted it in the *Mémorial.*

As Pascal studied the Scripture, he carefully consulted the commentaries of the rabbis,[73] and one of the concordances — *concordantiae utriusque testamenti* — which were already in wide circulation at the time. He made use of certain books of maxims, prayers, and Christian teachings, drawn from both Testaments, perhaps in manuscript form. One of his letters gives evidence of this.[74] We know also how frequently he read the same books as Jacqueline, and we know that in the course of her examination on August 22, 1661, she answered an investigator concerning the books she read: " At present it is the *Morales* of

[71] Jovy, E., " Pascal et la Bible," in *Etudes pascaliennes, op. cit.,* v. 8, p. 153.

[72] Benoist, R., *La Sainte Bible* contenant le Vieil et le Nouveau Testament traduite en françois in folio, Paris, 1566. Another edition in 2 v. in 4° was published in 1568.

[73] In regard to this, see especially *Pensées,* Section vii, Fr. 446, and the notes in *Œuvres,* v. 13, 359–363.

[74] Cf. *Œuvres,* v. 10, 55, 56, n. 1. In regard to the manuscript distribution of books long before formulated, cf. *Œuvres,* v. 6, 215, n. 3.

Saint Basil who is seldom translated." She was referring to the *Règles de la morale chrestienne,* selected from the New Testament by Saint Basil, with accompanying explanations by Guillaume le Roy. Finally, we know that Pascal was fearful of the charge of heresy. This accounts for the meticulous verification of all his Biblical inquiries by reference to the Fathers and to Tradition. This may be illustrated by Fragment 775 of the *Pensées,* which concludes in these words: " We must, then, follow the Fathers and Tradition in order to know when [we must explain *omnes* by *all*] to do so, since there is heresy to be feared on both sides." (He was concerned with two verses of Scripture, Matt. 26:27 and Rom. 5:12.) Pascal clearly manifested great scruple and caution in studiously searching Holy Scripture.

TRANSLATING SCRIPTURE

It should be understood that Pascal never claimed to give a full translation from the Bible. That was not his primary aim. There were indeed lengthy translations from his own pen, as in Fragments 682, 713, 722, 726, of the *Pensées;* but, whether long or short, these translations had but a single purpose, to probe into this or that point of Scripture either for personal edification or to shed light upon some matter with which Pascal was concerned at the time. It was Pascal's aim which determined the particular method he chose to employ.

Thus we see that his chief concern was, at one and the same time, to prove loyal to the message once delivered to the saints and intelligible to his own contemporaries by speaking in a language they could understand. Knowing the inadequacy of the translations at his disposal, he turned so far as possible to the originals, seeking to draw their message directly and in as literal a form as he could. At the same time, being an *honnête homme* in a cultured society, he omitted certain details which might have shocked his readers, and in certain instances adapted his phrases to the tastes of his time. In Amos 8:10, for example, he omitted the reference to the figure of a father mourning for his only son, with sackcloth on his back and his head shaven. In Isa. 49:23 he changed the words, " *Lick* up the dust of thy feet," to, " *Kiss* the dust of thy feet." He did not elaborate the detailed account of the idols, and passed over in silence the false gods and pagan sacrifices, when it did no injury to the sense of the passage.[75]

[75] Dan. 11:8; Isa., ch. 48; Isa. 65:3.

Whenever some point of doctrine was involved, however, Pascal was rigorously faithful to the text. Thus it was that he retained the entire description of the image in Daniel,[76] for this concerned an important point of prophecy. In his arguments one feels that he was drawing upon the legal tradition of his family, cutting out useless details, selecting and arranging the Scripture passages he needed in preparing for a verbal assault upon some position held by his opponent. Occasionally he introduced a relative pronoun or conjunction into the Scripture text, aiming to clarify some clause which required special emphasis. Isa. 41:23 came to read, at his hands, " If *ye are gods,* draw near, show us the things that are to come hereafter . . . ; *by this token we shall know* ye are gods." [77] Spurred on by the intuitive mind (*esprit de finesse*), the mathematical genius went so far as to introduce into Scripture a logical structure which was not originally there, or which at most was perhaps implied. In giving voice to this logic of the inner man, Pascal was once again a child of his age.

He would add emphasis to some word in the text, in a wholly Biblical spirit, in order to lend new force to its message. The " *Dabo vobis cor novum* " ("A new heart will I give you ") of the Vulgate thus became " *Je créerai en vous un cœur nouveau* " ("A new heart will I create within you "). Pascal shortens, omits, adds, annotates, comments, combines texts, and inserts his own interpretation. Obscure passages of prophecy are clarified by the light of history for this man to whom a measure of understanding has been granted by " the hidden God." Pascal's translation thus amounted to a paraphrase of Scripture. But, make no mistake, this habit of paraphrase was always for a reason, namely, to lead men to accept Scripture as nearly as possible in its literal form. This was in fact the method in use at Port-Royal, and Monsieur de Saci regularly employed it.

Let us see exactly how Pascal worked upon a passage such as Fragment 722 of the *Pensées,* which we mentioned above briefly. It has reference to Dan. 11:2: " ' The angel said to Daniel: There shall stand up (after Cyrus, under whom this still is) three Kings in Persia (Cambyses, Smerdis, Darius), and the fourth, who shall then come (Xerxes), shall be far richer than they all, and far stronger, and shall stir up all his people against the Greeks.' " [78] Now compare this with the Biblical

---

[76] Dan. 2:27–46.

[77] Antoniadis, S., *Pascal traducteur de la Bible*, Brill, Leyde, 1930, p. xii.

[78] *Pensées,* Section xi, Fr. 722, *Œuvres,* v. 14, 169, 170.

text: " Behold there shall stand up three kings in Persia, and the fourth shall be enriched exceedingly above them all: and when he shall be grown mighty by his riches, he shall stir up all against the kingdom of Greece." Pascal's version is briefer. He introduces it by the words: " The angel said to Daniel," and the direct nature of the divine message is made quite clear. The interpretation he adds for the sake of clarification: " There shall stand . . . three kings of Persia," and " the fourth." And Pascal goes on, by way of strengthening this point, to add, " Who shall then come," reaching the climax of this prophecy in disclosing the full prospect: " And shall stir up his people against the Greeks." Pascal was concerned for the quasi-mathematical exactness of prophecy, as it came to be verified point by point. To this extent translation became for him a form of Bible study, properly speaking, and the translation itself became a secondary concern. Let us now turn to this aspect of Pascal's work.

PROBING SCRIPTURE

As a student of the Bible, Pascal had his favorite verses, to which he continually turned. One of these was the famous text of Dan. 9:24. At the end of Fragment 692 of the *Pensées,* he summarized it in a concise, abbreviated form, which brings out the essential point. The reference to *everlasting justice,* however, strikes Pascal's religious consciousness, and he proceeds to insert a brief comment of his own: " *Eternal* justice, not legal, but eternal." [79] We know how often Pascal was to recur to this theme of true Justice, within the order of charity, which he held to be opposed to the notion of arbitrary, capricious, human forms of justice, within the order of the mind. This higher notion he took from the Bible, or perhaps he nourished from Biblical sources a notion already dear to him. In the study of his Bible, as we have said, he now gave the same attention to minute detail that he once applied in his study of nature. In Fragment 636 of the *Pensées* we see with what care he examined Mal. 2:2 and Isa. 1:19, probably in the light of Gen. 2:17. " *If* does not indicate indifference: Malachi, Isaiah. Is., *Si volumus,* etc. *In quacumque die.*" [80]

How was a man to understand Scripture? It required, indeed, the grace of God. But where did man's part begin? Put the question to Scripture itself: The mysteries have there been revealed to us in a cer-

[79] *Pensées,* Section x, Fr. 692, *Œuvres,* v. 14, 131.
[80] *Pensées,* Section ix, Fr. 636, *Œuvres,* v. 14, 79.

tain order. In the same way, this order must be followed in the case of every individual. The Jews learned the meaning of repentance before they learned of grace. John the Baptist came before Jesus Christ. In the same way, it is by repentance, again, that the individual Christian attains to faith, to charity, to grace.[81] The converse is also true, namely, that no one abandons the truth as it is in Scripture " save by abandoning charity."

What is needed, therefore, in *conversion* in the literal sense of the word? We " had our own will as our rule. Let us now take the will of [God]." [82] Repentance is thus the key to true understanding, and all valid psychology, having to do with human understanding as well as with other activity, derives its basic principle from the Gospel. " The veil, which is upon these books for the Jews, is there also for evil Christians, and for all who do not hate themselves." [83] Only a faith born of repentance is sufficient to break the vicious circle willed by a hidden God: Prophecies " are proofs only to those who know and believe them." [84] The paradox is a divine paradox. Blessed are those who have eyes to see!

In his study of the Bible, Pascal followed a method which is familiar enough to men of God: It consists in grouping a series of texts about a single question. Thus the author of the *Imitation of Christ* (III, lviii, 9) brings together two texts from Isaiah (ch. 60:22 and ch. 65:20), when he states the principle: " The least shall become a thousand, and the sinner of an hundred years shall die," aiming to point out that we must not seek to penetrate truth which is above us, nor the secret judgments of God. We find Pascal, similarly, examining such a question as sanctification in Section xiv of the *Pensées*. We find here thirty-five selected texts crowded into a single fragment.[85] Again we find him listing, within a single fragment, seven texts in less than ten lines, as he considers the Christian's triumph over death! [86] We could go on citing examples of this kind to illuminate his method. The *Abrégé de la vie de Jésus-Christ*, cited above in these pages, furnishes a choice example. Both in his quotations and in his translations, Pascal at one time is quite precise and complete while at another time he abbreviates; now he adds a phrase of

[81] *Pensées*, Section x, Fr. 661, *Œuvres*, v. **14,** 98.
[82] *Pensées*, Section x, Fr. 668, *Œuvres*, v. **14,** 102, 103.
[83] *Pensées*, Section x, Fr. 676, *Œuvres*, v. **14,** 112.
[84] *Pensées*, Section xi, Fr. 698, *Œuvres*, v. **14,** 136.
[85] *Pensées*, Section x, Fr. 682, *Œuvres*, v. **14,** 116–120.
[86] *Pensées*, Section xii, Fr. 782, *Œuvres*, v. **14,** 224.

comment, now he changes the order of words; now he groups together selections from varied passages by the same author; now he quotes Old Testament passages following those from the New, now he weaves together sections drawn from both; and then again he borrows from the commentaries in Vatable's *Polyglot Bible*. When he feels he must bring to a climax some argument, in which his quotations have found their place within a structure of pitiless logic, Pascal may suddenly disregard altogether the text of the Book he has been examining so meticulously, and rely for the time being wholly upon his memory. Dedieu has listed no less than thirty-eight passages in the first twelve sections of the *Pensées* [87] that are faulty in this respect. In such cases, the passionate Pascal is simply carried away by the end he has in view.

THE LAST PROPHET OF ISRAEL

All the while, however, there is no break in continuity, no interruption in the smoothly flowing style, so rich in the lifeblood it has drawn from the Bible itself. Pascal's style is now that of the prophet, now that of a poet, now that of an orator, then that of a man of law — or, we may say, a man of God's Law. After a section marked by gradual growth, there is suddenly an upsurge of energy overflowing in all its abundance. Such, for example, are the ejaculatory prayers like the *Mystère de Jésus*, in which, as Charles Du Bos finely describes it, " the somber rhythm of contrition is akin to a certain adagio in one of the later Beethoven quartets." [88] Ernest Havet felt with regard to Pascal's translation of Isa., ch. 49, that it was something of a masterpiece, gathering up all the inspiration found in this, perhaps the most magnificent text in the whole of the Sacred Writings.[89] With unfailing good taste, Pascal borrows from the Bible such words as may lend vivid color to his own discourse. Instead of the Greek $\chi \acute{a} o s$, he prefers $\dot{a} \chi \acute{a} \sigma \mu a$ which he translates *gouffre immense* (immense chasm). He selects from the Bible innumerable figures of speech, drawn in the language of flesh and blood, filled with vital energy. He enriches his diction with Hebrew phrases, and his style with a poesy flowing with robust strength and ample sympathy. The Biblical elements are so intricately interwoven

[87] Dedieu, J., *op. cit.*, pp. 80, 81.

[88] Du Bos, Ch., " Le Langage de Pascal," in *La Revue hebdomadaire*, No. 28, 32d year, July 14, 1923, p. 257.

[89] Havet, E., *Etude sur les* Pensées *de Pascal*, in ed. of *Pensées*, Delagrave, Paris, 1887, p. xxxix.

with the threads of his own thought that they lend an incomparable richness to the texture of his phrasing. He writes:

" Les Juifs avaient vieilli dans ces pensées terrestres, que Dieu aimait leur père Abraham, sa chair et ce qui en sortait; que pour cela il les avait multipliés et distingués de tous les autres peuples, sans souffrir qu'ils s'y mêlassent; que, quand ils languissaient dans l'Egypte, il les en retira avec tous ses grands signes en leur faveur; qu'il les nourrit de la manne dans le désert; qu'il les mena dans une terre bien grasse; qu'il leur donna des rois et un temple bien bâti pour y offrir des bêtes, et par le moyen de l'effusion de leur sang qu'ils seraient purifiés, et qu'il leur devait envoyer le Messie pour les rendre maîtres de tout le monde, et il a prédit le temps de sa venue.

" Le monde ayant vieilli dans ses erreurs charnelles, Jésus-Christ est venu dans le temps prédit, mais non pas dans l'éclat attendu; et ainsi ils n'ont pas pensé que ce fût lui." [90]

Translated: " The Jews had grown old in these earthly thoughts, that God loved their father Abraham, and the seed that came after him; that on account of this He had made them to multiply and had set them apart from all other peoples, and yet would not allow them to intermingle; that, when they were languishing in Egypt, He brought them out with all His great signs in their favor; that He fed them with manna in the wilderness; that He led them to a rich and fertile land; that He gave to them kings and a temple solidly built for them to make offerings of beasts, by the shedding of whose blood they should be purified, and that He would send them a Messiah to make them masters of all the world; and foretold the time of His coming.

" The world having grown old in its carnal errors, Jesus Christ came at the time foretold, but not in the expected magnificence; and thus they did not think that it was He."

Pascal was the very first author, before Bossuet, Racine, La Fontaine, Rousseau, or Chateaubriand, to introduce music, painting, and imitative harmony into French prose, together with all the wealth of imagery drawn from a life at once human and divine. " With him art passes into genius, to such a point that to call him an artist would be to do him an injury." [91]

In a splendid chapter on " Pascal as Poet," Dr. H. F. Stewart has

[90] *Pensées,* Section x, Fr. 670, *Œuvres,* v. **14,** 104, 105.
[91] Amiot, Ch.-G., " Impressions sur Pascal romantique et classique," in *La Revue hebdomadaire, op. cit.,* pp. 299, 300.

furnished us with a first-rate analysis to which the reader is referred. In a time when strong emotion was absent from verse, Blaise Pascal the prose writer was, according to Stewart, " an authentic poet, and most poetical when he drew his inspiration from the book which above all else he valued and studied, the Bible." Stewart insists, for example, on Pascal's use of prosopopoeia, a method of personification dear to the Hebrews. A further feature of Hebrew poetry, he adds, is " the parallelism which gives it its peculiar force and rhythmical music. This was congenial to Pascal's genius, and the practice of it colours many pages of his prose." The Bible provided Pascal also with a peculiar notion of *le cœur* (the heart), as being "the sense of the inner depth of human nature, of the seat of knowledge and will." This notion was indeed enriched by Pascal's own experience, and became strikingly similar to our notion of intuition. Its original meaning, however, roots deep in the Book. In his conclusion, Stewart praises Pascal's masterpieces " as literature immortal, and as language, setting the example whereby French prose has become the most perfect vehicle of lucid and persuasive speech which men have used since the days of Plato and Demosthenes." Pascal is " a living force." To read him is " an inspiration precisely because he speaks with the voice of the inspired prophet and poet, seeing the truth with the single eye which receives and radiates the light." [92]

The light which radiated from Pascal was, in fact, a light which he had received with singleness of heart through the pages of the Holy Book: " There is enough light for those whose only desire is to see," [93] he used to say modestly, once he had found his way to the Pool of Siloam.

[92] Stewart, H. F., *The Secret of Pascal,* University Press, Cambridge, 1941, pp. 79, 80, 85, 86, 87.

In 1942 Professor H. F. Stewart was invited to deliver the Annual Lecture on a Master Mind, Henriette Hertz Trust of the British Academy, upon Pascal. He took this opportunity to state once more his " conviction that the secret of Pascal's appeal to men of every condition lies in his marvelous style." He offered this precious suggestion: " It is in truth to the Order of Charity that we must assign Pascal's poetic view. Much of his prose is strictly of the Order of the Mind, and does not rise above it; but enter his bare and solitary chamber where he kneels in prayer and ponders passages of Holy Writ. It is there and then that the Muse visits him and raises him to sit beside the Hebrew prophets, teaching him to speak with their voice, yes, and often with the very rhythm of their periods." (*Blaise Pascal,* by H. F. Stewart . . . From the *Proceedings of the British Academy,* v. **28**, London: Humphrey Milford Amen House, E.C., p. 20 of the reprint.)

[93] *Pensées,* Section vii, Fr. 430, *Œuvres,* v. **13**, 337.

XVI

Running the Way of the Lord

*" I will run the way of thy commandments, when thou shalt enlarge
my heart."*

—*Ps. 119:32*

In a broad sense Blaise Pascal was committed as a writer to the cause of Christianity, and in this respect he belongs to his century. The great classic writers of the period, who seem at first glance to have been utterly removed from religious preoccupation, among them Descartes, Corneille, Racine, Boileau, La Fontaine, Madame de La Fayette, La Bruyère, and La Rochefoucauld, are in reality just as Christian as they are French. In their work there rise to the surface, more unconsciously than otherwise, certain " anxieties, scruples, revolts, and fine points of heroism or of perversity, that were either unknown to the ancients or completely scorned by them. . . . Chateaubriand's insight did not fail him when he recognized in the Andromache or in the Iphigenia of Racine the Christian wife and daughter." [1] More than once have Pascal's sisters, Gilberte and Jacqueline, reminded us of some of Racine's heroines. So Pascal himself exemplified the eagerness and profundity of the Christian man of letters.

A CHRISTIAN LAYMAN

This he showed more directly when he wrote the *Provinciales* and when he collaborated in the translation of the Mons edition of the New Testament, cited in the preceding chapter, and which, we remember, was chiefly the work of his spiritual adviser, Monsieur de Saci. [2] In Pascal, it was " the whole man " that brought to fruition the great, divinely appointed task of planting the love of Christ in the hearts of

[1] Feugère, A., *Le Mouvement religieux dans la littérature du XVII*e *siècle*, Boivin, Paris, 1938, p. vi.
[2] Cf. *Œuvres*, v. 9, 234.

men, a task which was to become his lifework. One of the first Christian laymen, Pascal revealed himself as that passionate lover of truth,[3] "that poet who preaches salvation with such despair, . . . that angel of light . . . , that inspired rebel," whom the modern Church distrusts.[4] He is the man of the Bible clutching by the lapel of his coat the freethinker whom he would shake into consciousness, the lost sheep who turns his eyes away from the only thing which counts in this world: the problem of human destiny and that other so completely inseparable from it, the problem of individual salvation. Pascal is the family man, the friend, true enough, the guardian of the weak in faith, the letter writer who offers spiritual advice. But above all, he is a committed Christian scholar who would devote the strength that is left him to writing on a new basis, entirely Biblical in inspiration, a vindication of religion. He is the elect of God, highly conscious of his responsibility.

He knows it: "From the one who has received the most, shall the greatest account be demanded, because of the power which he has through the help [of grace]."[5] He read that and meditated on it in Luke 12:47 and in Rev. 22:11. Henceforth, his greatest desire, according to a beautiful expression that we find in a fragment of his *Pensées*, is "to beget children for God."[6] He knows that the meaning of the Greek word ἁμαρτάνειν, to sin, is to err, to miss the mark, and he pities "those miserable lost ones who, having looked around and having seen some pleasant objects, have surrendered to such things, and have become attached to them."[7]

Certainly, he also knows quite well that it is grace which must bring about the transformation of the unbeliever, and engender faith in him.[8] He read in chapter 10 of The Epistle of Paul to the Romans, verse 17, "Faith then cometh by hearing; and hearing by the word of Christ." Preaching appears to him essentially a message of salvation which must

[3] "The love of truth . . . was always the dominating passion of Monsieur Pascal," writes Dom Clémencet, in § I of his *Vie inédite de Pascal*, quoted by Jovy, E., *Etudes pascaliennes, op. cit.*, v. 6, 8.

[4] Amiot, Ch.-G., "Impressions sur Pascal romantique et classique," in *La Revue hebdomadaire*, No. 28, 32d year, July 14, 1923, p. 304.

[5] *Pensées*, Section vii, Fr. 531, *Œuvres*, v. 13, 421, 422.

[6] We are taking here in its spiritual sense an expression borrowed from Fr. 923 of Section xiv of the *Pensées*, *Œuvres*, v. 14, 352.

[7] Cousin, V., "Rapport à l'Académie française" on the necessity of a new edition of the *Pensées* of Pascal, read at the meetings of April 1, May 1, June 1, July 1, and August 1, 1942, part two, in *Des Pensées de Pascal*, Ladrange, Paris, 1844, p. 115.

[8] Cf. *Pensées*, Section iv, Fr. 248, *Œuvres*, v. 13, 181, 182.

be announced. It is in this sense that we are laborers together with God. This state of things leaves, and Pascal admits it, an infinite part to mystery which we cannot claim to encompass. We already know to what point Pascal respects the apparent antinomies of the Scriptures: salvation comes from God, . . . work out your salvation. Yet he holds solidly to both ends of the chain, whose central links are not all visible to him. It is to misunderstand Pascal greatly, to suggest, by drawing arguments from his project of a " Vindication of Christianity," that in his heart he did not believe in election, and that on this point in particular he " did not belong to Port-Royal." Pascal believed in election for this very simple reason, i.e., that election is formally taught in the Bible, whether that pleases us or not, we who like to set ourselves up as little gods. The great battle of Christianity through all the ages is " being fought by two invisible armies, as they struggle to dominate the minds of men. The one army we might rightly call Supernaturalism; the other, with equal accuracy, we shall designate Naturalism." [9] In this battle, Pascal is clearly on the side of supernaturalism in all that touches questions of faith. That is why we have seen him oppose to scholasticism a theology strictly Biblical.

Unbelievers, exactly on this point, take argument from the objections which reason is bold enough to oppose to the Christian interpretation of the Bible. The fact is, however, that nothing should frighten them " like that revolt of reason against the authority of the Word of God revealed: is it not the sign that one is excluded and reproved? " [10]

According to Madame Périer, his sister, when Pascal conferred with unbelievers, he began by seeking to discover " if they were looking for truth with all their hearts." [11] Then he measured, disposed, and expressed what he had to say to them, to make it enter their spirit.[12] At

[9] Smith, W. M., *The Supernaturalness of Christ*, W. A. Wilde Company, Boston, Mass., 1941, p. vii.

We warmly recommend this work, whose greatest merit, as we see it, lies in pointing out that the best way to combat naturalism is to bring out the value of supernaturalism in its purest form, i.e., the supernaturalness of Christ. One destroys only that which one replaces.

These views do not invalidate in any way what is well founded of a naturalism which consents to keep to its place. Pascal has expressed his ideas on this matter in the unforgettable terms of his fragment of a Preface to the *Traité du vide, Œuvres*, v. 2, 129–145.

[10] *Œuvres*, v. 12, cxxxvi.

[11] *Ibid.*, ccxlvi.

[12] *Œuvres*, v. 1, 71.

the school of His Master, and in his name, he stood at the door and knocked. The door partly opened, he entered with an argumentation in which were found disposed for the greater glory of God all his acquisitions: "a whole unity of views on nature, science, and man," which *alone*, as he saw it, were in accord with "faith, once accepted," and which *alone* could "lead the indifferent or the unbeliever to faith." [13] It was thus that he was able to despoil theology "of a whole repulsive exterior apparatus and present it in an engaging manner, and to speak the language of the seventeenth century, in a *polite* way." [14]

For this God-appointed task, Pascal prepared himself with the greatest care. His *Pensées* on rhetoric testify to this. In his fragment *De l'Art de persuader*, he had, moreover, taken care, from the beginning, to set aside the divine truths as being so far above nature that only God Himself could introduce them into the soul in any way which might please Him. "I know," wrote Pascal then — probably toward 1658–1659 — that "in order to humiliate that superb power of reasoning which claims it must be judge of the things which the will chooses, and to cure that infirm will, [God wished] that these truths enter from the heart to the mind, and not from the mind to the heart." That is the reason one says of human things that one must know them before one can love them, while according to the saints one must love divine things in order to know them, for one enters into truth only through charity.

This psychological approach should be understood in the framework of the Pascalian orders to which we have paid so much attention in these pages. It appears to Pascal that "God established that supernatural order, quite contrary to the order which should be natural to men in the things of nature. They have nevertheless corrupted that order by making of profane things what they should have made of sacred things because we believe almost nothing except what pleases us. And from there comes the fact that we are so far from consenting to the truths of the Christian religion, absolutely opposed as they are to our pleasures. *Tell us agreeable things and we shall listen to you*, said the Jews to Moses, as if agreeableness should regulate belief!" [15] It is by

[13] Rauh, F., "La Philosophie de Pascal," in *Revue de métaphysique et de morale*, 30th year, No. 2, April–June, 1923, p. 307.

This article was published for the first time in No. 2 of the *Annales de l'Université de Bordeaux* (ed. E. Leroux).

[14] Hervier, M., "L'Utilité pédagogique de Pascal," *Revue pédagogique*, 1923, 2d sem., p. 85.

[15] Fragment *De l'Art de persuader*, *Œuvres*, v. 9, 271–273.

such pages that Pascal, after the author of the *Imitation of Christ*, has convinced us that all true psychology has its principle in the Bible.

Pascal's apologetics are Scriptural, in the spirit and in the letter. In his *Comparaison des Chrétiens des premiers temps avec ceux d'aujourd'hui*, Pascal asks that catechumens submit themselves not only to instruction, but also to penitence.[16] From their very first steps, Pascal would have those whom he touches know that they ought not to say, " I would soon leave my way of life if I had faith," but rather, " I should soon have faith if I were to leave my way of life." Pascal is closely attached to the family of Arnobe, of Lactantius, and of Saint Augustine. It is their true method which he found again through a happy intuition, the method which is originally in the New Testament and in Saint Paul, the one which the first Apostles and the first Church Fathers practiced, and which made the strength and the success of the apologists of the third and fourth centuries. " In the history of modern apologetics, Pascal is as great a name as Socrates in the history of ancient philosophy." [17]

For Pascal, it is not a question of more or less in " conversion " taken in its exact meaning: it is a miracle where " efficacious grace " intervenes, the very grace which brought Jesus back to life. And it is indeed a question of a passage from death to life for the regenerated man. The opuscule *Sur la conversion du pécheur* presents reminiscences of the Sermon on the Mount.[18] Pascal's opposition of the heart to the mind is a résumé of " the opposition between the action which God exercises on man and the action of which man reduced to his own strength is capable." [19] Thus, this opposition has a claim to the very heart of Pascal's apologetics.

For this Christian layman, every choice which daily life brings up

[16] *Comparaison des Chrétiens des premiers temps avec ceux d'aujourd'hui*, work not dated, published for the first time in the edition of the Abbé Bossut, 1779, v. 2, 510. This title has been generally accepted since Bossut. The text of this document will be found in *Œuvres*, v. 10, 411–418. The quotation which we have just given is found on p. 416.

[17] Boutroux, E., " Socrate, fondateur de la science morale," in *Etudes d'histoire de la philosophie*, Paris, Alcan, 1897 (quoted by Giraud, V., *Pascal, l'homme, l'œuvre, l'influence*, notes for a course given at the University of Fribourg, Switzerland, during the first semester of 1898, 3d edition, revised, corrected, and considerably enlarged, Albert Fontemoing, editor, Paris, 1905), pp. 170, 171).

[18] *Ecrit sur la conversion du pécheur, Œuvres*, v. 10, 422–426. See in particular, a reminiscence of Matt. 5:19, on p. 424.

[19] *Introduction à la seconde série des Œuvres de Pascal* [v. 4-11], *Œuvres*, v. 4, xxv.

is resolved by an appeal to the Bible. When it is a question of a proposed marriage for his niece, Jacqueline Périer, Pascal writes to her a letter filled with the doctrine of Saint Paul.[20] To Domat, who needs encouragement for the common struggle in the service of Jansenist truth, he addressed a message in which Saint John and Saint Paul are cited as testimony.[21]

What inspires him is Christian charity, victorious, if need be, over prejudice. We see him rendering the most gracious homage to a Protestant — in the person of the Doctor attached to Madame du Sablé, who has remained famous for her dread of contagion. Menjot, the Protestant Doctor, embarrassed by such homage coming from Blaise Pascal, wrote on this subject to Madame du Sablé: " If, on one hand, I consider the sincerity and the sublime knowledge of that great man, on the other hand I know that charity is the first of Christian virtues, so that I have difficulty in distinguishing between justice and grace principally in a person who doubtless puts it into practice with as much ardor as he sustains it." [22] Menjot was not mistaken: This took place in 1660, and Pascal had long since renounced the advantages which politeness alone can give in worldly relations: it was indeed Christian charity which inspired him above all.

A thing which inspired him still more, and which inspired his charity and all the aims and views which this charity crowned, was his idea of God the sovereign Good and Master of all things. A contemporary Protestant writer, Loraine Boettner, justly wonders at a letter of Pascal " to a bereaved friend." Instead of repeating the ordinary platitudes of consolation, Pascal develops here the beautiful Biblical theme of the decrees of Providence, in these terms: " If we regard this event, not as an effect of chance, not as a fatal necessity of nature, but as a result inevitable, just, holy, of a decree of His Providence, conceived from all eternity, to be executed in such a year, day, hour and such a place and manner, we shall adore in humble silence the impenetrable loftiness of His Secrets: we shall venerate the sanctity of His decrees: we shall bless the acts of His Providence; and uniting our will to that of God Himself, we shall wish with Him, the thing that He has willed in us and for us for all eternity." [23] Loraine Boettner is mistaken, however: The letter in

---

[20] *Œuvres*, v. **9**, 317 ff.
[21] *Œuvres*, v. **10**, 156. The quotations are from John 7:25 and I Thess. 5:15–18.
[22] *Œuvres*, v. **10**, 46.
[23] Boettner, L., *The Reformed Doctrine of Predestination*, 5th ed., Wm. B. Eerd-

question is the letter which Pascal wrote to his elder sister, Madame Périer, and to her husband, on the death of Etienne Pascal, their father, October 17, 1651. The translation which Boettner gives of it is incomplete and not always exact, as one can realize by referring to the original.[24] Yet these considerations take nothing from the value of the argument, and in certain respects accentuate its force. Sabatier, studying predestination in the Apostle Paul, noted in particularly fortunate terms, that it is " a normal product of religious faith," and that the feeling of predestination " never grows weaker without bringing or marking an equal weakening " of this very faith.[25] This assertion finds its full weight under the pen of a liberal Protestant. One must add, for the case of Pascal, the fact that theological determinism presents a particular attraction for a man of science.

In the political realm also, our Christian layman is dominated by this same viewpoint of the decrees of Providence. We find him, toward 1659, haunted by the idea of a theocracy of Biblical inspiration, apropos of *Trois discours sur la condition des grands*. Nicole had had the three opuscules of Pascal preceded by this notice: " One of the things on which the late Monsieur Pascal had many views was the instruction of a Prince, whom one should try to raise in the manner most fitting to the state where God calls him, and the most proper to make him capable of fulfilling all the duties and avoid all the dangers of this state. He has often been heard to say that there was nothing to which he desired to contribute more if he were to become engaged in it, and that he would willingly sacrifice his life for such an important thing." [26] In the meantime, he consecrated this life to bringing forth children for God and to making himself their spiritual guardian.

SPIRITUAL GUIDANCE

The best example of Pascal in this role is doubtless furnished us by the instance of the Duke and Mademoiselle de Roannez. Pascal led to God the Duke who, in his pursuit of saintliness, subsequently was to resign from his governorship of Poitou, and to give up his plan of marrying

mans Publishing Co., 1941, p. 330. The essential defect of this useful work is that too many quotations are given secondhand.

[24] *Œuvres*, v. 2, 537 ff.

[25] Sabatier, A., *L'Apôtre Paul, esquisse d'une histoire de sa pensée* [sketch of a history of his thought], 4th ed. revised and enlarged, Fischbacher, Paris, 1912, p. 350.

[26] *Œuvres*, v. 9, 361.

Mademoiselle de Mesme, a rich heiress. For those who know the views on the " bondage of marriage " to which Pascal had come,[27] the latter's influence on his friend the Duke is in this circumstance evident. The Count d'Harcourt, great-uncle of the Duke, knew this quite well. Doubtless it was he who had encouraged the wife of the concierge of the Roannez household to attack Pascal with a knife while he was in bed. The attempt was fruitless, however, for that morning Pascal had already left his bed to go to Church!

Mademoiselle de Roannez herself was to refuse the hand of the Marquis d'Alluyre. Already under the influence of her brother, and more or less directly under that of Blaise who perhaps in the course of his " worldly " period had cast his eyes on her, she nurtured vague desires to become a nun. It was during the mass celebrating the miracle of the Holy Thorn, in the course of which she had not ceased to shed tears, that Mademoiselle de Roannez had felt her vocation take form. And it was upon coming home that she had announced her decision to give up marriage and enter a convent. Her family were not able to make her change her mind. Pascal became henceforth the spiritual adviser of the brother and the sister: " I do not separate you two, and I think constantly of both of you," he wrote to them Sunday, November 5, 1656.[28]

These letters of guidance are a beautiful Christian inspiration. Upon reading them objectively, one can indeed find passages which could be interpreted in the light of an attachment not entirely forgotten of Blaise for Mademoiselle de Roannez.[29] But from there to the interpretations which Chamaillard solicits from the texts,[30] there is a far cry. What do we know specifically on the subject of Pascal in love? Let us answer in all frankness: absolutely nothing. And let us add, moreover, that if Pascal thought of marriage on several occasions, that fact would offer nothing whatsoever which could contradict the interpretation that we offer here of his life. On the contrary, it has always pleased us to recognize that Pascal knew all our human vicissitudes. On the subject of Mademoiselle de Roannez and her brother, if we respect the available

[27] See, for example, his letter to his niece Jacqueline Périer, Œuvres, v. 9, 317 ff.
[28] Extrait d'une lettre de Pascal à Mr. et à Mlle de Roannez, Œuvres, v. 6, 159.
[29] See, for example, another letter of November, 1656 [?], Œuvres, v. 6, 216, 217, n. 4 (and also 215, n. i); a letter of the 24th [?] of December, 1656, Œuvres, v. 6, 300, 301.
[30] Chamaillard, E., Pascal mondain et amoureux, Les Presses Universitaires de France, Paris, 1923, pp. 436–441. See also the exhortation of Chamaillard to those whom his book would not have convinced, ibid., p. 455.

texts, we can only affirm with Mauriac that Blaise Pascal belonged to his century, which was par excellence one of friendship.[31] The love of which he speaks, when he speaks of it abstractly, is, moreover, that noble Cornelian love which is based on esteem.[32]

The themes of Pascal's letters of guidance to the Duke and Mademoiselle de Roannez are rich in Christian counsel, for example, that the will of God must be our rule of life;[33] that renewal of heart gives fresh meaning to speech[34] — a Biblical expression taken from Ezek. 18:31; 36:26, and from Mark 16:17; also the theme of the death of the old man and the renewal of the new man who will be perfect only in eternity, when he will sing the new song of which David speaks in Ps. 149:1, the song of charity.[35]

Charlotte de Roannez was to enter Port-Royal in 1657, and remain there in spite of the violent objections of her family. Deprived of spiritual support by the death of Pascal in 1662 and of Monsieur Singlin in 1664, and because of other circumstances which we shall not discuss here, Mademoiselle de Roannez had herself relieved of her vows by Rome in 1665. Then, through the intercession of the King, she married the Duke de la Feuillade. The marriage had scarcely been consummated when she was to weep bitterly for her mistake before God. Her first child died at birth; her second was an invalid; her third, a dwarf, died at the age of nineteen years; the line then disappeared with the fourth. The poor mother had to undergo horrible operations, and these sad events make one diagnose a venereal disease in the Duke de la Feuillade, whose " gay " past was notorious. The Duchess died in 1683. At the hour of her death, her letters from Port-Royal were burned[36] and this destruction, as one may well think, has been shamefully exploited by those who are pleased to tell a romantic story of Mademoiselle de Roannez and Pascal. Supposing that there were in the drawer of the cabinet of the Duchess de la Feuillade " compromising " secrets, is it in good taste to

[31] Mauriac, F., *The Living Thoughts of Blaise Pascal*, Longmans, Green & Co., Inc., New York, Toronto, 1940, pp. 223, 224.

[32] Cousin, V., Unpublished fragment of Pascal " Sur l'Amour," article in the *Revue des deux mondes*, September 15, 1843, reproduced in appendix no. 11, *Des Pensées de Blaise Pascal*, new edition, revised and enlarged, Ladrange, Paris, 1844, pp. 408 and 412.

[33] *Extrait d'une lettre de Pascal à Mr. et à Mlle de Roannez*, November 5, 1656, *Œuvres*, v. 6, 159 (see also Fr. 668 of the *Pensées*).

[34] Letter of November 5, 1656, *cit.*, 160.

[35] *Ibid.*, 161.

[36] Cf. *Œuvres*, v. 5, 402.

speculate thus on the letters which an unhappy and repentant woman had burned on her deathbed? The seventeenth century certainly would not have pronounced *honnête* this way of doing things. It is true that we have evolved since then.

VINDICATION OF CHRISTIANITY

Further to spread the influence of his spiritual guidance,[37] Pascal was thinking more and more of writing a great work for the vindication of the Christian religion. His design took form in his mind toward 1658, when he consented to sketch in about two hours the outlines of his projected work for some of his Port-Royal friends. About eight years after Pascal's oral exposé, with the aid of the late scholar's notes, Filleau de la Chaise was to undertake to edit the *Discours sur les* Pensées in which Pascal's design appeared.[38] To carry out this plan, Pascal, by his own confession, would have needed ten years of good health. However, since the spring of 1658, his health, which had never been good, became very poor. It was in order to distract his mind from horrible headaches that

[37] Cf. Calvet, J., " Pascal directeur de conscience," in *Revue du Clergé français*, June 15, 1901, for a more strictly Catholic presentation of certain aspects of the subject that we are treating in this chapter.

[38] Cf. *Discours sur les* Pensées *de M. Pascal où l'on essaie de faire voir quel était son Dessein, Œuvres*, v. 12, cxcix–ccxxxviii. This *Discours* appeared in 1672, under the name of Dubois de la Cour. (Cf. Sainte-Beuve, *Port-Royal*, 5th ed., v. 3, 386.) See also Filleau de la Chaise, *Qu'il y a des Démonstrations d'une* " Autre espèce et aussi certaines que celles de la géométrie," reproduced in the *Revue de métaphysique et de morale*, 30th year, No. 2, April–June, 1923, pp. 215–220. This little treatise, reproduced from the text of the *Pensées de M. Pascal*, published by Desprez et Desessartz in Paris, in 1715, is commonly attributed to Filleau de la Chaise, and is found added in most editions of the *Pensées* to the two other *Discours* put under the name of Dubois, but which are very probably the work of Filleau. In an article of the *Revue bleue*, January 21, 1922, Victor Giraud showed that this must be the echo of a conversation of Pascal's. In n. 1, p. 205 of *La Vie héroïque de Blaise Pascal, op. cit.*, p. 257, the same author casts doubt upon the testimony which Etienne Périer is the only one to give, according to which the discourse of Pascal was " made thus on the spur of the moment, without having been premeditated or worked out." The *Discours* of Filleau de la Chaise are to be completed by the *Résumé des* Pensées *par Nicole* (*Traité de l'education d'un Prince*, second part, xli–xliii), reproduced in *Œuvres*, v. 12, ccxxxix–ccxli, and the *Plan de l'Apologie d'après Madame Périer* (Extract of Dr. Besoigne, *Histoire de l'Abbaye de Port-Royal*, v. 4, 469), reproduced in *Œuvres*, v. 12, ccxli–ccxlvi. All these data are arranged by Brunschvicg in his *Argument logique des Pensées* for the classification of his edition, *Œuvres*, v. 12, cclv–cclxxiii. For the comparison of his arrangement of the *Pensées* with that of the manuscripts and the other important editions, Brunschvicg has established an admirable *Table de concordance, Œuvres*, v. 12, cclxxvi–ccciv.

he turned again to mathematics and solved the insoluble problem of the cycloid.[39] The controversy which ensued lasted until the beginning of 1659 and tired Pascal a great deal. Before his death he had had at the most scarcely a year, and that in delicate health, to work on this " Vindication of Christianity " which he loved more than any of the other works which he had done up to that time.

Of his efforts, what remains for us? Piles of papers on which he had feverishly jotted down or dictated notes, maxims, analyses that were pasted on registers, and which Etienne Périer, nephew of Blaise, later had copied by secretaries. Port-Royal gave the first edition (posthumous) in 1670, which in its omissions and arrangements already constituted a Jansenist commentary on Pascal. In his superb edition, Brunschvicg presents to us the results of the examination of the manuscript copies; he tells us in detail about the preparation of the first edition; he gives us information on the composition of the examining committee and follows the fortunes of the later editions.[40] Each of these in some particular is found to be just another of the many commentaries on the thought of Pascal.

Modestly, Brunschvicg contents himself with classifying the fragments according to the main subjects which they treat. Doing this, he is obliged to separate thoughts which resemble each other in more than one aspect, even if they differ in others; on the other hand, he brings together other thoughts in ways that might distort the intention of the author.

The thought of Pascal thus broken up cannot but seem vague and incoherent! " Pascal incoherent! " cries Dr. Stewart indignantly: " He who was of an implacable coherence! " And the Cambridge professor submits a new suggestion which would consist in keeping of the *Pensées* only the fragments destined by Pascal to his " Vindication," by classifying them according to the plan of Filleau de la Chaise.[41] Brunschvicg,

---

[39] *Première Lettre circulaire relative à la cycloïde* (June, 1658), *Œuvres*, v. **7,** 337 ff.; *Seconde Lettre* . . . (July, 1658), *Œuvres*, v. **8,** 15 ff.; *Troisième Lettre* . . . (October 7 and 9, 1658), *Œuvres*, v. **8,** 155 ff.; *Histoire de la roulette* (October 10, 1658), *Œuvres*, v. **8,** 179 ff.; *Suite de l'histoire de la roulette* (December 12, 1658), *Œuvres*, v. **8,** 280 ff.; *Récit de l'examen et du jugement des escrits envoyés pour les prix,* November 25, 1658, *Œuvres*, v. **8,** 231 ff. See also the letters published in *Œuvres*, v. **8,** 147 ff.; 321 ff.; 325 ff.

[40] *Œuvres*, v. **12,** iii–xl.

[41] Stewart, H. F., " Vers une nouvelle édition de l'Apologie de Pascal," *French Quarterly,* September, 1921, 132–151. Quoted by Peyre, H., " Pascal et la critique

however, had already replied to that suggestion, that the *Discours sur les* Pensées " does not have sufficient authority " to permit the restoration in question, and he has basis for this objection.[42]

Professor Stewart, however, pursues his efforts in the direction he has indicated. Already, in his fine collection of sermons entitled *Holiness of Pascal*,[43] he had felt that the page on the three orders leads us to the very center of Pascal's thought. For Pascal religious certainty was of the order of charity, supernatural. Reason of itself could not attain unto it. All that it could do was to prepare the way, first by analyzing its own limitations, then by grouping auxiliary evidence, always sufficient in itself, that would confirm the intuition of the heart — this last word being understood in the Pascalian sense. This intuition, in turn, presupposes a man who proceeds in his search through laboring anguish. What Pascal wanted to do above all was to bring about both this labor and this anguish.

It is in following these broad outlines that Stewart, after so many others — among whom should be mentioned Strowski, Chevalier, Massis, Dedieu, Tourneur [44] — has just undertaken to finish the unfinished symphony, i.e., the " Vindication of Christianity." In 1942, he published at the Cambridge University Press the work which was to crown his noble efforts, under the title *Pascal's Apology for Religion Extracted from the* Pensées.[45]

It leaves one in deep thought to see what has here been selected as the " first *Pensée* " of Pascal, the fragment which, in the classification of Brunschvicg, is found under number 185. We must confess that it constitutes an excellent introduction: " The way of God, who does all

---

contemporaine," *The Romanic Review*, No. 4, October–December, 1930, v. **21**, 329. See n. 38 above.

[42] *Le Plan de l'Apologie, Œuvres*, v. **12**, liii, liv.

[43] Stewart, H. F., *Holiness of Pascal*, Cambridge University Press, 1915.

[44] Strowski, F., in his " Edition Définitive " of all Pascal, Ollendorff, Paris, 1923; and the following in their respective arrangement of the *Pensées:* Chevalier, J., Galba, Paris, 1925 (*Nouvelle revue française*, Paris, 1937); Massis, G., A la Cité des Livres, Paris, 1929; Dedieu, J., Librairie de l'Ecole, Paris, 1937; Tourneur, Z., Editions de Cluny, Paris, 1938.

[45] Stewart, H. F., *Pascal's Apology for Religion Extracted from the* Pensées, Cambridge University Press, 1942.

In a personal letter, dated December 15, 1943, Professor H. F. Stewart informs us that the second volume of his edition of the *Pensées* will be published as soon as circumstances allow. This second volume will open with *Le Mystère de Jésus* and the *Mémorial*. " Both belong, it seems to me, rather to the intimate thoughts of the man than to his apologetical effort," remarks the Cambridge scholar.

things in gentleness, is to instill religion into the mind through reasons, and into the heart through grace." [46]

We indeed grant this Cambridge professor that too many writers have strained the meaning by incorporating into the " Vindication " certain fragments which did not belong there. Certain fragments expressed the objections of freethinkers that Pascal reproduced or imagined; others constituted arguments attributed by Pascal to some imaginary conferee, but with which he was far from being in agreement. What final criterion do we have at hand which will permit us to exercise the necessary discrimination? And then, how many heterogeneous elements there are in the *Pensées!* We find there, for example, notes taken with the *Provinciales* in view, rough sketches of the same *Provinciales*, or of *Factums*.[47] Let us go farther. Here is something that appears essential to us: according to the most trustworthy testimony of Marguerite Périer, Pascal never forgot any of the ideas that crossed his mind, and he carried them in his memory up to the moment when he would make use of them. It was only in the last five years of his life — we would remind the reader of his fatigue and his deplorable state of health after 1658 — that, "in order to relieve his mind," he cast on paper the thoughts which came to him. Fragment 370 of the *Pensées* offers here a curious testimony: " Chance gives thoughts, and chance takes them away: no art to conserve them nor to acquire them.

" Thought escapes, I wished to write it; I write instead that it has escaped me." [48]

What we suspect Pascal to have noted in the course, let us say, of the last five years of his life, would not therefore necessarily be thoughts bearing the date of these five years, but resurgences, reminiscences of thoughts acquired during the course of a laborious evolution belonging to almost his entire life.

But let us take the question from another angle: Marguerite Périer — all of these Pascals are passionate people prone to exaggeration — stresses too strongly the fact that her uncle relied in normal times on his memory. We have had occasion to notice Pascal's habit of jotting rapid notes on tablets. He did this, for example, in the company of Méré, Miton, and Roannez at the time of their famous voyage to Poitou. Many of these notes must have been saved with the others. Certainly, he must

[46] *Pensées*, Section iii, Fr. 185, *Œuvres*, v. 13, 97.
[47] See, for example, *Pensées*, Section xiv, especially Frs. 902–958.
[48] *Pensées*, Section vi, Fr. 370, *Œuvres*, v. 13, 282, 283.

have drawn from them in writing his " Vindication " — he who used everything that came his way. But that is not the question as, from both sides, we arrive at the conclusion that *the papers found after the death of Blaise Pascal, and today published under the title* Pensées, *constitute essentially the " journals " of a life as brief as it was fertile and full of genius.*

We have waited for this point in our development to justify our drawing so liberally from the *Pensées* in the course of our chapters. *In a way, a biographical study of Pascal would provide an excellent basis for a classification and an interpretation of the* Pensées *according to a psychological method.* All true psychology, for Pascal, has its starting point in religion. Viewed in this light, the *Pensées* would then reveal their Biblical structure: *they constitute the mirror of a life lived and meditated more and more in the light of Scripture.*

Without doubt, since it is founded on facts, such an approach would explain, and consequently conciliate, numerous points of view. It is certain, for example, that there is a place, on the one hand, for an organic classification of all the *Pensées* considered as the whole of the journals of Blaise Pascal; on the other hand, for a selection of the type which Dr. Stewart is undertaking with a view to restoring the " Vindication of Christianity." Not only are all these efforts praiseworthy in themselves, but they constitute just so many commentaries on Pascal.

An essential prerequisite of any restoration should be the relative importance that the Bible has in the fragments considered; the most profoundly Biblical will reveal a later composition. Who knows? Perhaps a pertinent organic classification of the *Pensées* should take as its starting point (in memory of Pascal's childhood — which we have called his emergence) silhouettes of judges, of people in law courts, and the fragments treating a human conception of justice. Justice is a minimum of goodness and is only this world's conception of true charity. Our classification of the *Pensées* of this *honnête homme,* Blaise Pascal, would then be spread out between a human ideal, in large part inherited, and the soaring of the eagle's flight at the end. When Henri Bremond suggests that one take from " Pascal in prayer " fragments for a *Book of Hours,* he retains nothing for the Catholic heritage except the last outpourings of a consecrated soul longing for communion with the Christ.

It is a delicate task indeed to draw dividing lines in the midst of such abounding wealth. Let us therefore keep an open mind as we consider existing outlines of the *Pensées*, and we may thereby expect a truer perspective of the aims of Pascal.

BIBLICAL STRUCTURE OF THE " PENSÉES "

First of all, as we have said, the manuscript of the *Pensées* is a formless mass of papers. In a good article in *Comoedia*,[49] Strowski brings out the fact that these papers had been confided to a bookbinder — and at that time bookbinders did not know how to read. This bookbinder then cut and pared them down to make them occupy the least possible space. Next he pasted them hit-or-miss, like puzzles, on a big album of about five hundred pages. How idle, then, and misleading, is it to speculate on the varying margins of the manuscript!

The intimate history of the vicissitudes of a manuscript thus disposed is told us in detail by Guy de Pourtalès, in a carefully documented study,[50] which renders fine homage to the edition of Port-Royal. Laporte has no trouble in establishing that the doctrine of Port-Royal constituted the soul of the *Pensées* at least as much as that of the *Provinciales*.[51] For him, the different reflections of Pascal should be brought under three headings:

1. Presentation of the problem: or an appeal addressed to the conscience of the unbeliever to draw him out of his indifference with respect to religious matters, and to bring him to a search for true religion.

2. Statement of the solution: or an exposition of the Christian religion as the only one capable, through its dogmas and its ethics, of answering the anxiety and the needs awakened in the unbeliever.

3. Demonstration of the solution: or the development of the proofs which make the Christian religion appear not only satisfying to man, but divine and divinely revealed.[52]

Does this plan not constitute, as we have already suggested, the pro-

---

[49] Strowski, F., " Psychologie et accidents des manuscrits de Pascal," in *Comoedia*, 20th year, No. 5108, Saturday, December 25, 1926. We owe the possession of this rare number, as well as that of the precious number of the tricentenary of Pascal of *La Revue hebdomadaire*, to the kindness of our friend André Ferrier, founder and director of the Théâtre d'Art, of San Francisco. May he find here the expression of our gratitude.

[50] Pourtalès, G. de, " Les Editions originales des *Pensées*," *La Revue hebdomadaire*, No. 28, 32d year, July 14, 1923, pp. 278–286.

[51] Laporte, J., " Pascal et la doctrine de Port-Royal," *Revue de métaphysique et de morale*, 30th year, No. 2, April–June, 1923, p. 265.

[52] *Ibid.*, 267

jection into the realm of apologetics of the very experience of Pascal in which the Bible had come to have so much importance? Through these three essential headings, Laporte remarks, such an apology appears to have been taken from Jansenism. And what can this mean save that Jansenist views, strictly Biblical, were dominant in Pascal during the latter part of his life when God took full possession of him? The edition of Port-Royal, moreover, even though it constitutes a Jansenist commentary on Pascal, was eager to attenuate certain passages, or prudently to suppress them in the hope of religious conciliation.

The Preface of the Port-Royal edition reported the interview which Pascal had had with these gentlemen toward 1657 or 1659, and in the course of which he had sketched his design.[53] According to Pascal, " The Christian religion has as many signs of certainty and of evidence as the things which are received in this world as the most indubitable." [54] Starting — and this was something quite original — from a picture of man that will arouse the freethinker who would recognize himself in it, Pascal would have sent his interlocutor to the philosophers, then to the infinite number of religions in the universe and in all ages, to cap the climax. Next he would have presented the Jewish people and the " unique Book by which they are governed, and which comprises their whole history, their laws and their religion." And finally he would have unfolded the story of the Fall of man and the redemption in " this same Book," carrier of the Good Tidings.[55] And Pascal would exalt " this Book in which he has discovered the truth," " this same Book " where his interlocutor will find " the means of consoling himself." This exaltation of the Book knew no limits when one arrived at the fundamental proofs of the Christian religion.[56]

The *Discours sur les* Pensées (written by Filleau de la Chaise) likewise exalted in Pascal " the eloquence, the profundity, the intelligence of what is most hidden in the Scriptures." [57] Did Pascal not also know " how few men have intelligence fitted for metaphysical reasoning "? [58] He was to go through human philosophies in order to raise himself — or to be raised — to a Biblical argumentation. We have insisted enough

---

[53] *Préface de l'édition de Port-Royal, Œuvres,* v. **12,** clxxxii.

[54] *Ibid.,* clxxxiii.

[55] *Ibid.,* clxxxiv.

[56] *Ibid.,* clxxxv–clxxxvii.

[57] *Discours sur les* Pensées, *Œuvres,* v. **12,** cciii. Compare with the eulogy of M. Tillemont, v. **12,** ccxlix (Letter of M. de Tillemont to M. Périer, the son).

[58] *Ibid.,* v. **12,** cciii.

on the fact that Pascal had quite early turned from scholasticism to attain a theology drawn from the Scriptures. The *Discours sur les Pensées* presents, then, in beautiful order these Biblical themes in which Pascal had recognized himself in the course of the great moments of his experience: the Fall, and its consequences; the hidden God, his Book, which reveals man to himself and makes him see clearly the order in the world, the only Book which has revealed to man the true good and which has promised healing. This healing is not in the hand of man; and on this point the Jansenism of the *Discours* is certainly recognizable.[59] The greatest authority for attracting the belief and faith of men is the authority of miracles and of prophecies. By the obscurity of the latter, a hidden God made Himself incomprehensible to evil, and increasingly clearer to those who search for Him. From this observation we understand the two meanings of Scripture, blinding some and enlightening others. Himself enlightened, Pascal would then have shown us how, with the Old Testament serving as a cryptograph of the New, all Scripture leads to Jesus Christ and derives from Him full meaning.[60]

This same insistence on the Bible will be found in the résumé of the *Pensées* by Nicole: [61] " The Plan which Monsieur Pascal had, to restrict himself to the proofs taken either from the knowledge of man, or from the prophecies and from different remarks on the Scriptures, is the reason that one does not find others in his papers; and it is certain that abstract and metaphysical reasoning is quite far removed from this." [62] On this point, *Le Plan d'après Madame Périer* echoes Nicole, since according to Pascal, this kind of proof can lead only to a speculative knowledge of God, and to " know God in that way was not to know Him." [63] And Madame Périer explains at length that the God of Pascal was the Living God of the Bible, " the God of Abraham and of Jacob, the God of the Christians "; [64] that consequently it was necessary " to strive only to know Jesus Christ." [65]

In addition, one finds in the *Pensées* outlines of a plan in Pascal's own handwriting. Fragment 60, for example, presents to us a very simple plan of which the author has thought a moment:

[59] *Ibid.*, v. **12**, ccxiv.
[60] *Ibid.*, v. **12**, cxxiii–ccxxxi. Note the considerable place given to Jesus Christ.
[61] *Résumé des* Pensées *par Nicole, Œuvres*, v. **12**, ccxxxix, ccxl.
[62] *Ibid.*, ccxli.
[63] *Plan d'après Mme Périer, Œuvres*, v. **12**, ccliii.
[64] *Ibid.*, v. **12**, ccliv.
[65] *Ibid.*, v. **12**, cclv.

" First part: Misery of man without God.

" Second part: Happiness of man with God.

" In other words:

" First part: That nature is corrupt, the proof being drawn from nature itself.

" Second part: That there is a restorer, the proof being drawn from Scripture." [66]

This plan of the " Vindication " reduced to its simplest expression is very curious. Its purpose is here unquestionable in that it presents with highest evidence the keystone of Pascal's project as being Jesus Christ, the Redeemer according to Scripture.

Here are some résumés of " proofs " of the Christian religion, Fragments 289, 290, which are just so many outlines or searching for ideas.[67] The first fragment gives a central place to " the marvels of Holy Scripture," Jesus Christ, the Apostles, Moses and the prophets, the Jewish nation, the permanence of our religion, and " the doctrine which makes everything rational." The second fragment is much briefer: " Ethics — Doctrine — Miracles — Prophecies — Figures."

An examination of Fragments like 642 and 602 reveals that there are three ways of re-establishing unity between the Book of the Jews and the Book of the Christians: (1) The Old Testament has a literal sense and a figurative sense. (2) The Old Testament announced a spiritual Messiah. (3) Jesus Christ was this Messiah.[68]

Ah, certainly Pascal was faithful to the revelation of the *Mémorial!*

From this high place one can measure the profound incomprehension of the optimistic rationalism of the eighteenth century, of Voltaire and of Condorcet with regard to Pascal.[69] " What a chimera is then man? what chaos, what a subject of contradiction! " cries Pascal. And Voltaire comments, " *The true speech of a sick man.*" [70]

In our time, Paul Valéry echoes in his way Voltaire and Condorcet. All three of them regret to see the fine intelligence of Pascal lose itself in religion. They do not realize that it is " lost " there so as to find itself.

[66] *Pensées,* Section ii, Fr. 60, *Œuvres,* v. **12,** 61.

[67] *Pensées,* Section iv, Fr. 289, 290, *Œuvres,* v. **13,** 210, 211.

[68] *Le Classement des* Pensées, *Œuvres,* v. **12,** lix.

[69] Let us recall in particular the work of Waterman, M., *Voltaire, Pascal and Human Destiny,* King's Crown Press, New York, 1942, which sheds light on the question, with a great indulgence for Voltaire. We are pleased to render homage to this effort at comprehension.

[70] *Pensées de Pascal* avec les notes de M. de Voltaire, Geneva, 1778, v. **2,** 127, 128.

Pascal is frightened by the silence of infinite space. This cry makes the author of *Eupalinos* think of " that unendurable barking which the dogs turn toward the moon." [71]

Valéry does more than renew the Pascalian criticism of the eighteenth century: he attacks the romantic interpretation which, in the nineteenth century, made of Pascal " a kind of French Jansenist Hamlet, who weighs his own skull, skull of a great geometer, and who shudders and dreams." [72] Henri Peyre saw very well that the reproach of the highly intelligent Valéry proceeded from the vast and delicate comprehension of a humanist. The admirer of Leonardo da Vinci finds the Jansenist antitheses of Pascal artificial: geometry, finesse; grandeur, misery; Epictetus, Montaigne.[73] We believe that we have shown in these pages, however, that Pascal states antinomies in order to resolve them in a higher order.

The *Variation sur une* Pensée of Valéry is found to offer the best opportunity possible to study the basic antinomy which is established behind these debates: that of naturalism and supernaturalism. The superiority of Pascal lies precisely in the fact that naturalism is not foreign to him. He traversed it to attain the higher order. He stated the paradox in order to solve it by searching in a higher realm for the crux of the problem. And it was the Scriptures which uncovered this point to him. Valéry, on the other hand, considers that in the last analysis the search for the first cause is " an instinct which may be ascribed to our vertical position," [74] and that is as it should be. One must wager, said Pascal.

[71] Valéry, P., " Variation sur une *Pensée*," in *La Revue hebdomadaire*, No. 28, 32d year, July 14, 1923, p. 163 (art. reproduced in *Variété*, N. R. F., Paris, 1924, pp. 137–154). Jovy discusses the *Variation* of Valéry in his *Investigations péripascaliennes*, Vrin, Paris, 1928, v. 4, 43: *A propos d'une " Pensée " de Pascal.*

[72] *Op. cit., La Revue hebdomadaire*, 164, 165.

[73] Peyre, H., " Pascal et la critique contemporaine," *The Romanic Review*, No. 4, October–December, 1930, v. 21, 335.

[74] Valéry, P., *op. cit.*, p. 165.

For a presentation of the naturalistic outlook, see " A Few Remarks on One or Two Aspects of the Voltaire-Pascal Controversy," by Andrew R. Morehouse, in *Essays in Honor of Albert Feuillerat*, edited by Henri M. Peyre, *Yale Romanic Studies*, Yale University Press, 1943, v. 22, 149–162.

We disagree cordially with the author. If he is right, then many great men of the last two hundred years would have done well to make, at least once in their lifetime, the current joke about the news of their death being somewhat exaggerated. As far as our day is concerned we would refer Andrew R. Morehouse to *Who's Who in America*. He would find in the very latest edition an imposing array of qualified authorities unwill-

Every way leads to God provided that one takes the path. What the Christian layman wanted to obtain in his " Vindication " was to shake the torpor of the indifferent, to bring him to admit that God is not an impossibility, that it is only the refusal to orient oneself toward Him that makes Him appear such. The nature of the wager [75] of Pascal has been terribly misjudged by making it a variation of the theme *will to believe* which the peripheral theory of James and Lange was finally to elucidate.

The fact is that the argument of the wager, according to a method familiar to Pascal, catches the freethinker at his own gamble and addresses him at first in the only language he understands, that of " human reasoning." [76] God exists or He does not. In a domain beyond our reason, there is a game the meaning of which differs according as to whether God exists or not. You must take sides on this issue. You must bet. You have no choice. You have already embarked. Keeping your point of view, let us see now what you have to gain or lose, according to whether you wager that God exists or that He does not exist.

Now, the rule of probability and of the stakes proves to you — and Pascal establishes it [77] — that by wagering for God, if God does not exist, the player loses after all only a finite value of dubious quality; at the most he takes the risk of merely leading a life that is on the whole noble and advantageous; but in making his wager against God, if God exists, he will lose " an infinity of life infinitely happy " and vice versa. It is the decision for God, the supreme step, that Pascal wants to obtain from the indifferent whom he has just buttonholed; he wants a full and unconditional surrender.

Certainly, the reasoning of Pascal can convince the mind without

---

ing to admit that " the eighteenth century marks in striking fashion the final death and collapse of a culture founded on the hypothesis that God was the primary reality in the Universe, the source of life and knowledge, the creator, redeemer, sanctifier of all mankind, etc." — or that " the final rise of Pagan naturalism and of science in the sixteenth and seventeenth centuries dealt powerful blows to supernaturalism " — that " Pascal made a last great effort to revive it, but it was too late, etc." (*op. cit.*, p. 151).

[75] Pascal had many precursors in his argument of the bet: Arnobe (*Adversus nationes*, I, 53; II, 4); Saint Augustine (*De Utilitate credendi*, 12, 26); Raimond Sebonde, *Théologie naturelle*, trans. by Montaigne (ch. 68); etc.

[76] *Pensées*, Section iii, Fr. 233, *Œuvres*, v. 13, 145.

[77] *Ibid.*, v. 13, 147–151. See the important notes of Brunschvicg.

securing action. Lachelier has definitely shown that what is left to be done is to pass " from the formal absolute to the real and living absolute, from the idea of God to God." [78] But Pascal has well realized — and he is, in this sense only, a precursor of James and Lange — that action greatly overlaps the syllogisms of the intellect. From the moment the recently indifferent consents to live as a Churchgoing Christian, the very act of worship will generate in him the feeling and drive with which it was ordinarily associated, since this act of worship first brought them to life.

But more follows — and one cannot dwell on this sufficiently: since God exists, and since the searcher would not look for Him had he not already been found by Him, each step in the new way will give rise to a revelation which will henceforth make his walk firmer and his path easier.

Let us here recall a worthy argument according to which Pascal is said to have owed the idea of his wager to a Jesuit Father whom he had taken to task. However, we must now affirm in conclusion that the first fundamental idea had long since come to him from the Bible: " I call heaven and earth to witness this day, that I have set before you life and death, blessing and cursing. Choose therefore life, that . . . thou . . . may live." [79] And it is to the Bible that Pascal would finally refer the man whom he had just snatched from his gaming table.

CULMINATION IN CHRIST

In order to estimate to what extent the Biblical apologetics of the *Pensées* is basically in conformity with the real Tradition of the Church, it would be well to refer to the admirable work, *L'Art religieux du XIII⁰ siècle en France* of Emile Mâle.[80] The author shows here that since

[78] Lachelier, J., in *Du Fondement de l'induction*, 7th edition, Alcan, Paris, 1916, " Notes sur le pari de Pascal " (175–208), p. 199. The *Notes* of Lachelier had for its immediate cause an article of Dugas and Riquier, which appeared in the *Revue philosophique*, September, 1900. Dugas answered in the *Revue occidentale*, September, 1901 (*Le Pari de Pascal sur Dieu*). See the long note (*Appendice* for Fr. 233) in *Œuvres*, v. 13, 161–173. For the recent fate of the *Pari* in France, cf. Eastwood, D. M., *The Revival of Pascal, A Study of His Relation to Modern French Thought*, Oxford University Press, 1936, pp. 84–86.

[79] Deut. 30:19.

[80] Mâle, E., *L'Art religieux du XIII⁰ siècle en France*, Etude sur l'iconographie du Moyen Age et sur ses sources d'inspiration [a study on the iconography of the Middle Ages and on its sources of inspiration], new edition, revised and corrected, illustrated with 127 prints, Colin, Paris, 1902.

the days of the catacombs Christian art has spoken in type; [81] that the Old Testament appears to the thirteenth-century artist as a prefiguration of the New.[82] Reading from the great Bible of stone, as we might call the medieval cathedrals, Mâle discovers a profound harmony between the Old and New Testaments. And because the synagogue could not read the harmony therein, it is represented in the art of the thirteenth century as a blindfolded figure.[83] As circumstances in our profession have led us to read Pascal and Mâle at the same time, we have wondered many a time whether we were visiting Chartres, or if it were the Biblical structure of the *Pensées* unfolding before our eyes. " The Old Testament has meaning only with respect to the New," wrote Mâle as Pascal had done before him. And then he would add in the same spirit as Pascal: " This doctrine, which has always been that of the Church, is taught in the Gospel in the words of Jesus Himself." [84] Jesus Christ is the meaning and key of all creation, as well to the universe as to man. He is God incarnate, Redeemer and sovereign Master of the new Heaven and of a new earth wherein justice will dwell, and through it all is the key to the Bible. This is the *raison d'être* of Pascal's *Pensées*.

Pascal, the Christian layman, wanted to be the John the Baptist of modern times, to prepare the way for Him whose shoe latchet he felt himself unworthy to unfasten. Like John the Baptist, Pascal preached repentance: " One must realize both one's wretchedness and one's unworthiness as well as the need for a mediator." We cannot know Jesus Christ " without knowing at the same time both God and our wretchedness because He is not simply God, but God the healer of our miseries." We must then " strive solely to know Jesus Christ." [85] The whole Scripture culminates in Jesus Christ.[86]

Pascal denounces the philosophers who think they can attain unto God without Christ.[87] Christ alone is the *Way*, the *Truth*.[88] " Jesus Christ is a God to be approached without pride, and before whom one is humbled without despair." [89] Pascal summarizes Christ's message in

[81] *Ibid.*, p. 28 ff.
[82] *Ibid.*, p. 162 ff.
[83] *Ibid.*, p. 163.
[84] *Ibid.*, p. 163. Mâle supports his statement by quoting John 3:14; Matt. 12:40.
[85] *Vie* par Mme Périer, *Œuvres*, v. 1, 77–79.
[86] Cf. *Pensées*, Frs. 699, 705, 706, 707, 741, 762.
[87] *Pensées*, Section vii, Fr. 463, *Œuvres*, v. 13, 373.
[88] *Pensées*, Section vii, Fr. 466, *Œuvres*, v. 13, 376.
[89] *Pensées*, Section vii, Fr. 528, *Œuvres*, v. 13, 420.

these words: " Jesus Christ did nought but to teach men that they were lovers of themselves, that they were slaves, blind, wretched men and sinners; that He needs must free them, enlighten them, bless and heal them; that that could be done by hating oneself, and by following Him through the suffering and the death of the Cross." [90] Here we have, wonderfully summarized, the Good News, as our Christian layman announced it. Without being irreverent, we permit ourselves to add, addressing ourselves first of all: " Please copy! "

In Jesus Christ is " all our virtue and all our felicity. Aside from Him, there is only vice, wretchedness, wrongdoing, darkness, errors, death, and despair." [91] Through Jesus Christ we know God and " we can know God only through Jesus Christ. Without this Mediator, all communication with God is disrupted. . . . Jesus Christ is therefore the veritable God of men." [92] " Not only do we know God only through Jesus Christ, but only through Jesus Christ do we know ourselves; we know life and death only through Jesus Christ. Outside of Jesus Christ, we know neither what our life is, nor our death, nor God, nor ourselves.

" Thus, without the Scripture, which has only Jesus Christ as its object, we know nothing, and see only darkness and confusion in the nature of God and in nature herself." [93]

Pascal preaches Jesus Christ, and Christ crucified. Nothing can enable us to know and to love God, " except the virtue of the folly of the Cross, without wisdom or signs; and not the signs without this virtue." [94] What enables us to believe " is the Cross," [95] and in support of this, Pascal cites a fragment of I Cor. 1:17.

Pascal preaches Jesus Christ, and Him resurrected. In the sepulcher where He was shrouded by the saints, and where they alone could penetrate, Jesus Christ took on a new life — not that of the Cross. " This is the last mystery of the Passion and of the Redemption." Living, dead, entombed, resurrected, Jesus teaches.[96]

Blaise Pascal, Christian layman, preaches Christ in His entirety in the *whole* Bible.

Let us leave to the exegetes the concern of knowing how Pascal might

[90] *Pensées,* Section vii, Fr. 545, *Œuvres,* v. **13,** 428, 429.
[91] *Pensées,* Section vii, Fr. 546, *Œuvres,* v. **13,** 429.
[92] *Pensées,* Section vii, Fr. 547, *Œuvres,* v. **13,** 429, 430.
[93] *Pensées,* Section vii, Fr. 548, *Œuvres,* v. **13,** 431.
[94] *Pensées,* Section viii, Fr. 587, *Œuvres,* v. **14,** 29.
[95] *Pensées,* Section viii, Fr. 588, *Œuvres,* v. **14,** 30.
[96] *Pensées,* Section vii, Fr. 552, *Œuvres,* v. **13,** 533, 534.

have begun his " Vindication." We already know that he would have wanted it to bear the stamp of Jesus Christ, who would have been its central inspiration, as He is the central inspiration of the Bible, and for the same purpose. We also know how Pascal *came* to write his " Vindication." As Jesus Christ had become for him the measure of all things, Pascal, with the simplicity of a child, and often using the very words of the Bible, began to write an *Abrégé de la vie de Jésus-Christ*.[97] Faugère admits in the *Avant-Propos* of his edition (pp. 13, 14), that Pascal had the idea of publishing a *Vie de Jésus-Christ*, and that he doubtless regarded such a work as the essential introduction to his " Apologie de la religion."

In his *Abrégé*, Pascal closely followed the *Series vitae Jesu Christi* of Jansen; however, he lent to the contents a new emphasis, and he added to the summary of Jansen, by referring to the Biblical texts. He further enriched this historic exposé with commentaries borrowed chiefly from the *Tetrateuchus* of Jansen. But toward the end of his work, he abounded in personal reflections, reminiscent of the *Mystère de Jésus*.[98]

Although the very first part of the preface to the *Abrégé de la vie de Jésus-Christ* is a commentary on chapter 1 of The Gospel According to Saint John, the text is amplified by explanations borrowed for the most part from Saint Paul. For example, the Word is made man " in the fullness of time " (Gal. 4:4), assuming " the form of a slave " (Phil. 2:7). He suffered " until death and death on the Cross." Pascal does not use

---

[97] *Abrégé de la vie de Jésus-Christ, Œuvres*, v. 11, 1–94.

This work was published for the first time with much care in the *Revue ecclésiastique* of September, 1845, v. 88, 97–134; then edited for the second time by Faugère, published by Andrieux, Paris, 1846 (reprinted in *Pensées*, Leroux, Paris, 1807, v. 2, 445). The *Abrégé* was then inserted by Molinier in his *Pensées de Pascal*, Paris, 1889, v. 2. A critical edition was given by Michaut, Librairie de l'Université, Fribourg (Switzerland), 1897. Molinier, then Michaut (open letter from Michaut to Molinier in *Revue critique d'histoire et de littérature*, May 24, 1897, p. 414) have shown that Pascal was inspired by an ancient text; he followed closely the work of Jansen entitled *Series vitae Jesu Christi juxta ordinem temporum*, published at the end of his *Tetrateuchus, sive commentarius in Sancta Jesu Christi Evangelia*, authorization given at Louvain, May 10, 1639, published in Paris, 1655, 586 p. in 4°. Brunschvicg, by a publication *in extenso* of the *Series vitae Jesu Christi* of Jansen, accompanying the *Abrégé* of Pascal, *Œuvres*, v. 11, 6 ff., has shown not only that Pascal closely followed Jansen, but that he did so even when he was in disagreement with a similar work by Arnauld, *Historia et concordia evangelica*, Savreux, Paris, 1653, 445 pp. in 12°. (Cf. Introduction to the *Abrégé*: authenticity and sources, *Œuvres*, v. 11, 3–6.)

[98] *Œuvres*, Introduction to the *Abrégé*, v. 11, 4.

quotation marks, nor does he make any Biblical references to preceding lines. Such is his method as a student steeped in the Bible, having assimilated the very marrow and substance of the Holy Book. His style is fashioned by the Bible. Because his thinking is so closely identified with it, he uses Biblical texts unconsciously. Pascal's thought flows naturally into Biblical expression.

We are here dealing with the central message Pascal wanted to express without burdening himself with our present-day scruples concerning quotations and references. That he had a publication in view is indicated in the last paragraph of his preface: " If the reader finds here something good, let him give thanks to God, the only Author of all good. And for what evil he finds, let him pardon my infirmity." [99]

His didactic intention is again marked in the fact that Pascal inserts into his Biblical references dates and events which are not in the Bible itself, but which Jansen had worked out with precision in his *Tetrateuchus*.[100] However, errors slip in here and there: [101] The author writes, for example, " January " instead of " March "; " twenty-six " days after the birth of Christ, instead of " thirty-six." Pascal works between Jansen and his Bible, referring faithfully to the Holy Book according to the indications of his guide.[102]

In regard to this it is interesting to see what use Pascal makes of Scriptural references, as, for example, Luke 2: 41, *sq.*, cited by Jansen. He sums up twelve verses (Luke 2:41–52) in these few simple and beautiful sentences: " And twelve years later, His parents took Him to the feast at Jerusalem and He stayed in the Temple discussing with the Doctors. His parents searched for Him with a great anxiety. He told them that He must accomplish the things His Father had sent Him to do, and having gone back with them, He was subject to them, and grew in wisdom, in years and in grace before God and men." [103] Luke 2:41, 42 is thus summed up by Pascal in that twelve years after the birth of Jesus His parents took Him to the feast in Jerusalem.

The fact is that at the age of twelve each Jewish boy became a " son of the Law." As such, he was submitted to a course of studies and trained in fasting and in attendance upon public worship. This is what the parents of Jesus saw from the human viewpoint: that is to say, from the shortsighted viewpoint. But why this eclipse in their memory? Had

[99] *Œuvres*, v. 11, 9.
[100] *Œuvres*, v. 11, 10, 11.
[101] *Œuvres*, v. 11, 11.
[102] *Œuvres*, v. 11, 13.
[103] *Ibid.*

Joseph forgotten the warning of the Angel of the Lord seen in a dream (Matt. 1:20), and Mary, the visitation of the Angel Gabriel (Luke 1:26–38)? Many unbelievers have stumbled on this passage of Luke 2:43–45. Pascal doubtless saw there only human erring. In his sight, the spectacle is hardly edifying, so he ignores it.

His aim is that of an apologist. That is why, no doubt, he opposes to the legalism of the parents the fact that Jesus stayed in the Temple to *dispute* with the Doctors. Let us note the word *dispute*. The Latin text said, " *Audientem illos, et interrogantem,* " and Monsieur de Saci translates quite correctly, " Listening to them and interrogating." This method of question and answer was the usual form of rabbinical instruction. But, to an ardent believer like Pascal, Jesus had no need of such a course of study. He knew. He *disputed* with the Doctors. In this the contrast between the human infirmity of Jesus' parents and His already omniscient divinity is clearly seen.

To the astonishment of His parents, to the candid question of His mother, to the affliction of people of a stature out of proportion with His, Jesus answers, according to Pascal, by the affirmation of His mission. In his version of the Bible, Monsieur de Saci translated, " Ne saviez-vous pas qu'il faut que je sois occupé à ce qui regarde le service de mon Père? " (" Did you not know that I must be *occupied* with what concerns the service of my Father? ") Pascal's translation is much stronger: It is a question of things with which Jesus has been *charged* by His Father, and which must be *accomplished* by Him, Jesus. He was the One who was to come. Through Him the prophecies were coming to pass, and we well know to what extent Pascal could take advantage of such a situation. The parents of Jesus did not understand at all; and this fact is in accord with that shortsightedness already pointed out in them. Thus Pascal passes by v. 50: " And they understood not the word that He spoke unto them."

Jesus returned with His parents. This is said simply. It is the natural order of things. Monsieur de Saci declared that Jesus was *submissive* to His parents. Pascal is more specific: Jesus was *subject* to His parents, which implies, not a passive attitude, but the continuation of what must be accomplished according to the design of God, who ordains and allows for a short time this subjection to human order in His Son who was made flesh.

We do not think that we have strained the meaning of the text in the foregoing analysis. These few exemplary verses show clearly that

Pascal's aim was to vindicate Christianity in his didactic exposé, and it is not without reason that Molinier was to incorporate the *Abrégé* in his *Pensées de Pascal*. In its sources, in its ramifications, this fragment seems to have a real part in the mellowing of Pascal's last years, which would have given us a " Vindication of Christianity." Whereas Jansen is satisfied with some simple references, Pascal cites Scripture at length, but always to bring out the essence in a message destined to convince the elect that Jesus was indeed the Son of God, He that should come. Pascal knows how to keep to a strictly expository method of the Bible sufficient unto itself.[104] To him, a simple presentation of Scripture proves to be the best apologetics possible — truth with which our modern preachers would do well to imbue themselves.

When we come to the Passion, however, the commentaries are amplified, and the *Mystère de Jésus* recurs like the leading theme of a great minor symphony. " ' My God, my God, why hast Thou forsaken me? ' i.e., Why hast thou abandoned me to my human infirmity, to the tormenting of my torturers, without consolation? And He turns to God asking the cause of this abandonment; therefore [one sees] [105] that it is the sin of mankind that He was expiating in His innocent flesh." [106]

Pascal, the committed, does not leave Jesus in the tomb. His Jesus is the Christ, who died for our transgressions, was raised for our justification, and glorified in the bosom of the Heavenly Father, with the glory which He had before the world was. The Jesus Christ of the Pascalian *Abrégé* is not only He that should come, but also He that must return. In the glorious finale of his message, the style of Pascal is inseparable from the divine Book: " And this Kingdom shall be without end, where God shall be all in all." [107] Have we read this in The Epistle of Paul to the Colossians (ch. 3:11, *sq.*), or was it in the Epistle to the Ephesians (ch. 1:23)? Or could it have been a reminiscence of the " *Cujus regni non erit finis* " of the Nicene Creed?

But why try to analyze this irresistible surge of life bursting forth from the ardent heart of Blaise Pascal? It emerges from primitive Christianity, as did of old the volcanic lava from his native Auvergne.

And behold, it burneth ever!

104 For example, from 50 to 81, *Œuvres*, v. 11, 24–29.
105 Words restored by Faugère.
106 *Œuvres*, v. 11, 72.
107 *Œuvres*, v. 11, 94 (354).

XVII

Holy Anxiety

" Hold that fast which thou hast, that no man take thy crown."
—Rev. 3:11

In a letter dated Toulouse, July 25, 1660, Fermat expressed to Pascal his desire of seeing him in order to greet him and to converse with him for a few days; but as his health was scarcely better than that of Pascal, who was at that time resting in Clermont, he proposed to his friend to do him " the favor of coming half-way " between Clermont and Toulouse.[1] In his answer, dated August 10, Pascal showed himself touched by the honor which the greatest geometer in Europe was doing him. The real reason he desired to see Fermat, however, was that he enjoyed the wit and polish of the latter's conversation, and not that he cared for his position as a great geometer, for, he explained, " to speak to you frankly of geometry, I find it the highest exercise of the mind, but at the same time, I know it to be so useless that I make little distinction between a man who is only a geometer and one who is a clever artisan. Therefore, I call it the finest trade in the world, but it is only a trade: and I have often said that it is good in order to make the trial but not the use of our strength: so that I should not take two steps for geometry. . . . But now there is in addition this in me, that I am steeped in studies so far from that mentality, that scarcely do I remember that there is any such." [2]

Pascal was alluding, not only to his project of a " Vindication of Christianity," but to his Biblical studies and to his diligent efforts toward holiness. Henceforth, the only thing which counts more and more for him is salvation.

As we have stated before, Valéry comments: " He has exaggerated, frightfully and crudely, the opposition of knowledge and of salvation "; he had " found " — an allusion to the assurance which Pascal received

[1] *Lettres de Fermat à Pascal* (July 25, 1660) *et de Pascal à Fermat* (August 10, 1660), at the time of Pascal's stay in Auvergne, *Œuvres,* v. **10,** 1 ff.

[2] *Ibid.,* v. **10,** 4.

from Christ [3] — " but doubtless because he no longer sought." [4] The author of this horrible play on words would have profited by meditating on the principle formulated by Boutroux, addressed, it seems, to every student of Pascal: " Pascal, before writing, knelt down and prayed to the Infinite Being to submit unto Him everything that was in the suppliant, so that His divine Power might be in accord with the suppliant's abasement. Through such humiliation, Pascal surrendered to inspiration.

" It seems that he who would know a genius so high and so rare in its true essence must follow a similar method." [5] This reverent method, be it noted in passing, allowed Boutroux to write the best book we have on the philosophy of Pascal. The eminent teacher of Bergson [6] had understood these words from the *Discours sur les passions de l'amour:* " In a great soul, all is great." [7]

THE SAINTLINESS OF PASCAL

It is as a " passionate thinker " [8] that Pascal seeks for the last word of this problem of salvation which he approaches from the point of view of true conversion.[9] It is also as a utilitarian avid for what is certain, tangible, palpable. It is as a humble penitent who knows that God owes him nothing but chastisement, and that the slightest good received from on high is by pure grace.

This man, so great in all things, became as simple as a child with regard to piety, writes Gilberte [10] of her brother, Blaise. Those who saw

[3] " Console thyself, thou wouldst not search for Me, hadst thou not found Me," *Le Mystère de Jésus, Œuvres,* v. **13,** 438.

[4] Valéry, P., " Variation sur une *Pensée," La Revue hebdomadaire,* No. 28, 32d year, July 14, 1923, p. 170.

[5] Boutroux, E., *Pascal,* collection " Les grands écrivains de la France," 10th ed., Hachette, Paris, p. 5 [original edition, 1900].

[6] Bergson started from the thesis of Boutroux, *De la contingence des lois de la nature,* Baillière, Paris, 1874.

[7] *Discours sur les passions de l'amour,* in *Des Pensées de Pascal,* by Victor Cousin, new edition, revised and enlarged, Ladrange, Paris, 1844, Appendix No. 11, p. 397.

[8] The expression comes from Sophie Antoniadis, *Pascal traducteur de la Bible,* Brill, Leyden, 1930, p. xv.

[9] Clément Falcucci, in a thesis defended before the faculty of letters of the University of Paris in 1939, has shown well that Pascal, when he has once made up his mind for *true* conversion, fixes himself there, and when it is a question of judging men and situations, he returns to it constantly. [Falcucci, Cl., *L'Idée de vérité chez Pascal,* Didier, Paris, Privat, Toulouse, 1939.]

[10] *Vie* par Mme Périer, *Œuvres,* v. **1,** 102.

him regularly were astounded by it. There was in his ways of acting neither affectation nor hypocrisy. He knew how to raise himself to the highest virtues; he knew how to lower himself in the practice of the most everyday virtues which are the edification of piety. All things were great in his heart from the moment that they served to honor God. The curé of Saint-Etienne-du-Mont, who saw him in his last illness, admired that simplicity, and never wearied of repeating: " He is a child; he is humble and submissive like a child." [11]

Pascal masters pleasure; he masters suffering; he reduces almost to nothing the necessities of his poor body. He proscribes comfort, elegance, everything superfluous. The tapestries of his room are useless: he has them taken away. He renounces the pleasures of the mind as those of the senses. To pay attention to food is in his eyes a sensual thing. He consumes what is strictly indispensable, after regulating it once for all. He swallows the most repugnant medicines without showing the least disgust. Certainly his life is a *heroic life,* according to a pertinent title of Victor Giraud.[12]

Amiot himself speaks of heroism in connection with Pascal, finds in him its noblest and truest meaning. And since this heroism lasts a lifetime, it is " more beautiful than *Polyeucte,* a play which lasts but a day." There is nothing like it in Saint Catherine of Siena, not even in Saint François de Sales or in Fénelon.[13] It is the heroism of a man who knows that " the last act is bloody, however beautiful the rest of the comedy may be: one casts earth upon his head, and so forever." [14] Such heroism was to wring from bold Pierre Bayle the cry of admiration which has remained famous: " A hundred volumes of sermons are of less value than that life." [15] The principle of that heroism is made manifest with divine simplicity. Beurrier's *Mémoires* sum it up in the affirmation that Pascal had founded " the regulation of his life on evangelical principles," and that " he kept them ceaselessly before his eyes, and tried always to perfect himself more and more in them." [16]

The saintliness of Pascal is henceforth that of a man who hopes for nothing from the world, who fears nothing from it, nor wishes anything

[11] *Ibid.,* 104.
[12] Giraud, V., *La Vie héroïque de Blaise Pascal,* Crès, Paris, 1923.
[13] Amiot, Ch.-G., " Impressions et conclusions sur Pascal," *La Revue hebdomadaire,* No. 28, 32d year, July 14, 1923, p. 209.
[14] *Pensées,* Section iii, Fr. 210, *Œuvres,* v. 13, 128, 129.
[15] Quoted in *Œuvres,* v. 1, 47.
[16] *Mémoires* of Beurrier, II, 3, *Œuvres,* v. 10, 391.

from it; of a creature for whom, according to a fine contemporary Russian document, " the final Judge of every dispute is not man, but the One who holds Himself above man. It results that, in order to find the truth, one must be free from what human beings hold for truth." [17] Such piety, if rigorously consistent, may appear overdone; but as the great Protestant thinker Vinet very well says: " It is good that such vocations, such souls, should exist; it is upon such overabundance of spiritual life that the Christianity of the masses is nourished." [18]

The Pascal of the last years knows how to transpose human affections into the divine order. Detached from others, he wishes that they be detached from him. It is to the Creator that he wishes the heart of the creature to be consecrated. Any purely human affection constitutes a turning aside from that which one owes to God. Blaise even goes so far as to discourage by his coldness the attentions of his family. He seeks never to lose consciousness of what he considers an essential duty.

The proof of it is that, according to the testimony of his sister Gilberte, there was found on him a little paper, like that he was often seen to read, on which he had written: " It is unjust that anyone attach himself to me, although he do it with pleasure, and voluntarily. I shall deceive those in whom I shall awaken the desire; for I am not the end and aim of anyone, and I have nothing with which to satisfy him. Am I not about to die? Thus then the object of their attachment will die. As I should be guilty of creating belief in a falsehood, even though I should urge it gently, and although therein they should do me a pleasure; in like manner I am guilty if I make myself loved, and *if I draw people to me;* for they must spend their lives and their efforts in drawing near unto God, or in searching for Him." [19] It is we who have italicized the passage *if I draw people to me,* which appears to us, in Pascal, an assiduous reader of the Bible, as a reminiscence of the " *I shall draw all men to Me* " of Jesus. There is in this affirmation — take our word for it — the key to the motivating principle of Pascal. We have personally just reread the Bible from one end to the other, and what struck us most

[17] " *Der letzte Richter in allen Streitigkeiten ist nicht der Mensch, sondern Jener, der über den Menschen steht. Folglich muss man, um die Wahrheit zu finden, frei sein von dem, was die Menschen gemeinhin für die Wahrheit halten.*" (Schestow, L., *Die Nacht zu Gethsemane* [Pascals Philosophie], vom Verfasser durchgesehene Übersetzung aus dem Russischen von Hans Ruoff, *Ariadne* Jahrbuch der Nietzsche-Gesellschaft, München, 1925 [36–109], 40.)

[18] Vinet, A., *Etudes sur Blaise Pascal,* Kohler, ed., *cit.,* p. 10.

[19] *Vie* par Mme Périer, *Œuvres,* v. 1, 96.

forcibly was that the Commandment which recurs there most often, in one form or another, is the "*Thou shalt have no other gods before me*" of Mount Sinai. Looking closely into the life of Pascal, and its successive separations, we see there a more and more consecrated observance of this Commandment. The last separation, the hardest, was the detachment from his intimates. Hence this constant recalling of the little paper always within reach. Hence the future indicative of an unshakable resolution: *I shall deceive those in whom I shall awaken the desire* — the desire of attaching oneself to him, Blaise, of making of him a little god, despoiling all the more the only true God who will have no other gods before Him.

The preceding interpretation seems to us confirmed by a fragment of the *Pensées*, where Pascal, in dramatic style, appears to identify himself with the Old Testament as he writes: Let those who are of the earth, earthy and given over to the flesh, become surfeited with it and die in it. " But those who seek God with all their heart, who have no displeasure save in being deprived of the sight of Him, who have no desire save that of possessing Him, and no enemies save those who turn aside from Him other men, who are afflicted to see themselves surrounded and dominated by such enemies; let them be consoled. I announce to them good news: There is One come to liberate them." To others he will not show God.[20] To make the elect see God, such is his task, according to Scripture. This task is first of all negative: not to encourage idolatry. It will be carried out, with this immense reservation made, by directing his own affections in the way of the elect. Thus his affections are modeled according to the Bible.

Blaise, his sister Gilberte tells us, had " an extreme tenderness . . . for those whom he believed to belong to God." [21] This testimony is profoundly moving. Every Christian friendship is founded upon God. It is election in the truest sense of the word. Matthew Arnold was mistaken when he said that we are all islands; the novelists and dramatists who erect solitude into a dogma are mistaken. Solitude is for those who do not know God: and certainly no state is more fertile in dramatic themes. But the believer sees his solitude peopled by God's elect, peopled with holy friendships. These friendships, however, ought to be kept in constant reference to God who is their source and their only reason for being. All the rest is idolatry and sacrilegious spoliation.

[20] *Pensées,* Section x, Fr. 692, *Œuvres,* v. 14, 129, 130.
[21] *Vie* par Mme Périer, *Œuvres,* v. 1, 91.

To will what God wills — that is the source of all wisdom. Pascal was going to write a " Vindication of Christianity," and behold the specter of death standing before him! " Thy will be done, Lord, not my will! " It is for Blaise the supreme test. He accepts " like a child " the decision of the Father.[22] His sufferings redouble as the end approaches. Pascal confesses and accuses himself before God; he lays himself open to the suffering which purifies; he offers himself to holy pain; he sinks at the foot of the Cross and consecrates himself there. The admirable prayer asking of God the effective use of illness [23] closes thus, the ultimate mystic appeal to the unitary experience: " Unite Thyself to me; fill Thou me with Thyself and with Thy Holy Spirit. Enter my heart and my soul, to bear my sufferings from within, and to continue in me that part of the suffering of Thy Passion which yet remains to endure, which Thou art yet completing in Thy members until the perfect consummation of Thy Body; so that, I being filled with Thee, it is no longer I who live and suffer, but Thou who dost live and suffer in me, O my Saviour! and so that thus I may have some small part in Thy suffering, Thou mayest fill me wholly with the Glory that it has brought to Thee in which Glory Thou dost dwell with the Father and the Holy Ghost forever and ever. Amen."

In his ardor, Pascal passes unconsciously from involuntary mortifications to the ascetic penitence of a rebellious flesh. He who can no longer swallow except with the greatest difficulty not only takes the most repugnant medicines with smiling serenity, but he does not want anyone to feel sorry for him. He does not even want to be cured any longer, saying of the sickness of the body that it is the natural state of Christians. Meanwhile he encircles his bare flesh with an iron belt studded with sharp points — a fact to be discovered only when he was on his deathbed — and he thrusts them into his flesh to remind him of his duty as soon as he feels himself touched by a pleasure to his mind illicit, like that of conversation. Those acts will be recalled after he has

[22] *Introduction à la seconde série des Œuvres de Pascal* [v. 4-11], v. 4, xxiii.

[23] *Prière de Pascal pour demander à Dieu le bon usage des maladies* (1659?), *Œuvres*, v. 9, 319 ff.

With Madame Périer, Pascal's sister, Brunschvicg, and Bishop, we place this prayer in the last years of Pascal's life. The internal evidence — spiritual maturity of a text nourished with Biblical sustenance — appears decisive to us. The state of Pascal's health grew steadily worse toward 1657–1658. The *Prière* would then probably date from 1658 to 1662, and the fatigue following the controversy relative to the signature of the *Formulaire* and the death of Jacqueline (1661) inclines us to choose the last year of Pascal's life. We realize that this is an extreme solution.

uttered his last sigh. "Happy the man who can put a girdle about his conscience," comments Vinet.[24]

Not only does Pascal do "great spiritual exercises in penitence, silence, and the examination or very exact review of his whole life," but he sells all that he can and "gives all the money to the poor."[25] Doubtless these sales multiplied, each time drawing closer to that "total and sweet renunciation." Pascal gives everything. His love for the poor becomes such that he goes so far as to deprive himself of what is strictly necessary. Those about him grow anxious. He repeats gently: "I have noticed one thing. However poor one may be, one always leaves something behind upon dying." He suffers from not having more with which to help the poor, whose eminent dignity strikes him more and more. He sees in them Jesus: "I love poverty, because He loved it. I like wealth because it gives the means whereby to assist the needy."[26] He is persuaded that the spirit of poverty most agreeable to God was to serve the poor in a poor way, by a daily and individual assistance. "To do small things, like big things, because of the majesty of Jesus Christ in us, who lives our life; and the big things like small and easy ones, because of His omnipotence."[27]

Here are examples of both, if it is permissible for us to speak thus.

Madame Périer reports that three months before Pascal's death, as he was coming home from Church one morning, he was accosted by a beautiful girl of about fifteen who asked him for alms. Impressed by the dangers she was running, Pascal confided her to a priest, to whom he gave a purse, promising also to send a woman the next day to buy clothes for the abandoned girl and take care of her — which was done punctually. In spite of the keen desire which he showed at the moment, the priest did not succeed in finding out the identity of the benefactor.

Although great enterprises of charity were not Pascal's particular vocation, we have at least one example of his interest in such of these as he believed were set aside for God-appointed individuals. In 1658, standing on a street corner, he had noticed that a crowd of people were hurrying in the same direction. Why should they not be transported together by groups? Pascal had spoken of this to his friend the Duke

[24] Vinet, A., *Etudes sur Blaise Pascal*, Kohler, ed., *op. cit.*, p. 6.
[25] *Mémoires* of Beurrier, II, 3, in *Œuvres*, v. **10,** 391.
The sales of which Beurrier speaks here, "with the exception of the Bible, Saint Augustine, and very few other books," go back in part to January, 1655.
[26] *Pensées*, Section vii, Fr. 550, *Œuvres*, v. **13,** 432.
[27] *Pensées*, Section vii, Fr. 553, *Œuvres*, v. **13,** 440.

de Roannez. From these meditations was to come the invention of the omnibus. But one would misjudge the age in general, and Pascal in particular, were he to imagine that this invention was to remain theoretical. What finally came out of Pascal's reflections was an omnibus company, conceived with all the attendant circumstances related thereto. On Saturday, March 18, 1662, vehicles carrying passengers at five sous a ride started to run in the streets of Paris with full pomp and ceremony. As soon, moreover, as the affair of the omnibuses was arranged, Pascal asked for a thousand francs in advance on his share, in order to send them to the poor of Blois, who had suffered severely from a bitter winter.

Such an insistence on charity on the part of Pascal as for the Christians of his century, came, moreover, directly from the fact that the Vulgate translated the Greek ἀγάπη, which means *love*, by the Latin *caritas*, which itself means *love, tenderness*, and became in French, as in English, the word *charité* (charity). But *charité* in current speech means: virtue which causes one to do and to desire the good of others; hence, to do charity is to give alms. This meaning is indeed clearly implied in I Cor. 13:1, " If I speak with the tongues of men, and of angels, and have not *charity* "; but that is a derived meaning. In the Greek of the New Testament, the accent is on *love*. The passage, " Having *the same charity*," of Phil. 2:2, implies in the Greek text *ardent pursuit*.

This ardent pursuit, in the daily life of Blaise Pascal, is first of all translated by *alms, help to the poor, to Jesus who suffers in them*. " One should have no rest, one should not sleep " during that time, comments Leo Schestow [28] in a fine page inspired by the " Jesus will be in agony until the end of the world," of the *Mystère de Jésus*. Let it be remembered, finally, that according to Pascal's great page on the three orders, the order of charity is the supreme, supernatural order. It is the *only thing necessary* [29] where all human contradictions are resolved. It is the " key of the ancient feast " of which Rimbaud spoke.[30] Pascal becomes part of a noble Christian tradition, that of the author of the *Imitation of Christ*, for whom the order of charity is the order of

[28] " *Man darf nicht ruhig sein, darf nicht schlafen.*" Schestow, L., *Die Nacht zu Gethsemane, Ariadne, op. cit.* (see our n. 17), 101. The last paragraph of Schestow is superb.

[29] *Introduction à la seconde série des Œuvres de Pascal* [v. 4-11], *Œuvres*, v. 4, lv.

[30] Mauriac, F., " La Rencontre avec Pascal," *La Revue hebdomadaire, op. cit.*, 226.

grace: "This *grace* is a supernatural light and a sort of special *gift of God:* it is properly the distinguishing mark of the elect and the pledge of eternal salvation." [31] That is doubtless why, in the eyes of Pascal, charity establishes itself as " the only object of the Scriptures." [32] Man is free, but he cannot originate in his heart the love of God. To reach ultimately the order of charity, of grace, means, therefore, for Pascal that one should have the sign that one's election is confirmed. That is for him the *supreme implication of that page on the three orders, the laborious elaboration of which we have followed from the first pages of this book.*

We have come henceforth to the final grandeur of Pascal, to the hour when " the most impatient of geniuses yields to the saint." Yields? Let us say rather with Charles Du Bos, becomes only an " impetuous tributary of saintliness," in a fusion of " feeling " and of " vision." [33] In the detachment of saintliness, Pascal has left pleasures " only for others greater," according to the terms of a letter that he wrote several years before to the Duke and Mademoiselle de Roannez, appealing to the testimony of Saint Paul and Saint John, and interpreting the parable of the hidden treasure in The Gospel According to Saint Matthew.[34]

After the manner of the Jansenists, and contrary to an opinion commonly held, Pascal is not sad: he is joyous, even if his joy appears egotistic to Abbé Bremond.[35] Every thought of salvation, in a certain sense, can be so qualified; but is it the fault of the elect if it has pleased God to consider precious the human soul in particular, and to put salvation

[31] *De Imitatione Christi,* III, liv, 18: " *Haec gratia* supernaturale lumen et quoddam *Dei* speciale *donum est,* et proprie electorum signaculum et pignus salutis aeterne."

[32] *Pensées,* Section x, Fr. 670, *Œuvres,* v. **14,** 106.

[33] Du Bos, Ch., " Le Langage de Pascal," *La Revue hebdomadaire, op. cit.,* 261, 266.

See also *Port-Royal,* v. **3,** 338, and the chapter entitled " The Prayer of Pascal," v. **4,** of the *Histoire littéraire du sentiment religieux en France,* by Bremond (*op. cit.*) Consult, also, of this last named author, the study " Pascal et l'Eglise Catholique," *La Revue hebdomadaire, op. cit.,* 171–183.

[34] *Extrait d'une lettre à Mr. et à Mlle de Roannez,* November or December, 1656?, *Œuvres,* v. **6,** 220, 221.

The Biblical allusions are to I Thess. 5:16–18; John 14:27; 16:22; and Matt. 13:44.

[35] Bremond, H., *Histoire littéraire du sentiment religieux en France, op. cit.* The author, after asking himself if the Jansenist doctrine penetrated the interior life of Pascal (v. **4,** 319–322), discovers Pascal's joy, and the egotistical character, according to him, of this joy (v. **4,** 322–336), and concludes that there was no pessimism (v. **4,** 322, 323).

on a purely individual basis? The shadow of La Rochefoucauld hovers over this type of criticism. Would to God that the " egoism " of Pascal might spread abroad through the world! It is, moreover, very largely compensated for, it seems, by the charity of Pascal.

However, the objection of Bremond goes deeper, and is not lightly to be refuted: While orthodox Catholics say, " Christ died for all men; he died *also* for me," the Jansenists reason, " Surely, Christ did not die for all men, but he died for us." Here the quarrel concerning a proposition attributed to Jansen is rekindled. If Pascal asks himself the question, it is because the Bible posed it for him and in the most specific manner. Many fragments of the *Pensées* reveal to us Pascal sounding Scripture on this point.[36] He notes, for example, that Jesus Christ " never condemned without a hearing " (Fr. 780), but suggests that " Jesus Christ, in the quality of the Redeemer, is not perhaps the Master of all " (Fr. 781). It is to be observed that this last fragment is presented in dialogue form. For this reason, it constitutes, properly speaking, a piece of research, a *skepsis*. Fragment 774 is clearer: it opens with the proposition, " Jesus Christ for all," and ends with the proposition, " It belongs to Jesus Christ to be universal; even the Church offers sacrifice only for the faithful: Jesus Christ offered that of the Cross for all."

THE ANGUISH OF PASCAL

Pascal's joy, we see, is not unmixed, but that comes from the fact that he cannot entirely rest on the message of the Good News such as he finds it in his Bible, and such as the inner testimony of the Holy Spirit enlightens him with respect to it. What do I say? The blessed ambiguity of the Scripture, blessed because so willed by the hidden God, allows him to glimpse a whole divine strategy in which the assurance of his salvation lies in suspense: Am I or am I not called, until the end of my days, to be a part of the small flock of the elect? The notion of the perseverance of the saints does not succeed in taking full possession of him.

The elect will not know their virtues, nor the condemned the greatness of their crimes. " Lord, when did we see Thee hungry, thirsty," et cetera? [37] Faith is not within our power.[38] We must not expect it of our-

---

[36] For example, Frs. 774–781, Section xii, *Œuvres*, v. 14, 218–223.

[37] *Pensées*, Fr. 515, Section vii, *Œuvres*, v. 13, 414.

[38] *Pensées*, Fr. 516, Section vii, *ibid.*

selves. Quite otherwise, it comes when we expect nothing of ourselves.[39] It is in this sense that Blaise heard Jesus saying to him, " Thy conversion, 'tis my concern."[40] Here is truly the anguish of Pascal! A letter to the Duke and Mademoiselle de Roannez tells of Pascal's fright at the idea that one may fall from such glory. He appeals to I Cor. 9:27: " But I chastise my body, and bring it into subjection: lest perhaps, when I have preached to others, I myself should become a castaway." And he ends on the note of the psalmist (Ps. 3:1): " Blessed is the man that feareth the Lord."[41] Another letter specifies that anxieties do not come from the good which is beginning to exist within us, " but from the evil which is still there, and that we must continuously diminish." Henceforth Pascal prays God to enclose him within his limits, in particular not to let him become involved in the fear of the future: " The present is the only time which is truly ours, and of which we must make use as God wills."[42] However, does it not appear that Pascal's anxieties come from the past as much as from the future, and in particular from burning memories of his months of backsliding? Let no one accuse us of appealing too often here to the testimony of the writings from dates as far off as those of 1656 and 1660. In the words of Jacques Chevalier, if " the whole work " of Pascal moves toward true peace, it does so through a war to be preferred to " false peace."[43]

The question, then, is to discover whether Blaise Pascal ever knew serenity. On this point a contradiction which we must explain strikes us. On the one hand, the *heart* in the Pauline sense of the word holds a considerable place in Pascal's thought. For him, faith is " God perceptible to the heart and not to reason."[44] On the other hand, as far as we ourselves are concerned, we have been able to find in the *Pensées* only two occasions in which specific mention is made of the Holy Spirit. In Fragment 568, answering the objection that the Scripture is full of things not dictated by the Holy Spirit, Pascal replies that " the Church has never decided " that everything in Scripture was from the Holy Spirit. Let us

[39] *Pensées*, Fr. 517, *ibid.*

[40] *Le Mystère de Jésus, Pensées*, Fr. 553, Section vii, *Œuvres*, v. 13, 438.

[41] *Extrait d'une lettre à Mr. et à Mlle de Roannez*, Sunday, November 5, 1656, *Œuvres*, v. 6, 162, 163.

[42] *Extrait d'une lettre à Mr. et à Mlle de Roannez*, December, 1656?, *Œuvres*, v. 6, 300, 299, 298.

[43] Chevalier, J., " Des Rapports de la vie et de la Pensée chez Pascal," *La Revue hebdomadaire, op. cit.*, p. 208.

See also our section " Pascal on Peace," in Chapter XIV.

[44] *Pensées*, Section iv, Fr. 278, *Œuvres*, v. 13, 201.

note, in passing, this appeal to the jurisdiction of the Church in the matter. Pascal adds, moreover: " Even if the Church had decided that everything in Scripture was from the Holy Spirit, that could be maintained." [45] It would still be the supreme jurisdiction, i.e., the Church, which would be right. The other allusion to the Holy Spirit is found in Fragment 672: in the matter of circumcision, Saint Peter and the Apostles took into account only " the reception of the Holy Spirit in the person of the uncircumcised "; they did not consult the prophets. " They judged it to be more sure that God approves of those whom He fills with His Spirit. . . . They knew that the end of the law was only the Holy Spirit." [46] This second allusion shows us again a decision relative to the Holy Spirit, pronounced by Peter and the Apostles, that is to say, by the Early Church under the sign of the " Chief " of the Apostles. We do not have the right to draw an argument from only two texts — but they are the only ones available. We shall content ourselves with seeing in them an extremely characteristic symbol. Pascal holds on strictly to the Roman Catholic teaching on the subject of the Holy Spirit.

It is wishful thinking on the part of the Protestant Vinet when he writes: " Let one read the *Pensées* attentively, and then answer this one question: Is not Church authority simply a digression in Pascal's system? " The context indicates that he is sure of the reader's acquiescence. How, then, does he come to this conclusion? By identifying purely and simply the *heart* with the Holy Spirit according as it is a question of a " new heart with which the Holy Spirit provides us." [47] Truly one seems to be dreaming in reading this gratuitous transposition of Pascal into Protestant language. The author of this present work does not feel himself authorized to do anything of the sort. In his eyes, it is precisely such operations, which come from sentiments of conciliation praiseworthy in themselves, that have obscured so many similar questions. Let us allow only Pascal, his *Pensées*, his life, to speak. What do we find?

A MATTER OF USEFUL RELATIONSHIP

First of all, the profession of faith of the seventeenth *Provinciale:* " Thanks be to God, I have no bond on earth but to the Apostolic Roman Catholic Church alone, in which I am determined to live and die,

---

[45] *Pensées*, Section viii, Fr. 568, *Œuvres*, v. **14**, 14, 15.
[46] *Pensées*, Section x, Fr. 672, *Œuvres*, v. **14**, 107, 108.
[47] Vinet, A., *Etudes sur Blaise Pascal*, Kohler, ed., *op. cit.*, p. 153.

and in communion with the Pope, its sovereign head; outside of which, I am fully persuaded, there is no salvation." [48] That is clear enough. In November, 1656, Pascal made a similar profession of faith to the Duke and to Mademoiselle de Roannez: " We know that all the virtues, martyrdom, austerities, and all good works are useless outside of the Church, and the communion with the head of the Church who is the Pope.

" I shall never separate myself from his communion, at least I pray God to grant me this grace; without which I should be lost forever. I am making to you a kind of profession of faith, and I do not know why; but I shall neither erase it nor rewrite it." [49] Again a statement which is as clear as it is possible to make it!

May we be permitted to stress this proposition of Pascal that " all the virtues, martyrdom, austerities, and all good works are *useless* outside of the Church, and the communion *with the head of the Church who is the Pope.*" Just as we know God only through Jesus Christ, he believes, so we are in a *useful* relationship with Him, as far as our salvation is concerned, only through His terrestrial vicar, who is the Pope. For the Catholic Church, what is true with regard to Jesus Christ is also true concerning the Holy Spirit. " The Church has authority from God to teach regarding faith and morals, and in her teaching she is preserved from error by the special guidance of the Holy Spirit." [50] " The Saviour took measures that the Church teach us the essential truths without being mistaken and without deceiving us." [51]

It is not to the *testimonium Spiritus Sancti internum* that the Catholic Church appeals: it is to a quality by which the soul is transformed, becomes a child of God; it is on earth the *inchoatio vitae aeternae.* But here is " an essential feature: the faith that Jesus wishes to obtain is not only an individual act; the disciple of Jesus is not an isolated being, he must ' listen to the Church ' (Matt. 18:17); the Apostles are charged to preach through all the earth, and to baptize all nations; those who refuse to listen to them will be condemned." [52] For the Vatican council

[48] *Dix-septième Provinciale, Œuvres,* v. **6,** 343.

[49] *Fragment d'une lettre à Mr. et à Mlle de Roannez,* November, 1656?, *Œuvres,* v. **6,** 217.

[50] Gibbons, James, Cardinal, *The Faith of Our Fathers,* 94th carefully revised and enlarged ed., Burns, Oates and Washbourne, Ltd., London, ch. 7, " Infallible Authority of the Church," p. 65.

[51] Lesêtre, H., *La Foi Catholique,* 27th ed., Beauchesne, Paris, 1923, p. 91.

[52] Aigrain, R., in *Apologétique* [Catholic], published under the direction of Mau-

invoked by the scholarly Catholic apologist whom we have just cited, " beside the traditional method which seeks for proofs of the divinity of the Christian religion in ' divine deeds,' that is, the miracles and the prophecies, there can exist another, no less legitimate, which comes from the Church as a reality easy to observe and carrying with it the recognizable signs of its divine origin." [53] Pascal, who was so absorbed in the proofs of the Christian religion in the course of the last years of his life, seems to have been affected by this twofold proof.

This duality will prove not to have been foreign to the dualism which was to bring anguish to him as an assiduous reader of the Bible, and as a faithful Roman Catholic. We have seen this anguish reach its climax in an hour of crisis in the cry: " Lord Jesus, I appeal to Thy tribunal! " This antinomy was to be solved by obedience, by submission to the only earthly authority that was competent to judge the debate: the pontifical seat of Rome. Springing from a line of upright men of law, Blaise did not trifle with a matter of competent jurisdiction. Moreover, his own salvation was at stake!

Pascal, says Brunschvicg, remains " the Christian who devoted his whole life to the defense of the true religion and who never had consented ' to be separated from the altar,' to disavow the authority of the Church." [54] With his sister Jacqueline, he could have said: " As long as we do not erect Altar against Altar, as we are not unhappy enough to make a separate Church, as we remain within the limits of simple groaning, and of gentleness with which we endure our persecution, the charity which makes us embrace our enemies will attach us inviolably to the Church." It was a question, for Jacqueline as for Blaise, of not depriving themselves " of the effect of this union." [55] In this notion of an indispensable organic attachment, a condition of life, the parable of the Vine and the Branches is transposed into terms of the Roman Catholic Church and its loyal children. For Pascal it is a question of a " substantial unity from within," of a " sacramental life which assimilates the members to the head." [56] And the " head," of which it is an immedi-

rice Brillant and the Abbé M. Nédoncelle, Bloud et Gay, Paris, 1937, pp. 952, 953 [Nihil obstat, Paris, July 21, 1937 — Imprimatur, Paris, July 23, 1937].

[53] *Ibid.*, pp. 1017, 1018.

[54] *Introduction aux* Pensées *de Pascal, Œuvres*, v. 12, xiii.

[55] *Lettre de la Sœur Jacqueline de Sainte-Euphémie Pascal à la Sœur Angélique de Saint Jean*, June 22, 23, 1661, *Œuvres*, v. 10, 105.

[56] Blondel, M., " Le Jansénisme et l'anti-Jansénisme de Pascal," *Revue de métaphysique et de morale*, 30th year, No. 2, April–June, 1923, pp. 156, 157.

ate concern, is for him the visible head, the vicar of Christ on earth, the Pope. In his eyes, the Pope alone disposes of the nourishments of the sacraments which he needs in order to live. This will be seen clearly when death finally takes Blaise by the throat.

For a Catholic like Pascal, it is essentially the sacraments which aid in maintaining the state of grace. Thus their reality, verifiable, evident, and present, becomes precious for the child of Clermont, eager for what is sure, tangible, palpable.

The very subject of the present work might have led us to insist on the Bible to the point of falsifying the perspective of Pascal as a fervent Catholic, anxious to be lacking in none of the practices of his religion. Madame Périer, his sister, tells us that his principal " diversion," especially in the last years of his life when he could no longer work, was to visit the churches where relics were exposed or where there was some solemnity. To this end he procured an *Almanach spirituel,* which showed him the places where all the devotions were being held, and which indicated to the faithful the different feasts celebrated in the metropolitan and collegiate Churches, and in the parishes and monasteries of Paris.[57]

In the course of his last weeks, however, Pascal saw scarcely anyone except the curé of Saint-Etienne-du-Mont, who came to visit and confess him. In the month of June, 1662, he had received into his home a family of poor people, one of the children of which had the smallpox. Madame Périer, fearing for her own children, had wanted to have the little sick boy taken elsewhere. Pascal had decided that he himself would be the one to go away. He had therefore abandoned his home to the poor folk and had himself taken to the home of his brother-in-law in the parish of Saint-Etienne-du-Mont. It was thus that he had made the acquaintance of the Abbé Beurrier who henceforth assisted him.

[57] Jovy, E., " L'Almanach spirituel de M. Pascal," in *Etudes pascaliennes, op. cit.,* v. **7,** 59.

Jovy gives the facsimile of a page (v. **7,** 64).

This almanac was edited and put in order by a penitent monk of the Third Order of Saint Francis, of the convent of Nazareth, near the Temple, at Paris — Father Martial, of Le Mans. The said almanac had been appearing since 1646.

Professor Gilbert Chinard, of Princeton University, reminds us pertinently that although a mystic given to contemplation, Pascal was neither a recluse nor a solitary soul. (" Notes sur une Pensée de Pascal," in *Modern Language Notes,* Lancaster Testimonial Number, November, 1942, v. **57,** 511.)

In this way a great difficulty presented itself, at a time when Pascal felt more than ever that great need of spiritual assistance. The curé of Saint-Etienne scarcely knew him; he did not know the complex events of that great life which was to be so cut short. And then, how many contradictions for that curé whose mind was limited, if not confused! [58] Monsieur Pascal did not cease exciting himself against the false Christians who corrupted the Church.[59] Moreover, Monsieur Pascal seemed to blame those of Port-Royal for going too far into the questions of grace. The curé translated: they lacked submission to the Pope.

In a deposition dated September 4, 1684, the Duke de Roannez, the faithful friend of Blaise, explains that it was quite the contrary: Pascal meant that the Jansenists by their concessions in the matter of grace, showed too much submission.[60] The Duke specifies that because of his intimate relationship with Pascal he had had " a particular knowledge of his feelings on this matter." [61] It is a fact that his testimony coincides perfectly with that of Pascal concerning the signature of the Formulary — " The only debate worth mentioning which ever set Pascal and Port-Royal against each other," adds Laporte.[62]

Let us remember that the Formulary in question was a statement clearly condemning the Jansenist doctrine. In 1661, the Church of Rome required that this Formulary be signed by the clergy and the monastic orders. As the nuns of Port-Royal were profoundly disturbed by the pressure brought to bear upon their consciences, Arnauld devised for them a clever but ambiguous formula to be added to their signature. His phrasing allowed the nuns to preserve their Jansenist faith while paying lip service to the Constitutions. Pascal denounced such expediency as shameful and unworthy of true Christians, in his *Ecrit sur la signature*, then also in a *Grand écrit* which was subsequently destroyed. It was during these debates that Pascal fainted — an incident already

[58] Gazier, A., *Les derniers jours de Blaise Pascal*, Champion, Paris, 1911, pp. 55, 64.

[59] *Introduction aux* Pensées *de Pascal, Œuvres*, v. **12**, vii.

[60] *Œuvres*, v. **10**, 372. Cf. the complete publication of the record of the sickness and death of Pascal, *Œuvres*, v. **10**, 303–405.

[61] *Œuvres*, v. **10**, 372.

[62] Laporte, J., " Pascal et la doctrine de Port-Royal," *Revue de métaphysique et de morale, op. cit.*, p. 296.

recorded in these pages. Let us remember also that a short time before, his dear sister Jacqueline had denounced the tyranny of the Bishops, saying among other things: " Since the Bishops have a courage of maids, the maids should have a courage of Bishops." Under coercion she had attained unto the glory of martyrdom: " Unless I see at least a few people make themselves victims of the truth, I must succumb." She had succumbed three months after giving her signature, on October 4, 1661. When a messenger came to bring him the sad tidings, Blaise answered simply: " God give us the grace to die as well as that! "

We may now conclude on this whole unhappy matter of the signature:

There was disagreement with regard to the Formulary, not because Pascal disavowed his former opinions, but, on the contrary, because he found Arnauld and most of the others too moderate. It is a fact that Pascal had continued to go often to Port-Royal. At the end of June, 1662, it was Port-Royal which came to him. Outlawed, and running the risk of arrest, Nicole and Monsieur de Sainte-Marthe succeeded each other at his bedside,[63] where Abbé Beurrier, more and more confused, may have met them. It is to Port-Royal that Madame Périer was to turn in order to publish the *Pensées* of her brother. Laporte concludes his very remarkable study on *Pascal et la doctrine de Port-Royal* by the assertion that " Pascal does not let himself be separated from Port-Royal." [64] Three letters of 1682, preserved by the *Recueils Guerrier* and signed by Pascal's sister, consider the fact of a supposed recantation by her brother as " a calumny least worthy of belief for all those who knew Monsieur Pascal, and the most false indeed of any that has ever been imagined." [65]

The regrettable controversy had been brought about by the fact that in January, 1665, more than two years after Pascal's death, the former tutor of Louis XIV, Hardouin de Péréfixe, Archbishop of Paris, had sent for Abbé Beurrier to ask him why he had granted absolution and the sacraments to a Jansenist as notorious as Pascal. Beurrier justified himself by testifying to the orthodoxy of his parishioner. He added that Pascal had testified that he had retired from the party of Port-Royal because they went too far in the matter of grace and seemed to have less submission than they should for the Pope. Madame Périer and Pas-

---

[63] Gazier, C., " Pascal et Port-Royal," *La Revue hebdomadaire, op. cit.,* p. 159.

[64] Laporte, J., *op. cit.,* p. 304.

[65] *Œuvres,* v. 1, 46. (For the other letters, cf. v. 1, 44 ff.)

cal's friends having protested, Beurrier had formally retracted by a letter of June 12, 1671, to Madame Périer,[66] that we owe to Jansenist sources.

The debate continued from the seventeenth century without new evidence until in 1908 Jovy discovered in the Sainte-Geneviève Library in Paris some unpublished *Mémoires* of Beurrier in which the latter withdrew his own retraction. His penitent, he said in substance, had confessed to him that he had for some time " prudently " retired from the disputes of Port-Royal, " in view of the great difficulty of those very difficult questions of grace and predestination."[67] We know, indeed, that Pascal, after the affair of the Formulary, was to consecrate the rare hours of leisure which sickness left him to the preparation of his " Vindication of Christianity," to prayer, to reading the Bible, and to charitable works.

What else does Beurrier say to us? That Pascal found that these gentlemen of Port-Royal were going too far in the matter of grace. Of the clarification of Beurrier's lack of comprehension on this subject by the Duke de Roannez, Pascal's intimate friend, we have already spoken. Finally, the curé of Saint-Etienne-du-Mont declares that Pascal had only orthodox sentiments, and this we have never doubted. Father Petitot calls attention to the fact that all the Christians of Port-Royal were orthodox. Jovy himself published the will of Monsieur de Saint-Gilles, dated October 5, 1668, where the testator, calling himself " poor wretch," declares that he has " no other sentiment than those of my very dear mother the Apostolic Roman Catholic Church."[68]

Where, then, is the recantation of the Jansenist Pascal in all that? In that Pascal probably had a non-Jansenist end? Jovy, Strowski, and Jacques Chevalier uphold this, as well as Abbé Bremond, who introduces nuances and reservations into his opinion. For example, there was an evolution in Jansenism, which cannot be considered as a unit, and decadence developed after the Bull *Unigenitus* was issued. The " sect " became schismatic. Not so Pascal, who was " only a Catholic like the others."[69] With the Bull on the table, according to a letter of March 7, 1746, attributed by Jovy to Father Thomassin, it seemed that there

[66] Jovy, E., " Pascal inédit," *op. cit.*, v. 2, 454.
[67] *Mémoires* of Beurrier, *Œuvres*, v. 10, 387.
[68] MS. 4556, Mazarine Library, published as an appendix of Jovy, E., " Le Journal de M. de Saint-Gilles," *Etudes pascaliennes, op. cit.*, v. 9, 203, 204.
[69] Bremond, H., " Pascal et l'Eglise Catholique," *La Revue hebdomadaire, op. cit.*, p. 174.

was only one decision for the Jansenists to make. Now, " not one decided for obedience. The one who most closely approached it was Monsieur Pascal." [70]

We shall not pursue any farther the study of this controversy, in great part sterile.[71] In truth, the subject is somewhat repugnant. Even for a Doctor, respect for professional secrecy is sacred. What shall we say of the sacred character for a priest of the confession of a dying man? The Archbishop, Jovy says, " had promised Beurrier to be silent about his declaration: he hastened to make that declaration known." [72] Jovy said neither more nor less than " *the Archbishop* "! It is difficult for us, after that, to share the emotion with which the Abbé Bremond, preaching in the cathedral of Clermont on Sunday, July 8, 1923, for the third centenary of Pascal, cried out: " In the person of Father Beurrier, it is the whole Church which absolves the dying Pascal, and who recognizes him as hers." [73]

We believe, however, that we have read the essential material on this controversy, and we have integrated it as best we can into what we have already learned of Pascal:

The very concept of election, which is established at the basis of his interests, seems to incite him to seek with even more eagerness for the spiritual nourishment which flows from the organism of the Church through the sacraments. This concept of the election is often translated by saying: " I am one of the elect, therefore I persevere." Pascal sees things otherwise. One should rather suppose him to say: " I persevere, therefore I am of the elect." On the subject of grace, he did not change his opinion, but he changed his conduct. Doubtless, if he had been pressed to say what he believed about grace, he would speak again like Saint Cyran. Perhaps he would set up the antinomies. But, as Mauriac powerfully expresses it: " He no longer wants to be drawn into this thicket; he has no more time; death is very near; the wind of eternity

[70] Jovy, E., " Un Témoignage oublié du P. Thomassin sur Pascal " [work first given in the *Bulletin historique et scientifique d'Auvergne,* published by the Académie des Sciences, Belles-Lettres et Arts de Clermont-Ferrand, 2d Series, No. 5, May, 1924], *Etudes pascaliennes, op. cit.,* v. 3, 41, 42.

[71] It is thus that Reguron, *Pascal et l'anti-Jansénisme* . . . , Grenoble, 1934, takes up again and develops the thesis of Chevalier on the evolution of the doctrine of Pascal who is said to have gone as far as positive anti-Jansenism; Kelly, H., in *Studies* (Dublin) for December, 1937, questions again the possibility of the retraction *in extremis,* etc.

[72] Jovy, E., *Etudes pascaliennes, op. cit.,* v. 5, 11.

[73] Bremond, H., " Pascal et l'Eglise Catholique," *op. cit.,* p. 175.

strikes his face." [74] He hastens away from the land of struggle, throws away his arms and falls on his knees, wishing no more than to suffer and to pray while waiting for the instant fixed by God.

The Pope might have been mistaken, or deceived. What does it matter? What counts is not to have been cut off from the living organism of the Church through which he is nourished by Jesus Christ. What counts is to listen to " those who have the power to remit sins, to consecrate the host, to exile an unworthy man from the Holy Table." [75] The only thing that counts is salvation. It is the Church which disposes of salvation at this last hour. It has the power, at the supreme moment, to cause the crown of election, which is the only wealth for Blaise, to fall from his head.

Already convulsions shake him; already his throat closes. Oh, let the curé hasten to come to give him the viaticum and extreme unction! Yesterday he asked for the Abbé Beurrier several times. In his absence it was Monsieur de Sainte-Marthe who came to spend the night with him. He made his confession. Toward midnight a convulsion shook him from head to foot. Was this, then, the end? And what of the Holy Communion for which he was waiting!

In his night, Blaise saw the holy ciborium shining; his glance rested on the whiteness of the sacred host where he knew his Saviour was present in His glory.

" Here is He whom you have so much desired," the curé announced solemnly.

Blaise, with a superhuman effort of his own strength, half rose on his bed to receive with more respect the Word incarnate in spiritual flesh, the Word which was going to communicate Itself entirely, truly, really, substantially to his soul, to nourish it with life divine.

But first it was necessary that Blaise answer the questions on the principal mysteries of faith. And to all the questions he answered with a holy impatience: " Yes, sir, I believe all that, and with all my heart! "

And, his eyes bathed in tears, he then received the holy sacrament, extreme unction, and then the benediction of the holy sacrament: " May God never abandon me! " [76]

These were his last words, the cry of a hope in anguish until the end,

[74] Mauriac, F., *Blaise Pascal et sa sœur Jacqueline,* Hachette, Paris, 1931, p. 226.
[75] *Ibid.,* p. 231.
[76] *Œuvres,* v. **1,** 113.

echoing the " Let me not be separated from Him eternally " of the *Mémorial*.

For it is in this Catholic context that one must read that burning page of the night of November 23, 1654, and the " total submission to Jesus Christ and to my director " in which it culminated.

Convulsions seized Blaise and did not release him until the end. He breathed his last on August 19, 1662, at one o'clock in the morning. He was thirty-nine years and two months old.

His funeral rites were celebrated on Monday, August 21, at ten o'clock in the morning in the Church of Saint-Etienne-du-Mont.

There were there, around the family, the friends, the survivors of the former scientific group, the worldly companions, comrades of combat, converts, and those whom the Christian layman had helped, writers who had come to pay their tribute — Corneille, Molière, Bossuet perhaps. At the very back of the Church and in the aisles the crowds of poor were thronging. Among them were hiding the brothers of Port-Royal, who feared persecution.

The last liturgical chant having died under the deep vaults, everyone returned home. The will of Blaise was opened. As the man of law began to read it, this profession of faith stood forth: " First, as a good Christian, Catholic, Apostolic, Roman, the suppliant has recommended and recommends his soul to God, whom through the merit of the precious blood of our Saviour and Redeemer Jesus Christ may it please Him to pardon his faults and to join his soul, when it shall leave this world, to the number of the blessed, imploring to this end the intercessions of the glorious Virgin Mary and all the saints of paradise." [77]

[77] *Testament de Pascal* (August 3, 1662), *Œuvres,* v. **10**, 295.

XVIII

Meditation on a Death Mask

" And, lo, I am with you alway, even unto the end of the world."
— Matt. 28:20

In the words of a venerable man of God, the Reverend G. Campbell Morgan, " every century of consideration of the Word of Jesus proving as it has, that His teaching was not a deduction from appearances, but the uttering forth of eternal principles in the speech of man, has given to men a new conception of the authority of God, as based upon the necessity of the things that are." [1]

Pascal did not separate Scripture from Tradition. The experience of sixteen centuries of Christian life carried weight with him as he took his place in this Heavenly Fellowship. He would be surprised, in our day, to see disciples wait anxiously for the latest report of the philosophers and scholars on the Lord's earthly life, before finding out who He was.

Facing as he did the libertine's incredulity and sole concern, the leading of an easy life, Pascal devised a new method of apologetics designed to start from the point of view of the indifferent worldling and from the only premises the latter was willing to grant in reference to the Bible — namely, that the Scriptures were in part a historical record. Pascal went even farther in his scientific approach to the Book. He actually caught a glimpse of the problem of the Mosaic authorship of the Pentateuch. In fact, in more than one instance, he may be said to have blazed a trail for Bible criticism.

We should readily admit, however, that the Biblical theology of Pascal was formulated before Richard Simon and Jean Astruc inaugurated the methods of modern criticism, nay, before the impact of the new science of the universe, of man and society, had been felt. In the admirable Dictionary of Moréri completed in the middle of the following century

[1] Morgan, G. Campbell, *The Crises of the Christ,* Fleming H. Revell Company, London and Edinburgh, 1903, p. 436.

by Abbé Couget, there was no mention of matters such as Brahmanism, Buddhism, Confucianism, Sanskrit, Egyptian religion, Germanic mythology, et cetera. One hundred years after the death of Pascal there was still no discussion of linguistics, mythology, philology, prehistoric archaeology. Only in the second half of the eighteenth century would Diderot, d'Alembert and the Encyclopedists complete their integration of the data emerging from three centuries of modern erudition. Pascal died in 1662, thirty-two years before Voltaire was born. The latter's *Essai sur les mœurs et l'esprit des nations,* the first masterpiece of the new philosophy of history, was not published until 1756. Hume's *Essay on Miracles* came out in 1748. The German " professor " was as yet undreamed of.

Pascal, therefore, did not know the pangs and inhibitions of a Fundamentalist confronted with the flat contradictions of a daring Liberalism. To him " Bibliolatry " so-called was easy. His dividing line between subject matter pertaining to rationalism and naturalism on the one hand, and subject matter reserved for authority on the other, seems at first sight to have lost its meaning for us today. Ours is said to be a critical and scientific approach to the historical and literary problems of the Bible. More especially are we warned against retouching the portrait that objective Biblical scholarship paints of Jesus, lest we be " found guilty of trying to correct the Wisdom of God by the wisdom of men." [2]

And yet, out of a group of theologians who have restored the scene of the Crucifixion through the same tested methods of investigation some will take their stand beside the repentant thief; others will find themselves on the side of his fellow, unrepentant, and say to Jesus in their own way: " If Thou be Christ, save Thyself and us," because their naturalism calls for objective tests.

It may be that Blaise Pascal erred in not realizing with Calvin that the repentant thief on the cross became the brother of believers although he never partook of the Lord's Supper. What actually matters is that Pascal stood at the foot of the cross on the side of the repentant thief.

Having therefore removed the mote from Pascal's eye and becoming conscious of a beam in our own, we now understand that his supreme loyalty went out to the Incarnate Son, to the Supernatural Christ. Abbé Beurrier, who assisted Blaise during his last moments on this earth,

[2] Horton, Walter Marshall, in his Foreword to *The Intention of Jesus,* by Bowman, J. W., The Westminster Press, Philadelphia, 1943, p. vii.

understood his penitent far better than has generally been admitted: " Here is He whom you have so much desired," the priest announced solemnly as he at last gave the Holy Communion to the dying man.

To Pascal, the Vicar of Christ on earth derived his significance only from the existence of the Supernatural Christ. Pascal never mistook the means for the end. At a time of great stress, in one of those supreme crises that lay bare the very soul of man, grief wrung from him this out-cry of dereliction: " If my letters are condemned in Rome, what I con-demn in them is condemned in Heaven: to Thy tribunal, Lord Jesus, I appeal."

Through Scripture and Tradition he rediscovered the Jesus of early Christianity, a Jesus anterior to the formulation of Trinitarianism, that is to say, anterior to the Council of Alexandria, A.D. 362. To Trinitarian-ism indeed Pascal paid lip service. For all practical purposes, however, he held to a " binitarian " idea, to a Modalism of his own, by which we know God only through Jesus Christ. Blaise went even farther back than that. He actually saw and heard Jesus. He followed Him as the fish-ermen of His day had done because he believed in miracles, and because he had eyes to see in the Lord the fulfilment of prophecy. Nay, it was given him to behold the Flaming Bush that burned and was not con-sumed. And in this Flaming Fire he read three times the Name of Him who could say: " Before Abraham was, I am." [3]

Let us learn from Pascal, then, that Christianity is essentially a mat-ter of commitment; that theology is a matter of authority; and that in the last analysis the supreme authority in theology is that of the Incar-nate Son, the Supernatural Christ. He, the Living Word, is therefore the measure of all things spiritual, even of Scripture.[4] Let us once more realize, as in this final assurance we behold the serenity of Pascal's death mask, that the only true Church is the Communion of Saints.

[3] John 8:58.
[4] This faith has been forcefully vindicated in our day by Robert E. Speer in his admirable book *The Finality of Jesus Christ*, The L. P. Stone Lectures at Princeton Theological Seminary, 1932–1933. Fleming H. Revell Company, New York, London, and Edinburgh, 1933.

APPENDIX TO THE TORCHBOOK EDITION: RECENT RESEARCH

The task now remains to consider the bearing of the latest Pascalian scholarship on what has been said. Our aim is not merely to bring this book up-to-date. It is also to allow fresh information and new insights either to disclose areas of agreement, or to suggest rectification, modification in emphasis, and further amplification as necessary.

We need hardly remind the reader that our method of approach has been determined by the basic concept of emergence in the setting of the Pascalian perspective of orders. We have accordingly insisted that the rise of Pascal cannot be understood in terms of an anthropology of naturalistic inspiration. Probably the greatest culprit in this connection has been P. L. Couchoud whose sociological interpretation of New Testament Christianity may still be remembered by a few. Curiously enough, the man who dared appropriate a hallowed Pascalian title to dispose of the historical Jesus[1] has more recently called upon his naturalistic presuppositions to reduce Pascal's *Apology* for Christianity to a kind of "Discourse on the Condition of Man."[2] Neither his versatile scholarship nor the literary merit of his prose has succeeded in veiling the shakiness of his hypotheses.

Infinitely less impressive is the unfinished "infernal tale"[3] devised in his prison cell by the late monarchist Charles Maurras.[4] According to his fancy, the shade of M. de Saci in the nether world, having caught sight of Pascal being ferried across the Styx, hastens to reproach him for a number of things. Most of his complaints turn out to be unfounded distortions. Thus the well-worn accusations that Pascal meant to humiliate and belittle reason, and that the *Pensées* were notes for a book in which that most noble of all human faculties would be made

---

[1] In two articles published in the *Mercure de France* on March 1, 1923, and March 1, 1924, later amplified and published under the title, *Le mystère de Jésus,* 1924.

[2] Couchoud, P. L., *Discours sur la condition de l'homme;* ce qui reste du manuscrit en représentation phototypique et restitution, A. Michel, Paris, 1948.

[3] Maurras, Ch., *Pascal puni,* conte infernal présenté par Henri Massis, Flammarion, Paris, 1953.

[4] between 1945 and March, 1952. The former editor in chief of *L'Action Française,* the royalist Parisian daily newspaper, died in 1952, eight months after his release.

brutish and imbecile. Both Couchoud and Maurras may be said to symbolize the twilight of the naturalistic interpretations of Pascal in our time.

Now turning to more weighty works, we find the theme of emergence independently developed by the sensitive German *pascalisant* Romano Guardini. Writing from within the Roman Catholic fold, he insists that Pascal can only be rightly understood in terms of liberation —of a finite being's shedding of his limitations.[5] The same emphasis is found in Fletcher's attempt to locate Pascal within the mystical tradition by stressing the bearing of his encounter with God on the total pattern of his life. So genuine is this encounter, that it leaves Pascal to confess unequivocally to the mystery of the election of grace.[6] Once the emergence of God's elect is set within the context of the three orders, Fletcher's attention is increasingly focussed on the nature and function of grace. To trace the Pascalian view of faith to Jansenism, and even further back to the early Christian tradition, amounts to overlooking its uniqueness.

It is this *sui generis* quality that Jeanne Roussier has brought out in a masterly two-volume work,[7] one of the most outstanding produced on the subject in our generation. The first volume deals with Pascal's definition of faith as "God felt by the heart." This is done in two parallel sections, i.e., reason confronted by revelation, then the heart confronted by revelation. Whereupon the second volume directs the reader to the respective elements of tradition and originality detected in Pascal's understanding of faith. This volume is similarly divided into two sections. The first brings out the area of agreement between the Pascalian view on the one hand, and the traditional teaching of Port Royal on the other. The second section emphasizes the originality of the Pascalian conception henceforth coming into its own in a philosophy of faith—that is, in a genuine philosophy freed from any claim of self-sufficiency. No longer may Pascal the scientist be contrasted with Pascal the believer and mystic. Both come to expression in one and the same man, a thinker endowed with a spirit of submission to facts

---

[5] Guardini, R., *Christliches Bewusstein,* Versuche über Pascal, Hegner, Leipzig, 1935; new edition, Kösel, München, 1950.

[6] Fletcher, F.Th.H., *Pascal and the Mystical Tradition,* Blackwell, Oxford, 1954. Philosophical Library, New York, 1954, p. 150. It is unfortunate that this book is for the most part out of touch with recent research.

[7] Roussier, J., *La foi selon Pascal,* Presses Univ. de France, Paris, 1949, 2 v. A wellnigh exhaustive bibliography of the subject will be found at the end of v. 2, 431–440.

apprehended in their wholeness. This all-embracing apprehension conditions the attainment of certitude.[8]

A philosophy thus making light of philosophy no longer suggests in Pascal the agony of subjectivity later detected in the existentialism of Kierkegaard, Chestov or Fondane. The dramatic attitude of Kierkegaard is not more a Pascalian feature than Chestov's identification of reason with the Serpent. The plain fact is that neither Kierkegaard nor Chestov ever did justice to the mystics. Their tragic view had little, if anything, in common with the prophetic view of Pascal.[9] Strictly valid points of contact between Pascal and Kierkegaard may indeed be found in their strategy of evangelism, as shown by the late Denzil G. M. Patrick in his moving two-volume work *Pascal and Kierkegaard*,[10] yet hardly beyond this realm. The reader may remember that I have restricted the comparison of the two men to a common feeling of incompatibility between the Christianity of the New Testament and its modern version. With due tribute to a revered memory, it may be said that the holy frenzy of Kierkegaard was more congenial to Patrick than Pascal's quiet desperation could ever be. It is noteworthy that Patrick needed 402 pages to do justice to Kierkegaard, and only 223 pages to deal with Pascal. The reverse ratio might have come closer to the respective "size" of the two personalities and of their achievement. But then Patrick was one of our contemporaries, and the equalitarian spirit of our age is hardly conducive to a sense of values. Concluding on our main point, we would accept Paul Holmer's penetrating specification that Kierkegaard's faith was "in a tragic world,"[11] then further point out that Pascal's faith was in man's God-given faculty to transcend both himself and his wretchedness.

Jean Guitton has devised another study in contrast, this time between

[8] Ibid. v. 2, 428–29. On the same subject and in the same vein, see also Laporte, J.M.F., *Le coeur et la raison selon Pascal*, Editions Elzevir, Paris, 1950—a posthumous reprint of a valuable article published in *Revue philosophique*, 1927 (Laporte died in 1948). A glance at our Index will remind the reader that Laporte has been repeatedly quoted in this book. I have in fact stressed my indebtedness to him.

[9] For a study in contrast between the tragic view and the prophetic view, the reader may want to turn to Part IV and Conclusion of my recent book, *The Recovery of Purpose*, Harper and Brothers, 1959.

[10] Patrick, G. M., *Pascal and Kierkegaard*, A Study in the Strategy of Evangelism, v. 23 and 24 in the "Lutterworth Library," Lutterworth Press, London and Redhill, 1947.

[11] The phrase is actually a part of Holmer's own subtitle to his sensitive essay on Kierkegaard in *The Tragic Vision and the Christian Faith*, ed. by Nathan A. Scott, Jr., Association Press, New York, 1957. Cf. ch. 6, pp. 174–188.

Pascal and Leibnitz. As he sees it, these two men will always complete each other. They incarnate two traditions as old as Christianity—that of Paul (represented by Pascal), and that of John (represented by Leibnitz). Just as Albert Schweitzer brought out the perennial adaptability of Paul's thought, Guitton shows how Pascal transcends time, that is, history, even as the man in him infinitely transcends man. This is why every age has been drawn to him and has attempted to make him its own; it is also the reason he has never originated a school.[12] Such transcendence would further seem to invite a change of emphasis in the study of Pascal. Instead of stressing the features which point to him as the child of his age, we should increasingly give attention to those features which allowed him to free himself from it. A subtle, yet meaningful shift in this direction is becoming noticeable. Fortunat Strowski once devoted much time and scholarly thought to his three-volume classic *Pascal et son temps*, repeatedly quoted in these pages; now Gonzague Truc has more recently written a well-documented work on Pascal's time and our own.[13]

Thus emulating previous generations, our contemporaries have claimed Pascal as their own. Recent years have witnessed the publication of an impressive number of "Lives." This scientific age has claimed him. At least two lectures were devoted to him in the Palais de la Découverte in 1950 under the auspices of the University of Paris.[14] Philosophers have refused to let him go in spite of the seeming harshness of his views on their trade. They have been captivated by his uniqueness. Thus Pierre Delbet has contributed a fine character portrait,[15] and Albert Ducas has further plumbed the depths of Pascal's mind.[16] Georges Le Roy in a short introductory booklet listed in the "Initiation philosophique" series,[17] has revived the theme of the oneness of the savant and the believer, insisting that these two aspects can only be isolated at the cost of distortion. The same concern for wholeness was also shown in a concise pamphlet published in the Netherlands

---

[12] Guitton, J., *Pascal et Leibnitz,* Etude sur deux types de pensée, Aubier, Editions Montaigne, Paris, 1951. Cf. pp. 170–77.

[13] Truc, G., *Pascal, son temps et le nôtre,* A. Michel, Paris, 1949. (Cf. some recent works on Pascal, pp. 383–85, and Bibl. notes, pp. 387–93.)

[14] *Pascal mathématicien,* by Paul A. Montel, and *Pascal et la science de son temps,* by Petre Sergescu—both published in 1950 by Imprimerie Alençonnaise, Alençon.

[15] Delbet, P. L. E., *Le caractère de Pascal,* P. Caillier, Vésenay-près-Genève, 1947.

[16] Ducas, A., *La pensée et la connaissance de Pascal,* La Meditérranée vivante, Alger, 1952.

[17] Le Roy, G., Pascal, savant et croyant, Presses Univ. de France, Paris, 1957.

by David van Dantzig,[18] and more especially in a German work which stresses Pascal's preoccupation with the ultimate. My reference is to Wasmuth's *Die Philosophie Pascal's*,[19] of which many a page calls to mind the thinking of Paul Tillich. A profoundly human note has been struck in Jerphagnon's study of suffering in the setting of a working man's life, under the title *Pascal et la souffrance*.[20]

Because of this concentration of interest upon the personality of Pascal, the transition from philosophers to biographers is extremely subtle. The rich harvest reaped in this section once more testifies to a perennial interest in him. Although a great deal of duplication is involved in rehearsing the great life saga, the repetitive features of the presentations at hand are relieved by fresh insights gained from recent research. What current, biographical literature on Pascal is essentially doing is to mediate to the reading public the fresh information made accessible by scholars. Keeping this fact in mind, I limit myself to a briefly annotated bibliography of those titles which have a bearing on this Torchbook edition.[21]

The reader may remember that after examining the critical literature on the subject, I gave vent to doubt as to the ascription to Pascal

[18] Dantzig, D. v., *Blaise Pascal* en de betekenis der wiskundige denkwizze voor de studie van de menselijke samenleving, P. Noordhoff, Groningen, 1949.

[19] Wasmuth, E., *Die Philosophie Pascal's*, under besonderer Berücksichtigung seiner Leben von dem Unendlichen und dem Nichts und den Ordnungen, L. Schneider, Heidelberg, 1949.

[20] Jerphagnon, L., *Pascal et la souffrance*, Préface de Julien-Eymard d'Angers, Editions ouvrières, Paris, 1956.

[21] Cresson, A., *Pascal, sa vie, son oeuvre*, avec un exposé de sa philosophie, Presses Univ. de France 1947 (an elementary initiation); Chinard, G., *En lisant Pascal;* notes sur les Pensées et l'économie du monde, Giard, Lille, 1948 (critical studies in various aspects of Pascal's life and thought); Daniel Rops, H., *Pascal et notre coeur*, Leroux, Strasbourg, 1948 (a pamphlet whose subjectivism has been sharply taken to task by Albert Béguin in the P.S. of his Preface to Lafuma's *Recherches Pascaliennes*, p. 17); Mesnard, J., *Pascal, l'homme et son oeuvre*, Paris, Boivin, 1951 (a well documented, up-to-date biography which introduces the Roman Catholic point of view with an amazing subtlety; trans. under the title, *Pascal, His Life and Works*, Preface by Monsignor Ronald Knox, Philosophical Library, New York, 1952); Moussalli, U., *Le vrai visage de Pascal*, Préface d'Albert Béguin, Plon, Paris, 1952 (a sensitive pamphlet in the Ars et historia collection). Bourceret, A., *La vie brève et dense de Pascal . . .*, Regain, Monte Carlo, 1953 (some perceptive insights). Steinmann, J., *Pascal*, Edition du Cerf, Paris, 1954 (a substantial treatment). Spoerri, Th., *Der verborgene Pascal . . .*, Furche, Hamburg, 1955 (a journey within in quest of the thinker); Mortimer, E., *Blaise Pascal, The Life and Work of a Realist*, Methuen and Co., London, 1959; Am. ed., Harper and Brothers, 1959 (the brilliant conversation of a cultured reader who wellnigh incarnates Pascal's *honnête homme;* occasionally carried away by an admired interpreter; regrettable gaps in the documentation, especially in view of the recent date of publication); see also no. 1 of Cahiers de Royaumont; philosophie: *Pascal, l'homme et l'oeuvre*, Editions de minuit, Paris, 1956 (a rich harvest).

of the *Discours sur les passions de l'amour*, with the admission that "we never escape wholly from the mood of conjecture, in considering the *Discours*." (p. 103) Further taken aback by a jarring quotation, I had exclaimed: "Did Pascal himself really write that?" (p. 105) The answer has now been given by Louis Lafuma and it is an emphatic "No." Pascal is not the author of the *Discours* so long ascribed to him.[22]

Proceeding upon the well-ascertained fact[23] that all the passages in the *Discours* which resemble certain passages in the *Pensées* correspond to the 1670 Port Royal edition, he draws attention to strange discrepancies. Thus one of the first fragments under scrutiny proves to be, not Pascal's, but a gloss by one of the Port Royal editors.[24] This already suggests that the date of the *Discours* cannot have been 1652 or 1653 as claimed by those who ascribe the work to Pascal. While reminded of the fact that Pascal died in 1662, our attention is directed to borrowings posterior to 1670. For instance, there appear undeniable parallels between the *Discours* and the 1678 edition of the *Maximes* of La Rochefoucauld, the *Maximes* of Madame du Sablé (1678), and the *Works* of Méré (1668–77). The author of the *Discours* is even found to have "literally fed upon" Malebranche's *Recherche de la vérité* (1674–75).[25] Again he betrays a mondain's versatility in making up maxims on love, a game developed by Bussy-Rabutin around 1666. Having narrowed down his inquiry, Lafuma then points to the Marquis d'Alluye (1620?–1690) as the likely author of the *Discours*.[26]

The debt of *pascalisants* to Louis Lafuma extends much further than would appear even from his scholarly work on the *Discours sur les passions de l'amour*. In June 1944 he haply laid his hand on a small manuscript which had been on the desk of Sainte-Beuve at the time he was working on his monumental *Port-Royal* and was subsequently lost. Curiously enough, neither Sainte-Beuve nor Faugère, who had also used it, ever surmised its origin. Lafuma has identified it as that in which Louis Périer, one of Pascal's younger nephews, gathered various writings of his uncle. It had indeed been considered lost since the end

[22] Cf. Lafuma, L., *Recherches Pascaliennes*, Préface de M. Albert Béguin, Delmas, Paris, 1949, "Le 'Discours sur les passions de l'amour' n'est pas de Pascal," pp. 101–134.
[23] brought out by the Italian Néri in *Un portrait imaginaire de Pascal*, Turin, 1921.
[24] Lafuma, *op. cit.* p. 108.
[25] For parallel passages, see *op. cit.*, pp. 122–27
[26] Lafuma, L., *L'auteur présumé du Discours sur les passions de l'amour*, Charles Paul d'Escoubleau, marquis d'Alluye et de Sourdis, Delmas, Paris, 1950.

of the XVIIIth century.[27] What makes this manuscript valuable is its importance in the history of the publication of Pascal's works. It has actually provided all the heretofore unpublished texts between 1728 and 1779. Some of the most important among them, in fact, are only known through this manuscript, such as "The Mind of the Geometrician" and "The Art of Persuasion."[28] It further contains certain fragments of the *Pensées* which had been eliminated from the 1670 Port Royal edition,[29] as well as three fragments unknown until our day.[30] All three refer to the *Provinciales* controversy. The most striking of them reads, "They say that the Church says what she does not say and that she does not say what she says"—another thrust at the Jesuits! Still more valuable to the theologian are the unpublished parts of a writing on grace which the Périer manuscript provides in its entirety.[31]

By far the most important contribution of Lafuma relates to the *Pensées* and the witness they bear to Pascal's intended "Vindication" of Christianity, the famous *Apology*. The reference is of course to the papers found after Pascal's death on which he had feverishly jotted down or dictated notes, maxims, analyses—his *Thoughts*, as they are commonly designated nowadays. In his later years, he had planned to organize them and elaborate on them, with a view to writing a comprehensive work on religion.

In the Preface to the 1670 Port Royal edition, Etienne Périer testifies that an awareness of such a design led those concerned to gather the papers with great care. They were, he writes, "threaded all together in various bundles, yet without any order whatsoever, without any sequence." And so, "the first thing done was to have them copied just as they were, and in the same confusion in which they had been found."[32] These drafts were later pasted in an album with a green parch-

---

[27] a fact established by Lafuma in *Trois pensées inédites de Pascal*, extraites du MS. *de l'abbé Périer, son neveu*. Editions littéraires de France, Paris, 1945.

[28] now available in translation together with 43 others in *Great Shorter Works of Pascal*, translated with an Introduction and Chronological Reference Table, by Emile Cailliet and John C. Blankenagel, Westminster Press, Philadelphia, 1948, pp. 189–211. *Pascal's Short Life of Christ* has been published apart in Princeton Pamphlets, No. 5, 1950.

[29] Cf. Lafuma, L., *Pensées retranchées de Pascal*, Jacques Haumont, Paris, 1945.

[30] and published by Lafuma under the title *Trois pensées inédites de Pascal*. (see above, note 27)

[31] Pascal, *Deux pièces imparfaites sur la grâce et le concile de Trente, extraites du MS. de l'abbé Périer son neveu*, Introduction et notes de Louis Lafuma, Vrin, Paris, 1947. (This title does not adequately describe the content of this small book which presents one extract on grace, one on the possibility for the just to observe God's commandments, and a few fragments on grace which are also found in MS. 9,202.)

[32] Quoted by Lafuma, *Recherches Pascaliennes, op. cit.*, pp. 23, 24.

ment cover 43 cm x 28 cm, with a sticker on the back bearing the inscription, "Original des Pensées de Pascal." The document constitutes MS. 9,202 in the French Bibliothèque nationale. As for the copy mentioned by Périer, it was long believed to have disappeared and to have differed from other copies bearing the numbers, 9,203 and 12,449.

Taking his lead from Tourneur,[33] Lafuma focussed his attention on Copy 9,203.[34] He found it to be none other than the famous copy spoken of by Périer. Furthermore, this same copy turns out to present, up to page 188, a classification with Pascal's own titles, as if this first third of the *Pensées* had been prepared for publication by Pascal himself. It may be assumed that after 1658 poor health prevented him from completing his task.[35] Now it is significant that while second Copy MS. 12,449 thus far follows the order of first Copy MS. 9,203, the order of the two differs from page 188 on. The anomaly suggests that what happened to the Original MS. 9,202 must at a later date have also happened to first Copy MS. 9,203. Small sections of it are known to have circulated between the château Bienassis, near Clermont, and Paris toward the end of 1668 and the beginning of 1669;[36] that is, on the eve of the 1670 Port Royal publication of the *Pensées*. There is further evidence that Canon Louis Périer was then at Bienassis putting the finishing touch to the ordering of his late uncle's papers.[37] MS. 9,203 only took its final form after 1715 when dom Jean Guerrier had it bound somewhere in Limousin. And during all this while the second Copy MS. 12,449 remained unused and untouched. It therefore constitutes the most authoritative witness we have to Pascal's original intentions.[38]

As Lafuma proceeded with the research just outlined, his attention

[33] Tourneur, Z., *Pensées de Blaise Pascal*, édition paléographique, Vrin, Paris, 1942; *Une vie avec Pascal*, Vrin, Paris, 1942.

[34] *Recherches Pascaliennes*, "Ce que nous apprennent les manuscrits des 'Pensées'," p. 29.

[35] The gist of the demonstration will be found in *Recherches Pascaliennes, op. cit.*, pp. 21–100. See detailed comparative table indicating point-by-point comparison between the Copy with its 27 titled bundles and the original collection, pp. 149, 150. Also critical Preface by Albert Béguin, pp. 7–17, and Lafuma's observations on Béguin's critique; pp. 135–147.
On controversial aspects, see further, Lafuma, L., *Controverses Pascaliennes*, Editions du Luxembourg, Paris, 1952, with Bibl., pp. 187–89.

[36] from letters of de Brienne to Gilberte Périer, dated Nov. 16, 1668, and Dec. 7, 1668.

[37] *Recherches Pascaliennes*, p. 34.

[38] *Recherches Pascaliennes*, "Les deux 'copies des Pensées'," pp. 77, 78, Cf. Comparative table indicating the place of the non-classified texts in Copies 9,203 and 12,449 on pp. 80, 81.

was attracted to the "Discours sur les Pensées" by Filleau de La Chaise. It had until then been considered the report of a conference held at Port Royal in 1658, in the course of which Pascal outlined the plan of his projected *Apology*, that is, his plan for the *Pensées*. A great deal of mystery continued to hover over the occasion inasmuch as the *Discours*[39] relied on the recollections of a man nine years after he had attended the conference. How then to account for the order, quality, and precision of his relation?[40] Lafuma's answer is that Filleau's *Discours* not only follows the order of Copy MS. 9,203, but constitutes an epitome of it. Filleau, he points out, was a member of the editorial board entrusted with the 1670 Port Royal edition. He also was the secretary of the Duke of Roannez who was himself a member of the board, together with Arnauld and Nicole. Consequently Filleau had full access to the Copy, full access to the Pascalian perspective on the *Apology*.[41] His *Discours* therefore is one of the most reliable guides we have to an adequate view of the *Pensées*.[42]

The fresh information just brought to our attention has disposed of fanciful versions of Pascal's intended "Vindication" of Christianity, thus indirectly confirming what I have characterized in these pages as "the Biblical structure of the 'Pensées'." Lafuma himself hailed the liberation he had done so much to implement.[43] A more adequate edition of the *Pensées* now became possible. Hence Lafuma's own "Edition intégrale,"[44] followed by his up-to-date history of the *Pensées*.[45] What has just been said in praise of the outstanding research work by Louis Lafuma implies neither finality nor blind endorsement. My own feeling is that this scholar may have overemphasized external evidence, and that a renewed emphasis on internal evidence along the lines suggested

[39] probably written in 1667, published for the first time in 1672, and currently associated with the *Pensées* from 1678 on.

[40] I myself have relied on it in this Torchbook edition in conjunction with outlines of Pascal's plan suggested by Nicole's résumé of the *Pensées*, by Madame Périer who echoed Nicole and who knew the innermost thoughts of her brother, and by Pascal himself in certain fragments of the *Pensées* (Cf. pp. 326–28).

[41] *Recherches Pascaliennes*, "La source du 'Discours sur les Pensées' de Filleau de La Chaise," pp. 83–92.

[42] "He could not draw from a better source," *Ibid.*, p. 91.

[43] Cf. *Recherches Pascaliennes*, "Avant-Propos," p. 19.

[44] Blaise Pascal, *Pensées sur la religion et sur quelques autres sujets*, Avant-propos et notes de Louis Lafuma, Delmas, Paris, Copyright by C.A.E.L., 1947, 2 v.; *Ibid.*, Editions du Luxembourg, Paris, 1951, 3 v., illus.

[45] Lafuma, L., *Histoire des Pensées de Pascal* (1656–1952), Editions du Luxembourg, Paris, 1954. (A convenient presentation in 148 pages).

in the present book may yet bring us closer to the facts, more especially with reference to the restored *Apology*.

A clearer apprehension of the Pascalian view is likely to give the lie to those who suggest that apologetics has become obsolete in our time. They can only be right if they mean by apologetics a defence of propositions already accepted on authority. Let their view be straightened out by the Pascalian *Apology*. For as it now emerges in the light of recent research, it amounts to the presentation of the true landscape of reality, leaving to whom it may concern the obligation to draw the right conclusions. To this task our age has now turned.

In a work published under the auspices of the National Committee for Scientific Research, Julien Eymard d'Angers, has provided the needed framework, namely, a background study of the development of apologetics up to the first edition of the *Pensées*.[46] And since it remains true that the contention of the Christian outlook is with the libertines, as Pascal readily realized, the fresh insights of Jacques Rennes into this perennial condition are to be welcomed.[47] The crucial issue at hand remains the same: In a domain beyond the limitations of our infirmity, there is a "game" going on, the meaning of which differs according to whether God is or not. Our whole life is at stake in that game. Our prime concern should therefore be to find on what side of the issue we really are, for we *are* in the game. This is the gist of Pascal's argument of the Wager, recently made the object of an able treatment by Georges Brunet.[48] It is fair to say that a renewed concern for the vital problems raised by apologetics as Pascal conceived it, has become widespread. An over-all reassessment of the apologetical significance of the Pascalian *Apology* has been attempted in Switzerland, both from the Roman Catholic and Protestant sides. Thus Charles Journet has achieved an understanding appraisal of the truth inherent in the whole argument.[49] The Protestant scholar Arthur Rich has taken his subject from further back and followed the main line of development within the perspective of the three orders.[50] In this country, sister Marie Louise Hubert has with great care brought into focus her doctoral dissertation at

[46] *Pascal et ses précurseurs*, Nouvelles éditions latines, Paris, 1954.

[47] Rennes, J., *Pascal et le libertin*, Valois, Paris, 1950.

[48] Brunet, G., *Le pari de Pascal*, Préface de Jean Mesnard, Desclée, Paris, 1956.

[49] Journet, Ch., *Vérité de Pascal;* essai sur la valeur apologétique des "Pensées," Editions de l'oeuvre St. Augustin, St. Maurice, 1951.

[50] Rich, A., *Pascal's Bild vom Menschen*, Zurich, 1953.

Yale University under the title *Pascal's Unfinished Apology*.[51] Her approach is thorough and her documentation exhaustive. The book does credit to both Roman Catholic scholarship and to the department in which she worked. In England, meanwhile, the veteran Pascalian scholar of Cambridge University, H. F. Stewart,[52] has brought a noble career to a close with a bilingual edition of the *Pensées* meant to be a restoration of their original intent. This scholarly work marks the culmination of an independent quest of long standing.[53]

As this "hearing" comes to a close, our heartfelt gratitude goes out to those who have made possible here and there, either change in emphasis or amplification of treatment. New vistas have been opened. Large areas of agreement have come within view. In quite a few instances, this feature might be ascribed to some stroke of luck, were it not that the phrase is foreign to my Christian vocabulary. The plain fact is that both method of approach and general conception of the subject stand vindicated so far as I have been satisfied to practice self-effacement, and have allowed my naked soul to become one with the nakedness of Pascal's. Whatever lasting value may be found in this book should accordingly be ascribed to the fact that Pascal himself was satisfied to lose his life so that he might find it.

[51] Hubert, M. L., Sister, *Pascal's Unfinished Apology*, A Study in his Plan, Yale University Press, New Haven, 1952 (Yale Romanic Studies, 2nd ser. 3). See Bibl. pp. 150–59.

[52] See Index for further references to previous works.

[53] Stewart, H. F., *Pascal's Pensées* with an English translation, brief notes and introductions, Pantheon Books, New York, 1950.

For the sake of the record, I may say that the late Cambridge scholar had shown some concern after I had announced my intended publication of Pascal's "great shorter works" under the title, *The Heart of Pascal* which he himself was about to use. (Cf. his book under that title, Cambridge, at the University Press, 1945). I naturally yielded priority to him, and jokingly asserted the proviso that he should later develop into an English translation his previous *Pascal's Apology for Religion* extracted from the Pensées (1942) in which Pascal's texts were given in French. He took the proviso to heart. Hence the over-all Edition referred to in this note.

378

Molinier, 334, 337.
Mondory, 46, 49.
Mons Version, 148, 159, 291, 311.
Montaigne, M. de, 25, 39, 47, 107, 119, 170–173, 288, 329, 330.
Montalte, Louis de, name assumed by Pascal as he wrote *Lettres Provinciales*, see n. 1, 207, and Chs. XI–XIV (207–288).
Montel, P. A., 367.
Montferrand, 18, 22, 88, *see* Clermont.
Morehouse, A. R., 329, 330.
Moréri, 361.
Morgan, G. C., 361.
Mornet, D., 163.
Mortimer, E., 368.
Murphy, J., 30.
Mydorge, C., 43.
Mystère de Jésus, Jacqueline Pascal's, 87.
Mystère de Jésus, Pascal's, 90, 183–185, 205, 289, 307, 340, 346.
Mystic hexagram, Pascal's, 43, 44.
Mysticism, 22, 57, 134–136.

Names assumed by Pascal, 144.
Naturalism, 31, 63, 313, 329.
Neeser, M., 120.
Neo-Stoicism, 46, 47.
Nevers, Curés de, 284.
Newton, Isaac, 43, 106, 175.
Nicene Creed, 337.
Nicole, P., 159, 201, 216, 224, 271, 287, 320, 327, 355.
Niebuhr, R., 142.
Noël, Père, 32, 67–71, 73, 74.
Noris, Cardinal, 226.
Normandy, 49, 59, 86.
Northwestern University, 235.
Notre-Dame du Port, 17, 18.
Nouet, Father, 264.
Novelties, *see* Innovations.

Oiron, 98.
Omnibuses, 33, 346.
Oratoire, 48.
Orders, Theory of, 14, 15, 31, 32, 45, 52, 56, 64, 67, 100, 174–179, 309.
Origen, 57, 291.

Paganism, 57, 194.
Pagnino, Sante, 298.
Painting(s), 23, 158, 169.
Palinods, 47.
Pannier, J., 141.
Paris, 10, 40, 50, 61, 85, 86, 87, 105, 149; *see* Port-Royal-de-Paris;—University of, *see* Sorbonne.

Parlement de Paris, 80, 156, 277–288.
Parliament of Toulouse, 27.
Pascal, Antonia, 24.
Pascal, Antoinette (Bégon), 22, 23, 24, 25.
Pascal, Blaise (son of Etienne), 24.
Pascal, Etienne, 20, 22, 24, 25, 27, 28, 31, 32, 33, 40, 42, 43, 45, 46, 48, 49, 52, 53, 70, 73, 74, 78, 85, 86, 87, 153, 223;—Death of, 88–92.
Pascal, Gilberte (elder sister of Blaise, became Madame Périer), 21, 24, 25, 29, 30, 42, 50, 55, 58, 60, 64, 72, 80, 82, 86, 89, 93, 106, 123, 133, 143, 149, 181, 182, 235, 236, 237, 287, 311, 313, 317, 327, 340, 342, 343, 344, 345, 353–359.
Pascal, Jacqueline (younger sister of Blaise, became Sister Sainte-Euphémie), 24, 26, 46, 47, 48, 49, 58, 78, 80, 83, 85, 86, 87, 88, 92, 93, 94, 104, 105, 106, 132, 143, 144, 145, 149, 150, 151, 166, 167, 224, 235, 285, 311, 316, 318, 344, 352, 355.
Pascal, Jean (great-grandfather of Blaise), 20.
Pascal, Martin (son of Jean), 20, 21, 22.
Paschon, M., 26.
Pastourel, L., 132.
Patriarchal tradition, 24–26.
Patrick, D. G. M., 366.
Paul, 367.
Pelagius, Pelagianism, 57, 58, 164–166, 190, 192, 193–195, 226.
Pennsylvania, University of, 11, 126.
Pensées, 31, 32, 35, 47, 57, 64, 73, 76, 82, 85, 92, 93, 97, 99, 100, 101, 105, 106–115, 120–125, 146, 166, 169, 178, 179, 182–185, 188, 189, 199, 202, 203, 236–242, 247, 274, 279, 288, 289, 290, 291, 292, 293, 294, 295, 296, 300, 304, 305, 306, 307, 308, 309, 312, 314, 320–337;—Biblical structure of the *Pensées*, 325–331, *see* Vindication of Christianity.
Péréfixe, Archbishop, 355–357.
Périér, Abbé (son of Florin and nepew of Blaise Pascal), 133, 369, 371.
Périer, Etienne (magistrate, the eldest son of Florin, and nephew of Blaise Pascal), 55, 320, 321, 370, 371.
Périer family, the, 21, 93, 94, 105.
Périer, Florin (the husband of Gilberte, Pascal's eldest sister), 21, 74, 89.
Périer, Madame, *see* Pascal, Gilberte.
Périer, Marguerite (daughter of Florin, and niece of Blaise Pascal), 79, 132, 234–236, 287, 323.
Perrault's *Parallèle*, 225.
Perseverance of the Saints, *see* Grace.

383